The Playground

EXPLODING
THE PHONE

EXPLODING THE PHONE

The Untold Story of the Teenagers
and Outlaws Who Hacked Ma Bell

PHIL LAPSLEY

Grove Press
New York

FIRST EDITION

ISBN-13: 978-0-8021-2061-8

Grove Press
an imprint of Grove/Atlantic, Inc.
841 Broadway
New York, NY 10003

Distributed by Publishers Group West

www.groveatlantic.com

13 14 15 16   10 9 8 7 6 5 4 3 2 1

To the men and women of the Bell System, and especially to the members of the technical staff of Bell Laboratories, without whom none of this would have been possible

CONTENTS

CONTENTS

Phone phreak (n.)   1. A person who is obsessively inter-ested in learning about, exploring, or playing with the tele-phone network.   2. A person who is interested in making free telephone calls.

FOREWORD

FIRST LEARNED ABOUT phone phreaking from a magazine. In the fall of 1971 I stumbled onto an article that seemed like a bit of science fiction, about these groups of people who knew how to crack the phone system all over the world. I was young, only twenty years old, and I thought this was a really cool made up story.

I phoned Steve Jobs halfway through and started reading him the article. I just had to call him. We researched it and found out, "Whoa!" It made sense! Who would ever believe you could put tones into a phone and make calls free anywhere in the world? I mean, who would *believe* it? It was like we stumbled onto to some magical mystery that other people just didn't know about. And I had no idea the impact it would end up having on my life.

We just had to try it, to find out if it really worked. Over the next few months I started designing a "blue box," an electronic gizmo that made the tones you needed to control the telephone network. I put so much attention into trying to make it the very best blue box in the world. It was digital, unlike the ones that everybody else had, and it had some of the cleverest, most off-the-wall design techniques I've ever put into anything I've ever built, even to this day. It was great, and it was my passport into the phone phreaks' underground network.

I had grown up very shy and often felt left out of things. But for me, phone phreaking was a place in the world that I was like a leader. It was a place where I could blossom. And it's not that I could blossom as a criminal—it wasn't that we had lots of people to call or had giant phone bills or really wanted to rip off the phone company or anything. It's just that it was so exciting! When I went into a room and showed off phone tricks with a blue box, I was like a magician playing tricks. I was the center of attention. That was probably partly what drove me. But it was also the fascination of doing something that nobody would really believe was possible.

I was enthusiastic then about very few things, but this one I was enthusiastic about. Phone phreaking was one of the first big adventures I had in my life. And it made me want to have more of those adventures by designing more things like my blue box, weird things that worked in ways that people didn't expect. For the rest of my life, that was the reason I kept doing project after project after project, usually with Steve Jobs. You could trace it right up to the Apple II computer. It was the start of wanting to constantly design things very, very well and get noticed for it. Steve and I were a team from that day on. He once said that Apple wouldn't have existed without the blue box, and I agree.

Today a lot of people are computer hackers and a lot of them just want to cause problems for others—they're like vandals. I was not a vandal, I was just curious. But, boy, I wanted to find out what the limits of the telephone system were. What are the limits of *any* system? I've found that for almost anybody who thinks well in digital electronics or computer programming, if you go back and look at their lives they'll have these areas of misbehavior. And I think some of the most creative people have all, at some point, focused their creativity on doing things that they aren't supposed to do. But their goal is usually, oh my gosh, can I *discover* something? Is there some way to do something that is not exactly in books and not known? Hackers are the ultimate example: every hacker I've ever run into is always trying to explore the little tiny nuances of anything looking for a mistake, a crack they can get through.

The blue box was this magical, unbelievable adventure. The fact that nobody else knew about it and I did made it special knowledge.

But it was no good just to know it inside—it was *only* good when I shared it with others. It was playing with magical powers. I would say I had an awful lot of those experiences in my life, but the blue box was probably the most special of all.

I hope that getting to learn a little bit about phone phreaking turns out to be one tenth as much fun for you as it was for me to experience it.

Steve Wozniak
Cofounder, Apple Computer

A NOTE ON NAMES AND TENSES

ANONYMITY AND PSEUDONYMS have been a thorn in my side throughout the writing of this book. Despite my attempts to convince my interviewees that this all happened a long time ago, that the statute of limitations has long since expired, that the phone company doesn't care and the phone phreaks don't care and law enforcement doesn't care, several people have insisted on either being anonymous or being referred to by pseudonyms. For those who wished to be nameless, I have tried to make their anonymity obvious ("A source familiar with the matter recalls . . ."). Pseudonyms are marked with a footnote when they are first used to call attention to the shy. Each such footnote indicates whether the pseudonym is historical or modern, that is, whether the pseudonym used was the person's nom de phreak back in the day or is a more recent fabrication for purposes of present-day identity protection.

The identity of every source used in the book is known to me; there have been no "Deep Throat"–style encounters in which I have received late-night phone calls from truly anonymous sources telling me outlandish things or, for that matter, any things at all. I guess I'm just in the wrong line of work.

Finally, a note on verb tense: when I have used the present tense to attribute a quote in this book (e.g., "Acker recalls" or "Perrin remembers"), it means that the quote was taken directly from an interview I conducted between 2005 and 2012 or from a document published during that time. When I have used the past tense ("The memo stated" or "Draper said"), it indicates that the quote was taken from an older newspaper article, memo, FBI file, or other document, or from notes or audiotapes from the time in question.

One

FINE ARTS 13

THERE IT WAS again.

Jake Locke⋆ set down his cup and looked more closely at the classified ad. It was early afternoon on a clear spring day in Cambridge in 1967. Locke, an undergrad at Harvard University, had just gotten out of bed. A transplant from southern California, he didn't quite fit in with Harvard's button-down culture—another student had told him he looked like a "nerdy California surfer," what with his black-framed eyeglasses, blond hair, blue eyes, and tall, slim build. Now in the midst of his sophomore slump, Locke found himself spending a lot of time sleeping late, cutting classes, and reading the newspaper to find interesting things to do. Pretty much anything seemed better than going to classes, in fact.

It was a slow news day. The *Crimson,* Harvard's student newspaper, didn't have much in the way of interesting articles, so Locke once again found himself reading the classified ads over breakfast. He had become something of a connoisseur of these little bits of poetry—people selling cars, looking for roommates, even the occasional kooky personal ad probably intended as a joke between lovers—all expressed in a dozen or so words.

But this ad was different. It had been running for a while and it had started to bug him.

⋆A pseudonym.

WANTED HARVARD MIT Fine Arts no. 13 notebook. (121 pages) &
40 page reply K.K. & C.R. plus 2,800; battery; m.f. El presidente
no esta aqui asora, que lastima. B. David Box 11595 St. Louis, MO
63105.

Locke had seen similar classified ads from students who had lost
their notes for one class or another and were panicking as exams
rolled around. They often were placed in the *Crimson* in the hopes
that some kind soul had found their notes and would return them.
Fine Arts 13 was the introductory art appreciation class at Harvard,
so that fit.

But nothing else about the ad made any sense. Fine Arts 13
wasn't offered at MIT. And what was all the gibberish afterward?
2,800? Battery? M.f., K.K., C.R.? What was with the Spanish?
And why was somebody in St. Louis, Missouri, running an ad in
Cambridge, Massachusetts, looking for a notebook for a class at
Harvard? Locke had watched the ad run every day for the past
few weeks. Whoever they were, and whatever it was, they clearly
wanted this notebook. Why were they so persistent?

One way to find out.

Locke looked around for a piece of paper and a pen. He wrote:
"Dear B. David: I have your notebook. Let's talk. Sincerely, Jake."

He dropped the letter in the mail on his way into Harvard Square
to find something interesting to do.

An envelope with a St. Louis, Missouri, postmark showed up
in Locke's mailbox a week later. Locke opened the envelope
and read the single sheet of paper. Or rather, he tried to read
it. It wasn't in English. It seemed to be written in some sort of
alien hieroglyphics. It was brief, only a paragraph or so long.
The characters looked familiar somehow but not enough that
he could decipher them.

Locke showed the letter to everyone he saw that day but nobody
could read it. Later that evening, as Locke sat at the kitchen table in
his dorm room and stared at the letter, trying to puzzle it out, one

of his roommates came home. Shocked that Locke might actually be doing something that looked like homework, his roommate asked what he was working on. Locke passed the letter across the table and told him about it.

His roommate took one look and said, "It looks like Russian."

Locke said, "That's what I thought. But the characters don't seem right."

"Yeah. They're not. In fact . . ." His roommate's voice trailed off for a moment. "In fact, they're mirror writing."

"What?"

"You know, mirror writing. The letters are written backwards. See?"

Locke looked. Sure enough: backwards.

Locke and his roommate went to the mirror and transcribed the reversed lettering. It was Cyrillic—Russian letters. Fortunately, Locke's roommate was taking a Russian class. They sat back down at the table and translated the letter.

"Dear Jake," the letter read. "Thank you very much for your reply. However, I seriously doubt that you have what I need. I would strongly advise you to keep to yourself and not interfere. This is serious business and you could get into trouble." Signed, B. David.

Locke sat back. Someone had put a cryptic ad in the newspaper. He'd responded. They sent him a letter. In mirror writing. In Russian. In 1967. During the cold war.

Spy ring.

It just didn't get much cooler than this, Locke figured. Intriguing. Terrifying, even. And far, far better than going to class.

Locke mailed his reply that day—in English, and not in mirror writing. "Dear B. David: Actually, I do have your notebook and I would like to talk to you. Sincerely, Jake."

Four days went by before the mailman brought Locke an odd letter, a piece of card stock folded in half and taped at the top. The fold line was perforated so that it could be torn in half. The writing was in English this time.

3

"Dear Jake, if you have the information I need, you should be able to complete the other half of this card and mail it back to me. Then we can continue our discussions. Sincerely, B. David."

Locke looked at the other half of the postcard. It had a handful of questions on it:

Complete the following sequence: 604, 234, 121, ___
What does M.F. stand for?
What equipment were the students at Harvard and MIT using?

Huh?

Locke spent every waking hour over the next several days working on the postcard questions. The numbers repeated over and over in his mind: 604, 234, 121 . . . 604, 234, 121 . . . 604, 234, 121 . . .

604-234-1212.

A phone number? It wasn't directory assistance—Locke knew that would have been 555-1212—but it sort of sounded right. Worth a shot, anyway. He picked up the phone and dialed. A woman's businesslike voice answered on the first ring.

"Cleaner clean," she said.

"Excuse me?" said Locke.

"Cleaner clean inward," the woman repeated, more distinctly this time.

Locke hung up. He stared at the phone. Cleaner clean? Inward?

Where was area code 604, anyway? The phone book said British Columbia. And where was that? Western Canada. Locke looked around his dorm room, found an atlas, and flipped to the page on British Columbia. He scanned the map. The big cities had names he recognized, names like Vancouver and Prince George. The smaller towns had less familiar names. Names like Kamloops. Squamish. Quesnel. Chilanko.

Kleena Kleene.

★ ★ ★

At dinner that night Locke mentioned his phone call to Steve, another of his roommates. Steve said, "Huh. That's interesting. My girlfriend Suzy is an inward."

"What? What's an inward?" asked Locke.

"It's some kind of special telephone operator. You should talk to her, she might be able to help you figure some of this stuff out. She lives over in Revere. Give her a call."

Locke did. Suzy explained that an inward is an "operator's operator." When an operator needs assistance in making a call, she calls the inward operator for the destination city. The inward operator then completes the call to a local number.

"So how do I call an inward?" Locke asked her.

"You can't. Inwards have special phone numbers that only operators can dial. If you wanted to call the New York inward, you'd have to dial something like 212-049-121. So 121 is what gets you the inward, and 049 is a routing code inside of New York, and New York is the 212 area code. But you can't dial numbers like 049 or 121 from a regular phone."

Locke explained that he seemed to have found a way to call an inward operator from his regular phone by dialing 604-234-1212.

"Well," Suzy said, "I'm mystified. You shouldn't be able to. I don't know, maybe you found a glitch. But here's how you can tell. Call them up and ask them to complete a call to somebody. If they're really an inward, they'll be able to do it no problem."

"I don't know anybody in Canada," Locke said.

"That's okay. An inward can call anywhere. And we sometimes get calls from the test board within the phone company asking us to complete calls to places for testing purposes. Just tell them you're with the test board. Be confident and self-assured and act like you know what you're doing and they won't give you any trouble."

"Okay. I'll try that. Hey, any idea what 'M.F.' might stand for?"

"Well," Suzy replied, "it could be multifrequency."

"Multifrequency. What's that?" Locke asked.

"It's the system that operators use to make calls. It's kind of like those touch tones used for push-button dialing, but it sounds different." Locke's dorm phone was rotary dial, but he knew what touch tones were—they had been introduced just a few years earlier.

"Okay. Hey, thanks, Suzy." They said good-bye. He hung up.

Locke picked up the phone again and dialed 604-234-1212. Once again the businesslike female voice answered.

"Kleena Kleene inward."

"Hi, uh, yes," Locke said. "This is the test board. Could you connect me to 619-374-8491, please?"

"One moment." There was a pause. The long-distance hiss got louder. A click. Another pause. More hiss. Another click. Then a ringing signal.

"Hello?" It was his friend Dave in San Diego.

Locke chatted with his friend for a few minutes and then hung up. He felt as if he were floating. It seemed magical. "Act like you know what you're doing and they won't give you any trouble." It worked!

Two postcard questions down. One left: "What equipment were the students at MIT using?"

Once again, another roommate came to Locke's rescue—fortunately, Locke lived in a suite and had lots of roommates. "We're talking about phones and MIT students, right? I remember an article in the *Crimson* about a year ago about some MIT students who got in trouble for playing with the telephone. Could that be it?"

"Maybe," said Locke. "But how am I gonna find an old copy of the *Crimson*?"

"The library?" his friend suggested.

This was a challenge. Locke had never been to the university's library before.

Locke was surprised to find it was close to his dorm and that other students seemed able to direct him there. Soon Locke was flipping through page after page of old *Crimson*s. An hour later, in an issue from almost a year earlier in 1966, he found what he was looking for.

FIVE STUDENTS PSYCH BELL SYSTEM, PLACE FREE LONG DISTANCE CALLS

Five local students, four from Harvard and one from M.I.T., spent eight months making long distance and international phone calls as guests of the Bell System before they were finally discovered.

The telephone company accepted the news without bitterness, however, merely impounding the 121-page Fine Arts 13 notebook that contained the records of their "researches" and requiring them to submit a full report, which ran to 40 double-spaced pages, of what they had done.

Mesmerized, Locke read on, the words from the classified ad running through his head. The article described how, starting in 1962, the students had used inward operators—including one in Kleena Kleene—to complete calls all over the world. It tantalized with an infuriatingly brief description of how it was possible to build an electronic device to control the telephone system for "$50 of common electronic components." The article concluded abruptly, stating that the students were caught in April 1963 when a telephone company employee turned them in.

Locke was elated. Pieces were falling into place, and now he had enough to respond to B. David. But the article was short on details. He needed to find out more. He needed to talk to the original Harvard and MIT students. Locke jotted down the name of the article's author, another student at Harvard.

The next day he filled out the reply postcard and dropped it in the mail to B. David. Then he called the *Crimson* reporter to pump him for details. The reporter wasn't very helpful. He didn't know the names of the Harvard or MIT students, he said, and it turned out that he had gotten most of his information from an article in the *Boston Herald*. He had then talked to the *Herald* reporter to get some additional context.

"Didn't the *Herald* reporter know the names of the students?" Locke asked.

"Oh, sure, but he wouldn't give them to me. And I doubt he'll give them to you either," the *Crimson* reporter replied.

Back to the library. Locke dug up the *Herald* article. It described the Harvard and MIT students making calls to the president of Mexico and gave a name—"blue box"—to the electronic device that had allowed them to control the telephone network. It spoke of their staying up all night, of spending eighty hours a week on their research, of dialing ten thousand numbers over two to three days to find the information they needed. It even said the students were questioned by FBI agents who thought they were stealing defense secrets.

Locke looked up the telephone number for the newspaper. *Be confident and self-assured and act like you know what you're doing.* He drew a deep breath, picked up the phone, dialed the *Herald,* and asked to be connected to the reporter who wrote the article. When the reporter answered, Locke politely explained who he was and what he was looking for.

"This is Special Agent Stevenson with the FBI Boston Field Office. We've had a report that there has been some new activity related to an incident that occurred a few years ago with some Harvard and MIT students misusing the telephone system. We're trying to reach them to talk to them about this but we don't have current contact information for them. I saw your article about them from a year ago or so. Do you have telephone numbers for any of them?"

Not a problem, the reporter replied. He'd be happy to help.

Before Locke had a chance to call any of the students his phone rang. It was B. David and he wanted to know about the Fine Arts 13 notebook. Oh, yes, *that* notebook: the one that Locke didn't actually have. Locke did his best to keep up the charade. Well, he admitted, he wasn't actually one of the Harvard or MIT students but he knew them. He was a friend of theirs. He had participated in some of their "research."

B. David grilled him. It quickly became apparent that Locke didn't know as much as he was claiming. As Locke would later recall, "You can only fake things so far before they begin to crumble." Locke admitted the truth.

Surprisingly, B. David wasn't mad, and now that the cat was out of the bag the two had a pleasant conversation. B. David explained that there was an informal network of telephone enthusiasts like himself, and that he had been trying to reach the Harvard and MIT students to talk to them about their exploits. "Welcome to our world," he said. Locke asked for pointers. B. David demurred on details: "I don't want to give you too much information. I will tell you one thing, though: look for missing exchanges. Look for patterns. I'll give you a call back in a few weeks to see how you're doing."

This all seemed fascinating to Locke. He called the former MIT student—now living in Berkeley, California—whose number he had gotten from the *Herald* reporter. The student was friendly enough but, like B. David, was also reluctant to provide much information. The MIT student explained that he and his friends had been caught and interrogated by the FBI, although not actually prosecuted. He stressed that Locke could get in trouble playing with this stuff and that Locke should stay away from the whole thing. Locke pressed him for more information. Finally the MIT student told him, "If you really want to find out more, everything you need to know is in the library."

Great, thought Locke, a *third* trip to the library.

But what library would have the sort of information he was looking for? Some research led him to the physics library and something called the *Bell System Technical Journal*. The one term Locke knew to look up was "multifrequency." From the journal's index he quickly located an article from the November 1960 issue titled "Signaling Systems for Control of Telephone Switching." It was technical but not so technical that Locke couldn't understand a good chunk of it. It laid out in detail exactly how certain aspects of the telephone system worked, including the multifrequency signaling system. This article plus the *Crimson* and *Herald* stories, as well as his conversations with B. David and the former MIT student, gave him everything he needed to get serious about this stuff.

Locke started to spend a lot of time on the telephone. "Look for missing exchanges, look for patterns," B. David had told him. Locke knew that an exchange was the first three digits of a local telephone number. By making a careful study of the telephone book and doing a lot of dialing, Locke discovered that there were indeed missing exchanges in the downtown Boston area. When Locke found a missing exchange, he would start dialing all the telephone numbers in it. All ten thousand of them.

Weeks later Locke had three things to show for his efforts. The first was an indelible black circle around his index finger from his repeated dialing. Second was four livid roommates: because Locke was constantly on the phone, none of them could make or receive phone calls. But third was a collection of some very interesting telephone numbers. Some of these were odd test numbers, numbers that made weird *beeps*, *boops*, clicks, and tones. More interesting were so-called party lines. These were typically vacant number recordings ("We're sorry, you have reached a nonworking number . . .") whose audio levels were very low. All the callers to one of these numbers would be connected, and because the volume of the recordings was so low people could talk over the recordings. As a result, they served as primitive conference calls at a time when such things were unheard of.

Most interesting, though, was that several numbers went to inward operators in various places.

Locke's obsession grew. He decided he wanted to build one of these mystical "blue boxes" so that he, too, could directly control the telephone network. That meant he'd need to build electronic oscillators, circuits that would make musical tones. But Locke didn't know anything about electronics. Looking for patterns and missing exchange numbers was one thing; electronic circuit design was something else. Locke got a friend of his to introduce him to a graduate student in the physics department in order to persuade him to help build the oscillator circuits he needed for his blue box.

"What do you need them for?" the grad student asked.

Be confident and self-assured and act like you know what you're doing. "I'm a biology major and I'm studying the effects of high-frequency audio oscillations on fruitfly germination."

The grad student raised an eyebrow but helped Locke anyway.

Locke started haunting the electronics stores in Cambridge, looking for parts and guidance on assembling his blue box. Before long he linked up with students at MIT in the Tech Model Railroad Club, or TMRC, near the Kendall Square T Station. The TMRC was home to one of the most technically sophisticated model railroad setups in the country, possibly the world. MIT students had laid out some six hundred feet of track simulating ten scale miles of railroad amid painstakingly detailed scenery. The trains were controlled by a fantastically complex switching system based on many of the same principles as the telephone network. Indeed, the telephone company had donated equipment to the club for just this purpose, and the club's faculty adviser was in charge of MIT's telephone system, so it was not surprising that model train operators at TMRC used a telephone dial to select the train to be controlled. It was a veritable breeding ground for telephone enthusiasts.

With help from the more electronically knowledgeable students at MIT, and only a few soldering iron burns, Locke was able to piece together a blue box. By now Locke had been told by enough people that he could get in trouble for using his blue box and that he should be careful. So Locke *was* careful—when it was convenient, anyway. He used his blue box from the pay phone in his dorm quite a bit, as well as from friends' houses. As Locke figured it, the only thing he was doing with it was using it to learn about how the phone system worked. He didn't even really know anybody far away he wanted to call, so it wasn't like he was racking up thousands of dollars in free long-distance calls. He just couldn't imagine that anyone cared about his activities that much.

Incredibly enough, some people did care, as Locke learned upon returning to his dorm room in June 1967, just three months after seeing the Fine Arts 13 ad in the *Crimson*. He knew he was in trouble from the moment he walked in the door: waiting for him in his living room were three men. One of them was the crestfallen house master, the Harvard professor who was the head of Locke's dorm. Locke didn't know the other two, but he did notice that one of them was wearing a trench coat—strange, given that it was a warm summer day.

"The jig's up, Locke," the house master said.

Trying to stall for time, Locke asked, "Which jig?"

Based on the reactions of his three visitors, Locke surmised this was the wrong thing to have said.

"You know which jig we're talking about, Locke," said one of the men. "The telephone jig. We've been through your things." He held up Locke's blue box. "We need to talk."

One of his visitors turned out to be from the telephone company, AT&T security. The other introduced himself as a special agent from the FBI's Boston Field Office. They asked Locke to come downtown with them. The FBI agent told him that this was a very serious matter, that they had some questions they wanted straight answers to, and that they would arrest him if he didn't cooperate.

Locke spent the next twenty-four hours in what felt like a scene from a 1940s detective movie: a barren room with nothing more than a wooden table, a chair for him, two chairs for his interrogators, and a bare lightbulb dangling from the ceiling. Sitting across from him, the FBI agent and the telephone security man worked hard to get him to confess to using the blue box to make free telephone calls. Despite being scared to death Locke denied everything. He didn't know what they were talking about, he said.

After several hours of questioning, he finally admitted that yes, the blue box was his, but that he had used it only to learn about the telephone network. Locke expected them to start grilling him about how many free calls he had made, but his interrogators shifted focus. They wanted to know who had given him the technical information necessary for him to build a blue box. He explained that he had seen an article in the Boston *Herald* and then found the *Bell System Technical Journal* article and gone on from there. In other words, there wasn't anyone else; he had been all on his own. It took a long time, but he managed to convince them of his version of events.

Again the questioning shifted course. Okay, they said, you figured out this stuff on your own. Fine. Now tell us who you've been selling the boxes to.

Locke was flummoxed. Selling the boxes? What boxes? He had built only the one, and he hadn't sold it to anyone. The FBI agent grilled him. They were sure he had been selling them—or at least supplying them—to others. To whom, they wouldn't say. After hours of back and forth, Locke was able to get across that it was just him, there was just the one box he had built, and he hadn't been selling them. (In retrospect, Locke says he is glad he never thought of this. "The idea of selling blue boxes had never occurred to me . . . fortunately! It's not a bad idea.")

Locke spent the evening in the care of the FBI. In the morning he was told he could leave, but only after he prepared a written report describing what he had done and the techniques he had used. He spent the morning writing this report.

As he was leaving, Locke turned to the man from the phone company. His face slipped into a grin. "By the way," he said, "I'm not doing anything for the summer. You guys wouldn't happen to have any job openings, would you?"

TWO

BIRTH OF A PLAYGROUND

THE OBJECT OF Jake Locke's obsession—the telephone—recently celebrated its 135th birthday. Few products can say that. The telephone's staying power is testimony to our species' deep-seated need to talk with one another. For thousands of years we humans have tried every trick we could think of to communicate at a distance: torches on mountaintops were big with the Greeks, the Romans released carrier pigeons to report the results of chariot races, African bush tribes sounded drums, American Indians had smoke signals, and ships at sea hoisted signal flags to communicate with each other.

The problem, of course, was that these techniques all pretty much sucked; this is why you carry a cell phone in your pocket and not a signal flag or a pigeon. But we didn't get to cell phones overnight. It took repeated assaults on the problem to before humanity managed to make a dent in it.

In the late 1700s the new new thing in the world of communications was something called the optical telegraph. A network of windmill-like towers with pivoting shutters, blades, arms, or paddles that could be seen from a distance, the optical telegraph allowed reliable long-distance communications. Several systems were built but the best known was created by Claude Chappe and his brothers and deployed throughout France starting in 1793. The Chappe system used relay stations a few miles apart from each other. A station in Lyon, for example, would spin its paddle to send a particular signal. A few miles to the southwest, the operator at the Vénissieux station would be watching, perhaps with the aid of a telescope. He would spin his paddles to repeat the message on to the station at Saint-Pierre-de-Chandieu, a few miles farther on down the line. And so the message would go, one station—and one spin of the paddle—at a time.

It was as cumbersome as it sounds. It was expensive, laborious, and slow. Its use was limited to the government. It was also public—anyone could watch it, after all—and it didn't work in foul weather or at night. Despite this, the optical telegraph was the first successful telecommunications network, serving for more than sixty years. By 1852 the Chappe system boasted 556 relay stations and traced a network distance of some three thousand miles. Tributaries from the main network connected many of the capitals of Europe—Amsterdam, Brussels, Mainz, Milan, Turin, and Venice. News of Napoleon's coup d'état in 1848 would have taken just under half an hour to transit the network, slow by today's standards but fast for the time.

Then the electrical telegraph arrived. It was from the future and, like many things from the future, it made things from the present—things like the optical telegraph—look like they were from the past.

It was amazing. With a battery and a switch and miles of wire and a sounder—a thing that clicked when you ran electrical current through it—you could communicate over a distance. Instantly. Not half an hour to send a message but half a minute. Of course, it wasn't quite as easy as whipping out your cell phone and texting your friend, but you could write out a message—a telegram—and take it down to your local telegraph office, pay some money, and have it sent.

It was patented in both England and America in the same year, 1837. In America the inventor was Samuel Morse, whose his first functioning telegraph line went live between Washington, D.C., and Baltimore, Maryland, in 1844. Washington to New York followed two years later.

It seems incredibly primitive today. So primitive, in fact, that it is difficult to appreciate just how stunning this was at the time. It let loose a communications revolution that the writer Tom Standage dubbed the "Victorian Internet." Americans took to the telegraph like teenagers to text messages. By 1850 America had twelve thousand miles of telegraph lines served by some twenty companies. Only two years later this had just about doubled to twenty-three thousand miles, with another ten thousand miles under construction. A writer chronicling the telegraph's rapid growth at the time reported: "It is anticipated that the whole of the populous parts of the United States will, within two or three years, be covered with a net-work like a spider's web."

The prediction was right. The tendrils of the telegraph's spider-web spread rapidly, its threads vibrating with the dots and dashes of Mr. Morse's code. The web—the telegraph web, like its Internet great-grandchild a century and a half later—conveyed news, facilitated commerce, and whispered gossip. Romance blossomed over the telegraph; even weddings took place telegraphically. It reported stock prices and winning lottery numbers. Gamblers and scam artists used the telegraphic web as well, passing news of sporting events and devising schemes to cheat and defraud.

The spider that owned the web was the Western Union Telegraph Company. Formed by the merger of several competing telegraph companies in 1855, it controlled 90 percent of all telegraph traffic in the United States within just over ten years. But the telegraph's astonishing growth was just getting started. In 1867 the telegraph network carried 5.8 million telegraph messages and Western Union reported revenues of some $6.6 million—almost $700 million in today's dollars. By 1875 the number of messages had grown to about 20 million. So many messages, in fact, that the lines were becoming clogged. Expanding capacity by adding more telegraph wires was an expensive proposition. The network cried out for a way to transmit multiple telegraph messages over the same pair of wires, and riches awaited the man who invented the "multiple telegraph."

As a later observer put it, "Nothing, save the hangman's noose, concentrates the mind like piles of cash." Of the many minds that concentrated on solving this problem, one belonged to a Boston professor, amateur inventor, and teacher of the deaf named Alexander Graham Bell. Bell's take on the multiple telegraph came from his studies of hearing, sound, music, and human physiology. Bell knew that sounds, like music and speech, were made up of harmonics, that is, of different simultaneous frequencies. Perhaps it was possible to send multiple telegraph signals over the same wire using multiple tones of different pitch? Bell called his idea the "harmonic telegraph."

Bell worked intensely on the harmonic telegraph, even going so far as to accept an investment from Gardiner Hubbard, a Boston lawyer who would eventually become his father-in-law. But Bell's mind kept gravitating toward a slightly different—and slightly crazy—idea: if you could send several notes simultaneously down a telegraph line for a multiple telegraph then maybe . . . just maybe . . . you could send a human voice down the wires.

He became obsessed with this new idea, despite his investors' attempts to keep him focused on the piles of cash the harmonic telegraph was going to generate for them. The telephone "could never be more than a scientific toy," Hubbard told Bell. "You had better throw that idea out of your mind and go ahead with your musical telegraph, which if it is successful, will make you a millionaire."

But he couldn't. Bell was consumed by a puzzle that was stuck in his head, a puzzle that wasn't going anywhere until he figured it out. As the historian Tim Wu writes, "For him the thrill of the new was unbeatably compelling, and Bell knew that in his lab he was closing in on something miraculous. He, nearly alone in the world, was playing with magical powers never seen before." He was also the right man for the job, the key that fit the lock. Bell himself recalled later, "I now realize that I should never have invented the telephone if I had been an electrician. What electrician would have been so foolish as to try any such thing? The advantage I had was that sound had been the study of my life—the study of vibrations."

It took three years but on March 10, 1876, Bell finally succeeded: he managed to send speech through a wire and into the next room. His prototype telephone was an unlikely contraption. To use it, Bell spoke into the transmitter, a funnel-shaped mouthpiece that focused his voice upon a flexible diaphragm. Suspended from the diaphragm was a short length of platinum wire, half immersed in a jar of sulfuric acid, the same sort of corrosive acid you'd find in a car battery. A wire ran from the platinum to the receiver—a primitive speaker, basically—in the next room. From the speaker, a wire ran to a battery and then back to a brass pipe that was also immersed in the transmitter's acid bath. The acid was conductive and completed the circuit between the transmitter and the receiver. Here was the key innovation, the thing that made it all work: the louder Bell spoke into the mouthpiece, the more the diaphragm deflected and the deeper the platinum wire was plunged into the acid. The more wire dipped into the acid, the less electrical resistance there was in the circuit and the more current flowed to the receiver, causing the speaker to move proportionately. Using a jar of sulfuric acid Bell had created what would become known as a variable resistance transmitter. It was this that allowed his system to accurately mimic the volume fluctuations of speech over a pair of wires.

Bell, Hubbard, investor Thomas Sanders, and Bell's assistant Thomas Watson turned their attention to commercializing the new invention. Western Union, with its telegraph monopoly and millions of messages and hundreds of thousands of miles of wire, was the undisputed telecommunications giant of the day. It would seem to have been the natural home of telephony, an established company with a closely related business, technology, and relevant assets. Bell is said to have offered Western Union the rights to his telephone patent in 1876 for $100,000. Western Union's president is alleged to have responded, "What use could this company make of an electrical toy?" Well, then.

Bell and his associates pressed on with the telephone's commercial rollout. This often took Bell and Watson on the public lecture circuit in Boston and its surrounds, demonstrating their new invention to crowds that were usually enthusiastic but sometimes skeptical. As one newspaper wrote at the time, "It is indeed difficult, hearing the sounds out of the mysterious box, to wholly resist the notion that the powers of darkness are somehow in league with it." Despite such occasional press commentary they persevered. By 1877 the first permanent telephone wires were strung in a suburb of Boston, the first ads for telephone service appeared, and the first telephone rentals took place. The Bell Telephone Company itself was founded in July of that year.

If you wanted telephone service between your office in Boston and, say, your home outside of town, Bell would be glad to set you up. You would be able to call your office from the comfort of your home, and your coworkers could call you. But it wasn't much like telephone service today. Bell's offering was point-to-point: a telephone at your home, a telephone at your office, and a telephone line run directly between them. In fact, it was your responsibility to hire telegraph contractors to run the line between your home and office. If you wanted to talk to multiple shops or suppliers, you had set up multiple pairs of telephones—and wires—between them and you.

This was high-tech wizardry back in the day. But it suffered from some obvious drawbacks. The maximum distance you could cover was about twenty miles. Basic service was $20 per year for a pair of telephones for residences, $40 per year for businesses—equivalent to about $400 and $800 per year today. But the killer expense was telegraph line installation, which cost between $100 and $150 per mile, that is, between $2,000 and $3,000 per mile in present dollars. Note that telephones were rented, never owned outright; this was a key part of the Bell plan to maintain ownership over the entire telephone system.

Forget about all that, though, because these are all small potatoes compared to this: you couldn't call anyone you didn't have a connection to. Want to talk to Aunt Mabel? Better get the telegraph installers busy running wires between your house and hers.

Bell and others were aware of this problem and knew how to fix it. Instead of running wires directly from one place to another, why not run them all to a central place? When you wanted to make a call you'd pick up the phone and do something—push a button, turn a crank—to get the attention of someone at "central." There a person—an operator—would answer the phone. You'd ask to be connected to Mr. Smith (who needed telephone numbers when only a few people had telephones?). Central would ring Mr. Smith's telephone line. When Mr. Smith answered, the operator would connect the wires together, switching your call from central to your party.

As Bell himself put it in a memo from early 1878, "Instead of erecting a line directly from one to another, I would advise you to bring the wires from the two points to the office of the Company and there connect them together . . . the company should employ a man in each central office for the purpose of connecting wires as desired. A fixed annual rental could be charged for the use of the wires, or a toll could be levied. As all connections would necessarily be made at the central office, it would be easy to note the time during which any wires were connected and to make a charge accordingly—bills could be sent in periodically." He added, prophetically, "However small the rate of charges might be, the revenue would probably be something enormous." The switchboard, and with it the concepts of a telephone central office or exchange—to say nothing of your monthly telephone bill and its per-minute charges—was born.

The first commercial switchboard debuted in January 1878 in New Haven, Connecticut, connecting twenty-one subscribers over eight telephone lines to a single operator, all under license from Bell Telephone. The first switchboards were primitive affairs: pieces of wood with a handful of metal bits, something that a fourth-grade science fair participant would scoff at today. But they worked, quickly establishing their superiority over point-to-point connections.

Switchboards rapidly grew in size and complexity. The first switchboard operators? Teenage boys. As John Murphy writes in his book *The Telephone,* "It was believed that they would have the energy, dexterity, quicksilver reflexes, and mechanical know-how to connect hundreds of calls an hour on a switchboard composed of a bewildering maze of thousands of cords and jacks. It turned out, however, that they were often impatient, rude, and foul-mouthed to callers." Goodness, who could have predicted? The teenage boys soon found themselves out of their jobs, replaced by women. The ladies, Murphy says, provided a "warmer human voice for the phone company" and also injected some sex appeal for the telephone's primary user base: businessmen.

By now Western Union recognized its mistake in dismissing the telephone as a toy. Sure, Bell had three thousand installed telephones and Western Union had none. But Western Union was the largest company on earth at the time, with financing, engineering and operations skills, and 250,000 miles of installed telegraph wire. In December of 1877 it went head to head with Bell Telephone, launching the American Speaking Telephone company, with inventor Thomas Edison as one of its technical wizards. Within the year Western Union had surpassed Bell Telephone in several markets and looked poised to crush Bell entirely; it didn't even resemble a fair fight.

But Bell had something that Western Union didn't: the fundamental patent on the telephone. Bell sued Western Union for patent infringement in September 1878. It took more than a year but in the end Bell won. In November 1879 Western Union settled the lawsuit, agreeing to exit the telephone business and transfer its telephone exchanges and thousands of telephone subscribers to Bell. In exchange, Bell Telephone agreed to limit its involvement in the telegraph business and to share a portion of its telephone revenues with Western Union for seventeen years. By the 1880s Bell Telephone's publicly traded stock had become the belle of the

Boston Stock Exchange, where it traded under the ticker symbol "T"—for "telephone."

The legal victory also helped Bell go after a smaller but still vexing problem: people who had illegally connected telephones—some stolen, some leftovers from independent telephone companies—to Bell Telephone lines. "During the past few months the American Bell Telephone Co., of Boston, has had detectives at work in this city endeavoring to ascertain how many 'bogus' or outlawed telephones were in use here," an 1890 trade journal reported. "Over 200 have been discovered, and last Thursday the first batch of fifteen or twenty liverymen, doctors, dentists, druggists, and fuel dealers who have been using these infringing telephones were summoned to appear in the United States Circuit Court." As a Bell agent in Philadelphia said, "I cannot understand how many good business men can permit themselves to use what they know it is against the law to use."

Despite having to deal with the occasional pirate telephone user, Bell was now positioned to own the majority of the telephone network in the United States for the next one hundred years—but there was one problem. Bell Telephone's sacred patents would start expiring in 1894, opening the field for competition. To prepare for this coming onslaught, Bell Telephone formed a new subsidiary: American Telephone and Telegraph. AT&T's mission was to build long-distance telephone lines—"long lines," as they were called. The idea was to use the time remaining before its patents expired to develop the nation's long-distance telephone network. Then, when the patents ran out, the company would have a formidable barrier to would-be competitors. AT&T would be the only company with long-distance telephone service and it could either charge other companies for access to its long-distance network or simply refuse to let other companies use it.

AT&T's first long-distance line, between New York and Philadelphia (capacity: one call), went live in 1885. AT&T reached Chicago in 1892, St. Louis in 1896, Minneapolis in 1897, and Kansas City in 1898. The far west took longer, as telephone engineers struggled with the challenge of sending voice over greater and greater distances. But the engineers persevered; Denver was reached in 1911 and San Francisco in 1915.

Switchboards, meanwhile, still based on the same fundamentals as the piece of wood with connectors, became larger and more sophisticated. Electrical cords insulated in woven cloth were used to connect incoming calls to destination telephone lines; these are the "cordboards" you see in old movies, the ones where dozens of operators sit next to one another, arm by arm, plugging and unplugging wires into the large connector panels in front of them.

By 1888 a switchboard had been designed that could serve more than ten thousand subscribers in New York City. In the cordboard's eventual form, an operator would sit in front of about two hundred answering jacks and roughly three thousand calling jacks, that is, she could answer calls from about two hundred customers and connect them to about three thousand others. Multiple individual switchboards could be placed next to each other and ganged together, allowing one operator (with a certain amount of standing and stretching) to connect calls on the boards to her left or right, tripling her capacity. The result was that her two hundred subscribers could be connected to about nine thousand others. Put fifty of these switchboards and operators in the room and you had a complete telephone exchange: almost ten thousand people could be connected to one another.

But what if you want to talk to somebody served by an entirely different switchboard? To do this you need a way of connecting switchboards in different locations. Wires called trunk lines were installed between central offices for this purpose. The central offices are the branches on the tree and the wires connecting them form the tree's trunk. But Bell Telephone quickly ran into the same problem it had with the original telephone system: trunk lines are point to point. If you have ten central offices in a given city, and they all need trunk lines between them, you find yourself having to run forty-five lines due to all the possible combinations of central offices that need connections with each other—a big, expensive mess, and one that gets worse with each central office you add.

The tandem switchboard solved this problem. You can think of a tandem switchboard as a switchboard of other switchboards, a special switchboard in a special central office that was used only for connecting other switchboards together. Just like the original central offices had all the telephone wires for a given exchange brought to a central place, a tandem central office had the trunk lines from other offices brought to a central place. There an operator on a tandem switchboard could connect trunk lines from one central office to another. The network was starting to become hierarchical.

By 1903 there were about 3 million switchboard connected phones. The interesting thing about these millions of lines is that, in every case, a human being was the switch. It was the operator's hand, arm, and reach that switched an incoming call to its destination, and the operator's brain that told the hand and arm where to reach and what to do. Telephone switching was an intensely manual process, requiring warehouses full of people. By 1902 the Bell System employed some thirty thousand operators; by 1914 it was about a hundred thousand.

Humans as switches have lots of advantages, qualities such as judgment, sympathy, warmth—the personal touch that is part of customer service. But they have disadvantages too. For one thing, you have to pay them. For another, they're slow. Between a lack of long-distance capacity and humans having to put through the calls, a coast-to-coast call in 1922 might have taken fifteen minutes or more to be connected. They make mistakes, for instance, plugging the wrong cord into the wrong jack. And then there are their all too human frailties. They eavesdrop on conversations. They gossip. They have loyalties.

The last of these qualities, legend has it, was the straw that broke an undertaker's back. Back in the late 1880s Almon Strowger, a mortician in Kansas City, Missouri, noticed a disturbing drop in his business. As it happened, the wife of a competing undertaker worked as an operator at the neighborhood switchboard. She, the story goes, tended to connect callers to her husband's business—not Strowger's—when someone would call in and ask for the undertaker.

You can think of many solutions to such a problem. You could complain to the telephone company. You could have a friendly chat with your competitor. You could even sue. But Strowger could see through to the root of the problem: pesky humans. Eliminate human operators and you'd eliminate the problem. Strowger set upon inventing a system to make human operators obsolete. Who needs a bunch of people plugging cords in boards when a machine could do the work more quickly, more accurately, less expensively—and more honestly?

Strowger's first mechanical telephone switch was patented in 1891. It allowed telephone subscribers to "dial" their own calls without needing to go through an operator. The original Strowger system didn't involve an actual circular telephone dial; rather, each telephone had three buttons: one for the hundreds digit, one for the tens digit, and one for the ones digit. To call telephone number 315, you pressed the hundreds button three times, the tens button once, and the ones button five times. Inside, the fiddly bits of the switch worked together to connect you to the person you wanted. Look Ma Bell, no operator!

Strowger formed the Automatic Electric Company to build and sell his mechanical telephone switch. The first automatic telephone exchange, based on the Strowger switch, opened in November 1892 in La Porte, Indiana, with seventy-five subscribers and room for ninety-nine total.

Like many inventions, the first Strowger switch wasn't quite ready for prime time and required a great deal of additional work before it became a commercially solid product. But it got there eventually, and with tremendous success. Bell eventually began using Strowger switches from Automatic Electric in 1915, and by 1926 Bell had licensed the Automatic Electric design and was manufacturing the switches itself. Telephone switches based on the

Strowger switch—called "step-by-step" switches within the Bell System—would go on to become the dominant type of telephone switch for more than seventy years, seeing widespread use around the world. In the United States, the popularity of the Strowger switch reached its peak only in 1972 when more than 42 million telephone lines were connected to step-by-step switches descended from Strowger's original design.

Other types of automatic telephone switches followed the Strowger switch. The Bell System began a metamorphosis, from a purely human affair to a gigantic cyber-mechanical-human endeavor: a mix of operators and machines switching calls, supported in the background by still more humans designing, building, installing, and caring for the switching machines. Functions that were once the domain of human operators slowly became increasingly mechanized: switchboards became switching machines; tandem switchboards became tandem switches ("tandems" for short)—specialized machines designed to connect trunk lines from other switching machines, building up the long-distance telephone network link by automated link.

Bell Telephone's worries about competition starting when its patents began expiring in 1894 turned out to be well founded. Just ten years later there were more than six thousand competing independent telephone companies providing local telephone service. For Bell Telephone and its shareholders, this competition was bad enough. But in some ways it was worse for the customers. Prices varied considerably, with some telephone companies opting for flat-rate service in which customers paid a fixed yearly fee for all the local calls they could make, while other companies went with measured-rate service and charged customers per call (and sometimes per minute) for local calls. Worst of all, the telephone lines of independent companies didn't connect with those of the Bell System, or, for that matter, with other independents. Cities would have multiple telephone companies and subscribers to one company couldn't call those of another. Businesses had to have different phone lines installed from different telephone companies to support their customers.

Despite the chaos caused by these kinds of problems, the independents looked to be winning. By 1903 Bell had about fifteen hundred telephone exchanges and about 1.2 million subscribers. The independents had more than six thousand exchanges and about 2 million subscribers.

Bell Telephone fought back with everything it had. It drove independents out of business through what some would call predatory pricing, and it bought up many of those it could not drive out of business. It denied the independents the use of its long-distance network. And it engaged in more underhanded tricks, including bribing public officials to prevent the establishment of independent telephone companies as well as using company influence with banks to deny its competitors badly needed loans. It also launched an effort to dominate the telegraph industry, buying a controlling interest in its old nemesis Western Union in 1908. AT&T was described as a "ruthless, grinding, oppressive monopoly."

The U.S. Justice Department began an antitrust investigation against AT&T in 1913, culminating in a recommendation that the Interstate Commerce Commission dig into AT&T with an eye toward regulation. The possibility of breakup of the Bell System— or even government takeover of the telephone system—loomed. Such a possibility was not idle speculation. Britain had nationalized its telephone system in January 1912, and in 1913 the new U.S. postmaster believed that the telephone system should be owned by the government just like the postal system.

AT&T began a series of negotiations with the Justice Department to forestall such an outcome. By the end of 1913 AT&T vice president Nathan Kingsbury reached a compromise with the government, the first of what would be several over the next seventy years. Under what became known as the Kingsbury Commitment, AT&T agreed to do three things. First, it would divest itself of Western Union. Second, it would stop buying up independent telephone companies, at least without Justice Department permission. And third, it would allow independent telephone companies to connect to the Bell System's precious long lines, allowing customers of independents to make long-distance calls—for a fee.

The Kingsbury Commitment appeared to be a tremendous victory for the government and independent telephone companies, and a huge concession for AT&T. But appearances can be deceiving. Tim Wu writes, "The trick of the Kingsbury Commitment was to make relatively painless concessions that preempted more severe actions, just as inoculation confers immunity by exposing one's system to a much less virulent form of a pathogen." In particular, Kingsbury traded involvement in an old industry, the telegraph, for government-approved dominion of a new industry, long-distance telephone.

The Kingsbury Commitment started AT&T down the path of becoming a regulated, government-sanctioned monopoly. By 1925 the Bell System had coalesced into more or less the form that would carry the company forward for the next sixty years: American Telephone and Telegraph as the headquarters company and long-distance provider, Western Electric as its manufacturing division, Bell Laboratories as its research and development arm, and more than a dozen regional Bell telephone companies that provided local telephone service: New England Telephone and Telegraph, New York Telephone, the Bell Telephone Company of Pennsylvania, Pacific Telephone and Telegraph, etc. It employed almost three hundred thousand people and had annual revenues of $761 million in 1925—more than $9 billion in today's dollars. Its network connected about 50 million telephone calls each day for some 16 million telephone subscribers over 45 million miles of wire and cable.

AT&T's vast size, clever engineering, and distinct fusion of humans and machines made this communication network possible. What AT&T didn't realize was that, in building this network, it had also built an electronic playground.

Three

CAT AND CANARY

BY THE MIDDLE of the twentieth century the playground—
that is, AT&T's telephone switching network—was largely
formed, at least in its broad outlines. Millions of telephone subscribers used it to switch their calls across the country, and even
overseas, every day. Not one of them noticed that the telephone
system was anything more than a utility, a dull, drab, predictable
—and predictably expensive—service for getting calls from point
A to point B.

What the playground needed was someone to start playing with it.

David Condon* would turn out to be that person.

Condon was in a Woolworth's store in 1955 when he heard a
sound that transfixed him. Louder than the background noise of
the other shoppers in the store, it was also ear catching, increasing
in pitch and then decreasing. Not pure but warbling. If a pure
musical note was still water, this was water with ripples in it.

Condon scanned the store, trying to see past the other customers. Where was it coming from?

There.

He walked over to the counter, to the thing that was making
the noise.

A small electric motor and air compressor were connected to a
brightly colored plastic toy. It was a plastic flute, about ten inches

---

*A pseudonym.

29

long, with a small plastic bird in a small plastic birdcage on it. A plastic cat on the whistle gazed longingly at the bird. As part of the Woolworth's display, the motor ran the slide of the whistle back and forth while the air blew, producing the rising and falling pitch he had heard. A small metal clip inside the whistle added the warbling quality to the sound.

"Davy Crockett Cat and Canary Bird Call Flute," read the sign above it. A picture showed Davy Crockett in his trademark coonskin cap, playing his flute, while songbirds swooped down, attracted by the magical melody.

It was forty-nine cents.

It was perfect.

The whistle soon found itself under the knife. Wire cutters snipped off the plastic birdcage, freeing the canary. A soldering iron melted the plastic under the canary itself, freeing it still further—all the way into the garbage can.

Condon borrowed some equipment from the lab at the school where he was studying for his master's degree in chemistry. He took a motor from a chemical mixer—a blender for chemistry labs, basically—and mounted an aluminum disc on it. He placed some tape on the disc to make an insulated spot that would break an electrical connection as the disc spun. He adjusted the speed until a borrowed pulse counter told him it was rotating twenty times a second. He used a signal generator to feed a precise tone through this contraption. It made a warbling noise, a bit like a buzz but more pleasant. He adjusted the tone until it was centered in pitch about two octaves above middle C: a thousand cycles per second, or 1,000 Hz, as the engineers say.

He adjusted the slide on the Cat and Canary Bird Call Flute until it, too, made a 1,000 Hz tone when he blew it. Then he turned his attention to the bronze-phosphor metal clip in the whistle. He drilled holes in it until, by ear, it matched the pulses coming from his mixer-motor, wheel-counter setup: twenty pulses per second.

It was going to work, he was sure of it.

He waited for night to fall.

★ ★ ★

Say you travel back in time to 1955. You land in Miami, the weather is nice there, and you'd like to call your friend Bill in snowy Denver to rub it in. Bill's number, odd as it may sound, is Race 2-7209. If that doesn't seem like a reasonable telephone number to you, remember that you're from the future, where telephone numbers are, well, numbers—ten-digit-long numbers, at that.

It wasn't always that way. On the very early switchboards at the dawn of the telephone age you simply told the operator the name of the person you wanted to speak to and she connected you. Although numbers became necessary as telephone exchanges got larger, you didn't need seven- or ten-digit numbers; the original Strowger switching system used two-digit numbers to accommodate a hundred subscribers. And since the largest manual switchboard exchanges could handle only about ten thousand people, telephone numbers stabilized for a while at four digits. But of course a given city might have multiple telephone exchanges. Exchanges were named, not numbered, and often were christened with the name of the general area or street where they were located. So Bill might be in the Race exchange and I might be in the Atlantic exchange and Joe might be in the Filbert exchange, depending on which neighborhoods and local landmarks were prominent where each of us lived.

This system worked great back in the days when, even for a local call, you picked up the phone, the operator came on the line and asked "Number please?," you told her the number ("Race 2-7209"), and she connected you. No dialing involved. In some sense, this was the pinnacle of telephone service: as the Bell System's official history says of this approach to making a phone call, "[The telephone] user's operation had been reduced to the minimum effort ever achieved. He merely lifted his receiver and verbally informed the operator of his wishes."

This business of telephone exchanges having names created a problem when the rotary dial telephone arrived on scene: how are you going to dial the number Atlantic 3-3040? Is the telephone going to have a dial with twenty-six letters and ten digits? This problem befuddled AT&T for years, until 1917, when one of the company's engineers hit upon the system we're so familiar with today: the letters "ABC" would be associated with the digit 2, "DEF" with 3, and so on. Callers would use just the first two or three letters of the exchange name plus the telephone number to dial a call. So Race 2-7209 would be dialed as 722-7209. "[It] seems so obvious that it is unbelievable that it took so long to invent, and it is difficult to realize the tremendous significance of this proposal when it was made," according to an AT&T history. The result came to be called "two-letter, five-digit" dialing and it paved the way for telephone numbers made up entirely of digits.

But back to our 1955 long-distance call from Miami to Denver. By the mid-1950s the telephone system had grown into an interesting blend of humans and machines. In many areas of the country you could dial local calls yourself, but in other places you still might not have a dial on your telephone—in those places the operator would handle even local calls for you, just as at the turn of the century. And whether you dialed your own local calls or needed the operator to do it for you, in most parts of the country local calls were free or, perhaps more accurately, were paid for as part of your flat-rate monthly phone bill.

Not so long distance. It was expensive, of course, and, except for a tiny handful of cities with something called "direct distance dialing"—a newfangled service the telephone company had introduced in 1951—if you wanted to make a long-distance call you had to dial 211, where a special long-distance operator would arrange for your call.

So you dial 211 on your rotary phone to get the Miami long-distance operator on the horn. You tell her you want to talk to Race 2-7209 in Denver. Unfortunately for our operator—and for you—Miami has no direct circuits to Denver. This is not unusual;

cities don't have long-distance trunk lines to every other city. It's economics: long-distance trunks are expensive to string from place to place and, unless those lines are going to be reasonably well utilized, the telephone company just can't justify the expense.

Don't worry, though, your Miami operator has connections to operators in lots of other places, and one of those places probably has trunk lines to Denver. And if they don't, well, they'll have connections to other cities that will—kind of like the hub-and-spoke system airlines use today. Just like with air travel, if Bill lived in some tiny, faraway town that most people have never heard of, the route can get lengthy and complicated and hard to figure out, requiring multiple intermediate cities to get you there. A handy guidebook at the operator's switchboard position provides a quick memory jogger for the most common routes. For the unusual ones, Ma Bell provides a special rate-and-route operator that our Miami operator can call for advice when she's stumped. Rate-and-route is a phone company internal operator customers cannot call directly. She and her sisters are the mavens of call routing.

Denver is easy, though, it's a big city, and our Miami operator has that one memorized. Almost by reflex she reaches for a plug on her switchboard and jacks into an idle Atlanta trunk, connecting to her opposite number: the Atlanta inward operator. The Miami operator presses her "ring forward" button, sending a quick signal—*brrrrp!*—to get the attention of the operator up north. A light appears on the Atlanta operator's board and she answers by plugging into the corresponding jack. The operators have a quick, almost machinelike exchange.

"Atlanta."

"Denver, Race 2-7209."

"Right."

The Atlanta inward operator goes through the same process to move the call down field. She has a direct trunk to Denver; you can hear the hiss of the long-distance noise when she plugs into it. A similar mechanized conversation ensues.

"Denver."

"Race 2-7209."

The Denver operator does some quick plug-n-jack jujitsu. "Ringing."

Bill answers the phone. The operators drop off the circuit, their work done. You have a brief conversation. Remember, long-distance is actually expensive, so you can't afford to talk for too long. Your ten-minute call costs $5.90, about $48 in today's dollars.

As it happens, you've just experienced the best-case scenario: the breaks were all in your favor and everything worked just like it was supposed to. But lots of things could have gone wrong. All circuits could have been busy between Miami and Atlanta, or Atlanta and Denver, in which case the long-distance operator would have arranged to call you back when a circuit was free. Even if you got through Bill might not have been home. If his phone just rang and rang, that would be one thing; you wouldn't be charged a cent. But the worst would be if Bill wasn't home but his mom was. When she answered the phone, you'd get charged for the call, and you didn't even get to talk to Bill! Given how expensive this could be, that might be enough to scare you into not calling him at all.

The phone company doesn't like it when its customers are scared to make phone calls—it's bad for business. To avoid this, AT&T offered something called a person-to-person call. With a person-to-person call, you tell the long-distance operator not just the number to call but the name of the exact person that you want to speak to. If that person isn't home, you pay nothing. But the telephone company has just become a casino. If the person you're calling is home, AT&T charges you an extra fee—in some cases up to twice the cost of an ordinary station-to-station telephone call. This double or nothing scheme made long-distance calls more palatable for many, especially when calling places like dorms or boarding houses with lots of people and only one phone. Of course, person-to-person calls also created an opportunity to cheat the telephone company. Say you're a businessperson traveling across country and you want to let your spouse know that you're okay, but you don't want to pay for a long-distance phone call to your home. You and your sweetie agree on an imaginary name ("Josefina Q. Zoetrope") that means you've arrived and you're fine. When you arrive at your destination, you ask the operator for a person-to-person call to Josefina at your home telephone number. Your spouse answers and says that Josefina isn't there. The call was free and your spouse is relieved.

If Bill wasn't home but it was really important to reach him, you could have the Denver operator leave a message for him to call you. Of course, long-distance calls being expensive, Bill might not want to spend the money to call you back. That's okay, you can have him call you on your dime. The message left for Bill with whoever answered Bill's phone would be something like, "Please call Operator Eight in Miami, there is a long-distance call for you." When Bill got home, he could pick up his phone and ask to speak to Operator 8 in Miami. Long-distance cordboard magic would ensue and, when he finally reached Operator 8, he would give his name and ask if there was a call for him. Assuming she found his name in the pile of toll tickets on her desk, she would reply, "Yes sir, there is, let me connect you," and then would complete the call back to you in Miami. That call would cost you money but it would be free to Bill.

Darkness fell. It was time to test the modified Davy Crockett Cat and Canary Bird Call Flute.

Condon took his whistle to a pay phone. He dialed o and asked for Operator 6 in Kansas City. He knew his local operator didn't have direct trunks to Kansas City so she'd have to route his call through an intermediate operator in Chicago. He listened patiently as she set up the call.

Operator 6 in Kansas City came on the line. Condon gave a name—not his own—and said he had received a message that there was a call for him from Kansas City. The operator checked her toll tickets but couldn't find any record of such a call. Both parties expressed the requisite puzzlement—genuine on her part, feigned on his. Operator 6 in Kansas City disconnected.

The moment of truth had arrived. He put his Cat and Canary Bird Call Flute up to the mouthpiece of the telephone and blew it several times in quick succession. "*Brrrrp! Brrrrp!*" He listened to the hiss of the trunk line as moments ticked by.

A different operator's voice came on the line. "Chicago," she said. It worked!

It did just what he felt so sure it would do. He had modified his Davy Crockett Cat and Canary Bird Call Flute to generate the special "ring forward" signal—*brrrrp!*—used to get the attention of a distant operator. This was the signal that made the lamp light up on an inward operator's switchboard, the one that signaled an incoming call from another operator. Because it wasn't just a pure tone—it was 1,000 Hz modulated by a 20 Hz warble—he couldn't produce that signal with an ordinary whistle. The flute's warble was what had caught his attention in Woolworth's. The warble was what made the whistle so perfect.

With this whistle, he figured, he would be able to make free calls anywhere in the country. All he'd have to do was get a pair of long-distance operators on the line, get the distant one to disconnect, and then blow his whistle. That would get a new, different operator on the line at an intermediate city. And since she could be reached only by other telephone operators, he figured she'd pretty much be willing to connect him anywhere he wanted.

Although the term wouldn't be invented for more than a decade, David Condon was a phone phreak, that is, someone obsessed with understanding, exploring, and playing with the telephone network. In 1955 he was the only one. He was on his own and would be for years. Eventually others would follow, and among a select group of them his whistle, and his discovery, would lead to his phone phreak nickname: "Davy Crockett"—the original explorer, the King of the Wild Frontier.

Condon's hearing the Cat and Canary Bird Call Flute that day in Woolworth's was chance, of course. But somehow his mind made the mental plug-and-jack connection that linked it with the operator's ring forward signal the instant he heard it. As the old saying goes, "Chance favors the prepared mind."

Condon's mind started its preparations early, as early as three or four years old. "I was fascinated as a very young child by the fact that there was a switchboard somewheres, and when you picked up the phone, a voice said, 'Number please.' My mother used to tell me that that was an operator, that she was connecting you to other people." Young Condon was mesmerized by the idea that there was something "out there"—a whole network, in fact—that could connect him to others.

Born in Philadelphia in 1931 he gravitated toward science. "Mother had a first cousin who was a science teacher. I think she first got me started. One of my presents that she brought me for my birthday was a dry cell." That is, a large 1.5-volt battery, something that he could use to do basic science experiments—to make motors spin and lightbulbs light up. "That thing lasted me for years," he recalls.

His father was a banker and his mother, eventually, was the principal of a four-room school in rural Pennsylvania. Technical interests ran in the family; his dad was a ham radio operator. Condon recalls being eleven or twelve years old and listening to shortwave radio with his father at night during World War II. They could only listen, since ham radio transmissions had been outlawed during the war for fear of use by enemy spies. This listening could sometimes turn chilling. Every so often they heard the most famous rhythm of Morse code: dit-dit-dit, dah-dah-dah, dit-dit-dit—SOS distress signals from Allied ships in the Atlantic under attack by German U-boats.

His first telephone—at least the first one that was his own—came from an elderly couple who lived next door. "I used to go over there and empty the ashes from their fireplace and bring them a bucket of coal. They had no running water in their house except in the kitchen," he recalls. Despite their lack of modern conveniences, his neighbors had something he didn't. "They had two magneto telephones in their barn," he remembers, that is, telephones with cranks that you turned by hand to generate a ringing voltage. They were wall mounted, with a box in the bottom for wet-cell batteries, the kind you put sulfuric acid in, like tiny car batteries. When the elderly couple passed away he inherited the phones. He took the magnetos apart and used them as generators, amazing his school chums by making lightbulbs glow.

It will come as no surprise that chemistry and physics were his favorite subjects; reading, less so. When a book report was due he would make the trip into the central library in Philly to borrow a summary of the book and use that to write his report. Foreshadowing his extraordinary future efforts with plastic whistles, he recalls, "It was more trouble to do that than it was to read the book, but I thought I was getting away with something."

In 1950 he left for college in Greensboro, North Carolina, where he majored in chemistry and mathematics. There he discovered the school library subscribed to a magazine called the *Bell Laboratories Record*. Every month it summarized Bell Labs' latest innovations, from the invention of the transistor to upgrades to the telephone network. Intended for a general audience, it was easier to read and more accessible than the engineering-focused *Bell System Technical Journal*.

The *Record* provided Condon with a great education, one that had been difficult to get up until then. "How you gonna find out how the telephone works?" he asks. "The operators didn't have time to talk to you, they weren't allowed to get into conversations with customers." Sure, you could make friends with a repairman and learn a lot—and he did, pretty much every place he lived—but the *Record* was like a topical college seminar devoted to discussing the telephone network, one that was extraordinary for its breadth, depth, and currency. "They were proud, they tooted their own horn," Condon recalls.

If it seems incredible to you that a company would publish the details of its technical achievements and how its internal systems worked, if it seems as if today these would be stamped CONFIDEN-TIAL and locked away and used to crush competitors, you'd be right. Indeed, many telephone company documents were deemed confidential—or, AT&T's highest classification, RESTRICTED. But remember too that AT&T didn't have any serious competitors. It wasn't just any company: it was *the* telephone company, a government-regulated monopoly, a national institution. For reasons of corporate pride, national service, and, of course, public relations, AT&T felt an obligation to share its latest and greatest feats with the public.

Armed with his Cat and Canary Bird Call Flute, Condon set about exploring the telephone network. He was living in Knoxville, Tennessee, at the time but quickly found the perfect place to carry out his experiments: the town of Oak Ridge, some twenty-five miles away. Oak Ridge was a strange place, one that didn't appear on maps until just a few years earlier, despite having a population of more than seventy thousand people. During World War II, Oak Ridge was a secret town built by the Army Corps of Engineers and guarded by the military. Known at the time as the Clinton Engineer Works, Oak Ridge was home to three uranium separation and processing plants used for the Manhattan Project, America's crash program to develop the atomic bomb. After the war, the town gained its name and its freedom, unlocking its gates to the outside world for the first time.

Two things made Oak Ridge ideal to Condon. First, Oak Ridge had its own long-distance trunk lines. He figured the long-distance lines would be routed through Knoxville, the closest big city, "but no," Condon recalls, "the Defense Department didn't want that." For security reasons, he believes, "They wanted Oak Ridge to be autonomous in its access to the network."

The second part was even better. "They did not want the possibility of people listening to secure calls, so they didn't give the operators monitor keys," Condon says. In most cities operators had the ability to listen to a telephone call in order to monitor its progress. But not operators at Oak Ridge. "As long as you didn't flash"—that is, push the telephone hook switch up and down—"and didn't leave any indication that you were through, she would leave you alone! It was *wonderful!*"

The only fly in the telephonic ointment had to do with Condon's chromosomes. He was a man, in other words, and men weren't operators in the 1950s. This presented some problems, since his whistle hack revolved around the idea of getting an operator on the line and convincing her to do something for him. Fortunately, men were employed to do engineering and troubleshooting work on the long-distance lines. He quickly learned to pretend to be a test board engineer—"Oak Ridge number one test" was his standard dodge when challenged by an operator. "That sounded good," he says. "I don't know if there was such a thing as a 'number one test board' but they were happy to help me, once I made it sound like I was with the telephone company."

Still, there was nothing like a female voice to lull an operator into carrying out your bidding. Condon's solution: girlfriends. "I would train them on what to say. We'd go out to Oak Ridge and we'd get on a phone that wasn't monitorable, a pay station. You call an operator in a distant city, they don't have a call for you, and when the operator releases you, you ring and hand it to the girl! She knew what to say. I had written it down for her."

With a girl and a pair of pay telephones in Oak Ridge he was set for an evening of fun. Talk about a hot date! "You could even call back to Oak Ridge if you wanted," he recalls. "If there were two pay stations and you had a girlfriend with you, you'd call her back to Oak Ridge. You could ring back to Oak Ridge and talk to the person next to you over this circuit to New York, no ticket, no nothing!"

But why? What would motivate a person to do such a thing?

"Just to be able to do it," Condon recalls with glee in his voice. "That's the thrill of it, isn't it?"

Four

THE LARGEST MACHINE IN THE WORLD

WELL BEFORE DAVY Crockett was taking his girlfriends on hot dates to trick operators into making long-distance calls, the engineers at Bell Laboratories were working hard to get rid of long-distance operators. In fact, they were working hard to get rid of operators altogether.

It wasn't because they were concerned that people like Crockett would come along and imitate the ring forward signal and trick operators into making free calls for them. It was simply that they realized, early on, that the telephone network was going to grow to a point where it could no longer be supported by human beings plugging cords into jacks. In the 1920s Bell employed about a hundred thousand operators—a big number but one that could be made to work. By 1965, however, they figured the company would need closer to a million operators if it stuck with manual switching. An AT&T historian later noted that this was not a very meaningful figure because "the population could not have supported such a work force." Besides, even if AT&T could find enough women to staff a million operator jobs, the cost of paying them would be heart-stopping.

Just like Almon Strowger before them, Bell Labs researchers realized that automation was the way forward. Significant inroads had already been made for local calling. By the 1950s the Bell System had thousands of automated telephone exchanges using switching systems based on Mr. Strowger's step-by-step design, a Bell-developed system called "panel," and a new arrival—a switching system developed during the 1930s called crossbar. Dial switching systems were becoming smarter and able to handle more calls, automatically, even among multiple exchanges within a city. And while manual switchboards, with their operators and cordboards, were still in existence—indeed, in 1955 some 15 percent of telephones were still older models that didn't even have dials—it was clear their days were numbered. The machines were coming.

Long distance was the big holdout, the largest bastion of human switching. Even as late as 1960 operators were still used for about 70 percent of long-distance telephone calls. Automating it presented some huge challenges.

First, it took human intelligence to figure out how to route a call from place to place. Remember your call from Miami to your friend Bill in Denver and the gyrations that multiple operators had to engage in to get your call through? That was for an easy case. God forbid, what would happen if Bill had lived in the tiny town of Gerlach, Nevada, way off the beaten path? Figuring out the route for that call would be a much harder problem. It might have required a consultation with the experts at rate-and-route, who would have told your long-distance operator the four or five cities she needed to connect through in order to make Bill's telephone ring.

Now imagine trying to build a machine in the 1930s or 1940s that is smart enough to solve this routing problem in a few seconds. Given a starting city and a destination city, the machine needs to figure out how to get the call from here to there. While it's at it, the machine should come up with an alternate route in case the first route doesn't work. But before you go off trying to build such a machine, please remember that the computer hasn't been invented yet; heck, the transistor hasn't been invented yet. The tools at your disposal are what *Star Trek*'s Mr. Spock dismissed as "stone knives and bearskins," that is, vacuum tubes and relays and mechanical switches.

Second, even if you had magic switching machines that could figure out how to route a call across the country, your customers had no way to dial each other directly. Remember how, when you wanted to make a long-distance call, you told the long-distance operator the city name and the telephone number of the person you wanted? Well, the words *Denver* and *Miami*—to say nothing of the names of all the other cities in the United States—don't appear on telephone dials. Just as it took a while for AT&T to come around to the idea that telephones needed telephone numbers, and then to figure out that telephone exchanges needed numbers, it also took a while to realize that cities needed their own numbers too: area codes, they would come to be called. AT&T wouldn't have this so-called national numbering plan worked out until 1945.

Even with switching machines and area codes there was yet another problem. The switching machines would need to communicate with each other over long distances, just like operators did. Say you're in New York City and you want to call a number in San Francisco. The switching machine in New York first needs to be smart enough to know that it should get to San Francisco via, say, Chicago. Then it needs to connect to Chicago and communicate the digits of the telephone number you want to call in San Francisco. Chicago then needs to connect to San Francisco and pass the destination telephone number to a switching machine in the city by the bay. This was all information that human operators would have passed along by voice. AT&T researchers needed to figure out a way that switching machines could tell each other what number to dial and some other information, too, such as whether the person called had answered the telephone. In fact, they needed to build something resembling a computer network, a network over which switching machines could pass signaling information to one another. It's just that they needed to do it well before computers and modems and the Internet had been invented.

Finally, AT&T wanted to make money at this game—this is the telephone company, after all, not Mother Teresa—so it needed a way to bill customers. In the old days, when operators were manually switching calls, this was easy: long-distance operators wrote up a paper toll ticket for each call. These tickets were collated and processed by hand. But if machines are doing the switching and routing, machines need to be able to do the billing too. It wouldn't do to have an automated network that could handle millions of calls a day only to have the entire operation bog down because humans had to tally up the bills by hand.

All of this was an incredibly tall order in the 1930s. Yet the crazy thing is Bell Labs got right to work. It would take tens of years, thousands of engineers, millions of dollars, and buildings full of equipment to make it happen. In the end the telephone network would be transformed into something previously undreamed of: it would become the largest machine in the world, one that would eventually extend over the entire surface of the earth.

Perhaps the best way to follow this transformation is to start by putting your finger into the hole marked 7 on an old-school rotary telephone, maybe back around 1950 or so. Crank the dial —the actual metal dial—all the way over to the right until your finger is up against the dial stop. Remove your finger. A spring unwinds, spinning the dial back to the left. As it spins, over the course of about three-quarters of a second, your telephone sends seven electrical pulses down your telephone line, over the wires and cables in your neighborhood, and into one of several hundred Strowger switches in your local central office.

In movie terms, that Strowger switch was Frankenstein's monster writ small: able to follow simple commands—the simpler the better —but a little short on brains. Each Strowger "can" was a cylinder about sixteen inches high and about six inches in diameter, jam-packed with wipers and ratchets and pawls and blades and other mechanical clockwork. Your telephone dial directly controlled its musculo-skeletal system. Every one of those electrical pulses your phone sent down the wire made something twitch inside the Strowger switch it was connected to. "Twitch," by the way, is not figurative; it is an accurate description of what physically took place in the switch. The digit 7 that you dialed caused a pair of metal contacts to twitch upward seven times, so fast that it seemed to make a *brrrp* noise as it went. While waiting for your next digit, it rotated to the right, connecting your telephone line to the next idle Strowger switch it could find. That next switch would then accept whatever digit you dialed next, again twitching a mechanism inside up and to the right. This mechanized ballet continued until you had dialed all the digits of your number; your last digit connected you from the last Strowger switch in the switching train to the actual pair of wires running to the telephone you wanted to call.

The key thing about the Strowger system was that every pulse your telephone sent down the line caused something to happen in the switch—physically, immediately, and directly. This direct control system was innovative when it was invented in the 1890s. But in addition to having lots of noisy, moving parts that needed service and eventually wore out, it suffered from two fundamental problems. First, every digit you dialed tied up one Strowger switch for the duration of your telephone call. If telephone numbers in your local exchange were four digits long, then when you called your friend down the street and talked for an hour, you tied up four Strowger cans for the entire call. This meant the telephone company needed to cram a lot of these Strowger switches into a central office, and that was expensive.

The other problem was that, like Frankenstein's monster, Strowger switches were not the sharpest knives in the switching drawer. Because calls proceeded through a step-by-step switching system one digit—and one switch—at a time, no individual Strowger switch ever saw more than a single digit of the telephone number you were dialing. Nothing in a Strowger system had the big picture, and that limited what the telephone system could do.

The wizards of Bell Laboratories gave telephone switches a brain of sorts when they developed the successors to the Strowger switch. Both the panel and crossbar switching systems used a technology that the telephone company called common control. Instead of the telephone directly controlling a switching machine itself, your telephone would tell the switching system's brain what you wanted done and the brain would figure out how to do it. So, for example, in a crossbar central office, the digits you dialed on your telephone no longer caused the central office's switching system to twitch directly with every pulse your phone sent out. Instead, your digits were stored in a relay-based memory called a sender. Once you had dialed the full number, the switch's brain, the marker, could look at the digits and figure out what it needed to do to connect your call. Once it did this, it could forget about your call and move on to the next one, freeing up resources. And because the brain had the entire telephone number you wanted to dial in one convenient place, it could do clever tricks that a Strowger switch could only dream of. As Bell Labs' head of switching later wrote, "In a word, the [switching] systems were acquiring a form of machine intelligence."

The pinnacle of that era's telephonic mechanized brain was something called the #4A crossbar switch. It was another in a long line of creatively named products from AT&T, joining the ranks of the #1 manual switchboard, the #5 manual switchboard, the 500-series desk telephone, and the #1 crossbar switch. Who needs fancy product names when you're a government-sanctioned monopoly?

For what it was, the 4A deserved a grander name. Deployed in 1950, it was a triumph of common control switching, the most advanced switching machine created to that point in history. Even the word *machine* doesn't do it justice: it conjures up images of a mechanical contrivance, something bigger than a breadbox but smaller than a car; a lawn mower, maybe. In contrast, the 4A took up a good chunk of a city block. Built up of rack after rack of gray metal cabinets filled with crossbar switches, wiring frames, markers, senders, and relays, if the Strowger switch was Frankenstein's monster, the 4A was Godzilla. By 1960 there were fifty-nine of them throughout the United States; almost two hundred of these behemoths would eventually be installed, the last in 1976.

The 4A was to be the brains of the long-distance network, the magic switching machine that could automatically figure out how to route a long-distance call from one place to another. Its routing intelligence did not come from a computer but rather from a device called a card translator. Hundreds of thin steel cards, each about five inches wide and ten inches long, had patterns of 181 holes punched in them to indicate how a call should be routed. Based on the first six digits of a telephone number—the area code and the exchange number—electromagnets selected and dropped cards. Light shined through the holes. By seeing where light passed through and where it was blocked, the 4A could decide how and where to send the call as well as figure an alternate route if something went wrong with the first one. As the telephone network grew and changed, the 4A could be reprogrammed simply by changing out cards. Even if the 4A fell short of human intelligence, the telephone company knew that its common control systems were nothing to sniff at. "At the end of this era," wrote a former Bell Labs executive, "Bell engineers were able to look back on the automated network of switching systems as the largest distributed computer in world."

Just like human operators, the brainy 4A switches passed calls among themselves and their less intelligent brethren by talking to each other. And like human operators, there were only a handful of things the switching machines needed to tell each other: what number to dial, whether the called party answered, and whether either party hung up. The telephone company called these latter two items supervisory information, since they had to do with how an operator would supervise a call. They were critically important: you can't charge a customer for a call if you don't know that the call was answered or when the parties hung up.

AT&T enabled its long-distance telephone switching machines to talk to each other by teaching them two different signaling languages: single frequency and multifrequency. Both were based on the switching machines sending tones—musical notes, basically—down the telephone trunk lines to each other. The multifrequency language, or MF for short, used pairs of tones to communicate what digits to dial, much the same way that today you use touch tones to communicate to the telephone system what digits you want to dial when you make a call from a landline telephone. The other language, single frequency or SF, was simpler than MF, and although it was slower it could be used with less intelligent switching machines, such as the old step-by-step switches. SF used pulses of a single tone—2,600 Hz, or seventh octave E for the musically inclined—to communicate dialing information: one beep to dial a 1, two beeps to dial a 2, etc. In a sense, it was just like a rotary phone sending electrical pulses down a phone line, except that it sent beeps instead. Both SF and MF also used this 2,600 Hz tone for supervisory information, that is, to communicate when one machine wanted to make a call and when the person you were calling answered the phone so that billing should start.

Introduced in the 1940s, MF and SF were high tech for their time. The multifrequency system was speedy, taking only a second or so to transmit a ten-digit telephone number from one switch to another. The tones sounded like fleeting musical notes and customers could sometimes hear the quick little blips of MF digits as they waited for their calls to go through. AT&T began acting like a proud parent of a musically gifted child. Magazine ads in 1950 showed a musical scale with the pairs of notes that made up each MF digit and described the system as "playing a tune for a telephone number." Telephone bill inserts bragged about MF and the tones were featured in an educational AT&T movie as well. In a flight of fancy, one telephone company manager told the press that new AT&T switching machines "sing" to each other.

The cleverest thing about SF and MF signaling was this: they allowed the switching machines to communicate by using the exact same wires that humans used to talk to each other. AT&T had spent millions of dollars running long-distance cables all across the United States. These cables were designed to carry voice, since that's what AT&T's human customers and operators used speak to one another. Instead of building a separate computer network for its switching machines, AT&T realized it could reuse its existing long-distance telephone circuits to carry both human voice *and* signaling information for each call. This would cost less than building a separate network and would be faster to deploy. This approach, called in-band signaling, meant that signaling information was sent in the same frequency band and over the same wires that were used for voice. It was an elegant and economical solution to the problem.

With the crossbar switch and the multifrequency signaling system, AT&T could embark on the next phase of automating long-distance switching, something called operator distance dialing. The idea here was to allow operators to directly dial long-distance calls, even if customers couldn't. If you wanted to call coast to coast, you'd still call the long-distance operator. But instead of the operator having to plug cords into jacks and talk to other operators and build up a lengthy chain of connections, circuit by circuit, she would just key in the area code and telephone number on a keypad on the console in front of her. The switching machines would do the rest, routing the call and talking to each other with MF or SF to set up the intermediate links. If the place she was calling couldn't be reached by just keying a number into her console, she would use the machines to get her call as far across the country as she could and then enlist the help of a plug-and-jack manual inward operator who was closer to the final destination.

Operator distance dialing simplified and sped the dialing of long-distance calls—good for customers since their calls went through more quickly and good for the phone company because it needed fewer operators to handle more calls. But it also provided AT&T with an opportunity to work the kinks out of automated long-distance switching without having to directly involve its customers. The long-distance operators became the first users of the new automated long-distance network—beta testers, we'd call them today. Or, as they were called by an AT&T spokesman at the time, "guinea pigs."

The guinea pigs survived and AT&T decided the kinks had worked out enough to let the customers try it themselves. On November 10,

1951, the small town of Englewood, New Jersey, became the first place in the country where customers could dial their own long-distance calls. Instead of dialing 211 and telling the long-distance operator they wanted "Garfield 2-2134 in San Francisco," lucky Englewood residents instead picked up the telephone and dialed ten digits themselves: 318-GA2-2134. Their local telephone switch would take this number, find a trunk to the remote city, and then send the musical MF notes down the line to get the call across the country. In essence, the local telephone switch acted as a sort of translator, taking the digits you dialed with your rotary phone and converting them to the telephone network's internal language of MF tones. (It worked the same way when touch-tone dialing was introduced years later: the local switch translated the touch-tone digits you dialed on your phone into MF digits that it sent into the long-distance network; this was necessary because touch-tones weren't the same as the MF tones.) Best of all, all this happened in seconds, not the minutes that used to be required when operators were involved.

To start with, Englewoodians were able to directly dial some 11 million people in Philadelphia, Pittsburgh, Cleveland, Detroit, Chicago, Milwaukee, Oakland, San Francisco, and Sacramento. Over the next twenty years customer long-distance dialing—later known as direct distance dialing, or DDD—spread across the country, with more and more customers able to dial their own long-distance calls. The largest machine in the world was growing, and the engineers at Bell Laboratories were finally getting their wish: a fully automated long-distance network, one where calls could be dialed coast to coast without operator intervention.

It would turn out to be a classic case of that old expression "Be careful what you wish for."

Five

BLUE BOX

R ALPH BARCLAY WAS walking through the engineering library at Washington State College, just minding his own business, when it called out to him. He couldn't say why, it just did.

It was a booklet, about seven by nine inches and maybe half an inch thick, on display in the library's new periodicals section. Its pale blue cover proclaimed it to be the November 1960 issue of something called the *Bell System Technical Journal*. It had been out for less than a week.

Barclay looked at the table of contents printed on its cover. Most of the articles could put even the hardest of hard-core geeks to sleep at twenty paces: "Magnetic Latching Relays Using Glass Sealed Contacts," "Molecular Structure in Crystal Aggregates of Linear Polyethylene," and the ever popular "'Ionic Radii,' Spin-Orbit Coupling and the Geometrical Stability of Inorganic Complexes."

Yet one title caught his eye: "Signaling Systems for Control of Telephone Switching." He flipped to the article and started skimming. Minutes passed. His original purpose for coming to the library shelved for the moment, he sat down and began to read in earnest.

Barclay was just eighteen. Athletic and of medium build, with brown hair and blue eyes, Barclay had started his first year at Washington State's Pullman campus, about fifty miles south of Spokane, just a couple of months earlier. "I was living in the dorm," he remembers, "and a lot of people in the dorm are looking for ways to make cheap phone calls home to their girlfriends and parents and suchlike." One of the guys in the dorm had—"somehow," he says—acquired his own personal pay telephone. And although students weren't allowed to have telephones installed in their rooms, for some reason the dorm rooms had telephone lines in them.

Barclay's dorm had quite a few engineers in it, and engineers, Barclay allows, are a problem. The engineers soon determined that somebody had left the door unlocked to the building's telephone closet, the little room where all the telephone wires come from. In the dark of night an operation was mounted. Certain wires were cross-connected. *Et voilà:* a pay telephone line from somewhere on campus ended up connected to the personal pay phone in Barclay's dorm. Barclay and the other kids in the dorm could now make telephone calls by depositing money in the pay phone, as usual, but the difference was that the owner of the pay phone—apparently not a business major—was a nice guy and returned the caller's money after each call.

Maybe it was this pay phone hack that caused bells to ring in Barclay's brain when he spotted the article in the *Bell System Technical Journal.* It laid bare the technical inner workings of AT&T's long-distance telephone network with clarity, completeness, and detail: how the long-distance switching machines sang to each other with single-frequency (SF) and multifrequency (MF) tones, how 2,600 Hz was used to indicate whether a telephone had answered, what the frequencies were of the tones that made up the MF digits, how overseas calls were made, and it even included simplified schematic diagrams for the electrical circuits necessary to generate the tones used to control the network. It was all there. Nothing was hidden.

By the time Barclay finished reading it, the vulnerability in AT&T's network had crystallized in his mind: "I thought, this is a better way than using a pay phone . . . this is a way to get around all that other stuff and do it directly."

"It," of course, was making free calls.

The ability to absorb sixty-four pages of dry, technical mumbo jumbo and spot the vulnerability is a rare one. The engineers from Bell Labs who designed the system and wrote the article didn't see it. Thousands of engineers in the future would read that article and not see it. But eighteen-year-old Ralph Barclay did. The funny thing about it is, once the hole is explained to you, it's obvious. But until it's explained to you, most people would never think of it. Certain people have minds that are tuned in a particular way to see things like that. Ralph Barclay was one of those people.

To understand Barclay's insight we have to think back to the things that made up AT&T's automated long-distance network, things like the spectacularly named #4A crossbar switching system that was the brains of the long-distance telephone network and how the machines talked to each other by speaking in tones. Because that's what the *Bell System Technical Journal* described and that's where Ralph Barclay spotted the flaw. Here's what he came up with.

Say you're in Seattle and, as always, you want to call your friend Bill in Denver. With Barclay's hack, your first step is to pick up the phone and dial directory assistance in any city—let's say New York just for fun: 212-555-1212. Unlike today, calls to directory assistance were free back then.

Seattle and New York are both big cities and have direct trunk lines between them. On a given long-distance trunk line between Seattle and New York, the switching machine in Seattle sends a 2,600 cycle per second tone—seventh octave E—to New York to indicate that the line is idle. New York sends the same tone back to Seattle to indicate that the line is not in use on its end either. Remember how in a flight of fancy an AT&T manager described the switching machines as "singing" to one another? This is the boring part of that song; you can think of it as the machines monotonously whistling this single note back and forth. It's almost like they're keeping each other company, reassuring each other that they're both still there.

As you dial the last digit of the number for New York directory assistance, the fancy switching machines and their signaling systems spring to life to get your call through. Seattle finds an idle trunk to New York and stops whistling 2,600 Hz on it. New York hears the trunk go silent, indicating that Seattle wants to make a call. New York sends back a "wink" signal—really just a moment of silence, of no 2,600 Hz tone, for about a quarter of a second. This wink tells Seattle that New York is ready and waiting for Seattle to tell it a phone number to call. Using either the SF or MF signaling language, Seattle sends New York the digits 555-1212. In SF-speak, this is a series of beeps of 2,600 Hz. In MF-speak, it consists of nine quick little pairs of tones that sound like brief musical notes: KP, 555 1212, and ST. The special signal called KP ("key pulse") at the beginning tells New York to get ready, and the final note, ST ("start"), tells New York that it has all the digits and can start dialing.

Now that New York knows the number you want to call, it makes the local connection and the directory assistance operator's telephone starts to ring. Up until now everything that has happened has been perfectly normal, just like Ma Bell intended. But now you, using Barclay's hack, insert yourself into the process. Before the operator can answer, you—naughty you—hold a speaker up to your phone's mouthpiece and play your *own* 2,600 Hz tone down the line for a second.

It is loud and pure and it sounds like this: *bleeeeeeep.*

Seattle isn't paying any attention to this, but the switching machine in New York sure is. New York hears your 2,600 Hz tone loud and clear and thinks that the Seattle switching machine sent it. And since this tone indicates the trunk line is idle, New York figures that Seattle is done using that trunk line, probably because you hung up. New York disconnects the call to the directory assistance operator—maybe before she's even answered.

But now you stop sending your tone. When you stop sending 2,600 Hz, the long-distance switching equipment in New York City thinks that Seattle wants to make another call. Just as before, New York sends a wink back to Seattle to say it's ready for a new call. Due to the nature of the circuitry involved, the wink has a bright, metallic ringing quality to it. It sounds like this: *kerchink!*

The noise tells you that you have just fooled New York into thinking that a new long-distance call is coming in. Once again, the switching machine in New York is waiting for Seattle to tell it what digits to dial. But Seattle isn't going to tell it anything, because Seattle is blissfully unaware of everything that has just transpired. The only thing Seattle knows is that you haven't hung up—you're still on the line, after all—and Seattle believes you can make only one call every time you pick up the phone. As far as Seattle is concerned, you're still talking to New York's directory assistance.

You, on the other hand, know better: you possess guilty knowledge. Using a simple electronic circuit, you can generate the same pairs of tones that Ma Bell's telephone switches use to serenade each other. Once again holding up a speaker to your phone, you play the tones needed to send New York the digits KP + 303 722 7209 + ST—that is, the number of your friend Bill in Denver. Now, of course, area code 303 isn't in New York City, but that's okay. The telephone switch in New York is a brainy 4A and knows how to route calls from one place to another. After all, Bell Labs worked hard to give it the brains to be able to do that. New York happily finds a trunk line to Denver and puts your call through, sending out tones on your behalf to instruct Denver on what number to dial. Moments later Bill's phone starts to ring.

Congratulations, you've just hijacked a phone call to directory assistance in New York and rerouted it to Bill in Denver. But that's only half the trick. The other half is this: your phone call to Denver is free. Why? Because Seattle is responsible for the billing of your phone call. As far as Seattle is concerned, you're still connected to directory assistance in New York and directory assistance is a free call.

Barclay had three insights when he read that article in the *Bell System Technical Journal*. The first was that sending a 2,600 Hz tone down the telephone line resets the remote switch but doesn't affect the local switch. The second was that you could then reroute a phone call from the remote switch to wherever you want. And the third was that the local switch is in charge of billing, so it continues to bill you for whatever call it thinks you originally made. With these three insights he now owned Ma Bell's network.

A few weeks after reading the *Bell System Technical Journal* article Barclay made the three-hour drive west to his hometown of Soap Lake, Washington, population 1,200. Home may be where the heart is, but for Barclay home was also where his workbench, soldering iron, and electronic components were. "I was an electronic tinkerer for years and years and years," he says. A curious one too; his older sister remembers Barclay plugging a bobby pin into an electrical outlet when he was four. His father, a truck driver in rural Washington, used to bring him broken TVs to fiddle with, and his bedroom was littered with electrical equipment, telephones, and radios. Barclay landed his first job—repairing broken radios—when he was in the fifth grade.

Barclay's first box took a weekend to build. It was a simple affair, housed in an unpainted metal enclosure about four inches on a side and perhaps two inches deep. Inside was a nine-volt battery and a single transistor oscillator circuit. On the outside the box sported a surplus rotary telephone dial and a red push button. The red button would allow Barclay to disconnect a call in progress—to "seize a trunk," in both telephone company and phone phreak parlance—by producing a 2,600 cycle tone for as long as he held it down. When spun, the rotary dial would make short blips of 2,600 Hz. If Barclay dialed the digit 6, for example, it made six short beeps. In other words, it would allow him to send digits using the older single-frequency language.

"I was surprised!" Barclay recalls. "It worked fine the first time!"

As it happens, it also worked best the first time. Barclay quickly ran into a problem. By 1960 fewer and fewer trunk lines used SF signaling. In its push for progress and dialing speed, the Bell System was well on its way to converting most long-distance trunks to multifrequency signaling. And those trunks didn't respond to Barclay's single-frequency beeps. The red button still worked—he could disconnect a call in progress and hear the *kerchink* come back from the remote end—but dialing was often a problem. "It worked sometimes, not consistently," he says—maybe one in four calls.

"That's when I discovered I needed multifrequency," he says—that is, he needed to generate pairs of tones for each digit as well as for the special "key pulse" and "start" signals. Barclay started work on his multifrequency box over Christmas break. It was more complicated than the first box, what with more transistor oscillators and associated wiring and all that, so it took a bit longer to build.

Barclay added a rotary dial for making blips of 2,600 Hz, but that was just for old time's sake; the real way you'd dial with it, the modern way, was with push buttons. Touch-tone phones weren't a commercial reality yet, so Barclay had to come up with his own telephone keypad. He ended up using keys from an old mechanical Burroughs adding machine. Each key was fastened to a push-button switch mounted underneath it. There were twelve keys in all: ten for the digits 0 through 9, one for the KP signal that needed to be sent before the digits, and one for the ST signal that needed to be sent after the digits.

He had it finished by Easter and it worked like a charm. He and his device became popular among a small circle of friends in his dorm, where he made calls home for them. But mostly, he says, he used it to play with the telephone network, "to see where we could call." As Barclay remembers it, "There were very, very few calls I made that were actual phone calls"—that is, calls he made to somebody he knew and wanted to talk to.

His new device was housed in a metal box, twelve by seven by three inches, that happened to be painted a lovely shade of blue. Barclay did not know it at the time, but the color of his device's enclosure would eventually become synonymous with the device itself. The blue box had just been born.

Back home for the summer, Barclay ran into another problem: his hometown, Soap Lake, was served by GTE—General Telephone and Electronics—one of the independent telephone companies separate from the Bell System. For whatever reason, GTE's switching and signaling equipment just didn't work with his blue box. Fortunately, Barclay's summer job was at a television and radio repair shop in the town of Ephrata, some five miles down the road. Those five miles made all the difference for Ephrata was in Bell territory and his blue box worked like a champ there.

The shop where he worked was two blocks down the street from a friend's photography studio. In exchange for a few free calls, his friend was happy to let Barclay's blue box live in the rear of the studio. If Barclay felt like playing around he could pop over to the studio on his lunch hour, walking down the alleyway running behind the buildings so he could come in through the back door; no need to disturb customers at either business by going in and out the front door.

That summer was a fun and productive one for learning about the telephone network. Barclay made friends with a kid who lived in Seattle and whose dad worked for the telephone company. "He happened to furnish me with a copy of the 'Rate and Route' book," Barclay says, the loose-leaf binder of telephone routing information that operators used to figure out how to get calls from here to there. "I was able to use that to access more areas. We actually tried it for overseas calls and were able to do some calls to England." Unfortunately, Barclay reports, "I didn't know anybody in England to call."

Barclay had some other friends whose parents worked for the telephone company and he mentioned to one of them that he was interested in learning more about how the phone system worked. Was there any way he might be able to get some surplus telephone equipment, he asked? "Oh, sure," Barclay recalls his friend's dad saying. Pacific Telephone turned out to be in the process of converting a nearby switching office from three-digit dialing to a more modern five-digit system. "If you want to drive over there, I'll make arrangements," his friend's father told him.

Barclay recalls pulling up at the telephone company central office in his dad's pickup truck and chatting with the switchman there.

"What are you interested in?" the switchman asked.

"What have you got?" Barclay replied.

As it happened, quite a lot. "I ended up taking home the whole three-digit telephone exchange," Barclay says. It was soon set up in his garage.

Summer drew to a close. It was September 15 and Barclay was scheduled to return to Washington State College for his sophomore year. He dropped by the photography studio that morning to pick up his blue box. His friend the photographer asked if Barclay could leave it for a few more hours and come get it after lunch. There were some calls he needed to make, he said. No problem, Barclay replied. He returned to the TV repair shop.

About noon that day, two gentlemen entered the repair shop and asked for Barclay by name. This was unusual, since he was back-office help and not really known to the customers. The gentlemen then produced a warrant for his arrest on charges of bookmaking. This was even more unusual, given that he wasn't a bookmaker. The utter bafflement is evident in his voice even forty years later: "I mean . . . *bookmaking?*"

Barclay accompanied the men down to the local courthouse where he was interrogated by an assortment of unhappy-looking people: a sheriff's deputy, an FBI agent, a security agent from Pacific Telephone, a security agent from AT&T, and an engineer from Bell Laboratories.

Barclay recalls, "The first questions were, 'Who are you working for? Who's the head of this operation?' I remember spending quite a while trying to convince them that I wasn't working for anybody." His interrogators weren't buying. They knew that Barclay's partner—the guy who owned the photography studio, who had also just been arrested—spent lots of time on the phone talking about horses. (As it turned out, he owned a horse and photographed horse shows.)

"Finally," Barclay says, after several hours of grilling "they decided that maybe this wasn't a bookmaking operation and they started asking different questions." Questions like: where were you calling? "I repeatedly said, over and over and over again, to friends, to New York, to find out what time it was in New York." The time in New York? C'mon kid, you don't expect us to believe that, do you? Eventually the Bell Labs engineer cleared his throat and spoke up. The company had the details of all the calls Barclay made, he said, and he confirmed that very few of them were to actual people. Most were to test numbers, or recordings, or various oddball telephone company internal numbers.

The investigators threw up their hands. "We're not going to get any further on this," Barclay recalls the FBI agent saying. They turned to the Bell Labs engineer: "Find out where he got the information to make this stuff."

Barclay told them about the *Bell System Technical Journal*. "I remember one of them looked at the guy from Bell Labs and said, 'Could that be possible?' The Bell Labs guy said, 'Yeah, there was an article . . .'"

In the end the bookmaking charges were dropped, replaced with a misdemeanor: making a phone call without paying for it. It was a speedy trial, Barclay recalls.

The judge asked, "Did you actually do this?"

"Well . . . yeah," Barclay said.

"Where did you get the information?"

"Out of a book," Barclay replied.

The judge turned to the Pacific Telephone security agent and asked if indeed the phone company had published this information. Yes, they had, he said.

The judge turned back to Barclay. "Where's this blue box of yours?"

"The phone company took it," Barclay said.

Back to the security agent. "Is this true?"

"Well, yes," he said. "It's been taken back to Bell Laboratories for analysis."

"Will he get it back?" the judge asked.

"I don't think it's going to be returned," said the security agent.

The judge rendered his verdict. "When I was a kid," he said, "we used to freeze water into the shape of nickels to put into pay phones to make long-distance calls. This is nothing more than a new and ingenious way to do the same thing. I can't see making a big case out of this. You pleaded guilty. I'm just going to give you a suspended sentence."

"The [Pacific Telephone] investigator wasn't too happy with that," Barclay says.

An AT&T memo states that the Barclay investigation began when someone noticed "an unusual pattern of 555-1212 calls." Barclay can pin it down further: calls he made to a nonworking directory assistance telephone number in Canada.

"Back then the Bell System was trying to give good service," Barclay remembers. As part of that effort, directory assistance operators often answered on the first ring—sometimes, in fact, before the phone seemed to have rung at all. And that meant Barclay would have to whistle his 2,600 Hz when a live human being was on the other end of the call, something he didn't like. "I always was a little bit nervous about disconnecting when there was a real person on the line," he says. "I discovered in playing around that if you called information in the 407 area code, which was Alberta, Canada, you got a recording that said, 'This number is not in service.'" That seemed perfect to Barclay because it was a free call but didn't involve live human operators. 407-555-1212 became his go-to number.

Later, a contact he made at the telephone company in Ephrata told him that the switching machines were set up to print out a "trouble card" every time a call was made to a nonworking number. Before April 1961, his contact said, the nonworking information number in Alberta was getting about twenty calls a month from Barclay's area of Washington. In April it went to fifty calls. After April it went up to about two hundred calls a month for the rest of the summer.

"They didn't know where they were coming from," he says, but they started investigating more seriously. By the middle of August investigators had tracked it down to Ephrata. By September 1 they apparently had zeroed in on the photographer's studio.

That timing lined up with another thing, Barclay says. Sometime during the first week of September Barclay wanted to make a call using his blue box. He walked down the usually deserted back alley between the TV repair shop and the photography studio. "I remember, there was a black car that was parked in the alleyway with two guys that were just sitting there." Barclay entered the photography studio and made his call. When he came back out, he says, "the car was still there, and the two guys were still sitting there. I thought that was strange that these people were just sitting in the alleyway."

The vulnerability that Barclay had discovered with AT&T's network stemmed from decisions that Bell Labs engineers had made in the 1930s and '40s when they were designing the long-distance network. When they needed to find a way for their switching machines to communicate with each other, they decided to reuse the voice path that customers used to talk over. But this mixing of signaling and voice over the same channel carried with it a giant flaw: if you could hear the tones the machines were making, they could hear you. And that meant you could spoof them. All you had to do was mimic the tones they used.

Worse, AT&T had been deploying switching and signaling equipment based on this design since the 1940s. Now, twenty years later, there was a large installed base of equipment that had this hole in it. And this installed base was hardware, buildings full of machines and equipment and electronics. Today, when Microsoft finds a security flaw in its Windows operating system, it can push out a software patch and have things fixed relatively quickly. No such luck for AT&T's switching equipment back in the day. Its "operating system" was electromechanical, and updating it would require physical changes, possibly redesigning and removing and replacing the equipment wholesale.

It was a flaw that would cost millions, possibly billions, of dollars to fix. It would be discovered again and again over the following twenty years. The question for AT&T was: what do we do about it?

Six

"SOME PEOPLE COLLECT STAMPS"

I T WAS A Sunday morning—the last Sunday morning in April 1959, as it happens—and something approximating a miracle had just occurred. At least it seemed that way to Charlie Pyne, a fifteen-year-old high school student in Marblehead, Massachusetts. A few months earlier, a man from the telephone company had come to his family's house and replaced their telephones. The old phones had no dials. The new ones did: shiny black metal rotary dials.

The dials on the new phones didn't do anything at first. You could spin them and they'd spin back, the phone making a clicking noise from its earpiece. And that was all. But things changed that Sunday morning. The night before, somewhere in the bowels of the telephone company, someone flipped the million-dollar switch that enabled the metal dials on the phones in Marblehead. Yesterday, Pyne would have had to lift the handset of the telephone and politely ask the operator to connect him with his buddy Rick a few blocks away. Today, he could dial Rick's number himself: NEptune 1-1559.

To Pyne, this really was close to a miracle. The miracle part was because it was so cool not to have to deal with the operator. But it was only close to a miracle, because the dialing instructions from the phone company said that there were really only a handful of places you could call with these newfangled phones: Marblehead and three adjacent towns, Salem, Lynn, and Swampscott. That seemed lame. A real miracle would be if you could call anywhere with the new phones. *That* would be cool.

Charlie Pyne was a technical kid. Slightly heavy for his five-foot-nine frame, with respectably short brown hair and brown eyes, Pyne had been interested in electronics since a young age and had earned his ham radio license a few years earlier. He was no stranger to playing with things, to taking them apart, to seeing what they could do, to using them in ways that others hadn't thought of. Pyne played around a bit with the new phone that Sunday morning, first dialing his friends and later just dialing numbers at random to see what would happen. When he dialed a nonworking number he'd get what the phone company called a crybaby: a loud tone that went up and down and sounded sort of like *woo-ahh, woo-ahh.*

Pyne found himself wondering about the new phone. Did every number other than those in Salem and Marblehead get you a crybaby? Or were there maybe some other places you could get to that the phone company hadn't told them about?

If idle hands are the devil's tools, then a clever teenager with idle hands and a methodical personality is the devil's munitions factory. Pyne knew that the first three digits of a local telephone number were called the exchange and that there might be several exchanges in a city. He also knew that, for whatever reason, exchanges were never given the numbers 000 through 199. And he knew that exchange numbers didn't have 0 or 1 as the second digit.

Out of one thousand three-digit numbers, that left 640 possible exchange codes. Pyne made a list. And then he started dialing, one number in every exchange. 220-1212. 221-1212. 222-1212. And on and on. He ended every number in 1212 because, for some reason he can't explain, he found it easier than dialing 1111.

Pyne listened to a lot of crybabies—he was a persistent kid. On the ninety-second try, with a slightly sore index finger, something interesting happened. When he dialed 331-1212 he didn't get a crybaby. Instead, a woman's voice answered: "Boston."

Pyne hung up.

He continued his dialing experiments over the coming weeks. He found a few other interesting exchanges. He also spent a lot of time playing with the 331 exchange, eventually dialing most of the numbers in it. It was a strange place, populated with special telephone operators and weird tones and odd clicky noises. 331-1312 went to a directory assistance operator, 331-1412 was answered by a woman who identified herself as "rate and route," whatever that was, and 331-1020 gave a loud, continuous tone.

Pyne finally got up the courage to call back the operator who had answered the phone "Boston" at 331-1212. He asked her who she was. She said she was the Boston inward operator.

Pyne hung up again, having just learned a valuable lesson: you could know something's name yet still have no idea what it was.

A few months later Pyne was at an electronics junk dealer in Salem called Young Engineering. While browsing the surplus electronics on the shelves, he met another teenager who was also looking for cheap bits of used electronics. Paul Heckel was a tall, heavyset kid with a slightly unkempt appearance, a ready smile, and a funny, high-pitched laugh. Oddly enough, Heckel and Pyne had both grown up in Marblehead; they had attended the same high school, in fact. Their paths hadn't crossed until then because Heckel was a couple of years older than Pyne and was now off at MIT, majoring in electrical engineering.

They quickly became friends. Heckel took Pyne on a trip to see MIT's new IBM 7090 computer and to check out Eli Heffron's, the premier electronics surplus store in Cambridge. Pyne was soon telling Heckel about his dialing experiments. Heckel's sister was a telephone operator and was able to fill in a bunch of details for Pyne, such as what an inward operator was and what a rate-and-route operator did and what they could do for you.

Before long Pyne, Heckel, Heckel's sister, and Pyne's buddy Rick Turner were in Pyne's basement making calls via the Boston inward operator. Heckel's sister was an asset to their games: in addition to her knowledge of the telephone system, she was a girl. For most fifteen-year-old boys, that might be reason enough, but Pyne realized that her female voice meant that calls she placed went through unquestioned. The boys learned that they had to pretend to be engineers working on the test board.

There was just one problem: they didn't really have anyone to call. Indeed, most of their calls were to telephone company test numbers, to operators, or to one another. They were particularly proud of one call—so much so that they recorded it. It started with their old friend at 331-1212.

"Boston."

"Milwaukee inward please," said Turner.

Boston inward was suspicious that day. "Where are you calling from?" she asked, an edge in her voice.

"Marblehead test board," Turner replied, his voice 100 percent bored telephone company engineer.

There was a pause as she put the call through. Click. The noise on the line got louder. Ring.

"Milwaukee," said the distant operator.

"Milwaukee, this is Boston test board," said Turner. "Could you put me through to Portland inward please? Portland, Oregon?"

"Portland, right." Telephone company operators were trained to use the word *right,* much like military radio operators are trained to say *roger.*

Ten seconds went by. "Portland," said the operator in Oregon.

Turner had the Portland operator connect him to the Denver inward. Then he had the Denver inward call Little Rock. At Little Rock he asked to be connected to New York. And when he got to the New York inward he asked for Boston.

"Boston." The voice was buried in noise but the operator's Boston accent was still recognizable.

"Could you get me a number in Marblehead, please? Neptune 1-9819."

Ringing. "Hello."

"Hello, Charles!"

Turner had successfully routed a call from Pyne's house, across the country, and to a nearby pay phone—about 5,600 miles to go several hundred yards.

The junior and senior years of Pyne's high school career were spent at Governor Dummer Academy, an elite boarding school with a funny name twenty-five miles north of his hometown. Pyne describes Governor Dummer as near-Dickensian. "We couldn't go home on weekends," he says, and "we had to say prayers before meals." The worst part of being away at boarding school was being out of touch with his girlfriend Betsy. But thanks to 331, it didn't have to be that way; he taught Betsy how to call him at school by pretending to be an operator. "I was *soooo* scared that someone was going to come and arrest me," Betsy says. "I would go to a phone booth and put in my dime and dial 331-1212 . . ." Betsy would ask the operator to connect her to a pay phone in Pyne's building. The use of a pay phone on Pyne's end wasn't a security measure as much as necessity; he simply didn't have a phone in his room at school and a lobby pay phone was all that was available.

In 1962 Pyne left the confines of Governor Dummer and went on to enjoy the vast freedoms of Harvard University. That fall, Pyne made his way into the basement that housed Harvard's student-run radio station. He was a radio geek, after all, so getting involved with the radio station seemed like a natural extracurricular activity. Pyne didn't know it, but WHRB was much more than a radio station. As the journalist and alum Sam Smith wrote, "It also functioned as a counter-fraternity, a *salon des refuses* for all those who because of ethnicity, class or inclination did not fit the mold of Harvard. Other organizations sought students of the 'right type,' WHRB got what was left over. Eccentric WASP preppies, Brookline Jews, brilliant engineers, persons obsessed with a musical genre, addicts of show business or their own voices, seminal journalists, future entrepreneurs, prospective advertising executives,

and persons of heretofore unrequited imagination and energy fil-
tered through the door in the alley known as Dudley Gulch to
become part of The Network."

Pyne found a home in the WHRB engineering department. It
was there that he met Tony Lauck, a sophomore, and Ed Ross, a
junior. Similar to Pyne in build, Lauck had blue eyes and blond
hair that was slightly longer and a bit unruly, as opposed to Ross
who was thinner and taller but whose brown hair was already
receding; a girlfriend of his predicted it would all be gone by
the time he reached thirty. ("She was only about seventy percent right," he says.) Pyne recalls being impressed by his new
acquaintances: "They're the type of guys that came into college
with 1600 board scores and advanced placement." And while he
and Lauck were both ham radio operators and electronics tinkerers, Ed Ross was a music maven and mathematical prodigy
who prided himself on not knowing anything about electronics.
For example, to legally operate the radio transmitter at WHRB,
you were supposed to have a first-class radiotelephone operator's
license—called a "first phone" license—issued by the Federal
Communications Commission. The exam for this license was a
rite of passage for electrical engineers back in the day, requiring
a strong knowledge of electronics and radio theory. "Ed Ross
didn't even study. He went and took that test and passed it, just
from the logic of the multiple choice questions," Pyne says.

It wasn't long before Pyne realized something: "These guys are
going to be interested in telephone stuff."

The campus telephone system was their gateway drug. Back
in the day it was common for big organizations to connect their
telephone switches via "tie lines," that is, private trunk lines run
between the different telephone systems. So, for example, if you
dialed 83 on a Harvard telephone, you'd hear a pause and then a
dial tone. You were now connected to MIT's telephone system
via the tie line, allowing you to dial an MIT extension. This
allowed, say, a Harvard professor to easily reach a colleague at
MIT—often at a lower cost. But if you were Pyne or Lauck or

Ross, you saw a maze of twisty little telephone passages, all ripe with possibilities for exploration or prankery. Okay, dial 83 to get to MIT. Now what? What if we dial 83 here? Oh, look, that connected us back to Harvard! Hey, if we dial 83 repeatedly we can tie up all the lines between the two schools. Whee!

That was fun once. More interesting, though, was figuring out where else you could dial. The phones at WHRB provided the three convenient access to the campus telephone system. They spent lots of time dialing every code they could think of, just as Pyne had done several years earlier when he was exploring the telephone system in his hometown of Marblehead.

"From Harvard you could get a tie line to MIT, and from MIT there was one that went to Lincoln Labs, and from Lincoln Labs you could get to MITRE, and from MITRE you could get to IBM Kingston, and from IBM Kingston you could get to Stewart Air Force Base, and it went on and on, trying to put these connections together," Pyne says. "This whole process was mainly for our fun and amusement. We weren't too serious about making free phone calls or anything like that. It's not like we had a lot of people we wanted to call."

"The most useful technological discovery we made was that you should use a pencil for dialing, and not your finger," Ross remembers. "After a couple of hours it is much less painful if you're not putting your finger in the dial holes."

Dialing around the tie-line system was addictive, like solving a never-ending chain of puzzles. First you had to figure out a code to get you somewhere. Then you had to figure out where that somewhere was. And then you had to figure out if there was anywhere interesting you could get to from there. And sometimes there were interesting places to visit that you couldn't dial directly: lots of organizations had manual switchboard operators who could connect you to places you couldn't get to with dialing. "If you dialed 0, you'd get the operator," Pyne remembers. "Lots of times, you'd call the operator, you'd say, We're testing, we're doing this and that, can you tell me about your switchboard and what's on your switchboard?" With a few white lies you could find out all the places she could connect you.

At the start of his freshman year, Pyne had signed up for Fine Arts 13, Harvard's introductory art appreciation class, also known as "Darkness at Noon" for its darkened room with dozing students and slide shows of classical artwork. Within a couple of weeks Pyne decided it was "the stupidest thing I ever signed up for." His Fine Arts 13 notebook was unmolested, free of any writings except for the course title penned on its cover. It was quickly repurposed as the journal in which Pyne and his friends recorded their telephonic research; it would grow to more than a hundred pages.

They made a map, a diagram of circles and arrows, that showed who was connected to whom in the tie-line network. It wasn't just schools; the map made clear the close ties among academia, industry, and the military of the period. Indeed, the label on the very first circle on the map said, in capital letters, NIKE CONTROL—the control center for the Nike missile air defense site in New England.

At one point during their map making Pyne found himself connected to the operator at Hanscom Air Force Base outside of Boston. He did his usual routine, making a bit of small talk and then asking her for the names of the other places she could reach from her switchboard. She obligingly recited a list of locations, ending with ". . . and Stewart and Rome," in other words, Stewart Air Force Base and Rome Air Depot, both in New York.

Pyne misheard her. To him it sounded like she said ". . . and Stewart and Jerome." Why would an air force operator have direct switchboard connections to two guys named Stewart and Jerome? How utterly random.

The names rapidly became a running gag among the group. "We started joking about Stewart and Jerome, these mythical characters," Pyne says. "What are Stewart and Jerome doing today?" they'd ask each other. Ed Ross was particularly good at inventing Stewart and Jerome stories. "Oh, I talked to Jerome today," he would say, followed by a detailed soliloquy regarding Jerome's latest adventures.

★ ★ ★

"Over a period of time we realized there were any number of ways in which telephones and telephone systems were interesting," Ross remembers. "It was interesting to see how this strange and mysterious thing worked. And the more we got to know it, the stranger and mysteriouser it was." He adds, "Over the course of that academic year it became, as undergraduate things do, an obsession."

They soon graduated from tie-line dialing to harder drugs. Pyne told them about the 331 test number exchange and how he used it to reach inward operators. Before long they were making trips to Boston's Logan Airport to conduct their research; 331 was a local call from Logan, plus the airport was great because it had tons of pay phones and you wouldn't arouse any suspicion by constantly being on them. But 331 was somewhat limited: you could reach the inward operator and a few other places but not much else. And, besides, Pyne had already been through it with a fine-tooth comb. They wanted a bigger playground to explore.

Pyne had gotten his hands on a copy of the 1956 edition of a Bell System book called *Notes on Distance Dialing*. As Tony Lauck describes it, *Notes* "was an overview of the architecture of the long-distance telephone network that was written from the point of view of an engineer at an independent telephone company. So it described all the ways area codes were assigned, the way the various types of signaling worked, what the tones were, what the frequencies were, and all of this kind of stuff." It wasn't exactly secret but it wasn't widely available—unlike the *Bell System Technical Journal* or the *Bell Labs Record,* it wasn't in most engineering libraries.

The Harvard kids spent a bunch of time studying *Notes on Distance Dialing,* but they couldn't quite make the pieces fit together. For example, *Notes* talked about multifrequency signaling and even gave the frequencies of the two tones that made up each digit; it explained about the key pulse (KP) and start (ST) signals too. The good news was that WHRB had an audio oscillator, which they quickly pressed into service as a tone generator. The bad news was that WHRB had only one audio oscillator, so they couldn't generate the two simultaneous tones needed for multi-frequency signaling. They did have a tape recorder, however. Lauck recalls, "We had recorded one of the oscillators and we had dubbed it back on top of it on a strip of tape, all the various multifrequency tones. . . . We had tape rolls of zeros, and tape rolls of ones, and tape rolls of nines, and tape rolls of key pulse, and tape rolls of start. . . . And we could splice these together with splicing tape and play them through a tape recorder and it would sound very much like the tones you would hear when you were making a long-distance phone call in that era."

They tried mightily to use their spliced tapes to make calls using MF—to no avail. They would make a local call and press PLAY on the tape recorder and send their tones down the line. Nothing. They'd make a long-distance call and try the same thing. Still nothing. "We knew we had the tones right," Lauck says. "But every time we played these tones nothing would happen."

They kept at it. Lauck recalls, "On one particular day we swept the oscillator up to 2,600 while we were dialing into an information service someplace, or some sort of a useless free call. And we heard this . . . disconnect, a click, and then a *bomp* or a *babump* or some sort of a noise." They didn't know what it was, exactly, but they knew something important had just happened. "I looked at Charlie and he looked at me," Lauck remembers. "When we heard this thing go *kerbunk* we just sort of had this intuitive feeling that, yeah, now was the time."

A tape was cued up on the tape recorder, loaded with "KP 212 121 ST"—the eight quick MF tones required to call the inward operator in New York City. "When we heard this *bonk* sound we flipped the selector switch on the preamp and pushed play on the tape recorder. It went, *dee de de de de de de dup* and then the operator came on and said, 'New York.'

"After struggling with this tape for maybe two or three days and playing it in various ways and getting nowhere, all of a sudden when we heard this funny little sound, we had put the system in a new state. We knew that was it," Lauck remembers.

They had proven it could work. Now they needed to build an electronic box to generate the tones on command rather than dorking around with bits of audiotape. "We had some junk parts, Charlie had a bunch of switches," Lauck says. They built an audio oscillator, reusing the vacuum tubes from Lauck's stereo amplifier, basing their design on a circuit from the radio amateur's handbook. It was a bulky thing on a metal chassis, Lauck remembers, "But within twenty-four hours, 'cause we didn't get much sleep, we had this thing working and we could then key in whatever numbers we wanted."

Lauck believes it took them longer than it should have. "See, part of the thing that made it so difficult was that we didn't think it was really possible. We didn't think they would have been so stupid as to design the system where we could get into the signaling of the system. So even though we knew the signaling tones were in-band tones, we didn't think that was going to amount to anything. We didn't understand that the 2,600 Hz signal could be passed straight through. . . . We didn't think it was possible."

"The next idea was to make a more miniaturized one," says Pyne. "And that's where Heckel came in." Paul Heckel was two subway stations away at MIT, still majoring in electrical engineering. Heckel told them, "Not only can I make you one much more miniaturized and transistorized, but we'll pot it"—that is, the components would be coated in epoxy so that nobody would be able to tell what was in it. "Heckel was the main guy who built that," Pyne says, though Lauck and Pyne assisted in its assembly. Pyne remembers returning to Harvard on the first subway train from MIT's Kendall Square station around five a.m. after pulling an all-nighter in Heckel's dorm room working on the transistorized blue box. He vividly recalls spilling an assortment of resistors all over the floor of the train, scrambling around trying to find all the pieces and put them back in their container. Electronic component mishaps notwithstanding, they soon had a tidy little portable blue box, suitable for telephonic field trips.

Ultimately, they realized they could combine their blue box with the 331 test number: dial 331 plus any four digits, send a burst of 2,600 Hz down the link, and then use the blue box to MF whatever digits they wanted. The beauty of this setup was that 331 was a local call, and because the phone company didn't bill for local calls it didn't bother to keep records of them either. This, they figured, meant they were less likely to get caught than, say, calling 555-1212 in distant area codes.

"Now the only problem would be, sort of, 'Well, you've solved the problem!'" Pyne recalls with a laugh. "Now what do you do? You don't really want to *call* anybody." But, he says, "you still want to be researching more interesting things.

"Somehow that got us thinking, 'Well, what about receiving calls?'" They had figured out how to make free outgoing calls; indeed, they had solved that problem six ways from Sunday. But maybe they could figure out a way to receive calls that would make it free for the caller?

By now they knew that the secret to telephone billing was whether the called telephone answered, that is, went off hook. That's what 2,600 Hz indicated, after all: whether a phone was hung up or not. Pyne recalls their thinking, "What if you received a call but you never went off hook? Wouldn't that mean that the calling party wouldn't be billed for the call?"

Pyne says, "So we wound up building a very simple box, which was basically a capacitor on the line so you could pass the voice through but not the DC through." He knew that a change in direct current was how the phone system detected that a phone had answered, so if you blocked DC, you blocked the telephone company from knowing whether you had answered the phone. This approach worked, to a point. It did let them talk while the phone was still ringing it, but it also let the ringing signal through, and the ringing signal was much louder than the voice. As Pyne says, "You had to talk between the rings." And that, they all agreed, was lame.

They pressed on. "A lot of these things are just sort of by accident," Pyne says. At some point they were fooling with the circuit they had built and somebody took the phone off hook for a moment—the phone was picked up for a fraction of a second and then hung up again. The ringing instantly went away. But they could tell from the sound of the telephone line that billing hadn't started. They had discovered another unlikely glitch in the phone system: although the billing equipment and the ringing signal were both controlled by the phone going off hook—in other words, ringing stopped and billing started when you answered the phone—the timing on the two was different. The ringing signal stopped the very instant you answered the phone. But billing didn't start unless the phone stayed off hook for several seconds.

This gap in timing meant that they had just solved their latest research problem. "We said, *Oh!*" Pyne recalls. If they took the phone off hook for just a second, "it's long enough to make the ring go away but not long enough to activate the billing. So then we built this little box, you just go *click* [with a switch] and you get rid of the ring. And now somebody could call you and talk a little while and when they hang up they get their dime back or they don't get billed." Pyne and his friends didn't know it at the time, but this simple device had been discovered by others a few years earlier. The telephone company called it a "black box"; it would later come to be called a "mute."

They were rapidly running out of stuff to research. Bored and looking for something to do, they decided to borrow some musical instruments and see if they couldn't stage a live concert that would please the telephone system. If a blue box generated just two different musical notes, couldn't you do the same thing with a pair of flutes?

The trio soon found themselves gathered around a telephone, instruments in hand, trying to play 2,600 Hz followed by the MF tones for KP + 121 + ST. "We were able to generate the tones using some wooden baroque recorders"—flutelike musical instruments, Lauck says. "It actually did work," Pyne remembers. "The 2,600 was easy, you could just whistle that. The flutes weren't really a practical way to do it, but we proved that it could be done." Lauck adds, "We were laughing so much it was not very effective."

"We started getting maybe a little bored with it, and we started getting a little loose," Pyne remembers. "We started being a little bit more open about telling people what we had discovered." Everybody at the WHRB radio station knew about their playing with the phone system, for example.

It was around this time that, through some other students they didn't know very well, "we met a guy by the name of Ernie Reid," Pyne remembers. "Reid worked for the phone company, he was kind of like a repairman-type guy." Reid was very interested in what the Harvard kids were up to. "He said, 'This is very interesting, this is cool, what are you doing? I could get you keypads, I could get you equipment . . .' He kind of ingratiated himself with us and asked a lot of questions." At his request, they loaned him the Fine Arts 13 notebook.

Pyne didn't give any of this too much thought, as it was starting to dawn on him that he had other things to worry about. Ever since the group had been working on their telephone research, Pyne's grades had gone into the toilet. Sure enough, a bit later that month, Pyne got a phone call telling him to see his dean. With final exams right around the corner, there was no way a sudden request to speak to his dean could be anything good.

Pyne told Lauck about the meeting. "That's funny," Lauck responded. "I'm supposed to see my dean at nine a.m. tomorrow too."

Hmm. Lauck was an excellent student, so this wouldn't be about his grades.

Pyne and Lauck called Ed Ross. Sure enough, Ross had a nine a.m. appointment with the headmaster of his dormitory. The clincher? Paul Heckel also had a nine a.m. appointment, and he was at an entirely different school.

It didn't take a genius—much less several geniuses—to figure out they were busted.

"We had always realized that this stuff was not totally above board, people might look askance at our doing this," says Ross. Still, he says, "we never took it horribly seriously." The summons from the school officials suggested it might be time to reevaluate that sentiment. They scheduled an emergency meeting that evening at the Boston apartment of a mutual friend to get their stories straight. As Pyne recalls it, the gist for the group was: "What story are we going to tell these deans? Can we conjure up a story that will sound plausible and innocent?" After much discussion they concluded that, as Pyne puts it, "There's no story that you could make up that you could consistently tell that would be any more innocent than just the truth." So that's what they decided to do: they would simply tell the truth. They went their separate ways, the stress of the evening and tomorrow's impending meetings aggravated by Ross's car running out of gas on Boston's Storrow Drive on the way home.

At nine o'clock the next morning—May 10, 1963—each student went to his respective appointment. Each meeting was in a different location. Tony Lauck remembers that the staff in his dean's office "seemed pretty alarmed" when he arrived. Their alarm was caused by the two men there to interview him: "There was one tall one and one short one, they were both wearing trench coats, one was nice and the other was nasty, and they were both from the FBI."

The same scene played out in the other locations. No deans or headmasters, just Ross, Pyne, Lauck, and Heckel, each interrogated by two FBI agents. "I was totally flabbergasted by people flashing FBI badges," Pyne says. He was quickly introduced to the time-honored interrogation technique called good cop/bad cop. One of the two FBI agents interviewing him "was nasty," Pyne recalls. "He was pushy, he was questioning me. And the other guy was just the nicest guy in the world. The first guy would go out . . . and the second guy would say, 'Isn't it nice to be here at Harvard? And what are you studying?' He was just very pleasant. And then the other guy would come back in the room."

Periodically one of the agents would step outside and, apparently, coordinate with the other FBI agents by radio or telephone. The agents had done their homework, brandishing thick dossiers on the students. Indeed, the FBI had apparently gone to the trouble of tailing them, Ross remembers. The FBI agents knew about their meeting the night before, including their running out of gas on Storrow Drive. They tried to explain their research project as an innocent hobby; as one of the students put it, "Some people collect stamps." But they were thrown by the focus of the FBI agents' questions. "They were particularly concerned about the activities via MIT Lincoln Labs, MITRE, and the defense department phone system," Ross says. Ross felt this was the least technically sophisticated thing the group had done, so he wasn't sure why the FBI agents were so interested in it. After all, it was nothing special, just dialing around. Still, he remembers, "they concentrated on that."

It slowly dawned on all the students that the FBI was convinced that it had stumbled upon an espionage ring. The FBI agents, it seemed, didn't really care about AT&T and long-distance phone calls and blue boxes and whatnot. Rather, they thought Pyne and company were spies.

The agents drilled them on one point in particular, over and over again: Who else was involved? The answer they got back was always the same: "Just us!" The nasty one of Pyne's two FBI agents wasn't buying it. "What about Stewart and Jerome?" he finally demanded. "We know they're involved!"

"I almost broke up laughing," Pyne remembers. It was at that point, Pyne says, that "we knew that they had either read the Fine Arts 13 notebook, which mentioned Stewart and Jerome, or more likely had tapped our lines."

The FBI had been investigating Pyne and company for about three weeks, it turned out, ever since the telephone company brought the matter to their attention. Ernie Reid, the telephone company repairman who had befriended them and who had borrowed their Fine Arts 13 notebook, was the source of the trouble, passing the notebook on to the security department of New England Telephone and Telegraph. "His motives were to make a big deal out of this," Pyne says. "He told them things that weren't even true, that we were trying to get the keys to Franklin Street [the headquarters of the telephone company in Boston], that we were interested in defense things, and NORAD . . ."

If Reid's goal was to make a big deal, he succeeded. Within days Peter Mason, the head of New England Telephone and Telegraph security, and his deputy, John Desmond, had contacted the FBI. According to an FBI memo, Mason and Desmond had been reviewing the Fine Arts 13 notebook "and felt that this should be called to the attention of the FBI since it contains information concerning tie lines from various defense establishments in the Boston, Mass. Area, in addition to tie lines to defense establishments in other areas of the country such as Lincoln Laboratory, Raytheon Company, Arthur D. Little Company, Hanscom Air Force Base, Millstone Radar Installation, IBM, . . . MITRE Corporation . . . and General Electric Company."

The phone company's main concern was the specter of widespread electronic toll fraud. As the FBI memo put it, "Mr. Desmond furnished a copy of the subject's notebook . . . They requested that the information contained in this notebook not be disseminated at this time since it was felt by the telephone company that any dissemination outside the Bureau could lead to wholesale use of telephone company facilities at no cost."

In contrast, the FBI was more concerned about national security. The possibility that the Harvard kids were a spy ring was not entirely ludicrous; 1963 was a scary year, with charges and countercharges of espionage flying back and forth between the Kremlin and the White House. At the time, the FBI was deep into an investigation of a Soviet spy ring in New York and Washington, D.C., and just two years earlier the British courts had convicted five people in a damaging Soviet espionage operation. Indeed, Kim Philby, the so-called third man of England's notorious Cambridge Five spy ring, defected to the Soviet Union that very January; like Pyne and company at Harvard, the Cambridge spies had all attended one of their country's top universities. Could the FBI have stumbled onto the Harvard Three?

The Boston FBI office contacted the local U.S. attorney to see if the students could be prosecuted for making free phone calls. The answer was no. The U.S. attorney in Boston said that the facts did not constitute a violation of the Fraud by Wire section of federal law and that was the only statute he could see being relevant. But why were these kids so interested in defense facilities? On May 1, the Boston office asked FBI headquarters for permission to interview the students "to determine . . . any possible violation of the Espionage Statute." In Washington, the FBI polled each of its divisions—Domestic Intelligence, Special Investigative, Laboratory, and General Investigative—to coordinate their investigation.

A week went by. The phone company was getting antsy; according to an urgent FBI teletype message, "[Telephone] company is most anxious to learn today if Bureau desires to interview subjects before telephone company conducts own interview. States [Telephone] Company losing revenue and practice of fraudulent calls is spreading."

On May 7, the Domestic Intelligence Division decided it was time to interview Pyne and company. The memo from an FBI national security official was remarkably evenhanded, allowing that the students' interests might be perfectly innocent: "It is possible that this is an instance of two brilliant mathematicians [Pyne and Ross] embarking on an unusual research problem, finding initial success and now endeavoring to ascertain just how far they can go with this work." Still, the memo continued, "Their interest in defense establishments, however, does indicate [a] potential security problem. They or others, if full access to defense establishment lines is obtained, could cause the lines to be jammed or could use them to transmit false messages or tie up the circuits. In view of this possible harm to our national security, it is felt we should take steps to ascertain definitely why the subjects are engaged in their telephonic endeavors and, specifically, to determine what is their interest in the military installations involved."

The FBI agents came and went in one day. "I think they were maybe a little bit pissed that they were dragged into something that was a college prank," Pyne says.

Now it was AT&T's turn.

"We had to go see this guy by the name of Desmond," Lauck says. "He was some person in charge of AT&T security in Boston. . . . He was going to really nail our ass for stealing phone calls and all the rest of this. We were going to be prosecuted." This seemed ridiculous to Lauck. Stealing phone calls? Really? "We never actually made any phone calls that anyone in their right minds would ever pay two cents for," Lauck says. Ed Ross agrees: "None of us had anyone else in the world to speak to." The students soon invented a nickname for their telephone company tormenter. "We came to call him the Evil Desmond," Pyne says.

Tony Lauck had an uncle who was a lawyer and a banker in Philadelphia and who used to play golf with the head of Bell of Pennsylvania; a call was placed asking if he might be able to somehow smooth matters over. Similarly, there was an old friend of Charlie Pyne's parents who was the chairman of the New England Electric Company; perhaps he could help? The old friend said he knew the president of New England Telephone and Telegraph and would make a phone call and report back. Pyne remembers getting a phone call about ten minutes later, in which the chairman of New England Electric said, "Would you please call me back from a pay phone?" Pyne did so. "He told me that his friend the president of New England Telephone knew all about this," Pyne says, "and it was a big deal and in all likelihood our telephones were being monitored"—hence the request to use a pay phone.

Maybe it was the string pulling or maybe the telephone company had simply thought better of prosecuting Harvard students, something that might end up blowing up in its face. What the phone company didn't need, after all, was for the details of this to get out in the news so that more people would know about how easy it was to make free calls. Either way, Lauck recalls their next visit to the Evil Desmond. "He looked really pissed," Lauck says. "He was just seething with rage that these so-called rich kids or whatever were going to be able to get away with this and he was not going to be able to nail our asses for anything."

That did not stop Desmond from grilling the students. They were to write a detailed report for the telephone company, setting forth exactly what they had done, the details of the vulnerabilities in the system they had found, even giving suggestions for how to combat fraud in the future. And they had to get rid of their blue boxes. The transistorized unit that Heckel built wound up in the Charles River. As for the one that Pyne and Lauck had built using tubes from Lauck's stereo, Desmond and a sidekick showed up in person at Lauck's dorm room in order to watch it being dismantled.

In the end, the only serious result of the entire episode was that Pyne was told he needed to take a year off from Harvard. This was a pretty common occurrence, Pyne says: "You didn't have to do much to have them ask you to take a year off." An unexpected plus was that it stood him in good stead with his girlfriend Betsy—the girl he had taught to impersonate an operator to call him at boarding school—who says now, "I thought it was great. I thought, 'Oh my God, this is the most wonderful person in the world, he's so brilliant!'" Betsy's mother thought likewise. Pyne's mother was somewhat less enthused.

The Harvard students solved many mysteries during their research. But their discovery by the telephone company and the FBI solved one final mystery for Pyne's freshman adviser, Robert Watson, who wrote the following when he filled out the form for Pyne's year-end review.

> Pyne has been an enigma to me all year. I've spent more time with him trying to understand his problems than the combined time I've devoted to all my other freshmen advisees. In an attempt to arouse

his motivation I've used my entire bag of tricks to little avail. Then suddenly two weeks ago all was made clear when we learned from the FBI and Telephone Company of his tampering with the whole telephone system. Instead of studying, night after night all year long he and three other Harvard students with the cooperation of an MIT student have been discovering ways to beat the Telephone Company and how the whole system works. No wonder his studies have suffered. From what I now know he has been pursuing this interest for years. If he once settles down and really applies himself, there's no question in my mind that he can do the work. In fact, he possesses a vast knowledge of electronics in general and the telephone operation in particular. Surely this should stand him in good stead.

The evaluation form included a query about Pyne's probable academic concentration. "Engineering Sciences," Watson wrote.

The form went on to inquire, "Do you consider this to be a wise choice?"

Watson filled in the form honestly, if dryly. "I'm inclined to think so now," he wrote.

Seven

HEADACHE

I T WAS THE early 1960s and AT&T was starting to get a headache.
Actually, that should read headaches, plural.

First there was the growth-in-electronic-toll-fraud headache.
It wouldn't have been so bad if whiz kids like Barclay and Pyne
were the only ones who had figured out blue and black boxes.
But they weren't. Other people were starting to discover the holes
in AT&T's network. And no one, even within AT&T, could say
with any certainty exactly how widespread the problem was or
how fast it was growing.

Then there was the how-are-we-gonna-fix-our-network headache. In the past twenty years AT&T had already spent more than
$1.4 billion in building out its long-distance network, with its
2,600 Hz and in-band multifrequency signaling. This signaling
system was fundamental to the network in the same way that a
concrete foundation is fundamental to your house. For AT&T,
finding out that its network was vulnerable to teenagers with
tone generators was a bit like discovering that you've poured
the foundation of your house on top of a nest of some new kind
of concrete-eating termites. How much would it cost and how
long would it take to reengineer the long-distance network to
be immune to blue and black boxes?

Third was the how-do-we-deal-with-the-phone-phreaks headache. Should we have them arrested? Sue them? But it seems like
every time we do something, the newspapers pick it up and carry

a story about it. That means more people know about it. And that probably means more phone phreaks. Maybe it's better just to keep things quiet for now.

The icing on the cake was the oh-crap-what-if-it's-not-really-illegal headache. AT&T attorneys had studied the matter and were worried there was no federal law that clearly made these telephone shenanigans illegal. Most states had laws that were probably applicable, but these varied from state to state. This was a new kind of crime and the laws just hadn't caught up with it yet.

Where's that bottle of Tylenol again?

People were starting to discover Ma Bell's secret. Most were high school or college students, but it wasn't just Barclay and Pyne and the others at Harvard and MIT. In 1963 newspapers covered the story of a "brilliant but disturbed teenager" from Ohio who invented a device to "bypass operators" and had called all over the world. In 1964 there was a small epidemic of electronic toll fraud cases. Hoyt Stearns and friends at Cornell University, John Treichler at Rice University, a former engineering student who had attended Stanford and Columbia: all had figured out Ma Bell's secret. The stories were virtually identical: clever high school or college kids figure out the hole in AT&T's switching system, explore the network, are caught, and get slapped on the wrist.

Unfortunately for AT&T, college and high school students had no monopoly on clever. Another pioneer in the field was a Los Angeles–area businessman, electrical engineer, and former army communications officer named Louis MacKenzie. Perhaps you've been to the Los Angeles International Airport and heard the repeating tape recordings made famous by the 1980 movie *Airplane!*—the ones that droned on and on: "The white zone is for the immediate loading and unloading of passengers only . . ."? If so, you have MacKenzie and his company, MacKenzie Laboratories, to thank for the invention of the machine that allowed those recordings to play, twenty-four hours a day, seven days a week, fifty-two weeks a year.

MacKenzie was no stranger to the idea of using tones for signaling. His firm had been hired by Walt Disney in the 1950s to build tone-based equipment to remotely control animated special effects at Disneyland. Perhaps that was what gave him and a colleague of his the insight needed to spot the vulnerability revealed in the 1960 *Bell System Technical Journal* article. Sensing a business opportunity, he approached the phone company about it, offering his firm's services to fix AT&T's problem—for a price. AT&T declined. Soon thereafter, in 1963, MacKenzie's attorney appeared on the CBS evening news, waving around a blue box and talking about the giant flaw in the telephone system. MacKenzie, meanwhile, started a side business manufacturing and selling blue boxes, something that he would later note was legal in California at that time.

And then there were the people who built the mysterious "suitcase blue box," a thing of beauty that befuddled the boffins at Bell Laboratories. A small attaché case that looked like it came straight out of a James Bond movie, it was crammed full of cool telephone gear, all lovingly mounted: a rotary dial, a keypad, an audio level meter, switches, an auto dialer—a plug board that allowed you to program one frequently called number using a rat's nest of jumper wires—and, of course, a built-in blue box too. The workmanship was exquisite, as if it had rolled off the assembly line of a professional manufacturing facility—which perhaps it had. Bell Labs was certain that a number of these had been produced, possibly a large number, but was not sure how many or who was making them or where they came from. Investigators had leads suggesting that they originated in California, perhaps manufactured on a navy base somewhere. As to who was buying them, that they were convinced of: the mob. Who else could it be? What else could explain the cartoon—set smack in the center of the rotary dial on one of the boxes—of a laughing mobster chomping on his cigar?

If it were just a handful of clever people figuring this stuff out, that might be one thing. But the contagion was threatening to spread more widely via ads, like one that appeared in 1963.

Slash Communication Costs with TELA-TONE

You've been reading about it. Now you can build it yourself. No license required to operate. 5,000 mile range. Complete details, $5 or money back. Tela-tone, Box 4304, Pasadena, Calif.

Or the following gem from the January 1964 hobbyist magazine *Popular Electronics:*

TOLL Free Distance Dialing. By-passes operators and billing equipment. Build for $15.00. Ideal for Telephone Company Executives. Plans $4.75. Seaway Electronics, 6311 Yucca St., Hollywood 28, California.

"Ideal for Telephone Company Executives." Whoever got mail at 6311 Yucca Street in Hollywood seemed to have a sense of humor. Formerly the offices of *Variety,* Hollywood's leading newspaper, 6311 Yucca by the early sixties had become the mail-order headquarters of dozens and dozens of questionable enterprises, such as Seaway Electronics (blue box plans), Preview Records (vanity recording studio), Man International (false beards and mustaches), C. Carrier Co. (spy equipment), Holley Co. (old scripts from movies and TV shows), Vanguard Galleries (artwork); the list went on and on. AT&T had a chat with the owner of Seaway Electronics. "The advertiser has admitted that about 149 copies of these plans were mailed out," read a subsequent AT&T memo. "He increased the price of the plans to $7.50 and bulk-mailed at least 8,950 copies of [a one-page ad for blue box plans], mostly to amateur radio operators in New York, New Hampshire, Vermont, New Jersey, Massachusetts, Connecticut, and California."

Swell. So now that's almost nine thousand more people who know the network is vulnerable. Great, just great.

You would think that making a free call using a blue box or a black box would have to be illegal, right? I mean, how could it not? Oddly enough, however, no single law really nailed it.

Individual states had a variety of laws that were—or might be—applicable. But that meant AT&T had to become expert in the laws of fifty different states and, besides, it was crazy that it might be legal in one state and not in another. What AT&T needed was a single federal law that was broadly and clearly applicable and that made the whole enterprise illegal, end of story.

The law that came closest was Title 18, Section 1343, of the United States Code: "Fraud by Wire." Section 1343 made it illegal to transmit over a wire and across state lines any "writings, signs, signals, pictures or sounds" for the purpose of fraud. Now, what does a blue box do? It sends tones—that is, sounds or signals— over a telephone line—that is, wires. Usually these tones are sent across state lines—it's a long-distance phone call, after all—and usually the telephone company is getting defrauded of revenue in the process. Seems like an open-and-shut case.

Alas, when AT&T attorneys met with Justice Department representatives in February 1964, one of the Justice lawyers who actually helped write the Fraud by Wire law said he didn't think it was intended to apply to blue and black boxes. Section 1343, he said, was designed to protect people from being swindled over the telephone—something like a bad guy calling up your grandma and selling her bogus life insurance; that's what was meant by "fraud by wire." It was never intended to protect the phone company itself from being defrauded. In fact, there was a law similar to 1343 (Section 1341, as it happens) that covered mail fraud, and that law did not cover fraud against the United States Postal Service itself. Separate laws had to be written and enacted to deal with that problem.

Then there was the black box problem. Unlike blue boxes, black boxes didn't send signals or sounds down the wire. In fact, they actually *prevented* the sending of a signal that the phone had answered. Moreover, this signal usually didn't cross state lines as the signal was between a telephone and its local central office. So using 1343 to go after black box fraud seemed like tough legal sledding.

The Justice Department lawyers said the government was generally unwilling to prosecute toll fraud cases under Section 1343. Indeed, the most the boys at Justice would agree to was using 1343 to prosecute organized crime, if organized crime could ever be shown to be using blue or black boxes, and even that was only because the Organized Crime and Racketeering section wanted it done.

None of this was helping AT&T's headache. AT&T attorneys met with both the Federal Communications Commission—the FCC, the people who regulated the telephone system—and the Justice Department the next year. Their goal: get a federal law passed specifically prohibiting fraud due to blue boxes, black boxes, or any other colored boxes the bad guys might think up in the future. They even came with proposed legislation in hand: a two-hundred-word run-on sentence that made illegal just about any conceivable fraud perpetrated against a telephone company. While the lawyers were at it, their proposed new legislation also outlawed making, possessing, selling, giving, transferring, or offering for sale a blue or black box or any other "instrument or apparatus" that could be used for telephone fraud. AT&T argued that "a criminal sanction is needed which gets at the source of this fraud, namely, the clandestine manufacture and sale of these devices, which are now carried on with impunity."

AT&T's proposal was met with a cool reception. "The proposed legislation has too broad a sweep," wrote the FCC attorneys in an internal memo. "It would attempt to outlaw not only such physical devices but would purport to outlaw all other actions by ordinary users of the service that might conceivably be construed as a trick, scheme or false or fraudulent representation, pretense or credit device to avoid payment." The Justice Department was no more sympathetic: the chief of the Fraud Section of the Criminal Division expressed "lack of enthusiasm for the proposal on the ground that it would tend to make the [Justice] Department a collection agency for selected instances brought to them by the phone company." Who could blame Justice for not wanting to be AT&T's revenue rottweiler? The telephone company screws up and builds a network that's wide open and now somehow the Justice Department and the FBI are supposed to clean up the mess and go after the fraudsters?

AT&T left its meetings empty-handed, no new law in sight.

All of these things forced AT&T to think about the unthinkable: would it have to redesign the entire nationwide telephone network and install a new signaling system?

This was a huge question. The estimates of the costs for such a redesign varied from a quarter of a billion to a billion dollars (between $2 billion and $8 billion today). It would take years to deploy whatever new signaling system its engineers came up with. After all, the design of the original system had taken decades, starting in the late 1920s and with effort in earnest during the 1940s and '50s, and that deployment was still years from being finished. While the company was deploying whatever new system it came up with, the network would still be vulnerable.

Then there was the niggling question in the back of the minds of AT&T's leaders, namely, what if the new system also turned out to be vulnerable? As one person familiar with the matter put it, they had "no assurance at all that if we did modify [the signaling system], that that in turn would not be overcome, too."

None of this sat well with the executives at American Telephone and Telegraph in New York City. The directive to the engineers at Bell Labs from AT&T headquarters at 195 Broadway was clear: "You guys created this mess, you clean it up!"

Engineers are funny animals. If you tell an engineer about a problem, any problem, his first instinct is to measure it. Tell an engineer you don't love him anymore and he'll ask for a graph of your love over time so that he can understand exactly how big the problem is and when it started.

But there were no graphs of the extent of electronic toll fraud, at least not in the early 1960s. After all, the key thing that blue and black boxes did was to defeat AT&T's carefully designed billing system, the very system that kept tabs on the number and length of calls being made on its network. If there were no billing records for fraudulent calls, there was no way to know how many fraudulent calls there were or how long they lasted. And that meant AT&T was gazing into the abyss. Say the phone company catches some college students with electronic boxes. Fantastic! But elation is soon replaced by worry. Is that all of them? Or is that just the tip of the iceberg? Are there another ten college students doing it? A hundred? Are there a thousand fraudulent calls a year or are there a million?

Engineers *hate* stuff like this.

Bell Labs, filled to the brim with engineers, proposed a crash program to build an electronic toll fraud surveillance system and deploy it throughout the network. It would keep a watchful eye over the traffic flowing from coast to coast, ever vigilant for suspicious calls—not every call, mind you, but a random sampling of a subset of them, enough to gather statistics. For the first time Bell Labs—and AT&T's senior management—would have useful data about the extent of the electronic toll fraud problem. Then they'd be in a position to make billion-dollar decisions.

The project was approved; indeed, AT&T gave Bell Labs a blank check and told them to get right to work. Tippy-top secret, the program had the coolest of code names: Project Greenstar. Within Bell Labs Greenstar documents were stamped with a star outlined in green ink to highlight their importance and sensitivity. Perhaps as a joke, the project lead was given a military dress uniform hat with a green general's star on it, an artifact that was passed on from one team lead to the next over the years.

Greenstar development began in 1962 and the first operational unit was installed at the end of 1964. Bill Caming, AT&T's corporate attorney for privacy and fraud matters, became intimately familiar with the program. "We devised six experimental units which we placed at representative cities," Caming said. "Two were placed in Los Angeles because of not only activity in that area, but also different signaling arrangements, and one was placed in Miami, two were originally placed in New York, one shortly thereafter moving to Newark, NJ, and one was placed in Detroit, and then about January 1967 moved to St. Louis."

Ken Hopper, a longtime Bell Labs engineer involved in network security and fraud detection, recalls that the Greenstar units were big, bulky machines. "I heard the name 'yellow submarine' applied to one of them," he says. They lived in locked rooms or behind fenced-in enclosures in telephone company switching buildings. A single Greenstar unit would be connected to a hundred outgoing long-distance trunk lines and could simultaneously monitor five of them for fraud. The particular long-distance trunk lines being monitored were selected at random as calls went out over them. At its core, Greenstar looked for the presence of 2,600 Hz on a trunk line when it shouldn't be there. It could detect both black box and blue box fraud, since both cases were flagged by unusual 2,600 Hz signaling.

As Caming described it, "There were in each of these locations a hundred trunks selected out of a large number, and the [. . .] logic equipment would select a call. There were five temporary scanners which would pick up a call and look at it with this logic equipment and determine whether or not it had the proper [. . .] supervisory signals, whether, for example, there was return answer supervision. When we have a call, we have a supervisory signal that goes to and activates the billing equipment which usually we call return answer supervision. That starts the billing process and legitimizes the call, and if you find voice conversation without any return answer signal, and that is what it was looking for, it is an indication, a strong indication, of a possible black box that the caller called in; and if, for example, you heard the tell-tale blue box tone [. . .] this was a very strong indication of illegality because that tone has no normal presence upon our network at that point."

When Greenstar detected something unusual, it took an audacious next step: it recorded the telephone call. With no warrant and with no warning to the people on the line, suspicious calls were silently preserved on spinning multitrack reel-to-reel magnetic tapes. If Greenstar judged it had found a black box call it recorded for sixty to ninety seconds; if it stumbled upon a blue box it recorded the entire telephone call. Separate tracks recorded the voice, supervisory signals, and time stamps.

When the tapes filled up they were removed by two plant supervisors. "They were the only two who had access from the local [telephone] company," Caming says. Then they were sent via registered mail to New York City. There, at the Greenstar analysis bureau, specially trained operators—"long-term chief operators who had great loyalty to the system [who] were screened for being people of great trust," Ken Hopper says—would listen to the tapes, their ears alert for indications of fraud. The operators would determine whether a particular call was illegal or was merely the result of an equipment malfunction or "talk off"—somebody whose voice just happened to hit 2,600 Hz and had caused a false alarm. When these operators were finished listening, the tapes would be bulk erased and sent back for reuse.

"The greatest caution was exercised," Bill Caming recalls. "I was very concerned about it. The equipment itself was fenced in within the central office so that no one could get to it surreptitiously and extract anything of what we were doing. We took every pain to preserve the sanctity of the recordings."

Project Greenstar went on for more than five and a half years. Between the end of 1964 and May 1970, Greenstar randomly monitored some 33 *million* U.S. long-distance phone calls, a number that was at once staggeringly large and yet still an infinitesimally tiny fraction of the total number of long-distance calls placed during those years. Of these 33 million calls, between 1.5 and 1.8 million were recorded and shipped to New York to be listened to by human ears. "We had to have statistics," said Caming. Statistics they got: they found "at least 25,000 cases of known illegality" and projected that in 1966 they had "on the order of 350,000 [fraudulent] calls nationwide."

"Boy, did it perk up some ears at 195 Broadway," says Hopper. It wasn't even that 350,000 fraudulent calls was that big a number.

Rather, it was the fact that there was really nothing that could be done about it, at least not at once. "It was immediately recognized that if such fraud could be committed with impunity, losses of staggering proportions would ensue," Caming said. "At that time we recognized—and we can say this more confidently in public in retrospect—that we had no immediate defense. This was a breakthrough almost equivalent to the advent of gunpowder, where the hordes of Genghis Khan faced problems of a new sort, or the advent of the cannon."

The initial plan with Greenstar was simple: Wait. Watch. Listen. Gather statistics. Tell no one. Most important, don't do anything that would give it away. "There was no prosecution during those first couple of years," Hopper says. "It was so the bad guys would not be aware of the fact that they're being measured." It was only later, Hopper says, that AT&T decided to switch from measurement to prosecution. Even then, Hopper said, "The presence of Greenstar would not be divulged and that evidence gathered to support toll fraud prosecutions would be gathered by other means." Instead, Hopper relates, Greenstar would be used to alert Bell security agents to possible fraud. The security agents would then use other means, such as taps and recordings, to get the evidence needed to convict. "Greenstar bird-dogging it would not be brought out," says Hopper. "It was just simply a toll fraud investigation brought about by unusual signaling and you would not talk about the fact that there was a Greenstar device. That was the ground rule as I understood it. Any court testimony that I ever gave, I never talked about any of that." As another telephone company official put it, "If it ever were necessary to reveal the existence of this equipment in order to prosecute a toll fraud case, [AT&T] would simply decline to prosecute."

Bill Caming became AT&T's attorney for privacy and fraud matters in September 1965. Greenstar had been in operation for about a year when he was briefed on it. His reaction was immediate: *"Change the name. I don't even know what it is, but it just sounds* illegal. *Change the name.*" More innocent-sounding code names like "Dewdrop" and "Ducky" were apparently unavailable, so AT&T and Bell Labs opted for something utilitarian and unlikely to attract attention: Greenstar was rechristened "Toll Test Unit."

As the new legal guy at AT&T headquarters, Caming faced questions that were both important and sensitive. Forget how it sounded, was Greenstar actually *illegal*? And if it was, what should be done about it? Before joining AT&T Caming had been a prosecutor at the Nuremberg war crimes trials after World War II. He was highly regarded, considered by many to be a model of legal rectitude. Was there any way he could see that the AT&T program was legit?

There was. He later stated under oath that there was "no question" Greenstar was in fact legal under laws of the day—a surprising conclusion for what at first blush appears to be an astonishing overreach on the part of the telephone company. There were two parts to Caming's reasoning. The first had to do with the odd wording of the wiretap laws of the early 1960s; using this wording Caming was able to thread a line of legal logic through the eye of a very specific needle to conclude that the program was legal under the law prior to 1968. The second part had to do with his position at American Telephone and Telegraph. In 1968, when Congress was considering new wiretapping legislation, Caming was in a position to help lawmakers draft the new law. He made very sure that the new wiretap act didn't conflict with AT&T's surveillance program.

Caming even informed the attorneys at the Justice Department's Criminal Division about Greenstar in 1966 and 1967, in connection with some prosecutions. "Now, that does not say that they cleared it or gave me their imprimatur," he allowed. But then, he added, "we did not feel we needed it."

Years later, the Congressional Research Service agreed with Caming regarding the legality of the program—to a degree. While not going so far as to say there was "no question" that Greenstar was legal, it was concluded that "It is not certain that the telephone company violated any federal laws by the random monitoring of telephone conversations during the period from 1964 to 1970. This uncertainty exists because the Congressional intent [in the law] is not clear, and case law has not clearly explained the permissible scope of monitoring by the company."

This whole mess formed a challenging business conundrum for AT&T executives, the sort of thing that would make for a good business school case study. Put yourself in their shoes. You have made an incredibly expensive investment in a product—the telephone network—that turns out to have some gaping security holes in it. You have, as Bill Caming said, no immediate defense against the problem. You finally have some statistics about how bad the problem is. It's bad, but it's not terrible, unless it spreads, in which case it's catastrophic. Replacing the network will take years and cost a billion dollars or so. The Justice Department isn't sure there are any federal laws on the books that actually apply. And every time you prosecute the fraudsters under state laws, not only do you look bad in the newspapers—witness the *Milwaukee Journal*'s 1963 front-page headline "Lonely Boy Devises Way of Placing Free Long Distance Calls"—but the resulting publicity makes the problem worse.

AT&T played the best game it could with a bad hand. For now, it would quietly monitor the network, keeping a weather eye on the problem. When the company found college kids playing with the network, investigators would give them a stern talking-to and confiscate their colored boxes. Execs would start thinking about a slow, long-term upgrade to the network to eliminate the underlying problem. And if opportunity knocked and they could help out the feds with an organized crime prosecution—and in the process set a clear precedent for the applicability of the federal Fraud by Wire law—well, that would be lovely.

That opportunity came knocking in 1965. As it turned out, it used a sledgehammer.

Eight

BLUE BOX BOOKIES

IT WAS JANUARY 8, 1966, a cloudy winter day in Miami. Special Agent Heist rang the doorbell to Kenneth Hanna's apartment. Nothing.

Heist glanced down at the clipboard he was carrying where his FBI identification was clipped—along with arrest and search warrants. Standing next to Heist was Special Agent Roussell. Instead of a clipboard, Roussell was carrying a fourteen-pound sledgehammer.

"FBI!" Heist shouted. "We are here to execute a search warrant!"

Still nothing.

Heist looked at his watch. Seconds ticked by.

Heist pounded the door with his fist. He rang the doorbell a few more times.

Finally he turned to Roussell. "Hit the door."

Roussell swung his sledge. The door buckled but it didn't open.

"Hit it again," Heist ordered.

At the second blow the door opened. And with it so did a legal can of worms—worms that would, over the next four years, crawl all the way to the Supreme Court.

Special Agent Heist was there because of a blue box. But Kenneth Hanna—the guy whose door got sledged—was a bookie, not a phone phreak. If you're a bookie, the service you provide is accepting bets from your customers on a particular event—in football, say, maybe it's the upcoming Packers versus Patriots game. You charge a small commission for that service. But if that's the service you provide, your real business is a delicate balancing act. In aggregate, you need to get your customers to bet the same number of dollars on the Packers as they're betting on the Patriots. If they don't, if their bets are lopsided, then you're now running a risk: if the wrong side loses, you—personally—are on the hook for the difference.

Getting customers to bet evenly on both sides is tough to do if the Packers are widely expected to kick Patriot butt. So the way you even things out is with something called "the line." The line is the point spread, that is, the number of points by which the bookie claims one team is going to beat the other. Kind of like a handicap in golf, it aims to turn an uneven match into an even one. By adjusting the line, the bookie can influence which side his customers are betting on. But even then a bookie might still end up with lopsided bets and financial risk. When this happens, street-level bookies turn to higher-level "layoff" bookies: they lay off—outsource—some of their bets to a bookie higher up in the bookie food chain, someone with more financial wherewithal who is able to take on greater risk.

Even more than teenage girls, bookies are telephone junkies; good bookies are always on the phone. Not just to take bets from their customers but to stay in touch with their colleagues, from the casinos of Las Vegas and Atlantic City to informants in college football towns across the country. Did a big bookie in Vegas just change his line? Better figure out why. And if the Packers' quarterback bruised his shoulder in a fender bender, or Michigan State's star defensive end is drinking too much while pledging a fraternity, our bookie needs to know this ASAP. In the 1950s and '60s, before the Internet, the telephone was a bookie's lifeline. In fact, a bookie cut off from his sources is a bookie who will be out of business very quickly.

This telephone monkey on their backs gave bookies two problems. The first was just business, plain old profit and loss. If you were on the phone all day long to faraway places back in the 1960s, well, let's just say that AT&T was getting rich and you probably weren't. Money saved on your long-distance bill was money in your pocket.

The bigger problem was that pesky Federal Bureau of Investigation. While many FBI agents felt that sports betting was simply red-blooded American fun, the problem was organized crime. It turned out that bookmaking was one of the mob's most lucrative businesses; one estimate put U.S. betting at $20 billion in 1969, as much as one-third of which was pure profit for gangsters. Although there might not be anything wrong with betting a few bucks on the basketball game, the problem was, as one former FBI special agent put it, "it ends up feeding something else, like drugs, prostitution, loan sharking."

In 1961 Attorney General Robert Kennedy urged Congress to pass a suite of laws aimed at "the bankrollers and kingpins of the rackets," as part of a larger plan to go after organized crime by cutting off its finances. Several of these laws specifically targeted bookmaking. Shut down bookmaking, the logic went, and you cut off the mob's largest and most profitable revenue stream; cut off those revenues and not only do you hurt organized crime across the board, you limit its ability to invest in growth markets such as importing illicit drugs. And though not every bookie was mobbed up, the FBI knew a lot of the bigger layoff bookies were. So that's where the law focused.

But going after the bookies was tough. Bookmaking doesn't leave lots of physical evidence like dead bodies or stolen loot. The actual crime occurs only when you accept a bet, which might be done in person but more likely happened over the phone. Then, for it to be a federal crime under the new laws, the bet had to be placed across state lines. Even then, the law said, gambling across state lines was illegal only if you were "in the business of gambling," a vague term that was up to the courts to decide on a case-by-case basis. Merely placing an occasional bet with a far-away friend or two wasn't good enough. All of these requirements made it tricky to gather enough evidence to get a conviction. Who could the FBI turn to for help?

Who else? The phone company. Wiretaps were ideal for taking down bookies, but they were hard to come by—legally, anyway. Yet the phone company had something almost as good: long-distance toll records. Phone bills, in other words. Toll records provided the FBI with what the military code breakers at the National Security Agency would call "traffic analysis," answering the questions of who called whom, when, and for how long? Even if you don't wiretap the bad guys there's still a lot you can learn just from seeing the patterns of their phone calls.

Gil "the Brain" Beckley was a perfect example. "He was the number one layoff bookmaker in the U.S. and Canada. He was *the* guy," recalls Edwin J. Sharp, a former FBI assistant director who worked the Beckley case in his early years at the Bureau. Beckley, reddish-haired and handsome, was liked and respected by his fellow layoff bookmakers. His nickname came from his lightning-quick ability to calculate odds in his head, and he was known to take in more than $250,000 of bets in a single day. The government had been tangling with Beckley since the late 1950s and wanted to take him down. Badly.

"Beckley lived in a plush Miami Beach apartment house, five or six stories up, well insulated. There was no way to get in and do anything," Sharp says. "We were pretty well restricted to phone record checks." But the phone records were a treasure trove. Over a period of months Sharp amassed a 3x5 index card file—some twenty thousand cards' worth—of every long-distance number Beckley called. "We didn't know the term then," Sharp says, "but what we really needed was a computer database." Painstakingly, Sharp and his colleagues built a detailed map of Beckley and his associates. By combining this with other intelligence they formed a solid picture of his bookmaking operation.

The threat posed by telephone toll records wasn't news to the bookies, and they had developed several techniques to combat it. As early as 1950 bookies were using so-called cheese boxes to evade capture. The cheese box was a simple electronic circuit that bridged two telephone lines to form a two-person conference call. A bookie would get a pair of telephone lines installed someplace innocuous, such as an empty apartment, and install a cheese box there. The bookie would call one of the two telephone numbers and then just wait. At some point, one of his customers would call the other number and they would be connected. The beauty of this setup was that the customer never had the bookie's direct telephone number. Moreover, if the police took the telephone numbers to the phone company to get an address they could raid, they'd end up looking like chumps, because all they'd find was an empty apartment with a pair of telephone lines and some simple electronics in the closet.

Cheese boxes didn't solve the problem of long-distance toll records, however, because bookies still needed to make outgoing phone calls. Since the early 1950s bookies had been using every trick they could think of to make free and, more important, unrecorded long-distance telephone calls. One method was as simple as bribing telephone company operators and technicians to place calls for them so that the calls never appeared on their own telephone bills. Another approach took advantage of the fact that the phone company issued special telephone credit cards to its customers that allowed them to make phone calls while they were on the road. The bookies learned that it was possible to make up bogus credit card numbers, which both saved them money and guaranteed that records of the calls wouldn't wind up on their phone bills. In other cases bookies would establish legitimate telephone credit cards under different names and addresses and actually pay the bills. This latter method might not save them any money, but it did manage to keep long-distance calls off their own personal toll records, thus frustrating the Ed Sharps of the FBI with their thousands of 3x5 cards.

Around 1960 the bookies discovered a higher-tech approach. A former telephone company engineer named Walter Shaw seems to have been the guy who introduced the mob to the black box, the simple electronic circuit that makes it look like the telephone was never answered and that Charlie Pyne and his buddies rediscovered in 1963. A black box gets installed on the receiving end of a call but it benefits the caller: if you call a number that has a black box on it, your phone call is free and no record of the call is ever made by the phone company. It was easy to combine a black box with a cheese box so that bookie-bettor conference calls could be free and also leave no record that they had taken place.

Government law enforcement agencies got their first inkling of this new technology in 1960. Investigators at the Treasury Department had been investigating a large cross-country gambling ring with the standard technique of using long-distance toll records to map out the bad guys. They had recently received a tip that there was "some type of instrument or device through which gamblers are able to make long distance telephone calls but circumvent the recording of these calls by telephone company equipment." Not long afterward, the telephone toll records dried up; there was suddenly a "surprising decrease in their long distance telephone activities." Exactly what you'd expect to see if bookies started deploying black boxes to hide evidence of their calls. The next year Walter Shaw was arrested in Miami after a bookie raid a week earlier turned up a number of black boxes in Mamaroneck, New York, which the New York assistant attorney general claimed Shaw had been selling to bookies for $1,500 a piece.

Unfortunately—for the bookies, that is—black boxes weren't a panacea. A black box is a passive device for receiving calls. If you have a black box, then people calling you don't have to pay for their calls, nor do they have to worry about leaving a record that the call took place. But having a black box doesn't help you make calls; if you wanted to leave no trace of your outgoing phone calls a black box didn't help you.

Enter the blue box. Blue boxes were active devices: they allowed you to call people—anybody—without leaving a record that the call was ever made. It's not clear exactly when the bookies learned about blue boxes, or from whom, but the best guess appears to be about 1963 or 1964. One source was Louis MacKenzie, the electronics engineer who offered to fix AT&T's network, for a price, in the early 1960s. MacKenzie, who later became a witness for the government in several blue box prosecutions, sold blue boxes to bookies in 1965 or perhaps earlier. But it is certainly possible that organized crime members learned about blue boxes from another source, for example, Walter Shaw, the former telephone company engineer who provided the mob with black boxes.

Regardless of exactly where they came from, or when, blue boxes are what led to Special Agent Heist knocking on Kenneth Hanna's door on that Miami winter morning in 1966. About six months earlier, on July 19, 1965, AT&T contacted the Department of Justice's Organized Crime Division. AT&T's lawyer explained that the company had been investigating a toll fraud case and stumbled on something that the Justice Department might be interested in. Certain individuals had been "using devices to circumvent payment of telephone charges in the transmission of wagering information." The wording had special meaning to the feds, for transmission of wagering information across state lines was a federal crime, one made so by a law introduced just a few years earlier by one of Attorney General Kennedy's laws specifically targeting bookies and organized crime. The gambling network AT&T found certainly crossed state lines, spanning Boston, New Orleans, Las Vegas, Philadelphia, Miami, Washington, D.C., and Providence, Rhode Island.

The best part, though, was that AT&T had made tapes of the calls. "The Telephone Company investigation has resulted in obtaining various tapes and recordings, all in regard to gambling information," read the FBI memo regarding the meeting with AT&T. The phone company "indicated their desire to turn these items over to the Organized Crime Division."

From AT&T's perspective it must have seemed a master stroke. What better way to crack down on telephone fraud while simultaneously cementing good relations with law enforcement than to hand over the heads of mobsters on a platter? As Bill Caming, AT&T's attorney for privacy and fraud matters, describes it, AT&T

"put a blue ribbon around it and handed it to law enforcement. They would be delighted because the work was all done and the glory lay ahead."

Well, the work wasn't *all* done; the feds had certain niggling details to attend to, such as launching an investigation and then prosecuting the bad guys. A grand jury was convened in Philadelphia, thought to be the center of the gambling ring. TARCASE—"tapes and recordings," the FBI's code name for the investigation—was born.

It was about four months into TARCASE, on November 24, 1965, when Jerry Doyle's phone rang. Doyle, a former FBI agent, was a security officer for Southern Bell Telephone in Miami. The call was from the Internal Audit and Security Group at AT&T headquarters in New York City. The caller told Doyle that there were indications of a blue box in use on a telephone number in Miami and the company wanted Doyle to investigate it.

The telephone number in question belonged to Kenneth Hanna. The name was familiar to Doyle, who knew him to be a Miami-area bookmaker. So did the FBI. In fact, the FBI had been trying to connect Hanna with TARCASE for some months.

Inside the telephone company switching office, Doyle had a blue box detector installed on Hanna's telephone line. This was a device that listened for 2,600 Hz, the telltale tone emitted by a blue box to disconnect a telephone call. Each time it heard this tone it incremented a mechanical counter—a "peg counter"—to keep a running total of the number of times a blue box might have been used on Hanna's line. The peg counter quickly registered plenty of hits, strongly indicating that Hanna's line had a blue box on it. Doyle had the counter replaced with a tape recorder that was activated by 2,600 Hz. The recorder captured only the first thirty to forty-five seconds of each call, just enough to hear the blue box being used, to record what number was being dialed with it, and to get a few seconds of conversation, it was hoped enough to ID the people speaking. By limiting the recordings to just a minute or so at the start of the call, AT&T also hoped to avoid any later accusations that it had excessively violated its customers' privacy rights; the phone company would be able to tell the courts that it had engaged in the absolute minimum amount of recording necessary to catch the bad guys.

Within a day the tape recordings provided Doyle with all the evidence he needed ("beyond a shadow of a doubt," he would later testify) to prove that Hanna was indeed using a blue box. But for some reason—perhaps a desire to be extra thorough, perhaps a desire to help his former colleagues at the FBI, who knows?—Doyle left the tape recorder on Hanna's line for about a month. In all, some nine hours of Hanna's conversations were recorded, a minute at a time.

Toward the end of December, Doyle received a subpoena in the mail commanding him to turn over his tapes to the federal grand jury in Philadelphia. A few days later, Miami FBI special agent Bill Heist was handed the case—and the tapes. He spent hours listening to them. They contained everything he needed to go after Hanna and Hanna's partner, a New York bookie named Nathan Modell. Not only did the tapes make it clear that Hanna was using a blue box, Hanna and Modell's conversations captured on the tapes also made it clear that they were in the business of bookmaking and were transmitting wagering information across state lines. Even though the tapes had less than a minute of each conversation, the feds believed it to be more than enough to convict both of them for illegal gambling activities.

It was bad timing for Hanna and Modell but great timing for the feds because the FBI was just putting together a nationwide list of gamblers to raid that January. The Bureau planned to arrest bookies where there was evidence to do so and to execute search warrants to gather intelligence where there wasn't; agents hoped they could get grand jury indictments after the searches. Hanna and Modell were added to their list, joining an honor roll of about a dozen others, a list that started with a planned search of the apartment of Gil Beckley, the government's most wanted bookmaker.

On January 8, 1966, FBI agents executed raids in New York, Miami, New Orleans, Baltimore, and five other cities. As Special

Agent Heist and four other FBI agents crashed through the door of the apartment in Miami, Hanna made a dash for the bathroom. He was arrested moments later standing over a just-flushed toilet, the most incriminating of his bookmaking papers presumably making their way through the sewer system to Biscayne Bay. Still, the FBI recovered a blue box and other bookmaking paraphernalia from his apartment. That same morning the FBI arrested Modell at his hotel room in New York City. Hanna was charged with 18 USC 1343, Fraud by Wire, and 18 USC 1084, Interstate Transmission of Wagering Information; Modell, who only received blue box calls from Hanna, was charged only with Interstate Transmission of Wagering Information.

The raids in the other cities went off without a hitch. According to newspaper reports, FBI agents "used a chauffeur-driven Cadillac to get into the swank island apartment of Gilbert Lee Beckley . . . the chauffeur carried a carton of whiskey and was flanked by two agents disguised as the donors. Beckley looked through the peephole, saw the chauffeur, and opened the door." Although Beckley was not arrested, FBI agents obtained a wealth of gambling information. In the words of a Justice Department attorney in Miami, the operation was "most successful."

Then, just a few months later, in April 1966—and before Hanna and Modell even had a chance to get to trial—the phone company handed over to the FBI still more evidence of bookie blue box fraud. The setup was similar to the Hanna case in that gamblers and bookies using blue boxes to make illegal telephone calls were all caught on tape by the telephone company. The recordings this time were courtesy of AT&T's California subsidiary, Pacific Telephone, and they were of an alleged Los Angeles bookmaker named Al Bubis speaking with his associates throughout the country.

As in the Hanna case, Pacific Telephone had determined that Bubis was using a blue box. As Southern Bell had done with Hanna, Pacific Telephone installed a tape recorder on Bubis's line. But Pacific Telephone went further than the telephone companies back east that were involved in TARCASE. Instead of recording just the first thirty to forty-five seconds of each call, Pacific Telephone recorded the entire duration of all of Bubis's calls, both incoming and outgoing, from December 20, 1965, to March 24, 1966.

It was a gold mine for law enforcement: a chance to listen to three months' worth of telephone calls between Bubis and some of the FBI's most wanted bookies. Based on the Bubis tapes the FBI made simultaneous raids across the country on May 25, 1966. Sixteen alleged gamblers and bookmakers in nine different states were arrested; four more were sought as fugitives. As always, Gil "the Brain" Beckley was at the top of the list, and this time it was an arrest, not a search. Also arrested was Frank "Lefty" Rosenthal, a charismatic gambler whose career would later be reprised by Robert De Niro in the 1995 movie *Casino*. An FBI press release described the operation as a "crippling blow to the users of electronic devices designed to circumvent toll charges on long-distance telephone calls."

The bookies were not going down without a fight. Mob attorney Ben Cohen represented both Hanna and Modell in the Florida case as well as Gil Beckley and Henry Loman in the first California case to reach trial. Cohen was the brother of Sam Cohen, one of the five founders of Miami's notorious S & G Syndicate—the initials were said to stand for "stop and go," a reference to the syndicate's habit of suspending operations when things got too hot. At its peak, S & G ran a network of some two hundred bookies in the Miami area and raked in about $40 million a year.

Counsel Ben Cohen could switch instantly from smooth and charming to tough and intimidating. His balding head, horn-rimmed glasses, stout frame, expensive gabardine suits, and three-carat diamond pinky ring quickly became fixtures in Miami courthouses. The Senate's Kefauver hearings on organized crime reported in 1951: "Individual bookmakers understood that they would be arrested from time to time; that their fines would be paid out of the profits so that S & G would participate in one-half of the fine if the bookie did not have it; and that after the fine was paid, the bookmaking operation could continue unmolested.

The bookmakers were almost always represented by an attorney named Ben Cohen [. . .] There is concrete testimony on the record that Ben Cohen appeared on the scene of gambling raids almost immediately after the police, and the evidence indicates that S & G had information in advance about raids which were to be conducted."

By 1966 Cohen was an old pro; he had been at the bar for thirty-eight years and spent much of that time defending syndicate members. Together he and his young partner, Miami attorney James Hogan, assembled their blue box defense strategy. In both cases the key legal issue boiled down to this: Under what circumstances did the phone company have the legal right to wiretap your telephone line? And, when it did wiretap you, what could it do with the information?

In 1966 the law of the land on the subject of wiretapping was Section 605 of Title 47 of the United States Code. It read, in part: "No person . . . shall intercept any communication and divulge or publish the existence or contents of such intercepted communication."

This is fascinating wording. Under Section 605, merely intercepting a phone call is not illegal; it is interception *followed by divulgence* that is a crime. In other words, under Section 605 you could wiretap to your heart's content but you couldn't tell anybody about what you heard.

As far as Cohen and Hogan were concerned, this was precisely what the telephone company had done. That is, it had wiretapped Hanna's and Bubis's lines and then disclosed the results to the government. AT&T had violated Section 605, plain and simple. And, as such, all of the government's tape recordings—the entirety of the evidence, really—had to be thrown out. As Hogan argued to the judge in the Hanna case, "We submit that there are no exceptions to Title 47, Section 605; that we have proved interception; that we have proved divulgence." To Hogan, it was an open-and-shut case in the defense's favor: the telephone company's tapping of Hanna's line was clearly illegal.

Cohen summed it up this way to the judge.

Now, there is no omnipotence to the telephone company as far as
I am concerned. I can't see them being any greater than any small
corporation. They have no greater standing than the Government.
The President of the United States issued a proclamation that there
shall be no wire tapping except in national emergencies, and he did
not add, "with the exception of the telephone company." He didn't
add, "if they are being defrauded." Now, the telephone company
in this case decided there was probable cause. It was not done by a
court of law. It was they who decided there was probable cause to tap
the phone and divulge. The great telephone company decides what
their probable cause is. They decide whether or not they should tap
the phone, and then they send it over to the Federal government.
Now, Section 605 says, No one shall divulge what they hear over
a wire . . . they don't say, "Nobody but the telephone company."

Nonsense, responded the U.S. attorney prosecuting Hanna.
"The telephone company gets the right to monitor its lines under
certain circumstances because it is their lines . . . it would be
shocking and illogical not to permit them." And once they've
monitored and found hanky panky, they obviously need to be
able to tell law enforcement about it.

What is the telephone company to do with it? Are they not permitted to take the results of their own independent investigation
to law enforcement officials to see if these things can't be stopped?
People have been defrauding them of revenues. Are they not to
be punished? Are they permitted merely to monitor the line and
determine that Mr. Hanna has, in fact, a blue box on there and he
is defrauding them out of $500 or $1,000 of revenue per month and
do nothing about it? Do they not have the right to seek whatever
steps they deem appropriate in order to correct this situation?

The U.S. attorney in the Hanna case had another card up his
sleeve: a Supreme Court case called *United States v. Sugden*. In the
Sugden case the bad guys used radios while they were committing a

crime. The government overheard them on the radio and presented recordings of their radio transmissions as evidence against them in court. The defendants claimed that this evidence was illegally obtained under Section 605; as in the Hanna case, they argued that the government had illegally intercepted and divulged the contents of their communications and thus the recordings couldn't be used as evidence. The government countered that Section 605 didn't apply because the defendants did not have a license to use their radios, that they were on the air illegally. The government claimed that if you're using a communications facility illegally— just like Hanna was, for example, when he was using his blue box to make free phone calls—then Section 605 didn't apply. In other words, your right to privacy evaporates when you're on the line illegally. The Supreme Court agreed.

The blue box bookies lost both cases. Out in California, Bubis was convicted in August 1966, fined $2,000, and given a one-year suspended sentence. Loman, his codefendant, was acquitted. Beckley, the bookie the government had been after for so long, escaped on the thinnest of technicalities: the grand jury indictment against him had neglected to include the word *willfully* in a key sentence. In Florida, Hanna and Modell were both convicted on December 2, 1966, and sentenced to six months in prison and five years' probation. Hanna was also fined $10,000.

All three appealed.

Hanna and Modell's appeal focused mainly on suppressing the government's tape recordings. It hammered home the idea that Section 605 does apply to telephone companies, that is, that there is no special right that the telephone company has to monitor its lines. But it also alleged that the government was in bed with the phone company to improperly gather evidence on bookmaking. In California, Bubis's attorney argued that the telephone company had gone nuts. First, he said, the telephone company had disclosed to the feds that Bubis's telephone calls "sounded like gambling" before any subpoena had been issued to them—a clear violation of Section 605. Second, the telephone company had recorded not

just a few minutes of Bubis's calls but all of them—a gross violation of Bubis's rights.

On October 20, 1967, California's Ninth Circuit Court of Appeals derailed AT&T and the Justice Department's winning streak.
By listening to all of Bubis's calls over a period of months the
phone company had greatly overreached, the appeals court said,
and reversed Bubis's conviction. As the three-justice panel wrote:

> While we realize the result we have just reached means that the
> appellant will go unwhipped of justice, nevertheless, we reach the
> result on the ground that that fact is less important than that the tele-
> phone company should not resort to unreasonable and unnecessary
> practices which we deem contrary to the provisions of Section 605.

This was the first loss for the government and the phone company
on the subject of blue boxes. And, of course, the Hanna case was
still up on appeal. In fact, both sides in Hanna had just presented
oral arguments to the Fifth Circuit Court of Appeals in Florida.
Seeing this as either a great opportunity or a terrible threat, Hanna
and the government both rushed to file supplemental briefs with
the Fifth Circuit to persuade it that the Ninth Circuit was right,
or had lost its marbles, depending on which side was doing the
persuading.

Six months later, on March 5, 1968, the Fifth Circuit Court of
Appeals in Florida borrowed some poetic phraseology from its
Ninth Circuit brethren in California and handed the government
its second loss.

> Congress may have thought it less important that some offenders
> should go unwhipped of justice (and that the telephone company
> lose some long distance tolls) than that officers (or telephone com-
> pany employees) should resort to methods deemed inconsistent
> with ethical standards and destructive of personal liberty.

Yet the court's decision was strange. Although the appeals court
did direct the lower court to reverse its findings, each judge wrote

his own opinion on the case. Far from being unanimous, it was a one-one-one split: the senior judge sided with defendants Hanna and Modell, the second judge sided with the government, and a third judge took the position that while the telephone company might have the right to monitor illegal calls, it did not have the right to disclose the results of monitoring to law enforcement.

Faced with two reversals and a crumbling legal strategy, the government threw a Hail Mary pass: it petitioned for a rehearing, a legal move that almost never works. It emphasized that the court of appeals' ruling left the government and the telephone company at a loss for legal guidance going forward. It pointed out that of all the judges in the Fifth Circuit who had considered blue box cases to date, only one of them (the senior judge in the three-judge panel) felt that telephone company tape recordings were inadmissible. Moreover, the government argued, the Fifth Circuit Court of Appeals had neglected even to consider the Sugden case, the only relevant Supreme Court case in the matter.

Astonishingly, the appeals court agreed to rehear the case.

It was time to pull out all the stops. Bill Caming, AT&T's attorney, filed a detailed twenty-two-page "friend of the court" brief that took apart the Fifth Circuit decision piece by piece. He argued that illegally placed calls cannot enjoy the protection of Section 605, that there was no reasonable way to gather evidence in these cases other than by recording the calls, and that electronic toll fraud was a large and growing problem for the telephone industry. Caming elaborated in grim detail on this last point.

> Within the past few years the use of electronic toll fraud devices, which are relatively inexpensive to make, has grown at a disturbing rate. We estimate that blue boxes can be mass-produced at a cost of about $25 to $50 per unit, and "black boxes" at a cost of $1.00 or less per unit. Experience has shown these devices have a unique appeal to the criminal element. It enables them not only to evade the payment of lawful telephone charges, but also to falsify or avoid completely any record of the communications made in furtherance of their various illicit operations. [. . .]

We can only conjecture at the full scale of the substantial revenue losses sustained by the telephone industry and its ratepayers. Nonetheless, if the Court deem it desirable, we are prepared to show that since 1961 over 130 blue boxes, over 300 black boxes, and many "cheese boxes" have been seized. Some 224 different individuals were implicated. As in many criminal areas where detection is difficult, the instances of electronic toll fraud unearthed by the telephone companies represent merely that portion of the iceberg visible to the eye. [. . .]

The virtually unchecked use of toll fraud devices which could ensue if the threat of federal prosecution is removed would impose an unwarranted financial burden on the telephone industry and its honest customers. The latter would be required to underwrite the entire cost of these depredations.

On November 18, 1968, the Fifth Circuit Court of Appeals did something even more rare than granting a rehearing: it reversed itself. In a judicial mea culpa the court's opinion stated:

On original hearing, Judge Rives wrote what was intended to become the opinion of the Court. Judge Gobold concurred specially, and Judge Hughes dissented. On further consideration, it appears that Judge Rives' original opinion is in error both as to the facts and as to the law.

The court summarized where it went wrong—quoting liberally from Caming's brief—and concluded with the sentence: "The judgments of conviction of both Hanna and Modell are therefore affirmed."

The Hail Mary had worked. Caming recalls, "Outside of an opening salutation by the court, they adopted the nine pages or so of my brief as their opinion, not even mentioning that it was from my brief. That is the first and only time that ever happened to me. I couldn't believe it!"

Hanna and Modell must have figured that, if it worked for the prosecution, it could work for them. Two weeks later they filed a petition for a second rehearing. This time the court said no, so they appealed to the Supreme Court. On May 5, 1969, the Supreme Court declined to hear their case. More than three years after the FBI took a sledgehammer to Ken Hanna's door, the issue was finally settled. If you were making illegal calls you had no right to privacy. The phone company could tap your line and turn the recordings over to law enforcement.

For the phone company, the victory was about much more than convicting Hanna or Bubis. AT&T now had a case that had gone all the way to the Supreme Court, one that proved, definitively, that 18 USC 1343—the Fraud by Wire law that the Justice Department had believed wasn't relevant—did apply to blue boxes. Thanks to Hanna's failed appeal, the matter was now settled. AT&T finally had an arrow in its quiver to use against the fraudsters.

Throughout all of this legal drama one mystery remains: how had the telephone company found out about Hanna's or Bubis's blue box calls in the first place?

In the Hanna case, Miami telephone company security agent Jerry Doyle received a telephone call from the Internal Audit and Security Group at AT&T headquarters in New York asking him to investigate Hanna's telephone line for a possible blue box. How did investigators in New York know that somebody in Miami was making illegal calls? Hanna's attorneys asked Doyle this very question but Doyle said he didn't know.

There was a one-word answer that nobody was giving: Greenstar.

Hanna had been caught up in AT&T's toll fraud surveillance network. Imagine what would have happened if this had come out during Hanna's trial. After all, the Hanna case took almost four years to resolve and went to the Supreme Court based on tape recordings of each of his illegal calls. Think of the legal circus that would have ensued if Hanna's defense attorneys had learned that the telephone company had been randomly monitoring millions of telephone calls nationwide and recording hundreds of thousands of them.

This added considerably to the stress of prosecuting Greenstar cases. AT&T attorney Caming recalls, "That was the problem in the Hanna case! Fortunately, defense counsel never probed too far as to what our original sources of information were." With blue box prosecutions, he adds, "We were always on pins and needles as to what might spill over into the public press."

Fortunately for AT&T in the Hanna and Bubis cases their luck held. And although Caming wasn't a gambler or a bookmaker, he knew a thing or two about luck. In particular, he knew it didn't last forever.

Nine

LITTLE JOJO LEARNS TO WHISTLE

"**H**ANG UP THE phone and leave it alone!"
Joe was about four years old when his mother first shouted that phrase at him; it was a shout he would hear again and again as he grew up. His mother could be forgiven for raising her voice. She tried to be supportive, she really did, but sometimes her son's obsession with the telephone was just a little much for her. And besides, the shout didn't work. Joe soon turned the phrase into a little song, one he would sing over and over again to himself in a quiet, lilting voice: "Hang up the phone and leave it alone, hang up the phone and leave it alone . . ."

Joe was born in 1949. His given name was Josef Carl Engressia Jr. but his family called him Jojo. His mom, Esther, stayed at home and took care of Jojo and his sister, Toni. Dad—Joe Sr.—was a high school year book photographer. Though they struggled financially, they lived in a small but serviceable apartment in Richmond, Virginia. They had a car. They had a dog. In many ways the Engressias appeared to be a stereotypical postwar baby boom family.

But, as we know, appearances can be deceiving.

First there was the blindness. Joe was born blind, as was his sister. The doctors didn't know what caused it for either of them. It cannot have been an easy thing for Esther and Joe Sr. having two blind children. Any parent will tell you that having kids isn't easy. Having two blind kids is much harder, the sort of harder that make for stress, for anger, for fighting. "I won't lie to you," says Toni. "Our parents fought a lot."

Then there was the incandescence of little Joe's mind. When he was three Jojo would pester the adults to read aloud to him. Before long, he wanted them not just to read to him but to tell him how the words were spelled. Soon after that, he wanted the adults just to read the letters to him—he would piece the letters together and form them into words and sentences, handling the work of "reading" himself. "Before I was four I knew how to be read to with people spelling the words," he said. "So when I learned Braille I already knew how to read and learned in only a month or two."

Jojo didn't have much use for playtime. "I didn't like play," he said. "I told the kindergarten teacher, 'play stinks!'" Instead of play, "I wanted people to read to me by spelling the words."

Then there were the obsessions—many, many obsessions. Young Josef was famous for them. Shower curtains were one; he loved the sound that a plastic shower curtain made as it swished back and forth on itself. Jell-O was another. Jojo constantly asked his mom to make him a pot of Jell-O, saying repeatedly, "When is the Jell-O going to jell?" Then there was his fascination with brassieres. His sister recalls, "It was all I could do to keep him from going outside with Mother's bra wrapped around his head."

The greatest of his obsessions was the telephone. It started around the same time as he learned to read. "I used to ask what time it was, all the time, so Mother started dialing it on the phone. It entranced me, how I could hear another voice like that." The phone company used to offer a free recording you could dial that would tell you the correct time; in Joe's area that number was 737. Tired of dialing it for her son, Esther Engressia stuck pieces of tape on the 7 and the 3. Joe could run his fingers over the cool metal dial of their rotary phone, his fingers seeking the roughness of the bits of tape. With this, Joe could dial the time himself. Joe would dial 737 constantly, just to listen to the voice. One day Joe noticed that the 3 was three holes away from the dial stop and 7 was seven holes away. "I thought, well, if 3 is 3 away and 7 is 7 away, maybe 2 is 2 away and 4 is 4

away, and all that." Joe dialed a number at random, remembering
the digits as he dialed. He heard a ringing signal. A woman's voice
answered. "I asked, 'Is this 439011?' And she said yes, what do you
want? And I said, 'Oh *boy,* I just learned how to dial!'"

Play in the real world might stink, but play in the world of
the telephone was fantastic. The phone had interesting things to
listen to. It even had people who would talk to him! And it was
challenging: it made the ganglia twitch inside little Joe's mind.
It was more than a playground, it was a *laboratory,* a place where
a little kid could try things out and where he could conduct as
many experiments as he wanted. It was a world of possibility, a
world prefaced with that most intoxicating of words: *if.*

"The way I learned [how to dial] sort of characterizes the way
I've learned about telephone systems all my life," he said later.
"You make a theory . . . you think something." Then he'd try it
out. He'd perform an experiment. "Had that not worked I would
have either had to make another theory or see why that wouldn't
work," he says. Not simply trial and error but *guided* trial and error.
Although Jojo didn't know it at the time, the adults had a name
for this. They called it the scientific method. Years later, Nobel
Prize–winning physicist Richard Feynman would write, "The
principle of science, the definition, almost, is the following: the
test of all knowledge is experiment."

For Joe the telephone was much more than just an intellectual
playground. It was a warm electronic bosom, a source of comfort. It was never too busy to spend time with him. It was never
moody. It didn't fight with anybody. "Through the years the
phone has provided me so much," Joe said. "It was like a friend
and companion to me." His sister recalls that he would sometimes
just pick up the phone and listen to the dial tone, its warm drone
drowning out the angry voices of his arguing parents, arguments
that sometimes wound up with Esther in the emergency room.
"Most people take the little old telephone for granted, but to me,
it was like magic," he recalled. "I couldn't even describe how
important it was sometimes."

The sounds, the electronic playground, the people to talk to, a welcoming place that he could escape to—he was hooked. He remembers, "I was not quite four years old. I was crawling around the floor, running phone wire. The phone man had given me a big long piece of phone wire. Mother wouldn't let me run it on the wall anymore with the modeling clay, it made marks and stuff. I was humming, 'I'm a telephone man forever, I'm a telephone man forever,' and just kind of singing it to myself in the tuneless way of a three-year-old, and thinking about it, pretending I was driving the phone truck and all that. I told Mother that. I kind of credit that time to when I first really remember saying it out loud, that I was a telephone man."

His mother wasn't thrilled with the news. "She hoped that I would get over phones someday," he says. Still, she did her best to support her son. Joe amassed a collection of technical books and articles about the telephone system, documents he would ask his mother to read to him. "She hated phones, and she kind of hated to do it, but she did it anyway," he says.

He recalls, "We met a phone man and he gave us some books and Mother was reading to me about #5 crossbar"—the electromechanical telephone switch system that was a workhorse of local phone service. "It was a big thick book from 1955 called something like *The #5 Crossbar Job*," he says. "That was one of my first big, hard books." When a telephone man visited their house to install a telephone, Joe confided how much he was struggling to understand the book, how frustrating it was. He said, "I can't quite understand this #5 crossbar, I'm just stupid, it makes me want to cry." The telephone repair man responded, "There's guys who've been [at the phone company] twenty, thirty years who can't understand #5 crossbar!"

The Engressias moved a lot when Joe was growing up, from Richmond, Virginia, up to Saugus, Massachusetts, then back down to Florida: Fort Lauderdale, Pompano Beach, and finally Miami. ("Daddy hated the snow," says Toni.) Each new place exposed Joe to new telephones and new telephone switching systems. He was constantly on the phone in each new place, listening to the sounds and learning how things worked. One of his techniques was to call the technicians in the telephone company central office and ask them questions.

"I called up when I was almost eight years old and asked, what levels on your selectors are digit absorbing ones and which ones are absorbing repeatedly?" he remembers. (Levels and digit absorbing selectors are esoterica related to the old step-by-step switching system; you are forgiven if you do not have these terms close at hand.) "The guy said, 'Who is this, ma'am?'" Joe responded in his little kid's voice, "I'm not a ma'am, I'm Joe, and I'm nearly eight years old!" Joe got himself a tour of the telephone central office and a trip to a football game from the delighted switchman. "I learned a whole lot [from that trip]," he remembered. In fact, he was thinking so hard about what he learned that day that he was silent during the entire drive home—an event so unusual that his mother teased him about it later.

Although he didn't know it at the time—and wouldn't for ten more years—two of his telephonic discoveries would turn out to be pivotal, both to him and to a generation of phone phreaks.

The first of these was learning how to dial with the hook switch, the little switch that hangs up the phone when you put the handset back in its cradle. "I remember I used to hear the clicking of the dial. You could hear the clickings of the dial way in the background . . . When I hung up I could hear this tiny click in the background. I remember thinking, I wonder if the dial is the same as the receiver click, they both click. Maybe the dial is just faster clicks than the receiver button. . . . I thought about it and I said, if the hook switch and the dial are the same, then I should be able to hang up with the dial, and dial with the hook switch. It seemed impossible. But what if I did the hook switch real fast? And sure enough, I was able to dial." He went for his old standby, the 737 time number. Pressing and releasing the hook switch button, "I actually counted 7, and the 3, I had to do it a couple of times. But finally I actually got the time with the hook button." Joe had discovered that dialing a digit on a rotary phone is just like pressing the hook switch rapidly and repeatedly. Want to dial a 7? Press and release the hook switch 7 times in a row. (This still works on phones today, by the way; you can confirm the results of Joe's experiment yourself with most any landline telephone.)

Joe was far from the first person to discover that you could dial with the hook switch. But it tied into his second discovery, one that would become the basis for his future nickname. "I was seven or eight years old and I was sitting on a long-distance circuit, and I heard the background hum of the tone that controls it . . . I started whistling along with it and all of a sudden the circuit cut off!" How odd! "I did it again and it cut off again." Fascinated, Joe started playing around with this magic tone. He found he could consistently disconnect long-distance calls by whistling that tone—seventh octave E. At the time he wasn't quite sure why it worked, or even what exactly it was good for, but he recalls it had great potential for pranks. "[Mother and I] were walking one time and there was some guy on a pay phone and I just thought, in case it was long distance, I just whistled, it was when I could whistle really loud then, and we were like ten feet away, and he was going, Hello? Hello? And I said, I wonder why he's saying that? And Mother said, I think he got cut off. She didn't know about the whistling at that time. It was just amazing, that tone."

Joe didn't have many friends growing up, perhaps not surprising given his brightness and his very specific interests. When he was in the sixth grade he met another blind kid, Tandy Way, who shared his interests in technology, even including telephones. But, says Joe, Tandy "knew less than I did," and Engressia wasn't really able to learn anything from him.

Engressia got his ham radio license a year before he started high school in 1963. But phones remained his first love. Ham radio was "never as important as phones," he says, and, as for high school, "I never got into, like, dating or proms." He adds, "I'd much rather have a date with the pay phone than some girl or guy or anything." True to form, he says, his high school yearbook featured a photo of him in the school phone booth. "During breaks between classes that's where I'd always hang out," he said.

When Engressia was in tenth grade the unthinkable happened: a financial rough spot necessitated the removal of his home telephone. The high school pay phone booth became more important to him than he had anticipated. Joe began saving up money from his allowance to get his family's phone reinstalled. "I got $2.50 a week lunch money and I did without lunch twice a week for nearly two years and saved up $1 at a time," he said. "Back in twelfth grade I called up and got the phone installed." It was, he said, the only day he missed school in his whole senior year, but somebody had to be home to let the telephone installer in. "My parents decided that if I had that much persistence then they'd pay for it."

After high school Engressia began taking classes at Dade County Junior College. Then, in the fall of 1968, he transferred to the University of South Florida in Tampa. He lived in Beta Hall, one of the dorms on campus. A little over a month into his first semester Engressia mentioned to some other students that he could whistle free long-distance calls. *Yeah, right,* was the response. Faced with such disbelief, Engressia responded with words that would change his life: "I can whistle like a bird and get any number you want anywhere. I'll bet you a dollar I can."

Now then, some guy offers to bet you that he can whistle you a free long-distance call, using just his lips and nothing else, it's a sure thing, right? A dollar was wagered. Whistling ensued. Engressia emerged slightly richer, his fellow students with egg on their faces. At least they got a phone call in the bargain.

Engressia's whistling trick combined two of the things he had learned ten years earlier: hook switch dialing and whistling to disconnect a call. Engressia knew that if he whistled seventh octave E, that is, 2,600 cycles per second, he could disconnect a long-distance phone call. But then what? Engressia figured out that by whistling short bursts of 2,600 Hz he could mimic the telephone company's single-frequency (SF) dialing system, just like Ralph Barclay had figured out in 1961. To dial the area code 212, for example, Engressia would whistle two quick bursts of 2,600, followed by one quick burst, followed by two more quick bursts: *beep beep . . . beep . . . beep beep!* So the entire dance went like this. First, dial a call to a free long-distance number, such as directory assistance. Then give one long whistle to reset the long-distance trunk. Then whistle the pulses that made up the ten-digit phone number, one digit—one pulse—at a time. It was simply the whistling equivalent of the hook switch dialing he had learned as a little kid.

The trick gained him popularity. "The guys in the dormitory were calling me 'The Whistler.' Crowds of up to forty people would follow me around," he said. The students "begged me to make the calls." Engressia obliged, charging $1 for a whistled long-distance call to anywhere in the United States. Though it's not quite a free call at that point, Engressia's rates were still a bargain compared to AT&T's, which were then about $2.60 for a five-minute cross-country call—roughly $17 today.

While attempting to whistle a call to Long Island, New York, he "whistled wrong" and wound up connected to an operator in Montreal, Canada. This was an easy mistake to make. Long Island is area code 516, Montreal is area code 514; screw up by just two little beeps and you wind up two hundred miles north. Nonetheless, Engressia managed to convince the operator to connect him to the New York number. But the operator "was suspicious and monitored the call. Naturally the student I put the call through for talked extensively about the 'whiz kid' who had placed his free call," he said. "The operator broke in and managed to get the student to identify himself and where he was calling from."

An investigation ensued. Word eventually made it back from Bell Canada in Montreal to General Telephone, the independent telephone company in the Tampa area. GTE contacted the university, trying to identify the source of the whistled calls. Engressia was fingered. His sudden popularity came to an equally sudden end.

Despite having a crime and a culprit, GTE sensed a potential publicity black eye. As a security officer for the company wisely put it, the firm had nothing to gain by prosecuting a blind college student. Meanwhile, another GTE spokesman used the incident to pioneer what would become a standard response by the telephone company—and, years later, by high-tech software companies—when presented with claims of security vulnerabilities in their products and services: disbelief and denial. "It could happen—but did it really?" the spokesman said. "It would take a lot of sophisticated equipment and even then the probability of being able to do this is remote." Whether this was genuine ignorance, willful disbelief, or just a bit of misdirection to discourage would-be imitators is unclear.

As punishment for his crimes of whistling free telephone calls the USF dean of student affairs told Engressia that he would be "allowed to withdraw" for the rest of the term. If Engressia didn't want to withdraw, the dean said, he would be suspended. Engressia declined the dean's offer. "I didn't want to sacrifice all the course work I had done already this quarter," he said, and noted that his grade point average was between an A and a B.

Engressia was suspended from the University of South Florida on November 15, 1968. He appealed the decision soon after. Engressia's sister Toni was in her last year of high school in Miami when the USF whistling scandal occurred. She recalls coming home one day and being told by her mother, "Your brother has been doing something illegal with the phone. They say he's been whistling into the phone and making long-distance calls." Her mother explained about the dean's decision and Joe's appeal and said that they needed to go to Tampa to be with Joe. Toni, her high school boyfriend, and Esther made the five-hour drive, leaving Engressia's father home with his jobs and the family's dogs. Asked by a reporter what she thought of her son's telephone antics, Esther Engressia responded, "We're going to stick right by him. Anyone who can outsmart a computer—I'm with them."

On December 10, Engressia presented his case at a two-hour public hearing before the university's nine-member disciplinary appeals board, where he told his story with the help of a student advocate. He noted that he had stopped making the free calls on his own initiative. "It was a mistake and I'm sorry I did it," he said, "but not because I got caught. My action was totally irresponsible and it shouldn't be condoned, but I don't think I should be penalized for a first offense so severely that it practically cuts off my education."

The appeals board handed down its decision the next day. Engressia would be allowed to remain in school but would be placed on probation. The board also ordered him to donate $25—the amount he said he had made whistling calls at $1 apiece—to a worthy cause.

"I think the verdict was very favorable," Engressia told newspapers afterward. "I'm happy that I can stay in school."

Engressia's whistling scandal had another positive outcome. Shortly after his suspension back in November the press had gotten wind of things. It started when the *Oracle,* the USF student newspaper, did a story on him, Engressia recalls, "and then the AP or something picked it up, and then it was on the Huntley-Brinkley network news show." Indeed, the AP newswire story was covered in dozens of papers throughout the world. Calls began pouring in for him. "It was sort of exciting, people calling from Australia and all these places to talk with the Whistler," he remembers. The attention amazed and delighted him; it was a far cry from his mother's familiar shout of "Hang up the phone and leave it alone!" Of the publicity he says, "At that age I had never even thought of that, 'cause the phone was always something . . . oh, you know, 'talking about stupid phones all the time.' But people were actually excited about what I could do!"

Soon after the burst of media attention, Engressia received a letter in the mail with a Kansas City postmark. The writer had seen Engressia on the Huntley-Brinkley television show and wanted to introduce himself. Like Engressia, he was a ham operator and telephone enthusiast. Might they talk by phone, or make contact via amateur radio, and discuss certain items of mutual interest?

It was Engressia's introduction to B. David, the mysterious correspondent Jake Locke had met via the Fine Arts 13 classified ad at Harvard a year and a half earlier. Over the next year Engressia and B. David discussed all manner of things related to the telephone.

By April 1969, just four months after his disciplinary hearing at USF, Engressia was back to his telephonic games; this time he had tricked a switchman in a Miami telephone central office into wiring up a pair of telephone lines to form what was called an open-sleeve-lead conference. Essentially a cross between a cheese box and a black box, this circuit allowed two people to call into it and talk to each other without being billed. Engressia and B. David used this circuit to stay in touch between Miami and Kansas City, but they weren't its only users. A suspicious Southern Bell employee who discovered the setup and listened to the calls on it found "a good deal of discussion that students at the University of South Florida were being supplied pairs of numbers which would allow toll free conversations." Additional investigation revealed similar circuits had been set up in Orlando and other cities. The telephone company quietly removed them from service.

Then, on August 27, 1969, the telephone cord hit the fan. A Southwestern Bell security agent working a blue box case up in Kansas City discovered something alarming and called the FBI. Though he wouldn't tell Bureau agents how he had learned of it, he said that "B. David and Engressia have, through sophisticated electronic equipment, intercepted and monitored telephone toll calls." More disturbingly, he said, the two had also discovered a way to intercept calls on a "highly classified, Top Secret telephone system used only by the White House." He reported two other people in connection with this caper: an employee of United Airlines in Chicago and a young blind man named Tandy Way—Joe Engressia's sixth-grade pal down in Miami.

A flurry of urgent investigation ensued. FBI agents were dispatched to meet with Southern Bell telephone security in Miami and interview Engressia, B. David, and Tandy Way. It was a tempest in a teapot, said Miami telephone company investigators. Yes, they obviously knew of Engressia and had been following his and Tandy Way's activities for the past year or so, but basically they were considered to be harmless pests. Their investigation had not revealed that the two had intercepted any telephone calls or wiretapped any lines, civilian or military, and that "the activities of Engressia and Way have been strictly for their own amusement and harassment of the telephone company." For their parts, Engressia, Way, and David all told the FBI, in essence, that yes, they were fascinated with telephones but, no, they hadn't done anything wrong, and they certainly hadn't intercepted any calls and didn't know nuthin' 'bout no top secret White House telephone system. FBI headquarters called a halt to the investigation, but not before sending off posterior-covering letters to the White House, the secretary of defense, and the head of the Secret Service to let them know that their communications systems were alleged to be vulnerable. A few days later an attorney at the Justice Department blessed the FBI's stand-down: there was "not a sufficient indication of a violation under the Interception of Communications Statute to justify investigation," he said.

Engressia and company had gotten lucky; cooler heads had prevailed and decided this was all much ado about nothing. B. David, however, was not one to leave well enough alone. After his visit from the FBI, he concluded that the telephone company must have been illegally monitoring his conversations with Joe Engressia. In fact, he believed that the FBI agents had confirmed this during their interview with him. He proceeded to write an audacious two-page letter to the Kansas City FBI office citing chapter and verse of the Communications Act of 1934 and demanding that the Bureau turn the tables and investigate the telephone company for illegal wiretapping. It is unclear if the FBI ever gave David the courtesy of a response, but an internal FBI memo stated that B. David "is believed to be totally unreliable and his allegations are unfounded."

Despite his upbeat quotes to the press after his whistling incident was resolved, Engressia remembers his years at USF as far from happy. Partly this was a lack of focus. "I wasn't really sure why I was in college," he says. Engressia drifted from one major to another—business administration, mathematics, electrical engineering. "I didn't really know why I had come, except that was just the next step that you do. I hadn't really thought it through at the time, what I wanted."

The bigger part of his unhappiness was simply this: he was lonely. Thanks to the publicity surrounding his whistling escapades he had started getting calls from other phone phreaks in addition to B. David. "That was the first glimpse that there were even other people in the world interested in phones," he says. But now, even though he finally knew there were others like him out there, he couldn't talk to them—at least not on any regular basis. "In college I didn't have a phone where I could dial out direct," he remembers; students in the dorms weren't allowed to have their own telephone lines. For most this would be a minor inconvenience, but for Engressia it cut him off from the one thing that had provided him with years of comfort—and the thing that now promised to connect him to other people like him. His phone phreak fixes had to come from quick calls on the dorm pay phone, occasional trips home on weekends, and summer vacation.

"I did get on the phone some in college but I didn't have much money to speak of, $40 a month I think it was, of spending money where they gave me a state scholarship for the blind. It would be $6 to town for cab fare, so I didn't get out much," he recalls. "I might have stayed in college if I could have had the contacts, you know, on the phone and everything," he says. But as it was, he says, "I was so lonesome and depressed there, in college. It was just one of my sad times."

Engressia quit school and left USF about a year short of his degree, moving to Memphis, Tennessee, in March 1971. "When I left for Memphis, that was when my life started," he says.

He was determined to have his own apartment, one with his own phone, where he'd be able talk to other phone phreaks as much as he wanted. Too, he was tired of living off of his state aid-to-the-blind check. He wanted to be independent, to have a job, to be part of society—to "be a man," as he put it.

The apartment was easy. The job was harder. He applied at dozens of places, "as a switchboard operator, or just about anything, really." He heard one word a whole lot: *no*. The word wasn't always one syllable with two letters, n-o. "It came in a lot of forms," he said, but it always spelled the same thing in the end. We don't think it would be safe for you to work at our company, you might bump into a ladder and hurt yourself. We don't see how you could possibly be a switchboard operator—how would you dial?

The weeks slipped by. The *No*s wore on him. "I got desperate," he said, "$97-per-month welfare wasn't providing me a decent standard of living . . . I had heard that when you live on welfare you live on beans and baloney. Well, I went down to the grocery store and, you know, beans and baloney aren't so cheap anymore!"

Desperation is the mother of invention. Engressia invented a plan that can only be described as crazy: "I decided that since I had come so close to getting a job down in Florida by getting arrested—which was a mistake on my part, to have gotten caught, at that time—I decided to actually plan to get caught." He would engineer his own bust by the telephone company and use the resulting publicity to get a job. "I called it my great gamble. I knew it would either pay off or I'd fail."

Engressia set upon his task with urgency. "This was in late April and I only had money to last me until the end of July," he said. "I was running out of money and I needed to do something." Worse, much of his great gamble was out of his control. What if the phone company didn't do anything or took too long to do it? "I didn't want them to wait too long, either."

He called the telephone company and reported troubles with his line. He knew this would prompt somebody at the telephone company's test board to connect to his line to test it for problems. When he heard what he described as the "subtle impedance change" indicating that a test man was on the line, he began narrating a series of telephonic tricks for the benefit of his invisible audience. "I just said, 'Oh, I'm going to call Russia now.'" Calling through a satellite circuit, "I whistled up the U.S. embassy in Moscow and talked for about two hours pretending I was a talk show host and [the embassy operator] was a talk show [guest]. They heard that and then I made a couple of other free calls and gave my phone number and then used the blue box after it," he said. "Then," he said, "I called this place called NORAD headquarters, something to do with the military, and I called it on a priority circuit. For some reason it rubbed them the wrong way."

After the first evening Engressia felt sure that the phone company would soon wiretap his line. He hinted cryptically at his plan to get a job by getting arrested as he talked to his eavesdroppers: "I have only to July, so I must fly. Don't sit home and sob, blue box and get a job." He performed more stunts to impress the telephone company. "I remember one time they were playing around with my line and they cut the current off and the phone wouldn't work. So I hooked up a 30-watt amplifier and a microphone," he recalled. This he used to transmit his voice into the malfunctioning telephone line, betting that technicians in the telephone company central office or test board would be listening. "I wonder if a blind person himself could really hook up an amplifier in the dark all by himself?" he said into the phone line.

Engressia figured that, thanks to his attention-getting tricks, the phone company was probably now wiretapping his line on a continual basis. But he couldn't know for sure. And so, he said, "I hooked up a circuit so I could monitor the line while it was still on the hook." With this circuitry in place he could leave his phone hung up and yet still hear what the telephone company was up to as his line was being worked on. He quickly determined that the phone company was indeed monitoring him. Best of all, the phone company's monitoring circuit inadvertently worked both ways. "Their voice was leaking through the monitor that they had. I could hear them talking! They said, 'Did you hear what they said? He said something about hooking up a microphone!'

"In a sense I was tapping the tappers," Engressia gleefully recalled. "That made me feel good because I knew my plan was under way," he said. "I'm counting the days to my first paycheck."

★ ★ ★

The telephone company later admitted that it began investigating Engressia when he'd first reported troubles with his telephone line. A few weeks later they sent an undercover security agent posing as a magazine reporter to interview Engressia at his apartment in Memphis. The agent was "freely shown how the whistle calls were placed and the equipment in the young man's possession."

On June 2, 1971, as he was waiting on the sidewalk for a cab, a deep voice of someone nearby asked him if he was Joe Engressia. He said that he was. The voice replied, "You're under arrest."

He spent the night in jail. "I was gonna call some newspapers but two of them came to the jail, and then a TV network came to interview me the next day." His publicity plan seemed to be working but, even so, the experience of going to jail was unnerving. Everything might go perfectly or he just might end up stuck in jail. "You talk about a combination of emotions," he said. "I was happy, sad, excited, scared, nervous, everything imaginable lumped into one."

When the police searched Engressia's place that evening they found "complex telephone equipment devised by Engressia in his tiny apartment. It included pushbutton gadgets that could be programmed to transfer calls to neighbors' telephones."

Arraigned before Judge Ray Churchill of the Memphis City Court, Engressia was charged with two counts of fraud for making free calls. Despite entering an innocent plea to the charges, he told the court, "I've done wrong and the telephone company has every right to prosecute me." He added that he was "just fascinated with phones." Judge Churchill released him on $1 bail and ordered the trial continued until the next week.

"Some folks are on dope, I was on telephones," Engressia told reporters after his arrest. "I knew it would get me into trouble, but when I got lonely I would reach for the phone and it would be there."

Judge Churchill called Engressia's trial to order on June 8. Things did not go swimmingly for the prosecution. A telephone company security agent in court played a tape of some of Engressia's phone calls for the judge, Engressia recalls. During one of the calls an operator asked Engressia for his telephone number. "The operator would say 'number please' and I said 526-6156," Engressia remembers. Judge Churchill asked whose number that was. The telephone company security agents responded that, in fact, 526-6156 was Engressia's telephone number.

Judge Churchill exploded, Engressia says: "He gave his own number and you know who he called and you know how long he talked. Why didn't you just bill him for the call?"

The security agents responded that Engressia was a threat to national security. He calls through a satellite sometimes, they said.

Who owns that satellite? Judge Churchill asked.

The security agents admitted that they weren't sure of the exact ownership of the satellite.

Engressia recalls Judge Churchill's response: "You don't even own the satellite! I don't know, I oughta just throw this whole thing out. You know, if I had known what this is about, I wouldn't have signed the warrant."

The judge was "more sympathetic to my side than even I was," Engressia says.

Judge Churchill ultimately decided that there was not enough evidence to convene a grand jury. He reduced the charges to two counts of malicious mischief. "I can understand how he was driving them crazy," the judge allowed. In addition to a $10 fine, Judge Churchill sentenced Engressia to sixty days in jail.

"He paused awhile," Engressia recalls, and then the judge said, "Sentence suspended."

"Boy, it felt good to go out in the sun that day!" Engressia says. "That was enough to persuade me that stuff was over." From that point forward, Engressia decided, there would be no more illegal phone calls. In the future, he says, when there was a knock on his door he wanted to know that it would always be a friendly knock.

As for Engressia's great gamble, his plan to "blue box and get a job"?

"I got four job offers the next week," Engressia said. The min-
ing and manufacturing company 3M flew him up to Minnesota
for an interview and offered him a job in a research laboratory but
he declined; it didn't have anything to do with telephones and he
didn't want to spend his time "figuring out the right grain pattern
for sandpaper," he says. In the end he accepted a two-dollar-an-hour
job at a small but nearby independent telephone company called
Millington Telephone. "I guess they'll have me do whatever I can
that they need done; maybe I can work on the test board," he said.

"I don't recommend that method of getting a job," Engressia
said several years later, "but it worked for me."

Ten

BILL ACKER LEARNS TO PLAY THE FLUTE

IT WAS A conspiracy, obviously. A conspiracy organized by God himself, one made up of little blind kids out to drive the phone company crazy. What else could explain the fact that Bill Acker and Joe Engressia shared a birthday? What else could explain the fact that, like Engressia, Acker was born blind?

As with Engressia and his sister, the doctors didn't know what caused it. Acker's father, who had long suffered from seizures, killed himself in 1955 when Bill was two, leaving Bill's mother to raise him and his brother. Though his aunt Kaye and their extended Irish Catholic family were a big help to the three of them, Acker says, they were mostly on their own. Acker is quick to acknowledge that things were tough for his mom—"No kidding, she had it hard," he says—but he recalls his childhood as being "all about her moods, her emotions."

The public schools in Farmingdale, New York, weren't wholly prepared to handle a blind kid. "The one teacher didn't know what to do with me and let an itinerant teacher do it all. I sat in class and didn't really get any attention, except from the itinerant teacher," he says. "Even though I do remember that I was being ignored, I was fine with it. From my point of view, school was fine. I could daydream and do what I do. It didn't hurt my feelings that I wasn't getting an education." Unfortunately, says Acker, "I wasn't catching on to Braille," something thought to be very important for the blind in those days. So when Bill was not yet seven his mom sent him off to the Lavelle School for the Blind in the Bronx. Run by Dominican nuns, Lavelle was partly a residential school—along with several hundred other blind kids, Bill would stay there during the week and come home on weekends.

Educationally it may have been an improvement from being ignored, but it was far from paradise. "I was able to absorb enough stuff, but I was not motivated," Acker says. The nuns "branded me lazy over the whole Braille thing. That just sort of tuned me out. 'Okay, fine, if you think I'm lazy, what the hey . . .'" Some people might work hard to disprove an accusation of laziness but, Acker says, "unfortunately, I wasn't one of them." So he "skimped by on my education. That wasn't where it was at for me."

Where it was at for Acker was technology. He had been fascinated with technology for as long as he can remember. As a kid, "going outside was almost like a punishment," he says. "There was nothing for me outside. There was no technology outside."

Ah, but inside! Inside there was AM radio, shortwave radio, television. Acker spent much of his childhood learning about radios, how they work and how to make them work better. "DXing"—hunting down radio signals from places as distant as possible—was the equivalent of collecting baseball cards for young Bill Acker. DXing required patience, perseverance, and a solid understanding of how radio worked. Acker had these qualities in spades. Before he became a teenager, Acker needed almost no sleep and didn't like staying in bed. "There was an unspoken understanding: so long as I didn't disturb anybody I could stay up late—or wake up really early, like 3:30 a.m.—and do whatever I wanted," he says. So on many occasions Acker tuned old radios and searched for faint transmissions from faraway places in the wee hours of the morning.

In 1963, when Acker was ten, his mother thought her son needed to get out more. She pushed for him to attend Camp Wapanacki, a summer camp for blind kids in Vermont. Acker reluctantly agreed to go, he says, but only because he saw it as an opportunity to bring his radio and hear new DX signals from places he hadn't been able to receive in Farmingdale.

Inside had another piece of technology besides radio and TV: the telephone. "I remember being five or six years old and picking up the phone," Acker says. "If you picked up the phone and waited for the dial tone to go away, you got a high tone," a loud, incessant tone that indicated you had left your phone off hook and that reminded you to hang it up—designed to get your attention, in other words. The tone succeeded in getting Acker's attention. It intrigued him. What was it? How did it work?

In hindsight, this was probably not the kind of attention the telephone company wanted.

When he was fourteen, Acker decided it would be cool to find out where all the area codes were. He's not sure today exactly why he thought this would be cool, but teenagers are like that—it seemed like a good idea at the time. Acker remembered the telephone company commercial where a little jingle encouraged you to call 555-1212, the so-called universal information number, a free call in every area code. For Acker, free was good; his mother wasn't about to pay for him to make long-distance calls to every area code.

Acker's plan was straightforward. "I'll just dial every area code and 555-1212 and learn where the area codes were. I'd just talk to the operator and say, 'Where are you? Where are you located?'" The operators were surprisingly game for this. Several hundred calls later Acker had constructed an area code map of the United States in his head, a map that remains there to this day, revised, updated, and annotated with all the telephonic esoterica he's learned since.

His fascination grew. "Just being exposed to the network, how the different directory assistance operators sounded," he says, was like discovering a new world. The operators' accents differed from place to place, but even the sounds of the calls themselves—that is, the sounds that the telephone switching equipment made as the calls were being placed and routed through the network—well, those sounds varied almost as much as the operators' accents! Why was that? How did it all work?

In December 1968 someone pointed out to Acker an odd newspaper article about a blind kid at a university down in Tampa who could make free phone calls just by whistling a certain tone. Acker found the article interesting but figured it didn't apply to him. "I knew enough about the phone system by then to know that Tampa was independent," he says, meaning that its telephone service was provided by a telephone company other than AT&T and the Bell System. In contrast, Acker's community was served by Bell. "So I basically said, 'Gee, it's really nice if you could do those things if you're in an independent telephone company such as Tampa, but I guess that can't have much bearing on me. After all, I live in the Bell System, so it must work completely differently.'"

Acker continued his experiments with the phone system. He was fascinated by tones, by the sounds that the telephone system made. He tried lots of different things—just playing around, really. For example, Acker knew that every touch-tone digit is made up of two different tones that are added together. That is, when you press the 1 button your phone generates two different tones and adds them together. Equipment at your telephone company's central office hears these two tones and figures out from them that you dialed a 1. Acker says, "I discovered that if you added a third tone to a touch-tone, you could block the digits from being received. So if you pressed the digit one but you added some arbitrary tone on top of that, the central office wouldn't recognize the digit at all."

In other words, Acker had found that, with enough work, you can screw up your own dialing. My goodness, what a discovery! A normal person wouldn't think twice about this; come to think of it, a normal person wouldn't even think *once* about this. But phone phreaks aren't normal people. For Acker, the discovery that you could play a tone into the phone and goof up its operation gave him an idea.

He knew that when he made a long-distance call from his house he could hear the switching equipment sending tones down the line to complete his call. He knew these tones didn't sound like touch tones; they were something else. They weren't very loud. Probably they were far away, he thought. But, if he could hear them, maybe whatever equipment was listening to them could hear him. And if that equipment could hear him, maybe he could disrupt the tones, just like he could with his touch-tone phone at home. "If I make a very loud noise," Acker recalls thinking, maybe "I can block those tones from happening, and then I can substitute my own tones, by tape recording them and playing them back."

Acker looked around to find something that could make a loud noise. He figured he needed something really loud to disrupt the tones, given how faint they were.

"What I came up with was a little toy flute called the Tonette," he recalls. "The Tonette had a detachable mouthpiece and that made a very, very loud shriek if you blew it. I thought that shriek was the most perfect shriek I could make."

Acker dialed several long-distance calls. Each time he would wait until the switching equipment began its electronic concert, sending its quick little musical MF tones down the line. Each time he would jump into the concert, uninvited, playing his Tonette flute as loud as he could while the tones were being played. It was a jam session: he was trying to jam the switching equipment.

It didn't work. Try as he might, he didn't seem to be able to block the phone company's tones. The calls went through every time. His loud whistle was a loud bust.

Then something funny happened. Once, Acker recalls, "I kept that tone on too long after the call started to go through. And when I let go of the tone, the call didn't seem to want to go through. It went *chunk wink!* It made two clicks. And I didn't understand that. It stopped the call from going through, but I didn't feel like I had accomplished anything." While he might have succeeded in stopping the call from completing, he didn't know why. It certainly didn't seem to have anything to do with his blocking the musical tones the phone company was sending. In fact, it seemed to work best to stop the call if he played the tone *after* the call had started to go through.

After repeating the experiment a few times, some audio matching circuitry deep in Bill Acker's brain woke up and got out of bed.

The resonant, hollow sound of the long-distance circuit between the *chunk* and the *wink* that followed his whistling reminded him of something: the sound of an operator plugging her cord into an outgoing long-distance trunk. It all fell into place. "I realized very quickly that the 2,600 Hz stuff did apply to me, and that's what the Tonette squeal happened to be." Maybe it wasn't exactly 2,600 Hz, maybe it was a little bit lower or a little bit higher in pitch, but it didn't matter; whatever it was, "it was close enough to twenty-six to drop a connection reliably." The stuff in the newspaper article about the blind kid in Tampa *did* apply to him! "It seems strange in retrospect that I didn't get it as quickly as I could have," he says.

With this, Acker was able to disconnect a call in progress. But that's only half the game; you then have to be able to tell the switching equipment where you want your new call sent. His original plan to do this had been to tape-record the faint MF tones that the phone company's signaling equipment was sending out and then play them back. This plan was great in theory but suffered from one slight flaw in practice: he didn't have a tape recorder. But he figured he could do the same thing that the Engressia kid in Florida did: whistle bursts of 2,600 Hz to dial a call. Acker had no problem figuring out that his beloved Tonette whistle could be used to beep the appropriate number of beeps to dial a telephone number. The problem was finding a place in the telephone network that would accept this antiquated SF signaling technique. Lucky Joe Engressia just happened to live in a place where that worked. Not so Bill Acker.

"I knew it was my job to find a place that would take SF," he recalls.

Acker had a friend, John, who sometimes joined him on his telephonic explorations. Together, they started scouting out locations on the telephone network that would work for them. They dialed lots of places and tried to make calls using pulses of 2,600 Hz but didn't meet with any success. Then, one Sunday night toward the end of 1968, Acker happened to call Halifax, Nova Scotia (area code 902, if you're wondering). He noticed immediately that "it sounded like a very different kind of a system." Unfortunately, Acker had to go into school the next day, so he didn't get a chance to experiment with it that night. The next time he saw his friend he said, "John, try Halifax, it sounds a little different, maybe we'll be able to do it."

The next afternoon at school Acker was paged to the principal's office, saying that he had a phone call. Acker went down to the administration office, where he was handed the telephone. "So I pick up the phone call and I hear this long-distance noise on the line and a very excited John on the other end of the line saying, 'It works, it works! 902! You can do it!' So then we knew we were in." From then on, Acker says, "We routed all of our fun and games through Halifax, Nova Scotia." Acker would just dial 902-555-1212, whistle off, whistle the pulses for the number he wanted, and he was off to the races.

Using the Tonette whistle got old quickly. Acker needed a way to reliably make a controlled number of carefully timed pulses of 2,600 Hz. What better way than with a telephone dial? After all, that's exactly what your telephone dial does: it makes a controlled number of pulses on your telephone line. But, of course, he needed more than just a rotary phone, because a rotary phone just makes clicks or pulses and Acker needed beeps of 2,600 Hz. Fortunately, Acker was a ham radio operator and back in those days ham operators used Morse code to communicate. Acker rewired an old rotary phone and connected it to a Morse code practice oscillator that he had lying around. He tuned the oscillator to 2,600 Hz. *Voilà!* Now if he dialed a 7 he got seven perfect beeps at just the right pitch. No Tonette flute required. He didn't know it, of course, but Acker had just independently re-created the very first box that Ralph Barclay had built back at Washington State some eight years earlier.

The Morse code practice oscillator connected to the telephone dial was a great stopgap measure, but Acker wanted to get back to his original plan of recording the outgoing MF tones that he could hear the phone company equipment sending and then playing them back into the phone. Finally, early in 1969, Acker got his hands on a small Panasonic cassette tape recorder. Once he captured the phone company's tones on tape he could splice up the tape to select the particular digits he wanted and play them back—the network would be his oyster. Not only would this be easier than playing his Tonette flute or using the slightly clunky Morse code practice lash-up, it also meant he would no longer have to dial all his calls through Halifax as multifrequency tones were accepted pretty much anywhere in the network.

He ran into a problem, however. Although he could indeed hear and record the tones sent out by the switching equipment, he discovered that the tones were distorted. "It's all highs and no lows," Acker says. If you think of the phone network as a big stereo, it was as if somebody had cranked the tone control way over to one side, with the effect of toning down the bass notes and jacking up the treble notes. If you recorded these tones and tried to play them back, you'd be playing what Acker describes as a "very tinny" concert for the phone company; the remote switching equipment you were serenading "isn't really going to be interested," he says.

"So," Acker says, "I knew I had to do something to the audio. What could I do? The tape recorder was a cheap cassette machine with automatic level control," he recalls. There was nothing he could do to adjust it. "What you got, you got. I didn't have access to an equalizer, I'm not even sure if I knew such a thing existed back then. So I went to my junk drawer and pulled out a component." Unable to see the components, of course, he worked by feel. "I don't know what this is. It's a can, it has a lead at each end, it could have been a resistor, it could have been a capacitor. I didn't really know," he recalls.

"I put it across the output of the tape recorder. And that did a great thing!" Bill exclaims, excitement in his voice more than forty years later. "It did a wonderful job of rolling off the highs, it was much 'bassier,' and I was just *in*."

It wasn't too long before he came up with something even better than recording tones from the telephone company: an electronic organ. The Lavelle school had a Hammond organ that could be used to create the frequencies he needed to generate MF tones and transfer them to tape. "I used to go in there and record all the numbers I needed for the weekend," he says. Acker and his friends made a master tape from the Hammond. "You know, KP, 1, 2, 3, 4, 5, 6, 7, 8, 9, ST, and a lot of 2,600 Hz." With smaller tape recorders with pause buttons, "we could pretty much make tapes of whatever we wanted." What did his teachers think of his unorthodox use of the school's organ? "They had no clue!" Reflecting on it a bit more he allows, "I think the music teacher did know what we were doing but he kind of looked the other way." Either way, he says, it was "a bucket of fun!"

In May 1969, just ten days shy of his sixteenth birthday, Acker received a surprise telephone call.

"We had done something that I knew stood a chance of getting us in trouble," he recalls. In the old days, when you made a long-distance call and the person you were calling answered the phone, a supervision signal was sent back to the billing equipment instructing it to start charging for the call. If the phone just rang and rang without ever being answered, no supervision signal was ever sent back; that's why you didn't get charged for phone calls that weren't answered. The phone company also used this technique to make certain internal test numbers toll-free; the circuitry for those numbers was configured not to send back supervision. In phone phreak parlance, such calls were said not to "supe."

The telephone company did this on a large scale with the directory assistance number, 555-1212. Calls to 555-1212 were free because they didn't supe—from the telephone company billing equipment's standpoint, calls to those numbers never seemed to be answered.

But there's a subtle problem here if you're a phone phreak with a blue box or, like Acker, a phone phreak with tape recordings of blue box tones. If you call 555-1212 in a distant area code and then whistle it off and use your blue box or tape recordings to reroute the call to a normal telephone number, you've just given the phone company a clue that you're up to no good. Why? Well, remember, a call to 555-1212 never supes. Except that when you reroute the call to a normal telephone number and your friend answers the phone, the call *does* supe—the instant your friend answers the phone. Acker was starting his exploration of the network by dialing 555-1212, a number that should never look like it answered. "Yet when we were through with the call, it did, because we connected to things that answered."

At that point, the phone company billing records show something anomalous: here's a call to a number, 555-1212, that should never look like it answered and yet it does. The phone company doesn't like anomalies in its network, not so much because they think somebody might be messing with them, but just because anomalies probably mean that something is broken somewhere and needs repair.

"I knew that was an irregularity," Acker says. "My fear was, you know, if this registers on your tape"—Acker knew the phone company in those days used paper tape for billing records—"they'll be able to tell that [the call] answered, and they know it's not supposed to." Acker's fears were right on the money. The phone company was indeed using computer-generated reports of supervision irregularities to spot blue boxes. Along with Greenstar, these reports were a primary tool the Bell System used to detect such fraud and, due to Greenstar's secrecy, were among the most effective for prosecution.

Acker's surprise caller was a security agent from his telephone company, New York Telephone. The agent had already talked to Acker's friend John, likely because of 555-1212 supervision anomalies. But the reason the agent wanted to talk to Acker was more concrete. John had ratted out Acker to the security agent.

"He spilled his guts," Acker says. "That was just an inconceivable no-no to me. That pretty much trashed our friendship. Forever and ever." Forty years later you can still hear the intensity in Acker's voice. "When you get in trouble, you *don't squeal* on anybody."

Even today Acker still sometimes worries that the phone company may have caught some phone phreaks simply by surreptitiously monitoring Acker's telephone line. The thought that he might have inadvertently gotten people in trouble merely by talking to them on his home phone is bad enough, he says. "But to actually *give up* the name of another phreak was just . . . just horrible." Somehow Acker had picked up the concept of *omertà,* honoring a code of silence. "I don't know where I got that ethic. I believe it was the right ethic, but I don't know where I got it from," he says.

The New York Telephone security agent told Acker that his illegal dialing had to stop. "He was as firm as he had to be," Acker recalls. "He didn't go out of his way to scare us, but he laid it out for us. I don't even recall him saying, 'If you don't stop we're gonna send the FBI after you,' but he made it clear that it had to stop."

"I like learning about the network," Acker told the security agent.

"I can appreciate that," was the agent's reply. "It was nice of him to say that," says Acker, "but the bottom line was, you gotta stop."

So Acker stopped.

Or so it appeared, at least to all outward appearances; his fingers stopped dialing around the network and he quit playing with the MF tapes on his Panasonic tape recorder. But his brain just wouldn't stop thinking about this stuff. "I realized that 555 had gotten us in trouble," Acker says. What he needed, it seemed, was a safer way to access the network, one that wouldn't get him in trouble again. The telephone company delivered. Just a few years earlier the company had introduced an innovative new service, something called an 800 number. These numbers were free to the caller because the person or company being called paid the bill. That doesn't seem like such a big deal today, now that long-distance is so cheap, but back then, given how expensive calls were, it *was* a big deal.

Since calls to 800 numbers were free, like 555-1212, they were a good place to start a blue-boxed call. But 800 numbers didn't have the pesky problem that 555-1212 did. "When an 800 number answers, it answered. It went off hook, all the way back to you," Acker says. In other words, 800 numbers returned supervision.

Acker's theory was that if he used 800 numbers for blue boxing, "they looked like normal calls to an 800 number." That meant no telephone network anomalies for the phone company to investigate. And that meant no more phone company security calls to Bill Acker. Or so he hoped. Of course, it might look suspicious if you had too many calls to 800 numbers—normal people just didn't call that many 800 numbers back in 1969, or talk very long on them—but, says Acker, "it was obviously safer than 555."

The telephone call from the security agent scared him into going straight for a bit, he says. But it wore off. "That's the problem with 'scared straight,' it doesn't hold," Acker says. "It lasted for maybe a few months."

And then?

"And then I couldn't resist doing it again."

Eleven

THE PHONE FREAKS
OF AMERICA

JOE ENGRESSIA AND Bill Acker weren't the only kids playing with the telephone in 1968. As early as 1964 teenagers had begun to discover an interesting quirk of the telephone system. Certain telephone exchanges in some areas of the country, notably Los Angeles and San Jose in California, had busy signals that were shared among all callers. An example was San Jose's 291 exchange in the 408 area code. If you and I both happened to call busy numbers in 408-291 we would be connected, faintly, over the busy signal—along with anyone else who happened to have called a busy number at that moment. If we shouted we could hear each other. Of course, we'd be constantly annoyed by the *baaa . . . baaa . . . baaa* of the busy signal. And that busy signal was loud; our voices would be the background to the busy signal in the foreground. "It was an insane way to try to communicate," recalls Jim Fettgather, a teenager at the time in San Jose. But talkable busy signals were free and they became surprisingly popular. Lots of people could be on one at once and that made them a hangout, a great way for bored kids to meet each other and trade phone numbers. They also served as a sort of subtle introduction. "I didn't even realize that was the beginning of phone phreaking for me . . . I didn't realize it then," recalls Denny Teresi, another San Jose teenager.

Busy signals weren't the only type of low-tech conference call service the phone company inadvertently provided. Non-working number recordings—you know, "You have reached a number that is disconnected or no longer in service, please check the number and dial again or call your operator to help you"—on certain types of telephone company switching equipment also could be used in the same way: everyone calling in to nonworking numbers in such an exchange would be connected. As with the busy signal, you had to talk over the repeating announcement, but the voice announcements were less annoying than the busy signals, and the long silence between the announcements provided more opportunity for people to talk. Best of all, sometimes the announcement recordings broke down and didn't play at all. Highly prized, these so-called party line broken recording numbers were popular in the New York area in the early 1970s and remained so into the 1980s.

It turned out there was something even better than busy signal and broken recording conferences, something exciting and magical: loop arounds. These were pairs of telephone numbers that the phone company used for testing its circuits. Loop telephone numbers varied from one city to another, but let's use a pair from Los Angeles as an example: 213-286-0209 and 213-286-0210. The idea was that a phone company technician could call one number of the pair, say 286-0209, from one telephone line. This number would answer automatically and respond with a loud tone. The technician would then call the other side of the loop, the 0210 number, from a different telephone line. The tone on 0209 would go away and the equipment in the telephone company central office would connect the two lines, looping them around. The technician could now send a test signal down one line and hear it come back on the other line, allowing remote line measurements and troubleshooting.

Admittedly, this doesn't sound exciting and magical, but it was. Here's why. First, you could talk over a loop around. If you called one side of a loop and I called the other, we were both connected and could talk to each other. Second, because they were telephone company test numbers, many loop arounds didn't supe, that is, they didn't return answering supervision. To telephone company billing equipment, calls to loop arounds looked like any other unanswered call. And that meant calls to such numbers were free, and they were so from anywhere in the country.

Also, you could hang out on a loop around. You could call into one side of a loop and set the phone down on your desk and do your homework or whatever. Eventually somebody else would call the other side of the loop and you'd hear a ring-*clunk* sound followed by a voice saying "Hello?" Pick up the phone, stop doing your homework, and bingo: instant conversation.

Best of all, though, it was all anonymous. If we both called a loop around, you and I could chat and you never needed to give out your telephone number—heck, you didn't even need to give out your name. If you met somebody and wanted to stay in contact, but maybe didn't quite trust him entirely, you could always give them one side of a loop around. That way you could communicate but he wouldn't have your actual phone number—less chance of getting you in trouble that way. Loop arounds served the same function as the cheese box circuits that bookies had been using for years, a perfect electronic meeting place for clandestine activities. The difference was that these cheese boxes were part of the telephone network and came courtesy of the telephone company.

Rick Plath, a blind phone phreak from Los Angeles, recalls the spread of loop arounds among teenagers in the mid- to late 1960s. "Al Diamond hired Saul, a friend of mine," he says. Diamond, a phone phreak himself, ran a business in Los Angeles selling maps to stars' homes. His workers, all LA teenagers, hung out on likely street corners flagging down tourists, trading maps for cash. Rick had told Saul all about loop arounds. Saul quickly spread the word to the other map workers. "Saul was a friend of Dave. Dave got Aaron involved," Plath continues. "Aaron had a way of spreading the loops all over Fairfax high school. Through word of mouth it went through Fairfax and then into Beverly Hills."

Before long loop arounds had taken off in LA. "That's what got loops really started in the LA area. Between a bunch of us we got loops publicized in the LA area without knowing what we were doing," says Plath.

Mark Bernay,★ a Los Angeles–area telephone enthusiast and friend of Al Diamond, took the loop-around bug with him when graduated from college and moved to Seattle in 1967. The phone company certainly had loop-around telephone numbers up north, but Bernay was sad to find they were deserted and that nobody in Seattle knew about them. To help spread the word he printed up pieces of paper with loop numbers and put them on pay telephones throughout the area. Soon the loops in Seattle—they called them "hot lines" up thataway—were "constantly busy," recalls Seattle phreak Dennis Heinz. "Mark Bernay really brought phreaking to the Seattle area," he says. Loops were, in his words, the "social networking of the time," the "Twitter and Facebook of the day."

All that, taken together, was exciting and magical. As Plath recalls, "It was like CB radio over the phone. It's kind of cool that these circuits work the way they do. We didn't care why, we just knew that they did." Kind of cool. And incredibly unlikely. Consider that the phone company builds some obscure, mundane test feature into its network to allow technicians to do remote troubleshooting. Ma Bell turns her back for a second and the next thing you know a bunch of high school kids have remade it in to a free, anonymous communication system that the CIA would be proud of. It was almost as if loop arounds and broken recordings and talkable busy signals had been put there by the telephonic fates, a divine power that seemed to want kids to communicate—just not in ways that the designers of the telephone network had ever intended.

If such fates exist, John Draper believes they have not been kind to him. Actually, that's an understatement. It's more that he believes they are out to screw him over, repeatedly and without lube. The fates arranged for a phone call that would change Draper's life.

★The pseudonym he went by at the time.

The phone call would set events in motion that would first make him a countercultural legend and then lead him to prison. But the worst thing about the call, and the reason the fates were so clearly behind it, was this: it was a wrong number.

A year earlier, in 1968, he was Airman First Class Draper, five-foot-eleven and 170 pounds, with blue eyes, thick black GI-issue glasses, and a short military haircut. Draper was just finishing four years of active duty as a technician in the United States Air Force. He had grown up in rural towns in northern California, where he bristled under his father's strict control and got beat up a lot in school. As a kid he loved electronics, so it was natural that he wound up maintaining radar systems on airbases in Maine and Alaska for Uncle Sam's flyboys.

Now it was 1969 and he was John Thomas Draper, a twenty-six-year-old civilian. He could wear his hair long, dress a little more casually (some would say sloppily), and smoke some pot. He had an honorable discharge, some GI technical training, and was taking classes part-time at the local college. He had a job as an electronics technician and work was plentiful in the heart of what would come to be known as Silicon Valley. And it was much, much warmer in San Jose than it was at some stupid radar station up near the Arctic Circle. Things were looking good for John Draper.

Then the phone rang.

Draper had been expecting a call from an old friend who had just returned from Vietnam, but a few words into the conversation he realized that it wasn't his buddy on the line. It was a deep-voiced stranger, a guy named Denny, who had reached him by mistake. Despite the wrong number, Draper says, they struck up a conversation. Denny was "really interesting, especially when he mentioned he was into radio. For me, I was always interested in all aspects of radio, from the DJ end to the technical end," Draper recalls. In fact, Draper was a volunteer DJ at a local radio station. When he was in the air force he had built a low-power FM radio transmitter to entertain the bored servicemen stationed with him up in Alaska. He had even built a pirate radio station in high school.

Back in the day radio stations used to have listening lines, telephone numbers you could call to hear what was being broadcast by the radio station. They were used mostly by advertising agencies to check that radio stations were broadcasting the ads that their clients had purchased, but they were also sometimes used by radio fans to listen to faraway stations. Of course, they were long-distance calls, so they were expensive. Denny mentioned to Draper that he would call and listen to radio stations all over the country. He'd even call up the radio DJs and spend time talking to them too.

Draper commented that Denny must have a big phone bill. Nah, Denny said, I never pay for my phone calls. Really? How does that work? I know a million ways to make free phone calls, Denny replied. Draper wanted to know more, but Denny said he had to go. Before they hung up Draper got Denny's number.

Sometime later Draper called Denny. Or, rather, he tried to. Instead of "Hello?" he got an earful of tone—a loud, constant, high-pitched tone. Puzzled, he asked the operator to dial Denny's number for him. Same thing. She told him that the number he was calling was a telephone company test number. Had he written down the telephone number wrong? Whatever the reason, it looked like Draper's freak connection to Denny was a onetime thing.

The fates do not give up that easily, however. A few months later Draper and a friend were hanging out, listening to the radio, and they stumbled upon a pirate radio station. Intrigued, they decided to try to find the pirate broadcaster, not to complain, mind you, but to compliment him on his ingenuity and taste in music. They went for a spin around the neighborhood in Draper's trusty green VW van, trying to locate the transmitter. The fates guided them and soon they found themselves chatting with the bootleg radio operator. During their conversation they discovered that the radio pirate just happened to know Denny. Far out! Before heading home Draper made sure to get Denny's phone number from the pirate broadcaster.

Once again, Draper gave Denny a call. No earful of tone this time, they picked up their conversation where it had left off. Soon they arranged to meet in person. Draper got in his van and drove over to Denny's house in the suburbs of San Jose. A middle-aged man answered the door. Is Denny here? Sure, end of the hall and to the left. Draper walked down the hall and found a room with the lights out.

"Denny?"

"Yeah, buddy."

"Can I turn the lights on?"

"Sure, buddy."

Turning on the lights Draper set eyes on the mysterious Denny Teresi for the first time: "a chubby kid that looks like a miniature cowboy and sounds like Paul Bunyan and talks eighty miles per hour," Draper recalled. The sixteen-year-old didn't have much use for lights. Denny was blind.

The two continued their discussion from months back. What was up with that weird tone I got when I tried calling you? Oh, said Teresi, that was a loop around. Teresi explained how loop arounds worked, how you could call one side of a loop and somebody else could call the other side and the two of you could talk without ever having to know each other's telephone numbers. But one side often had a tone on it, and that was what Draper had heard.

Teresi had a wealth of seemingly incredible knowledge about the telephone system—how you could have conference calls by talking over broken busy signals and recordings, how you could use an electronic organ to make free phone calls, heck, how you could even just *whistle* free calls! Draper says he found it all un-believable. It couldn't be that easy. It just couldn't.

But it was, Teresi told him. To prove it, they drove over to Teresi's friend Jimmy's house. Jim Fettgather, also sixteen and also blind, was a talented musician who had a Farfisa electronic organ, the same type of organ that the Doors used on "Light My Fire" two years earlier. Fettgather was a virtuoso when it came to using his Farfisa to play those special notes that so charmed Mother Bell.

Wires spilled out the back of Fettgather's electronic organ and, through a pair of alligator clips, connected to the telephone line. Fettgather picked up the phone and dialed an 800 number. Just as it started ringing he whistled it off. *Kerchink!* He turned to his organ and, as Draper put it, "hammered out a call": two keys at a time, twelve times in a row. Jangly pairs of tones—not quite music —filled the room. Seconds later Draper heard the ringing signal of the rerouted call going through: an expensive long-distance call made free, thanks to a pair of blind kids with an electronic organ.

Draper was blown away. "He was *really* fast," Draper recalls of Fettgather's dialing. "I was just so flabbergasted that it was so simple. The whole network was controlled by tones! The whole long-distance network."

Teresi and Fettgather wanted to know if Draper could build them a multifrequency generator—an MFer, a blue box, a portable electronic gadget that would produce the same pairs of tones they were making with Fettgather's electronic organ. Draper said he could.

He returned home in a state of shock. "I *had* to build a blue box," Draper recalls. And that night he did. It was a crude first effort that was difficult to use. It had seven switches: one for 2,600 Hz and six to generate the tones that made up multifrequency digits. Just like Fettgather's electronic organ, you had to press two of the six buttons simultaneously to generate the right pairs of tones; it required practice to get the hang of it. But it worked. And Draper already had ideas for building more sophisticated boxes.

Teresi, Fettgather, and some of their friends were in the habit of taking "whistle trips"—trips to places with pay phones where they could explore the network just by whistling. Just as Acker had discovered, not all trunk lines were created equal: some were vulnerable to whistling, some weren't. San Francisco International Airport, thirty-five miles north of San Jose, happened to be wide open, and there was always somebody willing to give the kids a ride up to the airport in exchange for a few free long-distance calls. Several years earlier a Los Angeles phone phreak named Sid Bernay★ had discovered you could generate a nice, clean 2,600 Hz tone simply by covering one of the holes in the plastic toy bosun whistle that was given away as a prize in boxes of Cap'n Crunch cereal. Armed with their Cap'n Crunch whistles Fettgather and Teresi and friends would cluster around pay phones at the airport and go nuts. "We used to have a ball going up to San Francisco," Fettgather remembers. "I imagine we must have gotten quite a few looks . . . six or eight of us at these pay phones, whistling into these telephones, dialing long-distance numbers."

With Draper in the club the whistle trips expanded. The original trips were just to find and use whistleable pay phones, but the whistle trips soon morphed into what they came to call "phone trips"—the idea of going to some oddball location simply for the joy of playing with whatever telephone system they had there. Where could you call from there? What did the calls sound like? What techniques could you use to make free calls? What if you did this? Or this? Let's try it! It wasn't just Draper, Fettgather, and Teresi; other phone phreaks in other areas of the country made similar excursions. Mark Bernay in Seattle, for example, made a special trip to the northernmost town in Washington, right near the Canadian border, just to see how its telephones worked.

By late 1969 a network of phone phreaks had begun to develop. Like snowflakes forming out of moisture in cold winter air, it took just the right set of conditions for it to happen. Instead of humidity and temperature it was the presence of loop arounds and broken recordings and talkable busy signals—and, of course, people to talk on them. And, like snowflakes magically appearing, it was more accidental than planned.

★The pseudonym he went by at the time. As a pseudonym, the surname "Bernay" among phone phreaks indicated membership in the Mark Bernay Society—an inside joke stemming from a prank phone call placed in Los Angeles during the late 1960s.

Fettgather had been talking to other kids on talkable busy signals in San Jose since about 1964. He learned about loop arounds in 1968 when he was at Camp Bloomfield, a summer camp for blind kids down in southern California. Because many of the loop arounds didn't supe—that is, they were free calls—Fettgather says they "put all of us in San Jose in communication with folks all around the country." It wasn't long before Bill Acker in New York ran into Fettgather on the phone. Fettgather introduced Acker to Teresi. Teresi introduced Acker to Draper. The network expanded from there via word of mouth and chance telephonic encounters. The first time Bill Acker called a loop around and got another phreak on the other end of the loop, he recalls thinking it was the "coolest thing in the whole wide world!" You can still hear the amazement in his voice. "I was willing to work in isolation but to think that there were people out there that I could *talk* to . . ." Acker's mind boggled.

This was important, maybe more important than we might remember. Thanks to the Internet and the Web and Google, everything and everyone seems to be just a few mouse clicks away. Interested in something obscure, for instance, using hypodermic needles to water your Venus flytrap? Want to collect air raid sirens? Care to meet men and women who wear furry animal costumes and chase one another around hotel lobbies at science fiction conventions? Give 'em a Google, though perhaps you shouldn't Google that last one from your place of work. In every case you'll find there are websites and groups devoted to the topic. The Internet seems to be telling us: You Are Not Alone— no matter who you are or how rare your interests.

But in 1969, until he discovered loop arounds and talkable busy signals, Acker felt like he was Very Much Alone. Sure, he had friends at school who helped him out with his telephone hobby, but none of them were into the nitty-gritty like he was. "They were all happy to make free phone calls," Acker recalls. "I don't say that disparagingly. They just weren't into the guts of it." It wasn't just his schoolmates who liked free calls, by the way. For a time Acker's house mother at school was a woman from South

America and "every night for about four or five months she got to call home," Acker says, the joy audible in his voice.

"My brother was totally into different things," Acker says. "I couldn't tell him what I discovered, he wouldn't have gotten it." In fact, "He was older than I was, so the less he knew about the legally edgy aspects of it, the better."

Until he learned about the other phreaks, Acker recalls, as far as he was concerned, "I was pretty much the only one, and I was pretty much operating in isolation."

Loop arounds and talkable busy signals were unintentional—happy accidents that made for oases in the network. But other telephonic watering holes were planned.

Imagine for a second that you're a hardworking, businesslike caveman and you've just invented the pencil. Your cavemate asks you, What's it good for? You straighten up slightly, adjust the collar of your starched saber-toothed-tiger-skin shirt, and say, "Well, my goodness, this invention will propel us into the zeroth century! It will allow sharp-eyed cave dwellers—we'll call them accountants—to keep track of how many rocks and sticks we owe each other. With it, we will be able to record instructions for future generations regarding optimal hunting and gathering strategies. It will revolutionize the business of being a cave person!"

Your cavemate raises a skeptical eyebrow. And then picks up your pencil and begins sketching a beautiful drawing on the cave wall. You look on, dumbfounded, as you realize that the highest technology in the world at that moment—the pencil—has just been used to make art.

A telephonic version of this scene played out in Los Angeles in the 1960s. It went by funny names: "The Machine." "VERMONT." "Z, ZZ, ZZZ." "Superphone." All were telephone numbers you could call to hear tape-recorded audio performances. Most were comedy skits, some were horoscope readings, others were political commentary and humor. They were known as "joke lines" or "dial-a-joke" numbers. Most were run by high school or college kids. Once again, someone had taken the day's high technology—the telephone—and used it to make art.

In today's world it is tempting to dismiss telephone joke lines as quaint, even laughable. But think about it for a second. How many of the sites you visit during a day's surfing online are the figurative descendants of these telephone joke lines? The funny website or YouTube link that your friend emailed you today may have video or animation, it may be a lot flashier, it's probably more professionally produced, but basically it's the same idea as a telephone joke line: people sat down, came up with something they thought was funny, recorded it in some way, and put it out there for you to enjoy. Today you point and click, yesterday you dialed. Same deal. The impulse is as old as cave drawings.

Practically, though, there's a big difference between 1969 and now. Today you can go to Facebook or TypePad or Twitter and have a presence on the Web in five minutes. Video cameras are cheap and YouTube is free. But setting up a joke line in 1969 was another matter entirely. Until just one year earlier you weren't allowed to connect any non–Bell System electrical equipment to your telephone line—by any means. Ma Bell insisted that this had nothing to do with maintaining AT&T's telephone monopoly. Rather, she said, it was to maintain the integrity of the nation's telephone network, which AT&T built and that only AT&T understood. As the president of AT&T said in 1973, "The national switched telephone network is an interdependent, sensitive, highly sophisticated system. To work well, the system depends on technically compatible components. The phone network is not made of cans and string. It consists of intricate electrical switches and terminals, precisely configured, rigorously tested, and built to exact specifications. If consumers can plug anything they want into the network—any old piece of junk made who knows where—the system will break down. A faulty telephone in one house could conceivably disrupt service to an entire city. A system such as the switched telephone network is only as good as its weakest component."

This logic extended not just to telephone lines but to telephones themselves. Consider the case of the Hush-A-Phone. This was a product first manufactured in the 1920s by, you guessed it, the Hush-A-Phone Corporation. It was not a sophisticated electrical circuit that connected up to Ma Bell's fragile network. No, it was a molded rubber cup that fit over the telephone mouthpiece. It allowed you to whisper into your phone and thus gain a little bit of privacy from your house or office mates; you can think of it as the rubber widget equivalent of cupping your hand between your mouth and the telephone to keep others from hearing you.

AT&T didn't like it; tariffs were passed that made it a violation to use a telephone with "any device not furnished by the phone company." AT&T threatened to disconnect the telephone service of both vendors and users of the Hush-A-Phone for violating these rules. Hush-A-Phone Corporation complained to the Federal Communications Commission in 1948. In 1951 the FCC decided in favor of the telephone company. Hush-A-Phone objected; briefs were filed. The FCC took the matter "under advisement" for four more years. In late 1955 the communications commission officially sided with AT&T, saying that this sinister rubber widget was "deleterious to the telephone system and injures the service rendered by it" because its use sometimes "results in a loss of voice intelligibility, and also has an adverse affect on voice recognition and naturalness." Hush-A-Phone filed suit in federal court—and won. The D.C. court of appeals decided in 1956 that the tariff-imposed ban was "unwarranted interference with the telephone subscriber's right reasonably to use his telephone in ways which are privately beneficial without being publicly detrimental."

Eight years, a protracted FCC hearing, and a lawsuit to get the right to use a rubber cup on a telephone mouthpiece.

The beautiful thing about teenagers is that they rarely pay attention to this kind of stuff. And thus was born the Machine, one of the earliest telephone joke lines. It was the brainchild of two Toms in San Pedro, California: Tom Plimmer and Tom Politeo; born exactly one week apart, they were known as Tom 0 and Tom 1 by their friends. While the Machine may have been their creation, it looked more like something that Rube Goldberg would have designed. It consisted of an open-reel tape recorder and some custom electronics to turn it into an answering machine, with four thirty-second skits that callers could hear. Each caller would get the next skit in sequence until it repeated. Because it had to repeat, the two Toms couldn't use a standard cassette system. Reel-to-real audiotape ran at seven inches per second, so two minutes of audio translated into seventy feet of audiotape. This audiotape was festooned around Politeo's bedroom, fed through dozens of circular metal binder clips. When the Machine was playing an announcement, it was as if Politeo's bedroom had come alive, a whirling, reeling mass of moving audiotape.

The Machine launched on Tom 1's seventeenth birthday in September 1969. "Eight three three triple three nine" was the number. "A large part of what we were trying to do was to breathe more life into the phone system," says Politeo. The two Toms succeeded beyond their wildest expectations. Before long the Machine was receiving two thousand calls per day, an average of one call every forty-five seconds. A supervisor who worked in their local telephone company central office described to them the havoc the Machine's popularity was causing with the office's step-by-step switching equipment. Your local connector group has eight switches, he explained. Of these, one of them seems like it's permanently connected to your line. The other seven, he said, are permanently *trying* to connect to your line.

Of course, you don't build something like the Machine without knowing a little bit about the telephone system itself. Rick Plath, one of Acker's friends in LA, knew the two Toms through the Machine. Sensing kindred spirits, Plath told Plimmer he should call Bill in New York.

A few days later Acker's telephone rang. When he picked it up he heard a familiar sound: a long-distance call with unnatural routing. "Hi, this is Tom in San Pedro," the caller said. "Vancouverish," he

Samuel F. B. Morse, inventor of the electric telegraph, circa 1860. *Photo courtesy Library of Congress*

A Chappe optical telegraph station at Louvre, Paris. *Image courtesy Wikipedia*

A telegraph key and sounder, circa 1890. The electrical telegraph made the optical telegraph obsolete, sending messages across wires in an instant. *Photo courtesy Douglas Palmer*

Left: Alexander Graham Bell, inventor of the telephone, circa 1920. *Photo courtesy Harris & Ewing, Library of Congress*

Below: A re-creation of Bell's original telephone. *Photo courtesy Detroit Publishing Co., Library of Congress*

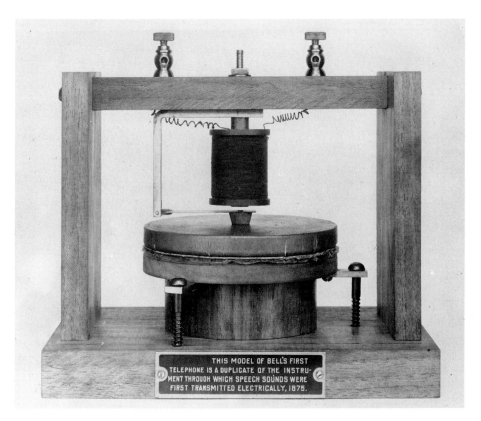

THIS MODEL OF BELL'S FIRST TELEPHONE IS A DUPLICATE OF THE INSTRUMENT THROUGH WHICH SPEECH SOUNDS WERE FIRST TRANSMITTED ELECTRICALLY, 1875.

The original Strowger switch from Automatic Electric Company, 1890. *Photo courtesy AT&T Archives and History Center*

Long-distance operators at "cord boards" circa 1945. Well until mid-century the operators' hands, arms, and brains were the workhorses of long-distance telephone switching. *Photo courtesy National Archives*

Above: A portion of the magnificent 4A toll crossbar switch, 1957. The brains of the long-distance network, the 4A would enable truly automated long-distance telephone calls that customers could dial themselves. *Photo courtesy AT&T Archives and History Center*

Left: The inner workings of a bank of Strowger switches showing the ratchets and pawls and assorted mechanical clockwork required to automate telephone switching in the early 1900s.
Photo courtesy Túrelio/Wikimedia Commons

Left: A 1950 magazine ad describing the multifrequency signaling system; the ad even went so far as to give the musical equivalents of the MF digits.

Below: A Woolworth's ad for the Davy Crockett Cat and Canary Bird Call Flute, circa 1955, and the genuine article itself—the toy that would be the basis for David Condon's whistled exploration of the telephone network.
Photos courtesy Hakes.com

Charlie Pyne (seated), Tony Lauck (standing), and Paul Heckel
(on the phone) as featured in *Fortune* magazine, 1966.
Photo courtesy Fortune

FRESHMAN ADVISER REPORT

PLEASE RETURN TO 3 UNIVERSITY HALL BEFORE MAY 1

1. Name of Student .... **Charles Francis Pyne** .... Class ... **1966**

2. Is his academic record so far about right, (below expectation,) above expectation? (*Circle one*)

3. Probable concentration **Engineering Sciences** Do you consider this a wise choice? ... **I'm inclined to think so now.**

   If not, what field would you recommend? ....

4. Comments on him as student and as citizen: **Pyne has been an enigma to me all year. I've spent more time with him trying to understand his problems, than the combined time I've devoted to all my other freshman advisees. In an attempt to arouse his motivation, I've used my entire bag of tricks to little avail. Then suddenly two weeks ago all was made clear when we learned from the FBI and Telephone Company of his tampering with the whole telephone system. Instead of studying, night after night all year long he and three other Harvard students with the cooperation of an M.I.T. student have been discovering ways to beat the Telephone Company and how the whole system works. No wonder his studies have suffered. From what I now know he has been pursuing this interest for years. If he once settles down and really applies himself, there's no question in my mind that he can do the work. In fact, he possesses a vast knowledge of electronics in general and the telephone operation in particular. Surely this should stand him in good stead.**

5. Any non-academic activities in which you expect him to make a *significant* contribution? **W.H.R.B.**

   Date ... **5/29/63** ... Signature ... *Robert B. Watson*

Pyne's Freshman Adviser Report at Harvard University, 1963.
Image courtesy Charlie Pyne

Joe Engressia, 1968.
Photo courtesy AP Images

Bill Acker, 1973.
Photo courtesy Bob Gudgel

Bob Gudgel, Jay Dee Pritchard, and John "Captain Crunch" Draper on a phone trip in Duvall, Washington, 1971. *Photo courtesy Bob Gudgel*

The Fine Arts 13 classified ad from the Harvard *Crimson*, 1967.

A Cap'n Crunch Bo'sun Whistle.
Photo courtesy Richard Kashdan

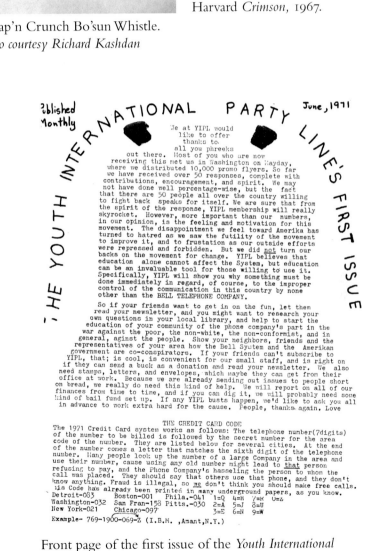

Front page of the first issue of the *Youth International Party Line.*

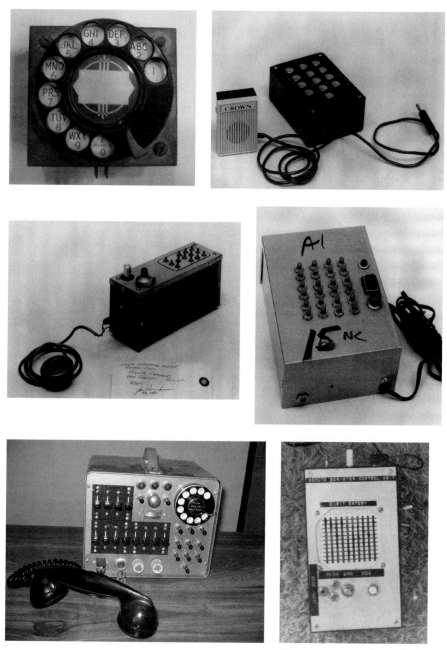

Assorted blue boxes, 1961 through the late 1970s.
Photos courtesy Ed Turnley or author unless otherwise indicated

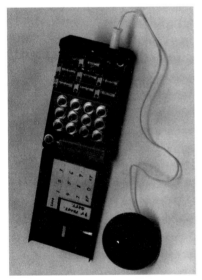

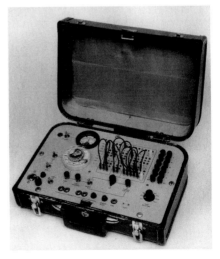

Steve Wozniak with blue box in the dorms at Berkeley, 1970s.

Wozniak's blue box. *Photo courtesy of the Computer History Museum*

Bernard Cornfeld and friends, 1974. The millionaire financier would eventually be convicted of Fraud by Wire for using one of Wozniak's blue boxes. *Photo courtesy AP Images*

Left: Chic Eder, the one-man crime wave and FBI informant who provided the feds with a tape recording of John Draper wiretapping their San Francisco office. *Photo courtesy FBI*

Below: A 16-button AUTOVON telephone, whose red-colored fourth column of precedence buttons made the military telephone network a sensitive and seemingly irresistible target for certain phone phreaks. *Photo courtesy Wayne Merit, JKL Museum of Telephony*

Security Agent Earl Conners and AT&T Attorney Bill Caming testifying before the U.S. House of Representatives after news of the Greenstar toll fraud surveillance system broke, February, 1975. *Photo courtesy George Tames/The New York Times/Redux*

Ken Hopper and Walter Heinze in the Telephone Crime Lab. *Photo courtesy Ken Hopper*

Stealing a phone call isn't a game.

Bell of Pennsylvania is sick and tired of being dicked by students who are always trying to beat the system. Well . . . . we're pissed now, and there's no stopping us! The next CMU student we catch stealing a phone call will be electrocuted! That's right. We're installing new security jacks into the Centrex system. That means that when we find a student up-to-no-good with his phone, we just have to push a button, and boom!!! He gets it right in the ear!

So you see, stealing a phone call isn't a game. it's taking your life into your own hands. BOOM!!!!

Bell of Pennsylvania

As this joke ad illustrates, the security department at Bell of Pennsylvania apparently had a sense of humor about the phone phreaks at Carnegie Mellon University. *Image courtesy Ken Hopper*

Bell Laboratories, Murray Hill, New Jersey, 1960s.
Photo courtesy AT&T Archives and History Center

Replica of the first transistor, invented at Bell Labs in 1947.
Photo courtesy AT&T Archives and History Center

MCI magazine ad, 1980, showing their long-distance rates to be about ½ of AT&T's.

added. Vancouverish? Between that odd word and the distinctive sound of the long-distance trunk, Acker knew instantly what was going on: Tom was calling him from San Pedro via Vancouver, just like Acker had learned to do himself from Farmingdale by routing his long-distance calls through Halifax.

"Tom Plimmer was one of my first constant connections," Acker recalls. "We would talk for hours."

The network continued to grow. Before long Acker and the other phreaks were regularly talking to some twenty or so people. Some were in Long Island, New York, like Acker, but more were in California. "California was the epicenter," Acker says. It was, he felt, the "capital of phreakdom." Acker's lack of a Long Island accent is testimony to California's influence. "It was at that time in my life where I decided I'd rather sound like the California phone phreaks," he says. "I needed to ditch my New York accent."

It was late January 1970 before they called the Old Man. They had all heard of Joe Engressia, of course, the blind whistling phone phreak mentioned in the newspapers a year earlier. But nobody had actually talked to him. Finally Bob Sirmons, a phone phreak in Los Angeles, took it upon himself to track down Engressia. It wasn't hard. Sirmons called Acker after reaching Engressia at his dorm in Tampa: I found him! He wants to talk to us! Here's his number!

Acker dialed Engressia's number. Acker's ears were well trained and he could tell one bit of telephone company switching equipment from another just by sound. As he listened to the clicks and clunks the network made during the ten or so seconds it spent getting his call from Long Island to Tampa, he heard something unusual. Acker knew that Engressia lived in an area whose phone service was provided by General Telephone, an independent telephone company. But the sound the network made right before Engressia's phone started to ring was that of a #5 crossbar telephone switch, a piece of Bell System equipment. In other words, it was a piece of equipment that had no business being down in General Telephone territory.

Engressia answered the phone. "Hey, where did General Telephone get a number five crossbar?" Acker asked him. Not just anyone would know that such a thing was unusual; indeed, most wouldn't have the ears to have noticed it at all. With a telephonic smile, Engressia explained that the #5 crossbar had come from Northern Electric—it was equipment from the Bell System out of snowy Canada, now enjoying its quasi-retirement in sunny Florida.

"It was clear we kind of liked the same things," Acker recalls. It was an understatement. That phone call was the first of thousands of hours he and Engressia would spend together on the telephone.

Many of these hours, at least in 1970, would be spent on a conference call that the phreaks called "2111." When they reached the 2111 conference they'd hear a distinctive, high-pitched hum. It wasn't so loud that you couldn't talk over it, but it was loud enough that you couldn't miss it. When they heard that hum, they knew just where they were in the network. As Bill Acker described it later, "The hum told us that we were home."

The hum came from an obscure little circuit called a TWX converter that lived deep in the bowels of a step-tandem switching machine in British Columbia. TWX stood for "teletype-writer exchange"; in the days before faxes and email, teletype machines were used by big companies and organizations to quickly communicate via the printed word over long distances. Clunky and electromechanical, teletypes sent data over the telephone line at then blazing speeds—typically forty-five words per minute—clacking away, each letter mechanically printed one at a time in ink on paper. In essence, they were big, remotely controlled electric typewriters, built by the Teletype Corporation, part of the AT&T empire.

The TWX converter was normally used for allowing different types of teletype machines to talk to one another. But somebody had left it slightly misconfigured, or maybe it had fallen into disrepair. Either way, it's kind of like that little door to the crawl space under your house: forget to button it up tight and you'll wind up with rodents living in your basement. Leave your TWX converter misconfigured and it'll get infested with phone phreaks.

The rodents like your basement because it's warm and dry. The phone phreaks liked the TWX converter because its misconfiguration turned it into a giant conference call, something rarer than diamonds in 1970. Its discovery was a mix of intention and accident, a happy offshoot from the phone phreaks' attempts to plumb the mysteries of the Vancouver step tandem by exhaustively dialing codes within it. One of the codes they discovered was 21: you'd call a number in the 604 area code, whistle off with 2,600 Hz, and then whistle 21 followed by any two digits; 2111 was popular because it was easy to whistle: *bleep bleep . . . bleep . . . bleep . . . bleep* and you're done. You'd be rewarded with an unusual dial tone, a constant tone that sounded like a continuous fourth octave B musical note. From this you could keep whistling digits to place a free call to anywhere you wanted.

The network of phreaks—Acker, Engressia, Draper, Teresi, Bernay, Fettgather, and the rest—had been using 2111 to make free phone calls via the Vancouver step tandem since the start of 1970. But something changed sometime around May of that year. The fourth octave B dial tone went away, leaving only the high-pitched hum. No more dial tone meant no more free calls. The phone phreaks were sad.

Then someone noticed something odd. If multiple people called 2111 at the same time they all got connected, forming one big conference call. In today's world of three-way calling and business and personal conference dial-in numbers, it's hard to remember just what an unusual animal an actual conference call circuit was back in 1970. Back then, about the only people who could afford conference calls were big businesses and the government. If you were a businessperson who wanted to have a conference call, you rang up a special operator and had her manually connect you to all the people you wanted on your call. You then paid AT&T's highest rate for each person you were calling, the so-called operator assisted rate, per person, per minute. If you were a phone phreak, you had loops and talkable busy signals and broken recordings, but loops supported only two people at once, and the others were annoying to use, what with busy signals and recordings interrupting your chatter.

In contrast, 2111 easily supported a dozen or more people; in fact, there seemed to be no limit to the number of people who could be conferenced together on it. Plus, 2111 had a built-in riffraff catcher, something to keep out the 1970s version of what hackers today would call script kiddies, that is, people who weren't serious about the hobby. This was because you couldn't merely call in to 2111 via a simple telephone call. You needed a whistle or an electronic tone generator to send the pulses of 2,600 Hz that the Vancouver step tandem wanted to hear before it would connect you to the conference.

By the late summer of 1970 the 2111 conference had become *the* electronic meeting place for a burgeoning collection of phone phreaks, their virtual home in one of the first virtual places—the long-distance telephone network. Together the 2111 gang formed an unlikely group, made all the more unlikely by a couple of things. The first was that these weren't the only phone phreaks, just the hard-core nucleus of a larger, wider, more casual network, one that stretched across the country. Who would ever have thought that in 1970 the obscure technical hobby of hacking telephones—an illegal one with no publicity to speak of—could possibly bring together dozens of like-minded young people throughout the United States?

The second thing was that more than half of the core group—Engressia, Acker, Teresi, and Fettgather—were blind. Theories abounded as to why this was so. To be sure, blind people spent a lot of time on the telephone, perhaps more than sighted people. Since there were relatively fewer blind people in the United States, their friendships tended to be more spread out. Thus suffering from higher-than-average phone bills, perhaps they were keener than most for ways to save money on telephone calls. Then too there was the "blind people have better hearing to compensate for their blindness" theory that suggested the sightless kids were better able to appreciate the subtle variations in tone, noise, and timbre of the long-distance telephone network, although there would turn out to be several sighted people with an equally acute appreciation of the sonic qualities of the telephone network. Finally, the telephone probably served as a great equalizer. On the telephone, after all, everyone is blind.

Regardless, the upshot was that if you were putting together a cast of characters for a hacker movie, you'd have a hard time doing better than the original 2111 gang. They began calling themselves phone freaks—back in those days, they spelled it with an "f"—and even went so far as to create an informal organization called the PFA: the Phone Freaks of America. Joe Engressia quickly found himself elected president and recalls his inaugural speech: "I said, 'Well, my pledge to you as president is that any knowledge I have I'll share with you and do my best to help people learn about phones, because knowledge shared is knowledge expanded, and that's enough of a presidential speech.' We were on a conference call and people clapped, probably because the speech wasn't so long that they would get bored."

It was a golden era, and it was the community that made it so. "The 2111 conference was just a blast," says Seattle phone phreak Bob Gudgel. "It was a huge part of my life. I met a lot of great people on it. I have really, really good memories of those days." One of the keys was that it was big enough to be fun but not so large that people had to be overly paranoid. Of course, this didn't stop some people from trying. Bill Acker recalls getting a phone call one day from a mysterious person who identified himself only as a representative of the International Society of Telephone Enthusiasts, or ISTE. Acker remembers this person's opening words: "We are concerned." Specifically, his mystery caller was concerned that Acker was talking to too many people and doing too many things and was somehow going to mess the whole hobby up for everybody. Acker later asked Joe Engressia if he knew anything about this. "Oh, that's just B. David," said Engressia. Engressia explained that he was an old phone phreak who seemed to love paranoia and spy stuff. Don't worry about him, said Engressia. Acker and Engressia went back to their conference calls.

It was on one of those conference calls that John Draper discovered a new identity for himself. For reasons of anonymity—and, honestly, just for the fun of it—it was common for phone phreaks to go by nicknames or handles. Bill Acker was "Bill from New York," Jim Fettgather was "Mr. Westin," the members of the Mark Bernay Society all had their Bernay handles—Al Bernay, Bob Bernay, Mark Bernay, Sid Bernay, etc. One day Draper and Engressia were talking about using a Cap'n Crunch whistle to make their beloved 2,600 Hz tone, Engressia recalls, when Draper suddenly said, "You know, I think I'll just call myself Captain Crunch. That'd be a good name." Engressia immediately liked it. "It just fit him somehow," he remembers. "It was just a good name for him. We called him 'Captain' a lot."

Captain Crunch was born.

Twelve

THE LAW OF UNINTENDED CONSEQUENCES

I'S A FUNNY thing, isn't it, how you never can tell where things are going to go. You set out to do some thing, some simple, straightforward thing. Let's say you even succeed at it. But because of some niggling detail you didn't think of, some connection you didn't quite anticipate, a freak chance that you didn't factor in, in the bigger picture things go totally off the rails.

It's called the Law of Unintended Consequences and it has sharp, pointy teeth.

It happened in the 1930s when Bell Labs was busy inventing the multifrequency signaling system. There they were, telephone company scientists and engineers just trying to figure out a way to put through long-distance calls quickly and efficiently and automatically. But they overlooked the fact that there were clever people out there and that their system was wide open to anyone who could generate a pair of tones. You can forgive them for this. Who knew from hackers in the 1930s or '40s? But the next thing you know, it's the 1960s and—*bleeeeep kerchink*—your network has blind kids and mobsters and college students making free phone calls with blue boxes.

It happened again in October 1970 when the phone company busted a guy in San Francisco for selling blue boxes. Al Gilbertson*

---

*The pseudonym he went by at the time.

had learned about blue boxes in the late '60s while he was a grad student at a prestigious East Coast engineering school. "I had heard a rumor about a blue box, that phone company people had these things," he says. "And apparently some bookies used them, this is what I understood. I heard a whiff of this. The next thing I heard was in the newspaper: a guy named Joe Engressia, a blind kid down in Florida, got busted for whistling 2,600 cycles per second down the phone line. Well, with those two pieces of information I went to the engineering library and looked it up in the *Bell System Technical Journal* and there were the goddamn codes." Gilbertson shakes his head in disbelief as he recalls his discovery.

About three days later he had built his first blue box. "It was amazing how much fun you could have with it," he says. Despite this distraction, Gilbertson somehow managed to complete his dissertation and finish graduate school. PhD in hand, he moved out to San Francisco. After a brief career as a physics postdoc, he decided to try something more entrepreneurial. Maybe he'd start a company, he thought. Maybe he'd make a product, perhaps an electronics product. Say, blue boxes.

"*That* was a mistake," he recalls with a laugh. "I wasn't a real sophisticated business guy at the time and I didn't understand the law." The venture ended predictably. "I got arrested by the phone company."*

From the phone company's perspective, it was about as straightforward as it gets. Some guy is using and making and, worst of all, selling blue boxes. Bust him. Check. What's next? Is it lunchtime yet? But it's on occasions such as this—the execution of simple, straightforward projects—that the Law of Unintended Consequences likes to kick in. It played out in slow motion over the next few months and it had two triggers.

---

*Of course, the telephone company did not have power of arrest, but getting "busted" or "arrested" by the phone company was a common phrase among phone phreaks in those days. It speaks to the telephone company's immense size and perceived power. Today nobody would say they "got arrested by Google," for example, but being arrested by the phone company made sense back then.

First there were the phone calls from the phone phreaks. For obvious reasons, news of a blue box bust was of great interest to the phreaks. Even though they didn't know Gilbertson, several of the phreaks, including Bill Acker, took it upon themselves to look him up in the phone book and whistle up a call to him. Their motivations were mixed. Partially it was to reach out to someone who might be a fellow telephone aficionado and get the details of what happened. As Acker puts it, "If the phone company's mad at him, he must be somebody we want to know!"

But their call was also to chide Gilbertson for selling blue boxes, something that the phone phreaks frowned upon almost as much as the phone company. By this time the phreaks had developed a sort of informal code of conduct. It was not universally agreed upon or followed within the phreaking community but, as Tom Politeo remembers it, it had three basic parts. First, don't seek publicity—the more people who know about phone phreaking, the more likely it was that the phone company would clamp down on it. Second, don't call during peak hours—this was to avoid busying out circuits, inconveniencing people, and drawing unwanted attention. And third, don't profit from phreaking. Anyone selling blue boxes was obviously violating this third commandment, and their customers would probably end up causing other problems too. "It sounds funny to say it about something that was already an illegal hobby," Acker says, "but those people gave phreaking a bad name."

Gilbertson was a bit older than the mostly teenage phreaks and his motivations were somewhat different. Acker remembers, "He didn't seem to love the phone the way we did." Regardless, the phone calls introduced Gilbertson to the cross-country network of phone phreaks and their reindeer games. "They were young and foolish and so was I," Gilbertson says. "We had tons of fun."

The second trigger to the Law of Unintended Consequences was Gilbertson's pride. He wasn't about to take his bust sitting down. Although he denies revenge was a motivation, he says that "I thought it made a great story, and I was interested in not just being snuffed out by the phone company." Moreover, his inner engineer was offended that the phone company had designed such a vulnerable system and then got huffy when people took advantage of it. "It was that they were so *sloppy*! What the Christ did they think, that there's not any bad guys in this world?"

Gilbertson complained to his attorney about this. "Well, I know these guys at *Esquire* magazine," Gilbertson recalls his attorney saying. "And I said, 'Well, call 'em up!'"

The phone company didn't know it yet, but that was the moment when things started to go off the rails.

Ron Rosenbaum read the story memo from an editor at *Esquire*. Some guy out in California had been busted for manufacturing something called a blue box, some sort of telephone fraud device. More interesting was the community it described—a "world of electronics whizzes, teenage blind kids, a whole network of people," Rosenbaum recalls. "You know, it sounded completely fascinating. These people had managed to create a sort of network, a parallel communications network, of their own."

Rosenbaum was just twenty-four, a few years out of Yale and in the early days of what would turn out to be a legendary writing career. For several years he had written for the *Village Voice*, New York City's hip alternative weekly newspaper. *Esquire*—"the magazine for men," as it billed itself, half a million readers strong—wanted to know if Rosenbaum would be interested in covering the phone phreak story.

"It immediately seemed to me to be a story I'd want to do," Rosenbaum says.

In the spring of 1971 Rosenbaum flew out to San Francisco to meet with Gilbertson and his attorney. "He showed me a blue box, told me the basics of how it was manufactured, how the tones worked, how you produce the phone company tones by merging two different cycles," Rosenbaum remembers.

Gilbertson passed on contact information for the kids in the network: Engressia, Acker, Teresi, Fettgather—the usual suspects. Soon, says Rosenbaum, "I started having running conversations with a bunch of phone phreaks." Rosenbaum recalls attending a meeting of phone phreaks in a suburb of San Francisco. "It was like entering this Alice in Wonderland electronic outlaw underground," he said.

He recalls being surprised by the breadth and depth of the network. "This network of people doing this was so extensive, and yet I hadn't seen anything about it in the media, I hadn't seen any reports about it, it was all new to me. It seemed to be fairly highly evolved and fairly . . . not well-organized, necessarily, but it just seemed to be a lot of people with a lot of interchange." In fact, it reminded him of fiction, he says. "I think I was also influenced in my vision of the phone phreaks by the Thomas Pynchon novel *The Crying of Lot 49,* which also describes this kind of underground communication network. They seemed to be living it out, in a way." Far from feeling that they were scary or weird, Rosenbaum says he felt "they were outside the mainstream of conventional America, but that was a reason for me to admire them, more than anything else. I admired their independent spirit and their sort of pioneering exploration and then their willingness to take risks."

"Then Captain Crunch injected himself into the publication," Rosenbaum recalls. "All throughout it, during the reporting of the story, he was injecting himself into the story. It was fairly clear that, with some justice, he considered himself if not *the* star, certainly a star in the phone phreak firmament. And he was always managing to interrupt calls I was having with other phone phreaks to check up on me, demonstrate his talents, stuff like that."

Rosenbaum's experience with Captain Crunch echoed that of many of the other phreaks in the 2111 gang. Indeed, John Draper had developed a second nickname among some of them: Mr. Intense. It was bestowed on him for his lack of manners, his rapid-fire speech, his supersize ego, and his impatience for anything that got in his way. Draper would often go nuts if he was trying to reach someone on the phone and encountered a busy signal, Bill Acker recalls. Draper would call the operator in such situations and, saying it was an emergency, demand to be cut into the line of whoever it was he was trying to reach. "Bell Labs invented call waiting for people like John Draper," Acker says. If Draper tried to call you and you weren't immediately available, he would often berate whoever answered the phone and insist that they go find you immediately, a behavior that did not endear him to the parents of his teenage phone phreak friends. In person encounters could be even more intense. Draper had a hatred of cigarette smoke, for example, and was famous for throwing tantrums when he encountered it at a restaurant. "He was pretty strange," says Jim Fettgather.

Draper claims that he warned the phreaks that talking to Rosenbaum was a bad idea and would get them all in trouble and might lead to the end of their hobby. He said he asked Rosenbaum not to write the article. "When I talked to Ron, I let him know in no uncertain terms that to publish this would cause major problems, not just for me, but for the phone company and all parties concerned, and did everything in my power to convince him not to publish this information." Rosenbaum's recollection differs: "At the time Crunch was very happy to be included in the story."

Rosenbaum concluded his West Coast interviews and flew to Memphis to spend some time with Joe Engressia. "He was a really fascinating character," Rosenbaum recalls, "a really likable guy." Rosenbaum returned home to New York to finish his assignment.

The picture on the cover of *Esquire* magazine's October 1971 issue was striking: a naked 1940s pinup girl on a swing, blond hair flowing behind her, breasts strategically hidden by her upraised arms. But for some readers, the really striking picture came on page 116: a full-page, full-frontal black-and-white photo—but not of a pinup girl. No, the photo was of a small plastic box with a silver metal face, four screws, and thirteen small buttons. The caption read, simply, "Actual size."

The photo was the lead in to Rosenbaum's article, "Secrets of the Little Blue Box." It followed the adventures of a fanciful mix of characters, members of an otherworldly underground network of phone phreaks. The soul of the network was Joe Engressia, a blind twenty-two-year-old from Memphis who could whistle free phone calls and whom Rosenbaum dubbed the "granddaddy of phone phreaking." Engressia, Rosenbaum wrote, sat like a sightless spider at the center of a web of other phone phreaks. A dozen teenagers—some blind, some sighted—formed the bulk of the network, each with his own odd nickname: Fraser Lucey from New York, Randy and Mr. Westin from San Jose, the Midnight Skulker from Seattle, the list went on. Rosenbaum chronicled their clandestine activities, their meeting like spies on anonymous loop-around circuits and their efforts to trick telephone company employees into manipulating switching equipment for them. The article spoke of an electronic mecca: a legendary conference call setup called "2111" that only phone phreaks could reach, one where dozens of teenagers would talk for hours, exchanging information on the telephone system and swapping tales of their adventures.

Their hobby may have been illegal but Rosenbaum portrayed most of the phreaks as possessing the innocence of monks, electronic seminary students studying the Bell System's long-distance network as if it were scripture. An older, worldlier character named Al Gilbertson injected hints of avarice and danger with his plans to Make Money Fast by selling blue boxes to the mob. And throughout the article a maniacal fellow referred to only as Captain Crunch kept popping up. Crunch appeared to be some kind of crazy superphreak who claimed to live out of his VW van as he traveled the country, using his wits and his blue box to tap phone lines and make calls that circled the globe from one pay phone to another—all while staying one step ahead of the telephone company and the FBI.

All in all, Rosenbaum's story read like a telephonic cross between an acid trip and *Gulliver's Travels*. It seemed like it had to be fiction.

Except that it wasn't—aside, perhaps, from some journalistic license. With the exception of Engressia, Rosenbaum gave the characters pseudonyms and brushed more than enough makeup over them to obscure their identities; some, in fact, were composite characters. Rosenbaum's distinctive writing style later caused several of the characters he portrayed to raise their eyebrows just a smidge when they read the article. "I thought he spiced it up too much," recalls Gilbertson. Bill Acker, who says he was the lion's share of the composite character "Fraser Lucey" in the article, agrees. "I didn't like the technical inaccuracies," he says.

Technical inaccuracies are one thing, Acker allows, and flavor another: "He captured the spirit of it wonderfully!" Indeed. The article's tone and style lent an air of mystery and hipness to an otherwise geeky hobby. Rosenbaum even coined a new word in the article: *phreak,* with a "ph." Although they had referred to themselves as phone freaks prior to the *Esquire* article, it had always been freaks with an "f." Now, forever more, it would be phreaks.

Readers with a slight bit of technical knowledge found the article intriguing, something worth investigating. The article gave enough leads to get people started, but not enough to hand it to them without some work on their own. In many ways, like the telephone network itself, it was a puzzle, a fifteen-thousand-word one that begged to be solved. To the right sort of reader, the rewards for solving this puzzle were intoxicating. It wasn't just the ability to make free phone calls but the promise of joining a secret society, one whose members could control the telephone network and con telephone switchmen into doing their bidding.

One part of the article described a phone phreak trick called tandem stacking. Remember that tandems were like intermediate stops on the telephone network: if you needed to call from Long Island to Chicago your call would likely be routed through at least one tandem switching machine to get there, and possibly a couple of them. The phone company spent lots of money and R&D effort in making the tandems smart enough to route calls automatically, like the hulking No. 4A switching machine that took up a city block, with its metal punch cards encoded with routing information. That was the intelligence that enabled the switching equipment to automatically route calls across the country. This is great news if you're a typical telephone user; you just want your calls to go through and you don't particularly care how they get there. But not if you're a phone phreak.

Phone phreaks like control, to be in charge of the network, to decide exactly how their calls get from point A to point B. For some this was a love of discovery. "What happens if I route the call this way? What does it sound like?" For others it was a flexing of electronic muscles, a feeling of power that came from exercising will over Ma Bell's billion-dollar network. And for still others it was just fun, a way to goof off, an interesting mental challenge followed by a lovely auditory experience.

Tandem stacking was possible thanks to a bug—some would call it a feature—in a particular type of telephone switch called a crossbar tandem. Crossbar tandems could be tricked with a blue box into sending your call via a particular route in the network. It might work as follows:

Say you're Bill Acker out in Farmingdale, New York. You dial an 800 number that goes to someplace out of state—California, let's say. The first leg of your call gets routed through a switching machine called White Plains Tandem 2, which happens to be a 4A tandem. Before anyone in California answers your call you send a burst of 2,600 Hz down the line and hear the *kerchink* come back from White Plains. This is the "wink" signal that tells you you've reset the call and are now talking directly to the White Plains 4A, which is waiting for you to send it MF digits.

Using your blue box you send KP 099 213 ST, a string of digits that doesn't look much like a telephone number. Within a given area code there are of course many different cities, and many of these cities had their own tandems. Partially as a holdover from the old days of operators plugging cords into jacks, each of these tandems was given a three-digit terminating toll center (TTC) code. In New York's 516 area code, 099 refers to a crossbar tandem in Poughkeepsie. So White Plains sees the 099 you sent, grabs a trunk to Poughkeepsie, and sends it the remaining digits: KP 213 ST. Poughkeepsie recognizes 213 as the area code for Los Angeles, so it takes this as a command to get southern California on the line. It connects you to a 4A tandem there called Los Angeles 2. But Poughkeepsie has run out of digits—that is, it has no further digits to send to Los Angeles—so while it establishes the connection to LA it doesn't do anything more.

Now it's your turn again. You and your blue box, via White Plains and Poughkeepsie, are now whispering into the ear of Los Angeles 2. You key KP 707 001 042 ST; 707 is the area code for the northern part of the San Francisco Bay Area and 001 is the terminating toll center code for Eureka, a small town in northern California. Los Angeles Tandem 2 recognizes 707 001 and grabs a trunk to Eureka and sends KP 042 ST. As it happens, 042 is the TTC code for Santa Rosa, California, so Eureka in turn grabs a trunk to Santa Rosa. But, like Poughkeepsie, Eureka has run out of digits, so the action stops for a moment. You're now talking to the Santa Rosa crossbar tandem via White Plains, Poughkeepsie, Los Angeles, and Eureka. Using your blue box you send KP 312 338 1975 ST, the number of your friend in Chicago. Santa Rosa finds a trunk to Chicago and sends it the seven-digit local number to dial. Your friend's phone begins to ring.

You've just placed a call that could have taken two hops through the network and traveled 750 miles and turned it into one with six hops over more than 5,000 miles. The call will now be way noisier than it needed to be and the audio distortion introduced by the extra crossbar tandems will make it sound like hell. Why on earth would you do this? Because you could. Because you're a phone phreak. Most of all, Acker recalls, because it was just plain fun.

When your friend in Chicago picks up the phone he will instantly know this is a special call—if he's a phone phreak, that is. He will first hear the hiss of the long-distance trunk noise, much louder than usual because of the peculiar call routing you've gone to such trouble to create. Over the course of the next couple of seconds he will hear a series of phantomlike *kerchinky* noises, one after another—about six in all—fading in volume as they go. It will be as if they are receding into the vapor of the network, almost as if they are running away from him. As it turns out, they are; these are the sounds of the supervision signal being sent from his phone in Chicago to the billing equipment in Long Island, a signal that is repeated by each intermediate tandem, each farther away from your friend and closer to you. When you hang up, the domino process will repeat, but this time the dominos will be falling toward your friend in Chicago, the *kerchinks* getting louder and louder as the supervision signal races toward him, repeated by each tandem as it goes.

Tandem stacking was simply a cool, harmless prank . . . until Captain Crunch made some hair-raising claims in the *Esquire* article, saying that just "three phone phreaks [could] saturate the phone system of the nation. Saturate it. Busy it out." This could be done, he said, by stacking tandems to tie up long-distance trunk lines between cities.

It was an alarming claim. It also happened to be nonsense, at least according to Bill Acker, Crunch's friend and the phone phreak probably most versed in long-distance call routing. "I don't know what John was smoking when he said that," Acker says. "I just don't know why he said things like that." According to Acker there were simply too many trunk lines between cities, the switching systems all supported the concept of alternate routing—that is, looking for an alternative route if the first choice was busy—and, finally, it was difficult to stack up more than about six or seven tandems at a time.

One of the other alarming things in the *Esquire* article was the suggestion that phone phreaks somehow had a preternatural ability to con telephone company employees into flipping switches in central offices for them. As it turns out, they did. When it came to the ability to BS telephone company employees, Denny Teresi— "Randy" in the *Esquire* article—was the undisputed master of the phone phreak phlimphlam, what would later become known as social engineering: calling someone up, pretending to be someone else, and getting them to do things for you, things they shouldn't oughta do. Teresi's targets were unwitting switchmen in telephone company central offices. Pretending to be another telephone company switchman or technician, his usual goal was getting his marks to wire up loop arounds or conference circuits or getting such circuits restored to operation when they had been removed from service. His patter might go something like this.

"Hey buddy, this is Fred in the network service center. How you doing? Hey, the loop around in your office seems to be busy. I wonder if you could take a look at it for me?" Depending on how green the switchman was, he might need some coaching. "Okay, let's find out what the trunk group is. On your computer type VFY-EXG-270100. Look for a TR02 message. Yeah. See it? Okay, in the TR02 message, you'll find on the third line down, on the left-hand side, you'll find the trunk group. Do you have that? Great. What is it? Fifty-five? Okay, now, we wanna find the TRZ in the trunk group. The way we'll do that is type TRK-TRZ-QT0055 . . ."

If you're wondering how the phone phreaks learned this kind of stuff, often all they had to do was ask. "Sometimes you'd call up and get a switchman who knew what he was doing," Acker says. "You'd ask him to do something for you and he'd jump right on it. Then you'd ask him to explain to you how he did it. You'd say something like, 'Wow, that's great, thanks! You know, I'm finding we're running into that problem a lot. Can you talk me through what you did to fix it?'"

Teresi explains his modus operandi this way: "I understood the equipment well enough. You just start trying it and see what happens. If you knew enough about it and you had the right tone, you could often get them to do it. Of course, you had to have the knack of BS a little bit, you needed to be able to convince them that, even though this was not a normal channels kind of thing, that it was still okay." One of his techniques involved reassuring his target. "For example, you tell them to choose the line links [i.e., where the wires should be terminated for a bogus conference call setup], and then you'd tell them you were immediately going to call Traffic [Engineering] and clear it with them, so they wouldn't reassign them." That way the target knew he wasn't going to get in trouble for whatever strange thing he was being asked to do. "We were doing things that were definitely nonstandard but it was just a matter of sounding authoritative enough to convince them that it was okay to do," Teresi says.

Teresi's task was made easier by the size of the telephone company and its sprawling geography, with its roughly one million employees spread out across virtually every town and city in the United States. The size and scope of the Bell System forced it to rely on its own product, the telephone, to perform its daily business; one historian estimated that some 95 percent of all telephone company internal business was conducted over the phone. And besides, say you're a telephone company switchman. Just how likely is it, really, that some kid is going to get your unlisted work telephone number and then call you up and ask you to do some obscure technical thing for him? And how could a kid possibly know enough about your job and the equipment you use to be able to convince you that he works for your company and that his is a legitimate request?

That was—and is—the sort of thinking that allows social engineering to work. "It's really kind of wild that we were able to get them to do it, but it was just a matter of sounding convincing enough," Teresi remembers. "If you got someone with not enough experience, they'd fall for it."

"Denny was the best," says Acker. The term "social engineering" hadn't been coined yet, so in Teresi's honor the phone phreaks invented a new verb: to DT someone was to bullshit them so thoroughly that they never suspected they'd been had.

Rosenbaum's writing skill coupled with *Esquire*'s circulation did more in one month to spread phone phreaking into the mainstream than anything before or after. The Law of Unintended Consequences could brush its hands together briskly. Its work here was done and the train was now fully off the rails.

John Draper remembers the publication of the *Esquire* article as if it were yesterday. A student at San Jose City College, Draper went to his first class that morning and then walked across the street to buy a copy of the magazine. "I went back to my car and

I read it cover to cover," Draper says. "I missed three classes. I had to read it. I could not go to those classes." When he finished, he remembers, "I said, 'Oh my God. Well, I guess that's pretty much the end of phone phreaking.'"

Draper drove home. He called Denny Teresi and read the article to him over the phone. Draper was certain that with this much publicity, with this many secrets being exposed, the telephone company would have to take action. Holes in the network would be plugged up. Things that used to be safe now wouldn't be. The phone company and the FBI could come swooping down on them at any moment. "I knew right then and there that phone phreaking as I knew it was ended," he recalled.

Worse, Draper was featured as one of the stars of the article. The good news was that he was under the alias Captain Crunch. But many phreaks knew his real name. And if there were raids, he figured he was likely to be the prime target. It was just a matter of time, he thought. Draper took his blue boxes and put them in a shed out back, where they wouldn't be discovered if the FBI searched his apartment. He made a decision, he recalls. From that moment on, "they don't live with me anymore."

Draper's instincts were right; as the saying goes, "Even paranoids have enemies." While the *Esquire* article was still being written the phone company was already beginning to step up its enforcement activities. In May of that year, after a three-month investigation, New York Telephone and the police arrested nine college students for blue box fraud in New York—eight upstate in Potsdam at Clarkson College of Technology and the State University of New York and one at the New York Institute of Technology; the NYIT student was referred to in the *New York Times* as a "boy genius." The very next day another ten students at Case Western Reserve University in Cleveland, Ohio, were arrested on similar charges. That August, eight more people were arrested by the FBI for blue box fraud in Billings, Montana. In September, four more people—including one telephone company employee, who claimed innocence—were arrested in Pennsylvania.

Draper's worries weren't helped when Maureen Orth's "For Whom Ma Bell Tolls Not" was published on October 31, 1971, in the Sunday supplement to the *Los Angeles Times*. The article, which was later reprinted in other newspapers, read like a shorter version of the *Esquire* story. It opened with a description of Captain Crunch in a pay phone booth at a gas station using his blue box to get the American embassy in Moscow on the line. It discussed the blind phreaks, Joe Engressia, tandem stacking and quoted an independent telephone company source as saying that the cost of blue box fraud might be as high as $50 million a year.

Just a couple of weeks after Orth's article appeared, Bob Gudgel (aka Bob Bernay), a seventeen-year-old Seattle-area phreak and a frequent 2111 conference attendee, had some unusual trick-or-treaters. Knocking on his door was J. C. VanInwegen, Pacific Northwest Bell security agent, and two other men. Wiggy, as he would come to be known to Seattle-area phreaks, was accompanied by an FBI agent and a United States marshal with a search warrant. They hauled away several radios, assorted electronic items, and a box of what Gudgel recalls as "telephone crap." The trio presented Gudgel with a subpoena commanding him to testify at a federal grand jury in Seattle a few days later. Gudgel wasn't the only one. In all, roughly half a dozen Seattle-area phone phreaks were called before the grand jury. "The phone phreaks are a public menace—not just a rip-off of Ma Bell," a telephone company attorney said, describing them as "mildly mentally unbalanced."

According to an internal AT&T memo, there were six electronic toll fraud prosecutions in 1970. In 1971 that number jumped to forty-five. The empire was beginning to strike back.

Draper wasn't the only one who studied the *Esquire* issue when it came out. The magazine's target audience was cool young men, guys who today would be called hipsters. But two middle-aged engineers who weren't in the magazine's usual demographic also found themselves carefully reading the October issue. They were

Charlie Schulz and Ken Hopper, members of the technical staff of the Telephone Crime Lab at Bell Laboratories.

Hopper's path to the Telephone Crime Lab was a circuitous one. In 1971 he was a distinguished-looking forty-five-year-old electrical engineer, a bit on the heavy side, with blue eyes, short brown hair, and glasses. Hopper had joined the Bell System some twenty-five years earlier, shortly after the end of World War II. Within a few years he had found himself at Bell Laboratories' Special Systems Group working on government electronics projects. The stereotype of government work is that it's boring, but Hopper was a lightning rod for geek adventure: wherever he went to do technical things physical danger never seemed far behind. There was the time he had to shoot a polar bear that had broken into his cabin while he was stationed up in the Arctic working on the then secret Distant Early Warning Line, the 1950s-era radar system that would provide advance warning of a Soviet bomber attack. Or the time he almost died in a cornfield in Iowa while building a giant radio antenna for a 55-kilowatt transmitter to "heat up the ionosphere" for another secret project. Then there's the stuff he still can't really talk about in detail, involving submarines and special tape recorders and undersea wiretaps of Soviet communications cables.

The Special Systems Group was a natural to help AT&T with the Greenstar toll-fraud surveillance network in the 1960s, Hopper says, and that work led to involvement with other telephone security matters. But the Telephone Crime Lab also owes its existence to the FBI. Hopper recalls, "In the mid-1960s the FBI laboratory came to our upper management and said they were getting electronic-involved crimes. They had no people in their laboratory that could examine evidence in these cases, especially related to communication systems, and they asked for Bell Labs' assistance. Upper management of Bell Labs agreed that this was in the public interest and that we would do that. The work was assigned to my organization, Charlie Schulz being the supervisor. We had just a few people, never more than two or three, working on this stuff.

Initially it was to be a five percent job . . . but within five years it was darn near a hundred percent job."

So it fell to Schulz and Hopper to study that month's *Esquire* magazine in detail. Their report to their bosses—and to Joe Doherty, AT&T's director of security—opened with a glum assessment. "The article entitled 'Secrets of the Little Blue Box' by Ron Rosenbaum in the October 1971 issue of Esquire Magazine is essentially factual," their memo began. "Some of his material is very recent and indicates an active inside source." It then went through the article, page by page, dissecting the phone phreak claims, some acknowledged, many disputed.

Hopper constructed a two-page appendix to Schulz's memo, a detailed table listing twenty-one names mentioned in the article, setting forth all the information Bell Labs had about each miscreant: age, whether blind or sighted, whether or not each knew Joe Engressia, physical description, and any other information they could glean from the article. "Fat, has been on LSD, experimenting with 2600 since age 8," read part of the entry for Engressia, for example.

The memo demonstrated that Bell Labs took the *Esquire* article seriously, that the phone company was not about to take this sitting down. But it also demonstrated just how poor a grasp the Bell Labs engineers had of the phone phreaks—in terms of both who the phreaks were and what they were capable of doing. Hopper's analysis of the names used in the article provided no useful information about any of the phreaks other than Engressia, and he was already well known to the telephone company. Worse, much of Bell Labs' technical analysis of the phone phreaking techniques revealed by the Rosenbaum article was simply wrong. For example, the Bell Labs memo discounted the phone phreak parlor trick of tandem stacking, claiming it just wasn't possible. "He talks about 'tandem stacking' as if he had the ability to deliberately select multilink routes and to keep adding on links," Schulz wrote. This was an "exaggeration"; the network simply did not work that way, the memo concluded.

In fact it was no exaggeration at all. The phone phreaks did have this ability and they used it to amuse themselves on a regular basis. It was a great example of how engineering insiders are often the last to know what is actually possible with the systems they design. Part of the problem was probably pride. Bell Labs had created the telephone switching network and, consciously or unconsciously, didn't want to admit how vulnerable it was; its engineers were, in some sense, spring-loaded to disbelieve reports to the contrary. The other part of the problem was both larger and more subtle. Compared to the phone phreaks, the Bell Labs engineers were laboring under a great disadvantage, for they understood how the system was supposed to work and that blinded them to how the system actually did work—and therefore how it could be made to do things it was never designed to do.

The result was that they could not see the holes in their network that sixteen-year-old blind kids could, even when Rosenbaum and the blind kids explained it to them.

Thirteen

COUNTERCULTURE

"FUCK THE BELL SYSTEM!"

THOSE FOUR WORDS, all in caps, formed the headline of a flyer handed out at the 1971 May Day demonstrations in Washington, D.C. More than thirty thousand hippies, Yippies, students, and radicals had camped out on the banks of the Potomac. They smoked dope, they listened to rock music, they marched, they protested—against the Vietnam War, against the military-industrial complex, against racism, sexism, the government, and Tricky Dick Nixon. It was, in some ways, the ultimate realization of Marlon Brando's reply in *The Wild One* when asked what he was rebelling against: "Whadya got?"

The flyer heralded the birth of a new newsletter: *YIPL, the Youth International Party Line.* Its name was a play on words that reflected both its roots and its focus. The "YIP" part made it known that it was an offshoot of the Youth International Party, the sometimes radical, sometimes comedic, but always theatrical countercultural movement and quasi-political party. Founded in 1967, the Yippies sought to radicalize the hippie movement and called for revolution in America—or, as they spelled it, Amerika: "We are a people. We are a new nation. [. . .] We want everyone to control their own life and care for one another. [. . .] We will provide free health services: birth control and abortions, drug information, medical care, that this society is not providing us with. [. . .] We cannot tolerate attitudes, institutions, and machines whose purpose is the destruction of life, the accumulation of 'profit.'" Despite the serious rhetoric, the Yippies approached their revolution with humor. Their flag was a marijuana leaf on a red star and, in 1968, at the Democratic National Convention, they announced the nomination of a pig— Pigasus the Immortal—for president of the United States. They were later referred to, aptly, as Groucho Marxists.

The "party line" part of *YIPL*'s name emphasized its focus on the telephone. Party lines were a form of telephone service used in rural areas in which multiple houses would share the same telephone line. Want to make a call? Better hope that your neighbor down the street isn't already using the phone. Want the call to be private? Better hope that neighbor isn't listening.

The connection between the Yippies and the telephone was this: *YIPL* was devoted to teaching Yippies and hippies and rebellious youth how to use the telephone as a tool of civil disobedience, specifically, how to make free phone calls to fuck the Bell System and, with it, the United States government.

YIPL was the brainchild of Alan Fierstein and Yippie founder Abbie Hoffman. Fierstein was an engineering major at Cornell University during the late 1960s who had long been interested in the telephone system. Based on his own investigations and through conversations with his fellow engineering students he had learned several ways to make free telephone calls. But Fierstein differed from many phone phreaks in one important way: he was strongly political. As a young liberal student at the end of a tumultuous decade he recalls feeling that his mission was to "end the Vietnam War and oppose Nixon in any possible way."

In his travels through the antiwar demonstrations at Cornell, Fierstein made the acquaintance of the famous and flamboyant Abbie Hoffman, who was then in the process of writing *Steal This Book,* the Yippie manifesto that taught its readers how to get free food, free postage, free weapons, even a free buffalo from the

U.S. Department of the Interior. Fierstein told Hoffman of the ways he knew to make free phone calls and Hoffman was quick to incorporate them into his stealable book. Hoffman, Fierstein recalls, "felt that the technology that I had would be useful in fighting the enemy, which in his case was the United States government. And while I had no love for the government, of course I also had a hatred for the phone company."

Understanding Fierstein's hatred of the phone company requires understanding a few things about the phone company itself—and the public's perception of it—in the late 1960s and early 1970s. Back then, AT&T wasn't simply the largest company on earth; it was the world's largest regulated private monopoly. People generally have little love for monopolies, associating them with high prices and poor service, and the telephone company was no exception to this general rule. "In a country indissolubly wed to free enterprise, AT&T stands as a corporate enigma, being a regulated monopoly and the only major phone company in the world not owned and run by a national government," New York Times business reporter Sonny Kleinfield wrote. "It is like some culture in a Petri dish about which scientists cannot agree whether it is harmful or beneficial."

As a regulated entity, the telephone company couldn't increase its rates without permission from its regulatory masters, the FCC and various state public utility commissions. But that didn't stop the company from asking, and AT&T became notorious for its rate hike requests. At first glance, this reputation seemed undeserved: AT&T's 1970 request for a 6 percent increase in telephone long-distance rates was its first in thirteen years. But AT&T's vast size meant that just about every year some part of its far-flung empire was asking some regulatory body somewhere for permission to charge its customers more money. In addition to a long-distance rate hike, the AT&T corporation wanted to increase rates for private telephone lines for things like teletype newswires in 1961 and, in 1968, for specialized high-quality leased lines for audio feeds used by radio and television broadcasters. Bell System local operating companies had their hands out too. Southern New England Telephone and Southern Bell both asked regulators for rate hikes in 1961, Chesapeake and Potomac Telephone in 1964, Pacific Telephone in 1966 (and then again in 1967), Pacific Northwest Bell and Southern Bell in 1968, New York Telephone and—once again—Southern New England Telephone in 1969.

Being frequently in the news asking for more money from rate payers does not endear you to the public. Nor did AT&T's insistence that all telephones were rented to customers, never owned by them outright. This policy, in place since the inception of the Bell System, wasn't just for telephone lines but extended to the telephones themselves. Want a single telephone line with two or three extension telephones in your house? Expect to pay the phone company every month for each telephone; prices varied across the United States, but figure about $1 per month per extension in 1970. Local telephone companies ran "ringer tests" at night using automated equipment to count the number of telephones on each line in an effort to spot unauthorized extensions; indeed, in the mid-seventies the Bell System went so far as to deploy a specialized telephone testing computer system called DUE—"detect unauthorized equipment"—to catch subscribers with unauthorized extensions. (A common technique to get around this was to install telephone extensions with their ringers disconnected so they couldn't be electronically spotted by the phone company.) Installers—or, more accurately, deinstallers—would be dispatched to remove offending instruments; repeat offenders could have telephone service terminated entirely. Needless to say, these were not the sorts of interactions that promoted warm gooey feelings toward the telephone company.

AT&T's reputation wasn't helped by the great service failures of 1969 and 1970. As a 1969 *New York Times* article put it, "Cries of frustration over erratic telephone service are being heard from more and more of the United States' major metropolitan areas. Although most of the attention has focused on New York, where Federal Communication Commission officials say the situation is the most severe, telephone customers in such cities as Miami, Boston, Denver, Atlanta, and Los Angeles are finding themselves inconvenienced and angered by a variety of troubles." Customer frustrations included the "inability to get dial tone for minutes or even hours; the rapid 'buzz buzz' that means all circuits are busy; the recorded voice that informs the customer the number he is calling no longer is 'in service,' when he knows it is; the line that unaccountably goes dead; the busy signal that intrudes before the caller finishes dialing; delays in getting telephones installed, and assorted misconnections, disconnections, and malconnections." As one writer described it, "A kind of surrealistic telephone chaos reigned, all too suggestive of a world gone mad."

The madness peaked in July 1969 when an entire telephone exchange—PLaza 8 on East 56th Street in New York City—failed completely due to overload; more than 10,400 telephones in that exchange became unreachable for large chunks of the day for several weeks. AT&T acknowledged that customer complaints had reached record numbers; a New York Telephone executive vice president publicly described service as "lousy." For its part, the telephone company blamed the problems on "unforeseeable expansion in demand for telephone use"—in other words, AT&T was the victim of its own success, for too many people were demanding telephone service and the company was unable to add capacity quickly enough to serve them. This caused some at the Federal Communications Commission to wonder, as the *New York Times* put it, "whether the telephone companies' management techniques are equal to the job of maintaining the United States' communication network in good order." An FCC investigation of telephone service complaints was launched.

Then there was the Bell System's reputation for discriminatory hiring and promotion practices. "For a long time," wrote one historian, "AT&T was the corporate personification of male chauvinism and racism. It had acquired a well-known tradition of hiring relatively few members of racial minorities, and while it was the biggest employer of women, it traditionally relegated them to low-level slots as secretaries or operators." Although the telephone company was able to offer some evidence that it was working to correct these problems, in 1970 the federal Equal Employment Opportunity Commission took an unprecedented step: it asked the Federal Communications Commission to deny a $385 million AT&T rate hike request until the telephone company ended its "callous indifference" to equal employment laws and stopped its employment discrimination against "blacks, women, and Spanish-surnamed Americans." The FCC responded by launching another sweeping investigation into AT&T, covering not only its request for a "major rate increase" but also its cost structure and "charges of discriminatory hiring practices." The feds weren't the only ones who were unhappy. Within a year, half a million telephone workers—members of the AFL-CIO Communications Workers of America and related unions—would be on strike for grievances including wages, pensions, health benefits, and the telephone company's "anti-feminist job policies."

Finally, there was AT&T's reputation as the world's most controlling and straitjacketed company, a company that prized conformance and discouraged creativity. "In this office," said an AT&T junior executive in 1967, "we call it 'The System,' and the use of the word 'the' means dogmatic finality. The wall comes up pretty fast when you start tampering with the way things are done within The System, and you either slow down and do things Bell's way or you knock your brains out." Another AT&T executive agreed: "We prefer to have our men use their own initiative, but we leave as little as possible to the imagination."

As part of its program to leave as little as possible to the imagination, AT&T created an exhaustive collection of manuals and how-to guides covering every conceivable situation. Called Bell System Practices or BSPs, they were the very embodiment of "The System," codifying precisely how AT&T equipment was to be assembled, disassembled, configured, and serviced and the exact way virtually any task was to be performed by Bell System employees. By 1952 there were more than nine thousand individual BSPs;

millions of copies were printed and distributed to the operating companies. A particularly illustrative example was Bell System Practice number 770-130-301 (revised), dated August 1952. Titled "Sweeping, General," this three-page document set forth the authoritative procedure for sweeping floors within the Bell System. It differentiated among light sweeping, heavy sweeping, stairway sweeping, and "pickup" sweeping, offered instructions for each, and provided a helpful list of tools required (including, not surprisingly, a broom, which it properly referred to as a "floor brush"). Finally, lest there be any confusion, it noted that smooth floors within Bell System buildings should be swept by alternative sweeping methods—methods described in detail in its two sister BSPs 770-130-302 and 770-130-303.

All this made the phone company a perfect target for mockery. In 1967, for example, the satirical comedy *The President's Analyst* starred James Coburn as Dr. Sidney Schaefer, the president's psychiatrist. A target for every spy agency on the planet, Schaefer goes increasingly crazy himself, reeling from one paranoid situation to another until he is finally kidnapped by the largest, most diabolical organization of all: The Phone Company—or TPC—which is run by a "robotic man in a three piece suit." As one reviewer wrote at the time, "I find it hard to fault a writer who has the gall to make the phone company his villain."

Then, two years later in 1969, Lily Tomlin introduced a new character to her comedy repertoire: Ernestine, a prissy, officious, nasal-voiced telephone company employee. Sitting before a switchboard on the controversial *Laugh-In* television show, Ernestine tormented famous personalities of the day, including "Mr. Milhous" (Richard Nixon), "Mr. Spiro" (Spiro Agnew), and "Mr. Hoover" (J. Edgar Hoover), her punch lines emphasized by her famous snort. "If we do not receive payment within ten days," she advised a "Mr. Veedle" (Gore Vidal) in one skit, "we will send a large burly serviceman to rip [your phone] out of your wall. I'd advise you to lock up the liquor cabinet, he's a mean drunk. Now, Mr. Veedle, wouldn't you rather pay than lose your service and possibly the use of one eye?"

Ernestine struck a chord not just with the public but also with the telephone company's rank and file, and she hit a nerve with their higher-ups too. Telephone operators in Southern California made Tomlin an honorary operator and presented her with a trophy, the Cracked Bell Award. "They love the character, Ernestine, but they said the phone company is a little uptight," Tomlin told newspapers at the time. A few years later, in a fake television commercial shown on *Saturday Night Live,* Ernestine captured the telephone company's perceived incompetence—"You see, the phone system consists of a multibillion-dollar matrix of space-age technology that is so sophisticated even we can't handle it"—and immortalized its perceived arrogance with the motto "We don't care. We don't have to. We're the phone company."

So, sure, lots of people disliked the telephone company back in 1970, Fierstein included. But what on earth did making free phone calls have to do with opposing Abbie Hoffman's enemy—that is, the United States government—and ending the war in Vietnam?

The answer lay in something called the telephone excise tax. Way back in 1898 Congress legislated a special tax on long-distance telephone calls to help fund the Spanish-American War. Although the tax has come and gone several times since then, it's come more than it's gone, and somehow it always seemed to be around whenever we were fighting a war. World Wars I and II both had their telephone taxes and Vietnam was no different. The 10 percent telephone tax was added to your telephone bill and collected by the telephone company, who in turn handed it over to the government. The feds netted more than $1.5 billion from the telephone tax in 1971, enough to cover about 10 percent of the costs of the Vietnam War that year.

So, the theory went, deprive the Bell System of long-distance revenue and you deprive the United States of telephone tax revenue that it needs to send young men off to fight and die in Southeast Asia. See? You can make free phone calls and feel good about it.

Fierstein recalls that, as a result of his discussions with Abbie Hoffman, "We decided that I would start a newsletter and I would introduce the newsletter to the antiwar community by distributing leaflets at the May Day demonstrations in Washington, D.C. So I took a bus down there, armed with a stack of a few hundred leaflets entitled 'Fuck the Bell System,' and putting in the connection between technology and many other cultural issues of the time, not just the war but racism, sexism, etc., worker conditions at big corporations, particularly Ma Bell."

"The response was, we got a few, I don't remember, maybe high dozens, maybe couple of hundred responses to our initial leaflet," Fierstein says. He started selling cheap subscriptions—$1 per year—to the *YIPL* newsletter. *YIPL* served as a bit of a Trojan horse, he recalls. "One of our main efforts was to try to make the average person who hated the phone company identify with that particular rallying point and use that as a way to sweep them into the exposure to countercultural ideas about these other subjects, you know, women's liberation, etc."

YIPL's first issue premiered in June 1971, with Fierstein writing under the pen name "Al Bell." Black and white, four pages long, its articles explained how to hook up extension telephone lines yourself (no need to pay Ma Bell an extra monthly charge) and how to make a simple circuit to conference two telephone lines together. It concluded with a bit on the telephone excise tax and War Tax Resistance, a group that sought to convince Americans not to pay war-related taxes.

The front-page story of *YIPL*'s first issue was titled simply "The Credit Card Code" and it told how to make free phone calls using made-up telephone credit card numbers. Telephone credit cards? Remember, it's 1971, and cell phones haven't yet been invented. But people still need to make phone calls when they're out and about. This, of course, is why God created pay phones. Long-distance phone calls are expensive, though, and if you're a traveling businessperson you'd prefer not to carry around $45 in coins in order to call your customers and home office when you're on the road. What to do?

AT&T's answer was the telephone credit card. This wasn't a general-purpose credit card like those offered by Visa (then

BankAmericard), MasterCard (then Master Charge), or American Express but rather was a credit card that could be used only to make telephone calls. You'd call the operator and ask to make a credit card call. She'd ask for your telephone credit card number, place the call for you, and then write up a billing slip. The cost of your call (plus a convenience surcharge) would eventually get added to your monthly telephone bill.

Telephone credit cards were big business for AT&T. During the month of March 1970 the telephone company billed almost $40 million in credit card calls. That's a tasty little revenue stream, and it's tastier still when it's growing at almost 10 percent a year.

Unfortunately for AT&T, almost a million dollars a month of these billings were "uncollectible." *Uncollectible* is one of those pleasant business euphemisms that means somebody is stiffing you for something. Sometimes customers don't pay their bills. Sometimes operators make mistakes, maybe writing down the wrong billing information. But the lion's share of uncollectibles was due to credit card fraud—people intentionally using bogus credit card numbers to make free phone calls. And the uncollectibles problem was rapidly getting bigger. Between 1966 and 1970 the percentage of uncollectible credit card revenue had increased 320 percent, and the pace was accelerating; the uncollectible percentage doubled in just one year between 1969 and 1970.

This runaway growth in fraud was possible because AT&T's credit card numbering system, securitywise, was a bad joke. In 1970 a telephone credit card number consisted of a single letter followed by a seven-digit telephone number followed by a three-digit "revenue accounting office" (RAO) code. The RAO code was fixed for each area of the country. For example, anybody who lived in the San Francisco Bay Area would have a credit card number that ended in 158. The letter that started a credit card number was the same everywhere in the country and it changed just once a year; the letter for 1970 was "S."

The upshot was that if you were only slightly craftier than the average houseplant, you could conjure up AT&T credit card numbers out of thin air. Perhaps you're a radical Yippie pinko who wants to annoy the local FBI office by sticking them with your long-distance telephone calls. Let's see, the FBI's number in San Francisco is 552-2155. Pick up the phone. Dial zero. "Hi, operator, I'd like to make a credit card call. My credit card number is S 552-2155 158 . . ." You get to talk to your friend and the FBI foots the bill; the left-wing Students for a Democratic Society did just this in 1973.

If that wasn't easy enough, a handful of bogus credit card numbers attained national prominence via radio programs and newspapers, especially college and underground newspapers. Starting in late 1966 a story popped up that would be repeated over and over in various forms, that the actor Steve McQueen (or Paul Newman or Sammy Davis Jr., depending on the story) had gotten into a fight with the telephone company. According to one version of the story, McQueen had won a million-dollar judgment against the Bell System and wanted to share the bounty, so he took out a newspaper ad and gave out his telephone credit card number, encouraging students and military servicemen to use it up. Another version had it that he had lost his battle with the telephone company but, refusing to give in, had taken out an ad in the newspaper giving his telephone credit card number to all and sundry; he would then refuse to pay the bill, sticking the phone company with the losses. A spokesman for McQueen stated, "Steve doesn't recall ever having a phone credit card. Besides, no man in his right mind would give out his credit card number." Still, both versions were great stories, and, like other urban legends, the fact that they weren't actually true didn't stop their spread. AT&T memos show that by 1970 more than a million dollars' worth of fraudulent calls had been billed to the two credit card numbers most commonly associated with the McQueen-Newman-Davis Jr. stories.

The utter lack of security in its credit card numbering system, coupled with the exponential increase in fraud, was not lost on the telephone company. "It is evident," a 1970 AT&T memo noted dryly, "that past endeavors to abate uncollectible losses have failed or have proven to be ineffective."

AT&T's solution was to introduce a new credit card system, one that would be harder for the bad guys to crack. The new, fraud-resistant 1971 credit card code looked like this: a seven-digit telephone number followed by a three-digit RAO code (same as last time) followed by the Big Secret: the "check letter." The check letter was the thing that allowed the operator to know if a credit card number was valid. It was the magic that would solve the fraud problem.

The Big Secret was that each year AT&T would chose a particular digit position—in 1971 it was the sixth digit in your telephone number—and that would serve as an index into a table of ten letters. For 1971 the letters, in order, were "QAEHJNRUWZ." If the sixth digit of your phone number was a 1, then the check letter was Q. If it was a 2 the check letter was A. And so on.

Obviously, protecting the Big Secret was key. "It is necessary that all employees in all departments understand the importance of protecting the integrity of the new credit card plan," read an AT&T memo. "Further, it should be made clear that under no circumstances should an employee disclose the characteristics of an acceptable credit card number to any unauthorized person nor should an employee ever divulge to a customer how she knew that a credit card was invalid."

The problem with the credit card code's Big Secret was, of course, clever people. If it's simple enough for operators to be able to figure out on the fly, it's simple enough for phone phreaks—or anybody else who was interested—to reverse engineer with a little bit of time, energy, and effort. While the network explorer type of phone phreaks may have looked down their collective noses at making fraudulent credit card calls, Bill Acker allows that they worked out the telephone credit card code each year just for fun, just by using pencil and paper and studying credit card numbers. It was, after all, both telephone-related and a challenge, so the phreaks went after it the same way others might solve crossword puzzles. But, Acker says, "With all the electronic means we had to get there, you don't need to mess with people's phone bills to make a free call."

Unfortunately for AT&T, the world is not made up of technically minded highbrow phone phreaks like Bill Acker; most people interested in the credit card code wanted to make free calls, plain and simple. The switch to the new credit card system was scheduled for December 1, 1970. The first underground and college newspaper articles appeared with the new credit card code just two months later. By April 1971 Abbie Hoffman was being interviewed on New York City's WNET-TV, channel 13, promoting *Steal This Book*. He read directly from his book into the camera: "This is going to be a public disservice announcement," he told his viewers. "To make your own credit card numbers, the 1971 credit card consists of ten digits and a letter. The first seven digits comprise any New York City telephone number. The phone company will bill this number, so make sure the number you use is nonexistent or the number of a large corporation. The next three digits are the credit card code. For New York City it's 021. The letter is based on the sixth digit of the phone number. If the sixth digit is one, then the letter is Q. If it's a two, it's A . . ." Hoffman went through the complete list and concluded, "For example, for New York, you would dial 581-6000-021-Z and Channel Thirteen would pick up the bill." The host of the TV show quickly disclaimed responsibility for this idea.

YIPL's first issue set the tone of the publication and subsequent issues offered a similar blend of technological hackery, counter-cultural politics, and antiwar and antigovernment rhetoric, all sprinkled with goofy illustrations. "I can't draw very well, as you can see from the first few issues," says Fierstein.

YIPL's second issue in July 1971 led with a tutorial on the blue box—what it was, how it worked, and how to use it. Inside it reprinted an open letter from the *New York Times* columnist Russell Baker in which Baker suggested that the Yippies' hatred of the telephone company was misplaced; on the opposite page, *YIPL* published a rebuttal from Hoffman that ended with, "Until AT&T and the other corporations really become public services rather than power and profit gobblers, we'll continue to rip them off every chance we get. If you want to discuss this further, call me up some time. Because of all the agencies claiming to have me under surveillance, it's one of the fastest ways to speak directly to your government." Issue no. 2 also introduced the first version of what would eventually become *YIPL*'s icon: the classic bell-shaped Bell System logo but one with a Liberty Bell–style crack in it.

Issue no. 3 in August 1971 raised the price of a subscription to $2 a year—"the best thing you can buy for two bucks," it proclaimed. Despite the price increase, the issue itself was thin on content, exhorting readers to send in information. "We tried to enlist, as much as possible, people to send in their own ideas because I had a limited amount of information I could write myself," Fierstein says. As *YIPL* got going, readers supplied letters, tips, ideas, technical information, and even finished articles; Fierstein did pretty much everything else himself. "I got friends to help fold newsletters," he says, but "ninety-five percent of it was from me, probably more than ninety-five percent, for the first twenty or thirty or forty issues." He continues, "I really did it all, I did the whole thing for many, many years—four years. It was a lot of work . . . I lugged the newsletters back from the printer, I brought the copies to the printer, I would paste them up, I would do everything." Still, he felt, it was worth the effort. "Every time I received a letter where people said they supported us, or someone would say, look, I really don't have much money but I'm enclosing a dollar to help the cause . . . I mean, it was so pathetically generous, a small amount of money but from someone who couldn't afford much."

YIPL grew rapidly, reaching a peak of between two thousand and three thousand subscribers. "We were caught between being smaller and wanting to be bigger," says Fierstein, "but at the same time not wanting to be so big that there would be an incentive for the phone company to act on us." There was, of course, no way to keep *YIPL*'s existence secret from the telephone company, and soon Bell Labs, AT&T, and the various telephone operating companies had purchased subscriptions—usually using assumed names and employee home addresses. By 1972 *YIPL* had become sufficiently prominent that AT&T security chief Joseph Doherty sent a memo to his security agents: "As you are aware, efforts are continuing to effectuate deterrent actions against publications which print detailed instructions regarding methods to commit toll fraud. It has been alleged that information published in the Youth International Party Line (Y.I.P.L.) newspaper was a source document for some acts of fraud. It would be helpful to acquire evidence to substantiate this allegation. Therefore, it is requested that signed statements (attesting to source of information) be obtained from fraud perpetrators who admit acting to defraud the telephone companies based on information appearing in the Y.I.P.L. newsletter." *YIPL* obtained a copy of this memo and printed it the next month.

Although Fierstein did worry that the phone company might try to shut him down, his spirits were buoyed by an ace in the hole. "Abbie lent us his lawyer Jerry Lefcourt," Fierstein recalls. Lefcourt was a young firebrand who had made a name for himself as part of the defense team for the Chicago Seven, a group of antiwar protesters (including Hoffman) who had been arrested for conspiracy and incitement of riot in 1968. "He promised to defend us in the unlikely event that the phone company would ever prosecute us and elevate our minuscule presence to a large-scale story, which we didn't feel they would want to do."

YIPL marked the beginning of the cultural hijacking of phone phreaking. Before this newsletter—and before the *Esquire* article, which would be published a few months after *YIPL*'s first issue—phone phreaking had been the domain of the Bill Ackers and Joe Engressias and Charlie Pynes and Ralph Barclays of the world: people who were obsessively interested in exploring the telephone network and understanding how it all worked. To be sure, these early phreaks weren't immune to the allure of making free phone calls, but that wasn't their primary interest. In contrast, Hoffman and Fierstein took the hobby in a new direction, one simultaneously more political and more utilitarian. If the old game was to understand, appreciate, and play with the telephone network, the new game was to make free calls and screw Ma Bell and the government.

The game was changing. Old Mother Bell couldn't afford to ignore this for much longer.

Fourteen

BUSTED

THE WOMAN WAS a busybody. The man was rude.

It was December 1971. They were at a discount gas station at the corner of Saratoga Avenue and Stevens Creek Boulevard in Sunnyvale, California, the very heart of the Silicon Valley. The woman had been waiting patiently to use the gas station's lone pay phone when the man cut in front of her and popped into the telephone booth.

The woman watched as he took out a small rectangular box. It had wires coming out of it, wires that went into something that looked like a mound of clay. The box had a label on its side. SPEECH SCRAMBLER. Strange sounds came from inside the booth as the man fiddled with the box. It all seemed very odd.

Curiosity piqued—and unable to make her phone call—the woman wandered over to the man's vehicle, a green Volkswagen van. She peered in the back, through the striped curtains, where she saw what looked like two large car batteries. She wrote down the van's license plate number, WB6EWU, and went to speak to the gas station attendant.

When she returned the phone booth was empty. The man was gone, along with his Volkswagen van. Nearby, a telephone company employee toiled, doing whatever it is that telephone company employees do. She walked over and told him about the rude man and his odd little box.

Months earlier, in April 1971, British Columbia Telephone took a wrecking ball to the phone phreaks' home on the network. In a bit of telephonic urban renewal, the old mechanical Vancouver step tandem—home to the 2111 conference—was replaced with a shiny new 4A crossbar toll switching machine. The old step tandem still existed but it was relegated to other, lesser duties. Unfortunately for the phreaks, the telephone company thoughtlessly failed to provide a phone phreak conference call setup in the new switching machine.

The 2111 conference really was something special. It was not the only conference circuit the phreaks had at their disposal but it was one of the best. It was easy to dial—you could use just a Cap'n Crunch whistle from many places—and it supported all the people they could pile on to it. In contrast, loop arounds were okay for meeting other phreaks but you could fit only two people on them, not much of a conference. Another conference bridge technique, pioneered by Joe Engressia, was something called an open sleeve-lead conference. This required either finding a miswired connection in a central office someplace or, more likely, fast-talking a telephone company switchman into miswiring such a connection for you. The former required luck; the latter, balls and skill. If you were particularly clever, you could engineer such a setup to be reached via an 800 number, creating a toll-free conference bridge that any phreak could dial into, whether or not he had a blue box. Bill Acker recalls setting up two of these, one in Charleston and one in Benton Harbor; the Charleston circuit supported up to seven people at once.

The phreaks searched the nooks and crannies of the network for a conference that would be as good as 2111. They did this via the time-honored technique of scanning. Using a blue box, they would connect to a tandem somewhere and start exhaustively dialing all the three-digit codes between 000 and 199—that is, the sequences that couldn't be the start of normal telephone numbers—to see what they did. The network was a varied thing in those days, so codes that worked on a switching machine in San Francisco, say, might be quite different from those in Peoria. It was tedious work, but it was the kind of tedious work that phone phreaks loved.

One of the tandems they scanned was White Plains Tandem 2 in the 914 area code of New York. In that tandem the code 052 was a bit of an enigma; if you used your blue box to dial KP + 914 + 052 + ST you'd be connected to something that gave you a short little beep—and nothing else. You knew you had reached something but nobody knew what. Pressing more keys on your blue box to feed it more MF digits didn't get you anything. Multiple phreaks had played with it and couldn't figure it out. It was the Sphinx of dial codes.

Then in January 1972 a phone phreak named Ray Oklahoma★ cracked the 052 code. Oklahoma, an engineering student from Long Island who was studying at Oklahoma State, had been a phone phreak for about a year. He had been fascinated by the musical notes he heard on long-distance calls and, like others before him, soon found himself headed down the phone phreak rabbit hole. For some reason, Oklahoma tried something that the others hadn't thought of: what if you connected to 052 and then sent it touch-tones instead of blue box tones? Bingo. Through a process of trial and error, Oklahoma figured out that 052 was actually an incredibly sophisticated conference bridge. Unlike 2111, this conference system allowed you to dial out. That is, you could dial in to 052 with your blue box and then, using touch tones, add other people to the conference by having the 052 conference system call them for you—for free! In fact, through an unintentional quirk, you could even use it to conference in people from overseas.

The 2111 conference was back in business; its new name was 052. It quickly became popular, hosting more than a dozen phreaks at a time, including some from the United Kingdom.

★The pseudonym he went by at the time.

That very same week in January, Bill Acker—then a senior in high school—received an unwelcome visitor, a man the New York phone phreaks would come to know well: Thomas J. Duffy, a security agent for New York Telephone. Duffy was one of roughly 650 Bell System security agents nationwide, some 10 percent of whom were former FBI special agents. Blue and black boxes—what the phone company called electronic toll fraud—took up only a tiny fraction of the average security agent's time. Mostly they focused on more common problems such as robberies and burglaries (a lot of people paid their phone bills in cash back in those days at telephone company customer service offices), coin telephone thefts, stolen vehicles, company car accidents, and even employee embezzlement. Where toll fraud was concerned, the vast majority were credit card and third number billing fraud. Still, Duffy seemed to be the security agent in the New York area assigned to electronic toll fraud cases, and, in particular, to dealing with the area's pesky teenage phone hackers—a group that had expanded since the days when Bill Acker felt so alone.

Acker wasn't entirely surprised to hear from Duffy, since Duffy had already had a few interactions with Evan Doorbell,★ another Long Island phone phreak Acker knew. What did surprise Acker —and annoyed him too—was that Duffy actually showed up at his school to talk with him, instead of visiting him in the privacy of his home. As a result of Duffy's visit, the officials and other kids at Acker's school now knew he was in trouble. "That was very uncomfortable," Acker recalls. "Which maybe was part of it, part of a 'shock-and-awe' approach"—an attempt to intimidate Acker and keep him off balance during their conversation.

The shock-and-awe approach didn't work out well for Duffy. "When Tom Duffy said, 'We want to talk with you,' I said the following thing: 'I have the right to remain silent, and I wish to do so,'" Acker remembers. Acker flat-out refused to talk to Duffy.

★The pseudonym he went by at the time.

"He wasn't expecting that," Acker says. After all, Duffy wasn't law enforcement, and he wasn't there to arrest Acker but just to get him to knock off his telephonic shenanigans. While he was at it, Duffy maybe figured he might be able to get some information on phone phreaking activities in the area. So why the silent treatment? "There was an element of 'screw you,'" Acker says. "'Hey, you're the telephone company, you're the enemy, you don't understand us phreaks.'" But there were two other things that made him keep his mouth shut. First, Acker says, "I knew I could talk to him as nicely as I wanted to, we could spend a couple of hours talking, but at the end of the day, 'Cut it out, kid, or you're gonna get arrested' was going to be the message. I knew that that was where the conversation was going to end up."

More important, Acker says, was this: "He was a trained interrogator. He wasn't law enforcement, but he was a security guy, that's what he did for a living. I was a kid. I couldn't guarantee that if we started talking I wouldn't let slip something about somebody else inadvertently. I didn't expect to be a match for him if he really was a good interrogator." Given his strong feelings about never squealing on another phreak, Acker says, "I just figured, 'Don't talk to him at all.'"

The right-to-remain-silent approach didn't work out well for Acker. "That *really* pissed him off badly," Acker remembers. The very next day, while Acker was still in school, Duffy drove to Acker's house, met with his mother, and drove off with Acker's most cherished possession: his blue box.

The busybody woman at the gas station in Sunnyvale was just the break the General Telephone security department had been hoping for.

"On several occasions during the year 1971," read an April 1972 memorandum from a senior special agent with General Telephone security, "information was received from the Security Department of British Columbia Telephone Company, Vancouver, Canada, that their long-lines department was observing illegal entry by parties dialing and multi-frequencing [*sic*] from points in the United States into their toll switching system and returning back to points in the United States." This was, of course, exactly what the *Esquire* phreaks had been using 2111 for back before it was a conference call, back when it still had a dial tone on it; they'd whistle into British Columbia via 2111, get a dial tone, and dial out again.

"Line traces were made," continued the memo, "and a number of them showed that some of the parties came through switching machines in the San Jose, California area. On 4/17/71, a new 4-A Type toll switcher was placed into service in Vancouver. During this cutover it was observed that a conference call of several hours duration was set up illegally, and a recording of a portion of this conference call was made." BC Tel sent a copy of this tape to General Telephone security. It was apparent that "one or more parties on the call were located in Los Gatos, California, served by Western California Telephone Company, a part of the General system."

When General Telephone security received the report from the busybody woman about the rude man with the box that made strange noises, agents ran the license plate number she'd given them through the Department of Motor Vehicles—something anyone could do back in those more innocent days. The registrant turned out to live at 16382 Robie Lane, Los Gatos. His name? John Thomas Draper. "In exchanging information between security departments throughout the United States and Canada," the memo noted, "the names John Draper and Captain Crunch were associated on a number of occasions in matters pertaining to fraudulent use of multi-frequency signaling."

"A night time line observation was made"—GT's euphemism for a tap-and-tape recording setup. One night's worth of recordings of Draper's home telephone line on March 27, 1972, netted "evidence of numerous attempts and completions of calls using multi-frequency signaling to points in California and to Sidney, Australia."

★   ★   ★

Draper had just finished up a nice long conference call with the other phreaks on 052 when his telephone rang.

The caller was an anonymous telephone company employee, a switchman at White Plains Tandem 2. He was calling to deliver an urgent message. They're monitoring this thing really, really closely, the switchman told Draper. They're recording everything. They're watching what you dial. You guys need to be careful about this. Bill Acker observed later that the switchman "stuck his neck out about a hundred and fifty miles" to deliver that warning.

While the call proved that not everyone in the phone company had it in for the phone phreaks, Acker and New York Telephone security agent Tom Duffy continued their cat-and-mouse games. Acker's ability to play with the network had been curtailed when Duffy took away his blue box; in particular, Acker needed it to call into the 052 conference. But Acker soon discovered a workaround. Due to a bug in his phone company's central office, Acker found he was able to dial a telephone number like 914 052 1211 and the switch would connect him—sometimes—to the 052 system. He could then use his touch-tone phone to control the conference, no blue box needed. It would have been better to have a blue box, to be sure, but this wasn't bad.

That April, Tom Duffy made another trip to Acker's house. This time he ripped out Acker's touch-tone phone, replacing it with a rotary dial one. Acker was aghast. "Rotary dial!" he wailed, but Acker's mom was actually kind of pleased. "She could never understand why anyone would want to push buttons when God intended us to spin a dial," he says.

It was May 4, 1972. Draper was in his VW van in the parking lot of a 7-Eleven in Los Gatos when the alarm bells began ringing in his reptilian hindbrain: the cars pulling up around him were predators. He wrestled with his fight-or-flight instinct for a moment, but neither option seemed like a smart move. He had no way to fight and a high-speed car chase pitting his Volkswagen bus against police cruisers seemed like a losing proposition.

Plan C, then. Draper got out of his van, walked around behind it, and—unobserved, he hoped—started dumping the contents of his pockets on the ground, ridding himself of incriminating electronics. The last item was a small magnet, which he stuck on the rear of his van. The magnet was a clever security precaution, used to activate a tiny magnetic relay inside his blue box. Draper's box would not emit even the slightest peep unless he held the magnet up against it in just the right place. The idea was that if a cop ever stopped him and started messing with his blue box, the box simply wouldn't work.

Plan C's execution did not go unobserved. The arresting FBI agents recovered every single item Draper had dumped, magnet and all. Their haul included Draper's blue box and a cassette tape containing "numerous multi-frequency signals representing telephone numbers in California and other states within the continental United States; inward operator route codes for all area codes within the United States; route codes to overseas sender points, foreign country codes, and foreign operator route codes." Between each series of numbers on the tape was a Morse code sequence identifying the person or place the tones were used for. The FBI also searched his van and, later that day, his apartment.

Draper was arrested for seven counts of violating 18 USC 1343, the Fraud by Wire statute, for making blue box calls to Australia, New York, and Oklahoma. The feds knew they were on solid legal ground using Fraud by Wire now, thanks to the Supreme Court's refusal to hear the bookies' blue box appeal under this law back in 1969. Draper was arraigned and released on his own recognizance the same day. On June 12, he appeared before U.S. District Court judge Robert F. Peckham and entered a plea of "not guilty." Not long afterward his attorney filed a motion to suppress the evidence. Captain Crunch was apparently not going to give up the ship without a fight.

The newspaper coverage of Draper's bust increased his fame from both the *Esquire* article and the Maureen Orth article, boosting his ego and status as a counterculture icon. The *San Francisco*

Chronicle described him as a "contemporary folk hero," an "over-grown, misunderstood kid with the mind of a genius"—though they also noted that he was "shy, shifty eyed, and slightly myopic." Both of the big newswires of the day, Associated Press and United Press International, covered the story and their copy appeared in smaller newspapers across the country. UPI described him as an "electronics whiz" and played up the Cap'n Crunch whistle angle.

The same month that Draper entered his not guilty plea, a magazine article appeared with an intriguing title: "Regulating the Phone Company in Your Own Home." According to its edi-torial lead, the article showed how "practically anyone who can change the plug on an electric toaster—using only a screwdriver, a kitchen knife, and four dollars' worth of readily available electric parts—can build in two or three hours a simple device capable of evading charges on long distance telephone calls." It explained to its readers how to build a black box, also known as a "mute," and its author was Ray Oklahoma, the discoverer of the 052 conference.

Now, it would be one thing if this article was to appear in *YIPL* or some obscure underground newspaper. But this was slated for publication in the June issue of *Ramparts,* the darling magazine of the New Left, circulation 100,000. *Ramparts* was unique among lefty publications for bridging the gap to the non–hippie-Yippie set. "It expressed radical left values in a way mainstream people could understand," said a former editor. It even did do it with style. It was printed on "heavy, shiny stock with classy graph-ics that looked good on a Danish Modern coffee table." In a few short years the magazine developed a scrappy reputation for railing against the Vietnam War and clashing with the Central Intelligence Agency, the National Security Agency, and the U.S. military. Its writers were talented and its reporting newsworthy; follow-on coverage of *Ramparts* articles by mainstream newspa-pers, even the august *New York Times,* was common.

AT&T usually had to react to the publication of phone phreak ar-ticles after the fact. With the *Esquire* article, for example, the phone company had no clue it was coming until it hit the newsstands, and then it had to scramble and figure out what to do. But this time the phone company caught a lucky break. *Ramparts'* contract printer in Milwaukee, perhaps worried about enraging Ma Bell, sent an advance copy of the June issue to the phone company.

The phone company was not amused. The friendly illustrations and reassuring text in Oklahoma's three-page article—"do not be intimidated by the spaghetti dish of wiring you see, only a small, identifiable portion concerns you"—enabled anyone to build a black box and receive long-distance calls without the caller being billed. The *Esquire* article may have inspired a generation of phone phreaks but at least it didn't give step-by-step instructions to all the world on how to make free calls with just a few dollars of easy-to-get components. *Ramparts* did.

This could not be allowed to happen.

AT&T chose its battleground wisely: California. *Ramparts* was headquartered in California but, more important, California had something that other states did not: section 502.7 of the California Penal Code. Added to California law in the early sixties, 502.7 made most telephone-related shenanigans illegal in the Golden State. But in 1965 telephone company lobbyists managed to get its scope dramatically expanded and the new 502.7 made it a crime to sell—or even give away—"plans or instructions" for any device that could be used to steal telephone service. And what was Ray Oklahoma's article if not plans or instructions?

The timing was tight. On May 12, after the June issue of *Ramparts* had been mailed out to subscribers and shipped to distributors but before it had hit the newsstands, Pacific Telephone contacted the magazine and its middlemen. The tone was polite but the company's demands were firm. To start with, *Ramparts* must recall its June issue or face civil and criminal charges, up to felony conspiracy charges for the magazine's editors. In addition, the magazine's editors reported later, "Telephone Company attorneys demanded that the copyright of the 'phone phreak' article be assigned to the Bell System so that they could prosecute underground or other publications that might reprint it; that the film and plates from which the article had been printed be delivered up; and that *Ramparts* agree never to print a similar article in the future." Finally, Pacific Telephone requested the *Ramparts* subscriber list "so that they could place those who had received our June issue under surveillance."

"In the past ten years," wrote its editors, *"Ramparts* has incurred the wrath of power in many forms." From *Ramparts'* perspective, regardless of what California law might say, this was a clear violation of the First Amendment, an affront to all that journalists held holy. It was prior restraint on a supposedly free press, an unacceptable tactic that the government had tried and failed to impose just a few years ago when the *New York Times* was set to print the Pentagon Papers—and that case was actually a matter of national security. In this case, it was just the telephone company whining. *Ramparts'* entire history and radical ethos had primed it for this fight.

And yet it caved. As its editors explained later, "We were willing to have the matter go to court . . . But the Bell System had hostages we had to consider. Their attorneys indicated that the whole network handling *Ramparts* was also vulnerable to civil and criminal charges. That meant that the over 500 wholesalers and thousands of retailers distributing the magazine could also be prosecuted. It was clear from our conversations that the largest corporation in the world lacked neither the will nor the resources to do it. To protect this distribution network, the lifeblood of this and other publications, we agreed to recall our issue."

The result was that some ninety thousand copies of the June issue never made it to newsstands or were withdrawn once they reached them; the roughly sixty thousand that had already been mailed to subscribers were unaffected. *Ramparts'* editors estimated the costs of the recall, including uncollectible advertising revenues, at almost $60,000.

"Within a week," its editors concluded, "American Telephone and Telegraph had achieved what the CIA, Pentagon, FBI and other targets of *Ramparts'* journalism over the last ten years hadn't been able to bring about: the nationwide suppression of this magazine."

Oddly enough, the 052 conference disappeared just about the time the *Ramparts* issue came out. As it turned out, the reason 052 had made such a great conference system was that it actually was a conference system, one intended for use by AT&T corporate executives. The suits at AT&T were less than amused at its appropriation by the phone phreaks, and telephone company security had been monitoring the phone phreak conferences on 052 since February.

Ray Oklahoma disappeared just about the time the *Ramparts* issue came out too; he was arrested by the FBI in Oklahoma City for Fraud by Wire and spent eleven days in jail before his father was able to come and bail him out. The charges were all related to using a blue box to call the 052 conference, he remembers. "As far as I know," he says, "they didn't know I had anything to do with the Ramparts article." He pleaded guilty and was given five years' probation. He also agreed to write an open letter to other phone phreaks discouraging them from the hobby. His letter ran in an Oklahoma newspaper and concluded with: "I know it looks easy but you will get caught. Look at me. My college days are ruined at least for now. I have lost money on bond and other expenses. Plus the anxiety and fear. I hope you don't make the same mistake. I can only hope you [. . .] don't do as I have done because I am sorry."

As the summer wore on, and phone phreaks and conference call setups were disappearing and people were being arrested, it seemed high time to take a vacation. National Airlines had been running a series of controversial television ads featuring attractive stewardesses in revealing minidresses saying things like, "Hi! I'm Tammy! Fly me to Miami and back with a stopover for only $100!" Miami was a good choice of destination in 1972. The Republicans and Democrats both had decided to host their national conventions in Miami Beach that summer—the Dems in July, the Republicans in August. Abbie Hoffman's Youth International Party seized the moment by hosting a pair of events in Miami on the same dates; true to form, the Yippie events would be part protest, part theater, part smoke-in. The publicity poster for the Yippie gatherings featured a hairy-legged Hoffman in a minidress in midflight, having just leapt into the air. The caption read, "High! I'm Abbie, fly me to Miami."

Unable to help itself, the front page of *YIPL's* June–July 1972 issue sported a cartoon telephone with wings proclaiming, "Hi, I'm Telly! Fly Me to Miami!" The *Youth International Party Line* capitalized on the Yippie gathering by announcing that the World's First Phone Phreak Convention would be held July 11–15 in Miami Beach. "The Celebration of Change will include, in addition, teach-ins on telephones, contests, meetings with nationally known phone phreaks," the newsletter reported. "Plus the unveiling of new devices never yet revealed. Courses are going to be held on Phone Politics, Phone rip-offs, establishment rip-offs, and peoples technology. [. . .] At the same time there will be other events too, such as antiwar demos, women's rights, health care, anti-smack information and actions, and many other happenings."

The *YIPL* issue reprinted a simplified version of the Ray Oklahoma article from *Ramparts* and concluded with an appeal to "Support Captain Crunch!" "As some of you might know from a recent *Rolling Stone* article, the FBI and the phone co. has arrested the supposed Cap'n Crunch of Blue Box fame for allegedly making a few Box calls. We are now setting up the Cap'n Crunch Defense Fund, for the benefit of such obviously political telephone busts. The money will go for support of those harassed and busted for phone co. specials, and for legal and bail fees. Please contribute what you can, it might be you next."

John Draper had to attend the World's First Phone Phreak Convention. How could he not? Thanks to the *Esquire* article and the publicity from his recent bust, he was probably the best-known phreak in the world at the time—more famous even than Joe Engressia, the man *Esquire* had dubbed the granddaddy of phone phreaking. Draper would enjoy the publicity and adulation he would receive at the conference; he always enjoyed being in the limelight. And afterward he would head up to New York City and visit Bill Acker, who was taking classes and staying at a YMCA in Queens. It would be a nice little vacation from his legal troubles.

Draper boarded a flight from San Francisco to Miami and, as his plane took off and banked toward the beaches of Florida, his legal troubles multiplied. Draper had overlooked one sniggly little detail. The terms of his release after his arrest required him to obtain the court's permission if he wanted to leave the San Francisco Bay Area, and this he did not do. John Draper didn't know it yet but he was now officially a fugitive.

An informant brought Draper's departure to the attention of the FBI a few days later. The FBI and an assistant U.S. attorney wasted no time in appearing before Judge Peckham, who immediately revoked Draper's recognizance bond and issued a bench warrant for his arrest on July 11. That very afternoon FBI agents raided Draper's Miami hotel room but missed him by scant hours. Unbeknownst to them, the phone phreak convention had been postponed and was now to be held in New York City later that month. Draper had already left for the airport, a witness told them, carrying—naturally enough—"a tape-recorder and a brown valise with wires protruding from the top."

FBI agents caught up with Draper the next day in New York City, arresting him at the YMCA in Queens where Bill Acker was staying. Appropriately, Draper was talking on the hallway pay phone when the FBI agents found him, his trusty tape recorder perched atop the pay phone and loaded with another cassette of blue box tones. Unable to come up with $10,000 bail, Draper spent the next several days in the care of the United States marshal service until he was flown back to California to appear before Judge Peckham. Peckham denied Draper's motion to suppress the evidence for his California bust and set a date for trial.

Despite the absence of its headliner, the World's First Phone Phreak Convention took place in New York City on July 29, 1972. The phreaks congregated in the basement ballroom of the Hotel Diplomat, a Times Square hotel that was developing a reputation for hosting rock 'n' roll shows and fringe political gatherings—Yippies, Communists, and Libertarians all had held conventions there. Alan Fierstein ("Al Bell") of *YIPL* was the master of ceremonies, presiding over attractions that included a black-and-white film showing three simple ways to make free phone calls from pay telephones, a presentation on the black box for receiving free calls, and breakout sessions on building answering machines and blue boxes. Yippie founder Abbie Hoffman led a workshop on the legality of phone phreaking and exhorted the attendees to support the Captain Crunch defense fund. A spy from New York Telephone later reported to the FBI that some seventy-five people were in attendance.

The telephone company and the FBI continued their stepped-up enforcement efforts as summer turned to fall. About a week after Labor Day, on September 12, 1972, the FBI conducted a series of raids across the country. Over the course of three days agents arrested fourteen people in eight cities, including Minneapolis, Dallas, Houston, and Memphis, charging them with manufacturing, selling, and using blue boxes. But here was the interesting thing: they weren't phone phreaks, or even bookies or hippies. This time the people arrested were all upstanding members of society, including real estate agents, stock brokers, two executives with a vending company, and the president of an air freight firm. A subsequent news release from AT&T described it as follows: "Cheat Ma Bell! Rip-off the phone company! Beat the system! Popular phrases like these were quite fashionable not so very long ago. Just about everyone attributed them to well-known anti-establishment types, to the New Left, and to the self-styled phone phreaks." It went on to note, "The 14 persons [arrested] were not those type-cast as the rip-off set. Rather, they were ordinary middle to upper-middle class Americans. Everyone seemed to be getting into the act. While the arrests pointed out that toll fraud is geographically as well as socially and economically wide spread, another more important fact became crystal clear—the Bell System was cracking down on the problem which had reached epidemic proportions. [. . .] Some people who wouldn't dream of stealing from a candy store seem more than willing to commit theft by wire."

"For years," the release continued, "Bell System companies were quite lenient with persons who committed toll fraud. Whenever possible, the company would first attempt to stop the calls, collect on them, and stay out of court. But that was before more than $20 million per year was being lost. Overnight, it would seem that the lamb has turned into the lion. Today, the Bell System is a vigorous—and successful—prosecutor."

True enough. By the end of 1972 AT&T was on track to chalk up a total of fifty-seven electronic toll fraud arrests. The numbers might look even better if the company could convict Captain Crunch before the end of the year. That wasn't looking like too much of a stretch. Despite Abbie Hoffman's best fund-raising efforts, the Captain Crunch defense fund failed miserably, netting a total of $1. Unable to continue to pay for a private attorney, Draper would have to be represented by the public defender's office.

Draper's trial was November 29, 1972. Of thirty-three prospective jurors, two were named Bell. "Don't think that didn't give us pause," one of Draper's attorneys remarked later. The evidence against Draper was extensive. First there were the tape recordings of his illegal telephone calls. Then there was the expert witness testimony from telephone company security agents. And there were the friends he'd called who would testify that it was indeed Draper who had made the phone calls, and even that Draper was indeed the infamous Captain Crunch. It wasn't so much that Draper's friends were rats; it was more that they had little choice. Before trial the FBI had tracked down and interviewed some of the people who Draper had called. In each case the FBI asked if they remembered receiving any calls from Draper. Not surprisingly, most people suffered sudden attacks of amnesia and were unable to remember anything. The FBI would then play a tape recording of the call, with Draper and the person's voice clearly audible. In most cases the person would then agree that his "recollection had been refreshed" and that now he did, in fact, remember receiving such a call. The FBI agents would then hand their new witness a subpoena to testify at trial.

"Draper didn't look very legendary as he stood with his head bowed while the prosecution offered its overwhelming evidence gathered by investigations from San Francisco to Sydney," wrote the reporter from the *San Francisco Chronicle*. Outgunned, Captain Crunch gave up the ship, changing his plea from "not guilty" to "no contest." The judge sentenced him to a one-year suspended sentence, a $1,000 fine, and five years' probation, during which he was required to "refrain from illegal use of the telephone or other electronics devices for fraudulent means." As part of the plea deal, all but the first of the seven counts against him—the one charging him with an illegal call to a radio station in Sydney, Australia—were dismissed. In essence, Draper would pay $1,000 for a two-minute overseas call.

Judge Peckham concluded Draper's sentence with a promise of sorts: "Your electronic gymnastics may have been thought to be a prank, a frivolity, or a harmless vocational endeavor, but on the next occasion—if there ever is one—you will receive a prison sentence."

If only Draper had heeded the good judge's warning.

Fifteen

PRANKS

LIKE THE FLAP of a butterfly's wings causing a hurricane half a world away, the ripples of unintended consequences from Ron Rosenbaum's "Secrets of the Little Blue Box" continued to spread. "You know how some articles just grab you from the first paragraph? Well, it was one of those articles," Steve Wozniak recalls. "It was the most amazing article I'd ever read!"

Wozniak happened to pick up a copy of *Esquire* from his mother's kitchen table the day before starting classes at Berkeley in the fall of 1971. Rosenbaum's article "described a whole web of people who were doing this: the phone phreaks. They were anonymous technical people who went by fake names and lived all over the place," he recalls, how they were "outsmarting phone companies and setting up networks that nobody imagined existed." It seemed unbelievable. And yet, he says, "I kept reading it over and over, and the more I read it, the more possible and real it sounded."

Oddly enough, part of what made the article seem so real to him were the characters. Despite their fanciful nature and funny names, Wozniak remembers, "I could tell that the characters being described were really tech people, much like me, people who liked to design things just to see what was possible, and for no other reason, really." There was something about the whole thing that just rang true, despite how crazy it seemed. "The idea of the Blue Box just amazed me," he says. The article even gave a few of the frequencies it used. As for Joe Engressia being able to whistle free calls? "I couldn't believe this was possible, but there it was and, wow, it just made my imagination run wild."

The twenty-year-old Wozniak put down the magazine. He picked up the phone and called his friend Steve Jobs—then a seventeen-year-old senior in high school—to tell him about it. Less than an hour later the duo were on their way to raid the library at the Stanford Linear Accelerator Center. SLAC was the atom smasher at Stanford University. It had a great technical library, Wozniak says, and he had a long history of sneaking into it to look stuff up. "If there was any place that had a phone manual that listed tone frequencies," he says, it would be SLAC.

The two dug through the reference books and before long they struck pay dirt: an international telephone technical standard that listed the MF frequencies. "I froze and grabbed Steve and nearly screamed in excitement that I'd found it. We both stared at the list, rushing with adrenaline. We kept saying things like 'Oh, shit!' and 'Wow, this thing is for real!' I was practically shaking, with goose bumps and everything. It was such a Eureka moment. We couldn't stop talking all the way home. We were so excited. We knew we could build this thing. We now had the formula we needed! And definitely that article was for real." Jobs agrees: "We kept saying to ourselves, 'It's real. Holy shit, it's real.'"

That very day Wozniak and Jobs purchased analog tone generator kits from a local electronics store; this was the Silicon Valley in 1971, after all, and such things were easily available. Later that night they had managed to record pairs of tones on cassette tape, enough to make a blue box call. But it didn't quite work. They were able to disconnect a call to 555-1212 with 2,600 Hz—they heard the *kerchink!* of the trunk—but their MF tone tape recordings didn't do anything. They worked late into the night trying to figure out what was wrong. In the end Wozniak concluded that the tone generator just wasn't good enough to make the telephone network dance to his tunes.

Wozniak started classes at Berkeley the next day. But he couldn't get his mind off of blue boxes and phone phreaking. "I started posting articles I found about [phone phreaks] on my dorm room wall. I started telling my friends what these phone phreaks were all about, how intelligent they must be, and how I was sure they were starting to take over the phone system all over the country," he says.

He thought more about the analog blue box that he and Jobs had tried to build. The problem with analog circuits is that they are imprecise. This is because the components they are constructed with—resistors and capacitors and inductors and such—are themselves inexact. For example, if you want an analog circuit to generate a tone at a particular frequency, as you would for a blue box, you might need a resistor of 1000 ohms and a capacitor of 0.1 microfarads. Unfortunately, when you buy a resistor, you can't get one that is exactly 1000 ohms; rather, it is guaranteed to be only within 10 percent of that value. If you want to spend more money, you can get ones that are more accurate—ones whose values vary by only 5 percent or even 1 percent—but there is always some inaccuracy in the individual components. When you combine them to build a circuit the inaccuracies often compound. Worse, the component values vary with temperature. So you might spend time tuning your blue box in the warmth of your dorm room and get it all working and then go out to a pay phone in the cold night air only to find that it doesn't work anymore.

Steve Wozniak had been designing electrical circuits for years; just a year earlier he had designed his own tiny computer, the "Cream Soda Computer," so named because he and a friend drank tons of cream soda while they were building it. Computers are made out of digital circuits, circuits that deal with 1s and 0s rather than the full range of values that analog circuits can handle. While this may seem like a limitation, it gives digital circuits a huge advantage. Digital circuits are exact and their building block components don't vary from one to another, nor do they vary with temperature. With this in mind Wozniak started thinking about how to build a digital blue box, which would be made up of the chips used to build computers, not analog components such as resistors and capacitors and transistor oscillators. It would use a quartz crystal, like those used in the then newfangled digital watches, for ultimate accuracy and rock-solid stability.

By early 1972 Woz had his design worked out. Even more than the fact that it was digital, he was particularly proud of a clever trick he used to keep the power consumption down so the battery would last longer. "I swear to this day," says the man who would one day design the revolutionary Apple I and Apple II computers, "I have never designed a circuit I was prouder of." It took a day to build. When he and the other Steve tested it, it worked the first time.

Finally they had joined the ranks of phone phreaks. Woz adopted the phone phreak handle "Berkeley Blue" while Jobs became "Oaf Tobar." "I would have died to meet Captain Crunch, who was really the center of it all. Or any phone phreak; it just seemed so impossible that I'd ever meet anyone else with a blue box," Wozniak says. But through a happy coincidence involving a friend from high school they tracked down the Captain at radio station KKUP in Cupertino. They arranged for Draper to meet them in Woz's dorm room at Berkeley.

Woz recalls the fateful meeting. "Captain Crunch comes to our door, and it turns out he's just this really weird-looking guy. Here, I thought, would be a guy who would look and act just far away and above any engineer in the world, but there he was: sloppy-looking, with his hair kind of hanging down on one side. And he smelled like he hadn't taken a shower in two weeks, which turned out to be true. He was also missing a bunch of teeth."

Hoping against hope, Woz asked his visitor if he was indeed Captain Crunch.

"I am he," was Crunch's reply.

"He turned out to be this really strange, funny guy, just bubbling over with energy," Woz says, "one of these very hyper people who keep changing topics and jumping around . . ."

Draper and Woz and Jobs and a few friends spent the next several hours trading blue boxing techniques and circuit designs; Woz was particularly pleased that Draper taught him how to call overseas using a blue box. They continued the conversation over pizza until about midnight when they went their separate ways. The two Steves got in Jobs's car and began the hour-long drive from Berkeley to Jobs's home in Los Altos.

About halfway home their car suffered a complete electrical failure. They managed to pull over and the two walked to a gas station, where they tried to use their blue box to call Draper and ask him to rescue them. But for some reason the blue box call wouldn't go through. Worse, the operator came back on the line. They hung up and tried several more times but it just wouldn't work. They started to worry that their blue box had been detected.

"All of a sudden," Woz recalls, "a cop pulled into the gas station and jumped out real fast. Steve was still holding the blue box when he jumped out, that's how fast it happened. We didn't even have time to hide it. We were sure that the operator had called the cops on us, and that this was the end for sure."

The cop and his partner spent some time rooting through the bushes, presumably looking for drugs that the two hippies had stashed; "I had long hair and a headband back then," Woz remembers. Finding no drugs, the cops turned their attention to the blue box. What was it, they wanted to know? It was an electronic music synthesizer, Wozniak said. He gave a demo of a few tones. What's the orange button for, the cops asked? Unfortunately for their story, the orange button was the one that generated 2,600 Hz and it didn't sound very musical. "Calibration," Jobs replied.

Woz and Jobs explained that their car had broken down. The cops told them to get in the back of their patrol car and they would go "check out the car story." As Woz put it, "In the back seat of a cop car, you know where you're going eventually: to jail." As the cop car pulled out, one of the police officers handed Woz back his electronic synthesizer. "A guy named Moog beat you to it," he said. Apparently the two Steves weren't going to jail after all.

It wasn't long before the more business savvy of the duo smelled an opportunity: selling blue boxes. "Steve Jobs suggested we could sell it for $170 or so, he came up with the price pretty early in there," Wozniak recalls. Before long the two were peddling blue boxes in the dorms at Berkeley. Their sales technique was inspired. They would knock on random dorm room doors and ask for an imaginary person with a made-up name. When the confused occupant would respond "Who?" they would say, "You know, the guy who makes all the free phone calls." Depending on the occupant's reaction they might add, "You know, he has the blue boxes." If the person they were talking to lit up and got excited, they knew they had a solid sales prospect who wasn't likely to turn them in.

In addition to going door to door they had another sales channel through a random phone phreak acquaintance in Los Angeles. Wozniak and Jobs had dialed into a loop-around circuit in southern California one day and found themselves talking to a young teenager named Adam Schoolsky. Their friendship blossomed. Schoolsky, better known as Johnny Bagel in Los Angeles phone phreak circles, had been introduced to the hobby by LA phreak Al Diamond and his telephone joke lines. As it happened, Schoolsky had an older friend who was well connected in Hollywood. Through this connection—and Schoolsky's help in assembling and manufacturing the boxes—Jobs and Wozniak found themselves handling a couple of "quantity orders," that is, orders for perhaps ten boxes at a time. Many of these wound up in the hands of various Hollywood stars and glitterati.

"Sales went on through the summer," Wozniak recalls, but eventually they dwindled off. He had a job at Hewlett-Packard and it took a lot of time to build a box, Woz says—it worked out to a "low paid salary." That fall Jobs started at Reed College and lost interest in the business. In all, Wozniak guesses, they sold maybe thirty or forty boxes; Jobs remembers it as more like a hundred.

Every blue box that Woz made and sold came with a unique guarantee: a small piece of paper was tucked inside the box and bore the words, "He's got the whole world in his hands." If one of his boxes ever failed to work and it came back to him with the little note inside, he would repair it, free of charge. Offering a guarantee on an illegal product in such a quirky way appealed to Wozniak's sense of humor. "It's kind of strange in itself, it's kind of unusual, but I felt it was worth the joke," he says.

Between 1973 and 1975 several of Oaf Tobar and Berkeley Blue's customers were caught red-handed with their blue boxes. The boxes wound up at the FBI Laboratory where they were disassembled and analyzed. On the whole, the FBI has never been known for its sense of humor. In each case, Woz's little bit of paper with its inscription—sometimes handwritten, sometimes typed—was carefully noted in the FBI's report and photographs. The feds knew that this tied the boxes together in some way, but fortunately for Woz and Jobs—and perhaps for the rest of the world—the FBI never linked the blue boxes to the two of them.

Like most phone phreaks, Woz spent time exploring the network, using his blue box to figure out how the telephone system worked. But he soon found another use for it: pranks.

Wozniak had always loved pranks, especially clever, high-tech ones. For example, his first year in college he built a small circuit that jammed televisions, which he would use to annoy his dormmates by surreptitiously messing with the reception on their shared TV set. When the TV went fuzzy, eventually one of the people in the room could be counted upon to get up and try to fix things. That era's TV sets had adjustment controls for fine tuning that you could fiddle with, and many TVs had rabbit ear antennas whose reception could vary quite a bit depending on how the antenna was oriented and where people and other objects were in the room. As soon as his victim was in an awkward position—say, with his hand directly in front of the TV screen—Wozniak would stop jamming the signal and the picture would clear up. The other students would shout at the victim to hold that position since the TV apparently liked it that way. Woz recalls one evening's particularly successful jamming prank: "The dozen or so students stayed for the second half hour of *Mission Impossible* with the guy's hand over the middle of the TV!" Later, when Steve Jobs was graduating from high school, Woz and Jobs and a friend worked hard on a graduation present for Homestead High School. It was a large banner featuring a middle-finger salute with the words "Best Wishes"; the idea was that it would be unrolled dramatically and anonymously during the graduation ceremony. Sadly, another student discovered it and it was taken down before it could be unfurled.

His blue box, Wozniak realized, had great potential for practical jokes. For reasons he can't quite recall he got it in his head one day that they should try calling the pope. Using his blue box he managed to route his call to the Vatican. "In this heavy accent I announced that I was Henry Kissinger calling on behalf of President Nixon. I said, 'Ve are at de summit meeting in Moscow, and we need to talk to de pope.'" The Vatican responded that the pope was sleeping but that they would send someone to wake him. Woz arranged to call back in an hour.

Woz recalls, "Well, an hour later I called back and she said, 'Okay, we will put the bishop on, who will be the translator.' So I told him, still in that heavy accent, 'Dees is Mr. Kissinger.' And he said, 'Listen, I just spoke to Mr. Kissinger an hour ago.' You see, they had checked out my story and had called the real Kissinger in Moscow."

Of course, Wozniak wasn't the only phone phreak with a love of pranks. Charlie Pyne and company at Harvard had used their blue box to try to reach the president of Mexico at two o'clock in the morning on a similar lark some ten years earlier. As suggested by the slightly misspelled Spanish in the Fine Arts 13 classified ad of the *Harvard Crimson*—"El presidente no esta aqui asora; que lastima"—they did not succeed. But the phone phreak prank that generated the most publicity and consternation occurred on November 10, 1974. Readers of the next day's *Los Angeles Times* were introduced to the gag via the reassuring headline, "Santa Barbara Is Still OK; A-Blast Report Just Hoax." Callers to Santa Barbara, California, the day before received no such reassurance. Rather, people calling in to Santa Barbara from out of town found their calls routed to someone who identified themselves either as an emergency operator or as a Marine Corps officer. In either case, the caller was told, "There has been a nuclear explosion in Santa Barbara and all the telephone lines are out." The prank lasted for only thirty minutes, reported the *Times,* "but the effects continued throughout the day, with alarmed calls to General Telephone Co. and to Santa Barbara police from as far away as Florida and Alaska, demanding details of the 'tragedy' and asking, in some cases, if World War III had begun."

This horrifying prank was the work of a pair of Los Angeles–area phone phreaks. The hack they used to pull it off was the result of a bug that the phone company called "simultaneous seizure"; it could be exploited in a couple of different ways. One way involved old-school step-by-step switching equipment, which was still quite prevalent in the telephone network of the 1970s. Under the right conditions, if two separate calls were made simultaneously, step-by-step equipment could become jammed partway through dialing the calls. In essence, two different sets of switching equipment in the central office would both attempt to seize the same circuit at the same time, hence the term. The upshot was that the two calls would be inadvertently connected. This was an extremely rare occurrence—the conditions had to be just right and, after all, very few things truly occur simultaneously in this world. When it did happen, it wasn't that big a deal. The two callers would be surprised to find themselves connected—halfway through dialing a number—to somebody they didn't call; they would curse the phone company and its incompetence and then both would hang up and try again. The system would reset and all would be well.

But what if one of the people didn't hang up?

Because of a quirk in the step-by-step switching system, the person who didn't hang up would be left in limbo, the call halfway complete. And there the call would stay, until eventually some new call would come in and attempt to seize the circuit in use by the first call. Once again, the two calls would be connected. How long it took for this to happen depended on exactly where in the switch the call failed and how many other calls needed to go through that portion of the switching equipment.

And though it's true that most things don't occur simultaneously in nature, sometimes you can stack the deck in your favor. What if, for example, you had two telephone lines and connected them both to the same rotary dial? This would take a bit of electrical wiring, of course, but when you spun that dial you would be sending dial pulses into two separate telephone lines in the same step-by-step switching office at exactly the same time. It might take a few tries, but using this method you were likely to succeed in jamming a step-by-step switch.

Another place that simultaneous seizure could occur was on the long-distance network, when two long-distance tandems simultaneously seized the same long-distance trunk to make a call to the other. For example, imagine a long-distance trunk line between New York and Los Angeles; this is a bidirectional trunk, so it can be used for calls in either direction. If the switching equipment in both New York and Los Angeles happen to grab this trunk line to make a call to the other, and do so at the same time, two unrelated calls will be thrown together. Phone phreaks could cause this situation to happen by making a long-distance call and then whistling off with 2,600 Hz and continuing to send 2,600 Hz down the line, thus mimicking the idle line condition. At some point the remote tandem would route a call back to the phone phreak who could then prank the hapless caller.

Once you had jammed the switch, you could lie in wait for incoming calls. If you were a bit clever, you could influence what part of the switch you jammed and thus what types of incoming calls you would be getting. For example, phone phreak Mark Bernay—who had had nothing to do with the Santa Barbara prank, it should be pointed out—was fond of jamming incoming directory assistance calls. Sometimes he would prank the callers, but more often he would actually look up telephone numbers for them, just like a directory assistance operator would, leafing through LA-area phone books as quickly as he could. "We would

sit there trying to look things up fast enough to satisfy the customers," he remembers. "It was really hard to do. I became very
impressed with directory assistance!"

One of the pair of phreaks who pulled off the Santa Barbara
A-bomb pranks recalled that they stayed on the lines about half
an hour, telling callers that their calls to Santa Barbara had been
intercepted due to a nuclear explosion. "We didn't even know
what we were going to do—it was all impromptu. . . . It was for
the reaction, just to see how people would react." In retrospect,
he said, "It's not something I would ever want to repeat again."

Perhaps the ultimate phone phreak prank belongs to Captain
Crunch and a friend of his, though their material came courtesy of
Johnny Carson's joke writers. The year 1973 had been a rough one
for the United States, what with the ongoing Watergate scandal and
the energy crisis and gas rationing. Carson, the host of the popular
Tonight show, watched by millions of people every evening, joked on
TV in late December about the latest crisis facing the United States:
"You know, we've got all sorts of shortages these days. But have
you heard the latest? I'm not kidding. I saw it in the paper. There's
a shortage of toilet paper." The next day Americans rushed to buy
toilet tissue, emptying shelves in stores. Carson later apologized
for the joke and clarified that there was no toilet paper shortage,
except that now it seemed as if there actually were one, since people
could see for themselves that store shelves were bare. The rumor
took hold and it was months before the situation worked itself out.

With that as background, Crunch's prank began with a call to
a particular toll-free 800 number. Back in the 1970s, 800 numbers mapped to regular telephone numbers. In fact, each prefix
within the 800 system translated to a particular area code. For
example, 800-421 mapped to area code 213 in Los Angeles, 800-
227 mapped to area code 415 in the San Francisco Bay Area, and
800-424 mapped to area code 202 in Washington, D.C.

Now, if you're a phone phreak and want to scan for interesting
numbers, what better place to dig through than Washington,
D.C.? There are only ten thousand numbers to dial and it doesn't

cost you anything to call them—they're toll-free, after all—and it should be a natural hunting ground for interesting things. Before long the phone phreaks had discovered a toll-free number that went to the White House: (800) 424-9337. Draper believed this was the "CIA crisis line," that is, the CIA's hotline to the White House, and he claims that he was able to eavesdrop on it using his blue box. One evening, Draper says, he and a friend were listening to this line and, through their wiretapping, learned that the code name for the president was "Olympus."

"Now we had the code word that would summon Nixon to the phone," Draper says. He and his friend wasted no time in dialing the 800 number, though he claims they were careful to first route their call through several tandems in order to make it difficult to trace back.

"9337," said the person who answered the phone.

"Olympus, please!" Draper's friend said.

"One moment, sir."

About a minute later, Draper recalls, a man who sounded "remarkably like Nixon" asked, "What's going on?"

"We have a crisis here in Los Angeles!" Draper's friend replied.

"What's the nature of the crisis?" the voice asked.

In the most serious voice he could summon, Draper's friend responded, "We're out of toilet paper, sir!"

"*Who is this!*" Draper recalls the Nixon-like voice demanding. Draper and his friend quickly hung up.

"I think this was one of the funniest pranks," Draper says, "and I don't think that Woz would even come close to this one. I think he was jealous for a long time."

Sixteen

THE STORY OF A WAR

NATIONAL PUBLIC RADIO host Jim Russell's authoritative baritone delivered the ominous news. "This is the story of a war," he intoned. "This war finds small bands of guerrillas attacking an enormous conventional army. While the large conventional army has been quick to publicize its victories, there is still great uncertainty about who is winning."

NPR listeners could be forgiven for thinking this was yet another story about the Vietnam War. In January 1973 Vietnam was on the minds of Americans everywhere; after on-again, off-again peace talks with the North Vietnamese, President Nixon had just ordered a massive resumption of B-52 bombing raids over the Christmas holidays.

The story wasn't about Vietnam, however, it was about phone phreaks. "The Telephone Company You're Dialing Has Been Temporarily Disconnected" was an hour-long special featuring the likes of Al Bell, Al Gilbertson, and Joe Engressia. Over jangly background music made up of MF tones—a song called the "MF Boogie," composed on an electronic organ during a conference call by the musical phone phreak Kim Lingo—the program gave its listeners a thorough, if slightly exaggerated, introduction to phone phreaking. It covered blue and black boxes, international dialing, conference calls, toll-free loop arounds, the *YIPL* newsletter, phone phreak conventions, Captain Crunch's arrest and conviction, and even early computer hacking.

For balance, it included counterpoint from Joe Doherty, AT&T's director of corporate security—the man NPR described as the "ranking general in Ma Bell's war effort against the phone phreaks." Doherty admitted that much of the phreaking problem was a self-inflicted wound. "The candor with which we have published technical information through the years, especially the early years, as to how the system works has come back to plague us to some extent," he said. But he also emphasized that the game had changed: "At one time, to be perfectly frank, we were, in my view, somewhat overly lenient, in that we would just caution these people, slap them on the wrist and give them a deterrent interview. We did not prosecute to any great extent. We have changed that policy. We are prosecuting as a rule now, rather than an exception." In addition, the network would eventually be modified to make phone phreaking obsolete. "It's a tradeoff between the cost of prevention and what we're losing," he said. "We are restudying the most economical way to modify the network at the present time."

The NPR program seemed to underscore the fact that phone phreaking had reached a tipping point. Thanks to the *Esquire* article, NPR, and other media coverage, coupled with the rise of the New Left and the hippie-Yippie "rip off culture," phone phreaking—at least the sort of phreaking that was interested primarily in making free phone calls—was spreading to the mainstream. The host of the NPR program went so far as to suggest that there were "tens of millions" of potential phone phreaks due to widespread hatred of the phone company.

But it was too soon to count Ma Bell out. Its newly acquired penchant for prosecution, coupled with improved technology that was proliferating throughout the network, would give the phreaks a run for their money.

One of these bits of technology had been invented more than twenty-five years earlier. On a workbench in Murray Hill, New Jersey, in 1947 three Bell Labs researchers—Walter Brattain, John Bardeen, and William Shockley—had lashed together a setup that looked about as unlikely as Alexander Graham Bell's original telephone back in 1876. It looked a bit like a high school science fair project, to be honest. It was a plastic wedge with a sharp edge that was pressed against a small chunk of germanium. Trapped between the wedge and the germanium were two small strips of gold foil.

Three tiny wires came away from the thing. One, attached directly to the base of the germanium, was a control input. If you applied a voltage to this wire, electric current could flow between the other two wires connected to the gold foil strips. This odd action happened because germanium was neither fish nor fowl. It was a semiconductor: not quite a conductor but not quite an insulator either. And though its semiconductor properties were not well understood at first, the practical implication was immediately clear. The little widget could be used both as an electronic switch and as an amplifier, just like a vacuum tube or a relay. But unlike vacuum tubes and relays, this thing could be turned on or off almost instantaneously. It was tiny, it had no moving parts, it consumed little power, and it didn't wear out.

The researchers called it a transistor, and less than ten years later the trio would be awarded the Nobel Prize in physics for its invention.

It was not lost on the engineers at Bell Labs that the transistor might be the ideal thing to form the fabric of a new telephone switching system, the technology the company needed to replace the old step-by-step and crossbar switches. Indeed, the first proposals within Bell Labs for a transistor-based telephone switching system came as early as 1952. Years earlier Strowger switches, with their rotors and pawls, had begun to replace operators who used plugs and jacks to make connections between pairs of telephone wires. They were in turn replaced by relays and crossbar switches. Now transistors would replace these electromechanical contrivances. No longer would telephone company central offices be filled with the clicks and clacks of physical switching as calls were placed; transistors would silently and electronically connect pairs of wires to one another. This new approach was dubbed "electronic switching."

Bell Labs' first foray into electronic switching began in 1954. For a variety of technical reasons, the transistor itself would not be used as the electronic device that would actually connect pairs of telephone wires together. Instead, transistors would make up the logic—the brains—that controlled the switches; in this role transistors were replacing the relays that had been used as the control logic in the crossbar system. But by 1955 the engineers working on the prototype electronic switching system at Bell Labs had run into problems. The control circuits had grown complex and unwieldy. Worse, every time the requirements changed—and given that they were building a pie-in-the-sky prototype system, requirements changed frequently—the engineers would have to go back and redesign surprisingly large chunks of the hardwired control logic.

During the summer of 1955 one of the Bell Labs engineers read an article that described a newfangled thing called a digital computer. He was "struck by the similarity of what the computer could do and the actions required of the [telephone switch] control circuits." Within a few months Bell Labs had abandoned its approach of using transistors to create hardwired logic to control the new telephone switch. Instead, researchers would use transistors to build a programmable digital computer. The computer and its program would control the telephone switch. They christened this concept stored program control, or SPC. If it worked, SPC promised a much more flexible, capable telephone system. New features could be added quickly and telephone switches could be upgraded simply by reprogramming them, instead of by rewiring or replacing physical hardware. Moreover, they hoped, such switches would be cheaper in the long run: computer-controlled electronic switching systems could serve more telephone lines than their electromechanical brethren, which in turn meant fewer central offices would be needed.

It was a risky approach. Bell Labs had never built a computer before and its engineers had never written a line of computer code. Yet now they were proposing to stake the development of the company's next-generation switching system on this new and unproven architecture.

Development took years, culminating finally in the 1960 trial of the world's first electronic telephone switching system—a trial that was fully a year behind schedule. Known simply as "Morris" after Morris, Illinois, the city that hosted it, it served only a few hundred telephone lines.

Now, at some fundamental level, computers haven't changed that much. At their most basic, computers still consist of central processing units (CPUs) and memories. The CPU executes instructions, that is, simple low-level commands that tell it what to do. These instructions direct the CPU to do things such as load a value from memory, store a value to memory, perform an arithmetic or logic operation, compare the result of an operation to some other result, or branch—execute some other set of instructions—depending on some previous result.

Today if you want a computer you can buy one for a few hundred dollars. Your computer will probably have a central processing unit—a processor—that executes somewhere between one billion and three billion instructions per second. This is made possible by about a billion transistors on a piece of silicon about the size of a postage stamp. Your computer will probably have several gigabytes of memory, that is, more than 10 billion bits, the zeros and ones that make up binary data. It will likely take less power than a pair of 100-watt lightbulbs and be smaller than a toaster.

In contrast, the computer that controlled the Morris switch consisted of twelve thousand individual transistors connected to one another by a spider's web of wires. It executed its programs at a then blazing three hundred thousand instructions per second—in other words, about five thousand times slower than a typical PC today. For reliability, Morris had two complete CPUs running in sync with each other. If one detected an error in its computations, it would take itself out of operation and pass control to its twin, ideally never dropping a telephone call in the process. The entire program to operate the Morris telephone switch took about fifty thousand instructions, including things such as maintenance tasks; the portion used for typical phone calls was smaller. This number was large by the standards of the day but is tiny now. Microsoft's popular word-processing program Word is about one hundred times larger, and that's not counting the gigantic Windows operating system.

Morris's program memory—the place where its programs were stored—looked like something out of a 1950s science fiction movie. Called the "flying spot store," it consisted of four ten-inch by twelve-inch glass photographic plates with thousands of tiny black dots on them. A cathode ray tube—like an old-school television picture tube—moved a spot of light across the plate. As the beam of light flew across the dots, lenses and photodetectors decided whether they were seeing a "1" (a transparent spot) or a "0" (a black spot that blocked the light), enabling the bits of Morris's program to be read out. Morris's data memory—the "barrier grid store"—was similarly Frankensteinian, using electron beams generated by cathode ray tubes to deposit charges on an insulating plate. These charges could be changed on the fly to store 0s or 1s of binary data. The individual electronic components that Morris was built out of, such as transistors and diodes, were often designed in-house by Bell Labs and produced by Western Electric, AT&T's manufacturing subsidiary. In total, Morris consisted of four rows of metal cabinets chock-full of components; each row was about seven feet tall by two feet deep. Oh, and thirty-five feet long.

Perhaps the most amazing thing about Morris was that it actually worked. Fundamentally, Morris demonstrated two things. First, the stored program control concept was viable, and a computer could in fact control a telephone switching system. Second, however, it demonstrated just how much more there was to be done before electronic switching was ready for prime time.

Bell Labs folded the hard-won knowledge from the Morris trial into an effort to develop a production-quality electronic switching system (ESS). It took five more years of hard work; a senior Bell Labs employee described the ESS development effort as a "traumatic experience." But the new system, called—naturally—the No. 1 ESS, went live in 1965 in Succasunna, New Jersey. Though the No. 1 ESS differed in many ways from Morris, it retained the basic concepts of stored program control and dual processors for reliability. By the end of 1967 some eighteen No. 1 ESS switches had been deployed throughout the network, with many more to follow in the 1970s.

Development of a commercial-grade electronic switching system had taken ten calendar years, a staggering four thousand man-years of engineering effort, and cost $500 million—more than $3.5 billion in today's dollars. It was a perfect example of the sort of thing that the Bell System could do, thanks to its being a regulated monopoly with a guaranteed profit and no competitors to speak of. In the words of the former AT&T historian Sheldon Hochheiser, "Absent competition, Bell Labs and AT&T took the time to get an innovation right (as an engineer would define right)." Or, as one observer of the ESS effort put it, they could "take the problem and trample it to death."

Deploying computer technology throughout the network would take still more time and money, but the deployment was inevitable; henceforth, computers and telephone switches would be joined at the hip. Even old telephone switches weren't safe from the computer revolution, not even the venerable 4A crossbar switch, the workhorse tandem of the long-distance network. Designed in the 1950s, 4As were purely electromechanical affairs, with vacuum tubes and relays and mechanical card translator systems that looked up routing information by shining light through steel punch cards. AT&T set about upgrading these switches, replacing their relay-wired control logic with computers to allow the switch to make faster, smarter decisions. As early as 1969, just four years after the debut of the No. 1 ESS, Bell started upgrading 4As with new brains. Called the SPC No. 1A, these brains were essentially clones of the computers used in the No. 1 ESS. It would be the final evolution of Bell Labs' cherished concept of common control—the idea that the smarts of the telephone switch should be separate from whatever mechanism did the actual switching. By 1976 more than 132 of the 4As had been upgraded to computer control.

From the telephone company's perspective, the No. 1 ESS was eventually quite successful, though not without some initial teething problems. It was physically smaller than electromechanical telephone switches, offered vastly more features (such as call waiting and conference calling), and in the end cost less and could handle more calls. As far as phone phreaks were concerned, the No. 1 ESS was a mixed bag. On the plus side, these ESS installations often had more trunks to more places, and that meant more routes to explore. And No. 1 ESS had loop-around circuits that didn't supe, meaning that they were free calls from anywhere in the country. Finally, No. 1 ESSes usually came with something called a touch-tone demonstrator. Believe it or not, there was a time when most telephone lines supported only rotary dialing; special circuitry had to be installed at the central office to enable touch-tone dialing on a given line, and this created a sales problem for the phone company. If you were a telephone installer and wanted to convince Mrs. Smith to upgrade her phone from rotary to touch tone (for which the telephone company charged an extra monthly fee), you had no way to show this new service to her, since her line probably didn't support touch-tone dialing. A touch-tone demonstrator was a number that an installer could call with a rotary phone that would then connect to a second line, one that had touch tone enabled. This way the installer could demonstrate to Mrs. Smith how convenient touch tone was by using it to dial a call with a touch-tone phone, thereby closing the sale. Since there was no password on a touch-tone demonstrator, anyone could use it to make free calls as soon as the number leaked out.

On the minus side for phone phreaks, the No. 1 ESS rendered black boxes obsolete. Mostly black boxes didn't work at all with them, and even if you could get them to work a little bit you were limited to about thirty-eight seconds worth of conversation before you were cut off. And although the No. 1 ESS didn't make blue boxing impossible, it did make it more difficult. After you whistled

off a long-distance call on a No. 1 ESS you had about eleven seconds to key the number you wanted to call on your blue box and
hope that the network put your call through and the person you
were calling answered the phone within that time; if that did not
happen, you'd wind up listening to dial tone.

If the potential impact of the transistor was not lost on the
Bell Labs engineers in the 1950s, neither was it lost on some of
the phone phreaks in the 1970s. "Bill Acker said something so
prophetic," Joe Engressia recalls. "I think it was in about 1970 or
'71. I didn't really believe it or understand it at the time. He said,
right now, we have more control over the phone system than we
ever will have again."

Acker was right. As the computer revolution began to pro-
liferate through the network, the network began to change. It
didn't happen all at once. Slowly, over the course of the decade,
the network began to homogenize. For example, a "precise tone
plan" would make sure that things like ringing and busy signals
sounded the same in every city throughout the network. And
the various bugs the phreaks had counted on in the telephone
switches began to disappear. But it was a slow process, and there
was enough older installed equipment throughout the network to
provide years more fun for the phreaks. The playground hadn't
been shut down just yet but it was certainly changing.

One of the new toys that the kids brought to the playground was
featured in *YIPL*'s February 1973 issue: the red box. Keeping up
with the Bell System's new, increasingly computerized network,
the red box was a new twist on an old hack. For many years pay
phones had had actual physical bells in them that communicated
to the operator how much money the customer had deposited:
a nickel was one *ding,* a dime two *dings,* and a quarter was *dong.*
When you needed to make a long-distance call at a pay phone,
the operator would tell you how much money to deposit and
then would listen to—and count—the *dings* and *dongs* as the coins
you deposited struck the appropriate bells; imagine the patience

required of an operator when a customer wanted to make a two-dollar long-distance call using forty nickels.

For as long as pay phones had been making noises like these, people had been figuring out ways to mimic the noises to avoid paying for calls. One low-tech approach required two pay phones right next to each other, a common enough setup back in the day. You'd deposit your money in the next-door neighbor pay phone while holding the handset of your pay phone up to it so the operator could still hear the sounds of the bells; since you weren't actually making a call on the other pay phone, it would return your money once you were finished. A higher-tech approach that came into vogue in the late 1960s used a portable tape recorder to play a recording of the bells for the operator.

One of the problems with the dings and dongs, of course, was that they were labor intensive for the phone company; a live operator, after all, had to sit there and count bells. Paving the way for automation, AT&T began introducing pay phones that went *beep* instead of *ding*. The beeps were electronically generated tones: one beep for a nickel, two beeps for a dime, and five shorter beeps for a quarter. The new beeps weren't any more secure than the dings and dongs but they had the advantage that they were easier to generate electronically—no bulky bells required—and, eventually, they could be detected by a computer instead of a human being.

Of course, the fact that the beeps were easier for AT&T to generate electronically meant that they were easier for phone phreaks to generate electronically, too, and that's where the red box came in. The red box was simply a tone generator, producing one, two, or five beeps of the appropriate duration. To start with, it was a single tone—2,200 Hz—but later AT&T mixed in a second tone, 1,700 Hz. The phone phreaks quickly modified their red boxes to follow suit.

The red box, like the black box, really had no use in exploring the telephone network. It was, plain and simple, a way to make free phone calls. "To me, a red box was unethical," says Seattle phone phreak Bob Gudgel, "because it was actually stealing quarters and dimes and nickels"—in contrast to a blue box, which actually had some intellectual purpose. Indeed, *YIPL* was not particularly popular among the network explorer–type phone phreaks. Some of this was intellectual snobbery. They felt that *YIPL* catered to the lower echelons of phone phreaks, kids who didn't know very much and were only able to follow the instructions of others. But the other problem was both larger and more practical, and had to do with the size of *YIPL's* mailing list. If some cool network feature, say a conference bridge or something, made it into the pages of *YIPL,* the next month it would have thousands of people calling it, and the month after that it would be gone.

So while the network explorer phone phreaks may not have had much use for *YIPL* or the red box, the fact was they were rapidly becoming the minority. Indeed, the phrase "phone phreak" was becoming synonymous with someone interested in making free phone calls. There seemed to be a lot more interest in beating the system—whatever the system was—than in exploring it.

YIPL understood its audience and their love of free things. By August 1973 it had changed its name: it was now *TAP,* the Technological American Party. As "Al Bell" wrote in the introduction to that issue, "No fancy excuses: we changed our name because we want people to know where we really are and what we hope to become. Technological American Party is rapidly becoming a people's warehouse of technological information, and a name like Youth International Party Line simply didn't ring a bell, even if you were trying to find out how to contact the phone phreaks, except of course for the Party Line. We've been receiving so much information lately about gas and electric meters, locks, even chemistry, that a name change is definitely in order. We seriously doubt that phones will cease to be our main interest, but it really isn't fair to ignore the rest of what science has to offer."

YIPL—er, *TAP*—didn't know it but it had dodged a bullet. At the urging of Pacific Northwest Bell, the FBI had investigated the newsletter in 1974 but found nothing that it could be prosecuted for.

Indeed, the FBI learned, "the legal department of [New York Tele-phone] has gone as high as the N. Y. State Attorney General's office in Albany but was told that no action could be taken against 'TAP' for to do so would constitute a violation of 'freedom of the press.'"

Not every group that wanted to publicize phone fraud tech-niques was located in a state that shared New York's love of freedom of the press. For example, in 1974 Michigan Bell had a misdemeanor criminal complaint filed against the Detroit un-derground newspaper *Fifth Estate* for publishing "Taming the Telephone Beast"; essentially a reprint of the *Ramparts* article, it also gave the details of the 1974 telephone credit card code.

Then there was the *Telephone Electronics Line* newsletter, or *TEL*. Started in 1974 and run out of Los Angeles, *TEL* was the creation of Jack Kranyak, whose company, Teletronics of America, also sold electronics plans via mail order. For $6 per year, *TEL* subscribers could read something like a more technical and less political ver-sion of *TAP*, one focused solely on topics telephonic. "How to Call Long Distance for Free," "Modern Phone Phreaking," "Detection: How to Avoid It," "Overseas Dialing Techniques," and "Trash-ing the Phone Company—A Look at Ma Bell's 'Garbage'" were some of the articles published over the course of seven months. Considering the provisions of Section 502.7 of the California Penal Code—the law that made it illegal to publish plans or instruc-tions for telephone fraud, which Pacific Telephone had brandished when it had suppressed the *Ramparts* article—it was a miracle that *TEL* lasted as long as it did. After its eighth issue, Teletronics, Kranyak, and several others associated with the newsletter were sued by Pacific Telephone in 1975. The telephone company won, obtaining an injunction against *TEL*. Under pain of a $100,000 penalty, Kranyak and company were prohibited from publishing any further information about defrauding the telephone system. In addition, Teletronics was required to turn its mailing list over to the telephone company. Soon some eight thousand people—both former subscribers to *TEL* and people who had just requested a catalog of plans from Teletronics—received an odd note from

Pacific Telephone in the mail. "Dear Telephone User," it began. "Your name appeared on a list (provided under court order) of subscribers, or potential subscribers, to material previously published by Teletronics Company of America." It went on to remind the Telephone User that it was a violation of state and federal laws to steal telephone service or to "provide information to any person which is useful for such purpose." It concluded, "Accordingly, you are urged to destroy any and all written material or device you may have which may violate any of these laws."

One recipient of this missive wrote a letter to the editor of *Radio Electronics,* a hobbyist magazine in which Teletronics had run ads. The Pacific Telephone letter, he wrote, "would appear to me to be saying that dissemination or mere possession of information which *could be used* for disapproved purposes is a criminal offense." He concluded, "I am committed to the position that *curiosity alone* is sufficient 'need to know' and that it is a fundamental freedom that criminality must be judged by what an individual *does,* not upon the knowledge which he has acquired or what he *could* do with it."

Phone shenanigans, it turned out, weren't confined to the shores of the United States. In January 1973 London's *Sunday Times* ran a front-page exposé charging that employees of the British Post Office, which ran the nation's telephone system, had installed special circuits—so-called fiddles—inside telephone company central offices that allowed those in the know to make free or reduced-rate long-distance or overseas calls. The article claimed that at least seventy-five telephone central offices had been fiddled and the cost of the theft was almost 2 million pounds each year. A post office spokesman described it as "serious national problem" and a "nationwide telephone fraud that has cost a vast but unknown sum in lost revenues."

That was all internal fraud, however, even if widespread and headline grabbing. England's first big, public run-in with real live phone phreaks came later that year, in October 1973, with the trial of nineteen young men at Old Bailey, London's central criminal court. Arrested at a phone phreak tea party at a flat in London a year earlier, the phreaks included Oxford and Cambridge graduates and the prosecutor in the case allowed that they were all "men of intellectual stature." The charges went back to 1968 when their fun and games began and covered a variety of offenses, including conspiracy, fraud, and theft of the government's electricity. Unlike the fiddlers within the British Post Office, these gentlemen were in fact network explorers with little or no interest in fraud. As was revealed at trial, on the day of the tea party the phreaks had made a total of 222 calls using a variety of techniques, including the use of ten different "bleeper boxes." Of these calls, exactly three went to live human beings, and those three had all been made legally. The trial went on for more than a month. In the end, charges were dismissed against one defendant, ten pleaded guilty partway through the trial, and eight were acquitted. To the acquitted the judge remarked, "Your trial is over and now I can congratulate you. I never did think you were dishonest, and I never said so." But, he added, "Do exercise some care and judgment in the future because men of your distinction ought never find themselves in the dock at the Central Criminal Court."

Back in the United States, phreaking continued its push into mainstream society. If anything, in fact, it overshot and landed among the stars. In 1974, for example, rock star Ike Turner was arrested along with three others for using a blue box from a recording studio in Los Angeles—a blue box that was later said to have come from Steve Wozniak and Steve Jobs.

Then there was the case of Bernard Cornfeld, the flamboyant financier who had built a $2.5 billion hedge fund called International Overseas Investors that eventually ran afoul of securities regulators; he was charged with fraud and spent almost a year in a Swiss prison until he was eventually acquitted. Cornfeld lived a lavish lifestyle, surrounded by women as he jetted between his castle in France and his mansion in Beverly Hills. But in January 1975 his Los Angeles mansion was raided by the FBI and his secretary was charged with blue box fraud. "Unfortunately [for the FBI] they just missed the shooting of a *Playboy* center spread," he joked to a reporter. Cornfeld himself, cracking fewer jokes this time, was arrested on the same charges about six months later. In all, FBI agents seized five blue boxes from Cornfeld's mansion, four of which, according to FBI files, had Wozniak and Jobs's telltale "He's got the whole world in his hands" notes inside them.

Then Lainie Kazan—singer, actress, and a former *Playboy* model—pleaded guilty to blue box charges in November 1975 and was fined, ordered to make restitution to the phone company, and placed on eighteen months' probation. The blue box suppliers? Woz and Jobs.

Finally, in December of that year, police said, Robert Cummings—an Emmy Award–winning actor with more than fifty movies to his credit, including *Dial M for Murder*—was arrested in Seattle with blue box in hand. It was like a little celebrity blue box crime wave, a good chunk of it from the two Steves and their Los Angeles connections.

Its movement into mainstream society had changed the culture of phreaking once already, shifting it away from curiosity and into the realm of outright thievery. But now, even among the hobbyist network-explorer types, it began changing again. In some ways the NPR announcer had been right—it really was the story of a war and like any war, this one was not without its spies and paranoia. Informants seemed to be everywhere, or so many phone phreaks believed. This notion began to change the way the phone phreaks interacted with one another.

The first evidence of this was the breakup of the phone phreaks into smaller and more isolated groups made up of people who knew each other personally. Of the many such groups across the country, one of them centered on David Condon—the legendary Davy Crockett, the man who, with the help of his girlfriends and his Cat and Canary Bird Call Flute, had tricked long-distance operators back in the 1950s into making free calls for him from Oak Ridge, Tennessee. Now, almost twenty years later, in 1973, Condon had moved to California and found himself the nucleus of a cell of half a dozen phone phreaks, mostly students and staff from UC

Berkeley. Several were gifted electrical engineers and one was also a talented chef. Together they spent many evenings in a house on Colby Street in north Oakland exploring the network with fancy blue boxes after equally fancy meals. "We'd cook dinner and then we'd play until the wee hours of the morning. It was a real circus!" Condon says. They delighted in finding new ways to outfox the network, including an unlikely but successful scheme that involved running high-voltage electricity directly into the telephone line to confuse the switching equipment.

But the cuisine and calls were served with a healthy side dish of paranoia. Although Condon's group had occasional interactions with other phreaks—Bill Acker was someone Condon respected and trusted and occasionally talked to—they kept to themselves as much as possible. They avoided conference calls and loop arounds, preferring to do their own research rather than trade information with people who might be informants. And as a rule universally agreed upon within their group, they avoided John Draper and his friends like the plague. "I tell you," Condon says, "Draper was the kiss of death. He was asking for it, he was looking for trouble." Well, Condon admits, perhaps Draper wasn't really looking to get caught, but he was so boastful and careless and public about everything he did that he might as well have been. "He was very flagrant," says Condon.

A similar cell formed on the East Coast around the same time. Called Group Bell it included, among several others, New York phreaks Evan Doorbell and Ben Decibel.★ Yet there was one New York phone phreak it specifically did not include: Bill Acker. "They explicitly excluded me, because they felt I was not going to keep their secrets," Acker remembers. "My exclusion from Group Bell was really Ben Decibel saying, 'This guy Bill is a little too free with who he trusts.'"

Being excluded hurt Acker's feelings, especially after having believed he'd been alone in the wilderness for so many years. It

★The pseudonym he went by at the time.

"was just nasty," he says. Still, he is not without sympathy for the underlying problem. The gems that the phone phreaks found in the network tended to be lost as soon as they became widely known —just look at the 2111 and 052 conferences. The more people who knew about a particular vulnerability, the more likely it was that someone from the phone company would find out about it and fix it, and possibly get them all in trouble in the process. "I think if I found something that was really cool but that obviously would go away if word of it got around, I think I'd be a little more selective about who I told," Acker says. Similarly, he says, he was perfectly willing to keep something confidential if someone asked him to. Not so Joe Engressia. Acker says, "He didn't want any part of that. His attitude was, nobody's going to put restrictions on anything I do." Information wants to be free, the saying goes, but it turns out that certain information also wants to be kept secret. And therein lies the tension. The more people you knew and talked to, the more you were likely to learn interesting things, but it was also more likely that you might get caught or the cool things you knew about would go away. "It was a struggle," Acker recalls.

In retrospect, perhaps it was the phone company that should have been paranoid. Some phreaks were becoming bolder in their quest to understand the network. One such phreak in New York recalls making friends with a fellow named George,* an operator at the AT&T overseas switching center at 32 Avenue of the Americas in Manhattan in 1975 or so. George provided him with a copy of the quick reference guide used by the international operators, giving the phreaks valuable international routing codes. Before long the phone phreak had talked George into loaning him his telephone company ID card, allowing him to slip inside and wander the switching center, looking for desirable manuals and reference books. "Later, after I pointed out the location of the books to him," the phone phreak recalls, "he put them in a

*A pseudonym.

garbage bag, which he placed in the freight elevator along with the other garbage. And yes, I went searching for it. It was my first time going through the telephone company's garbage, but not my last."

Still, the phone phreaks' increased paranoia wasn't without reason. In addition to celebrities, some of the original phone phreaks were being busted too. Blind San Jose–area phone phreak Jim Fettgather's arrest came in 1973. "The [Telephone Company] chief special agents kept warning us over and over again," Fettgather remembers. "They really were actually friendly. They were not mean in any way. They talked with my folks, they talked with me," Fettgather says, all to warn him to stop phreaking. "They knew what was happening. I don't quite know how they found out, but they knew we were doing all this MFing and muting and so forth. We were given ample warning, there's no question." Finally, he says, the phone company must have had enough. The local police showed up with a search warrant and Fettgather spent a night in jail. "The whole thing was pretty ugly," he says.

It was Denny Teresi's turn next. Teresi, the blind kid with what the *Esquire* article described as the "voice of a crack oil-rig foreman," the phreak with the otherworldly skill at getting telephone company switchmen to wire things up for him, had gone one call too far. "What finally nailed me was something that I had wired up in San Francisco," he says. "It was a touch-tone demonstrator, where you dial in to one number and it would grab dial tone from another line . . . You could make outgoing calls, and all the calls were billed to an unassigned test number. That was up for a while. When they took it down I had the balls to call back in and get it wired up. I probably would have gotten nailed sooner or later anyway, but that was just the final straw. When I called back to have it wired in, they went ahead and wired it up for me, but they set it up and then they watched that line for three weeks and they billed me for all of the calls. I probably should have let well enough alone and just let it go away."

Like Fettgather, Teresi agrees that the Pacific Telephone security agents had given them more than their share of breaks. "For the longest time the chief special agent, in this case George Alex, they had working on the case in San Jose, he was calling my parents or Jim's parents or whatever, and he'd let them know what's going on and he'd try to get us to cut it out. That went on for five years," he says. "I guess they figured that would be enough of a slap on the hand to get us to slow it down or stop." Teresi was fined $150 and had to pay for $320 worth of phone calls.

For the year 1973, an AT&T internal memo noted, there were 119 arrests for electronic toll fraud—more than double of the previous year. By 1974 the number had jumped to 158. By 1975 it was 176. Joseph Doherty, AT&T's director of corporate security, was as good as his word: "We are prosecuting as a rule now, rather than an exception."

Seventeen

A LITTLE BIT STUPID

O N JUNE 21, 1975, John Draper did something a little bit stupid. That day he entered a telephone booth in New York City and dialed an 800 number in Oakland, California. While the call was going through he held a blue box up to the phone and pressed a button, sending a burst of 2,600 Hz down the line.

"*Bleeep!*" said the blue box. "*Kerchink!*" responded the telephone network.

Draper pressed more buttons. Key pulse. 127 552 2155. Start. A few seconds later the telephone network rewarded him with what sounded like a bad imitation of Donald Duck talking to one of his nephews. If you squinted your ears and used your imagination you might think it sounded almost—*almost*—like two people talking.

Draper pressed another button and sent another quick blip of 2,600 Hz down the line. Donald Duck was replaced by the clear voices of two people talking about a work-related matter. Draper was now in the middle of their conversation, listening quietly. He eavesdropped for a few minutes and then hung up.

Draper had just used his blue box to hack into an internal telephone company service called verification. The need for this service sprang from one of the most annoying sounds in the world: the repetitive *baaa . . . baaa . . . baaa* of the busy signal. Although it's less common to run into them today, what with call waiting being a standard feature on every mobile phone, it wasn't that long ago that busy signals routinely drove people up the wall, especially if you were trying urgently to reach somebody with important news—somebody who, let's say, had a teenage son or daughter who was constantly on the phone. When your frustration boiled over in such cases you could call the operator, give her the number you were trying to reach, and ask her to verify if someone was indeed talking on the line. After all, perhaps the person you were calling had simply forgotten to hang up the phone properly. If a conversation was actually in progress, you could ask for an emergency interrupt, in which case the operator would barge into the conversation and announce to your party that you were trying to reach them. Naturally, the Bell System charged for both of these services, typically 25¢ or so in the 1970s.

Busy line verification service had been around since the early 1900s. It was kind of a spooky thing, since it allowed operators to monitor and break in on private telephone calls. For security reasons, in most places only special operators had access to busy verification trunks, and these were limited to a particular city or area or telephone exchange. That way, an operator in Kansas City couldn't eavesdrop on someone in San Francisco, for example.

It didn't take phone phreaks long to start playing with verification, and by 1970 or so they had learned that you could call an inward operator, pretend to be someone from the test board, and—if you had the right voice or maybe just got lucky—talk her into "putting you up" (that is, plugging you in) to a verify trunk. From there, with a blue box, you could select the particular telephone line in that area or exchange that you wanted to eavesdrop upon.

As with everything else in the telephone network, verification started out as a manual affair but eventually became automated. By 1972 phone phreaks like Bill Acker, Ray Oklahoma, and Joe Engressia had discovered that verification circuits in some places could be reached with just a blue box, no operator required, from anywhere in the country. Telephone calls in parts of Miami, Dallas, San Francisco, and Long Island, New York, to name the four that the phreaks had discovered, could all be eavesdropped upon this way. As scary as this sort of security hole seems, the phone phreaks viewed verification access primarily as a harmless prank, the sort of thing you might do to your pal as a joke.

Or maybe for bragging rights. So believe it or not using verification to eavesdrop on a telephone conversation wasn't the little-bit-stupid thing that John Draper did that day. No, the little-bit-stupid thing was the telephone number he had chosen to eavesdrop upon. Because 415-552-2155 was the telephone number of the San Francisco field office of the Federal Bureau of Investigation.

It would be a couple of more days before Draper did something *really* stupid.

Draper lived in California but was visiting New York, hanging out with his buddy Chic Eder. Eder was a burly, forty-five-year-old ex-con whose slightly bulging eyes perched above a bushy mustache and underneath a balding head, surrounded on both sides by long, straggly hair. Outgoing, friendly, intelligent, and intense, Eder was a dope dealer's dope dealer, given to introducing himself to strangers with a handshake and the phrase, "Chic's the name, smoke's my game." An acquaintance of the stand-up comic Lenny Bruce—"It was my best friend in LA who sold Lenny the smack he OD'ed on," Eder is said to have claimed—Eder had become a staple of the New York City drug scene: friends with everybody he met, unafraid to wander into the toughest neighborhoods, sure that he could take care of himself in any situation. This confidence came from hard-won experience. Eder was like a one-man crime wave, one whose rap sheet spanned almost ten pages. It went as far back as 1950 and detailed offenses such as fraud, reckless driving, vagrancy, possession of a concealed weapon, possession of narcotics, burglary . . . the list went on. Eder had spent years behind bars in some very tough places. His most recent legal woes stemmed from his involvement in the firebombing of a police station in Santa Barbara, California, an act that appeared to be connected to the Weather Underground organization, a political offshoot of the New Left dedicated to the violent overthrow of the United States. In 1971 Eder was convicted of possession of marijuana and a firebomb and sentenced to spend up to fifteen years enjoying the hospitality of the California state prison system.

It was hospitality he apparently didn't care for. Eder busted out of prison in late 1972, only to be apprehended six months later. Yet somehow, despite a lengthy original sentence and subsequent prison escape, he was granted parole and released just a year and a half later. He moved to New York City where he began working with his friend Albert Goldman, a professor and writer, helping research an article on the dope-dealing trade. Eder's contribution to the effort included buying and selling drugs in New York's roughest neighborhoods.

Draper had already told Eder about phone hacking—free calls and the various colored boxes that phone phreaks used. This was, after all, four years after the *Esquire* article and it's not like this stuff was that much of a secret anymore. Besides, keeping quiet was never one of John Draper's strengths. It wasn't too long before Draper was telling Eder about his eavesdropping on the FBI.

And that was the *really* stupid thing. Because Chic Eder was an informant for the feds. Eder's career as an informant began with a letter to the FBI, written just three months after being back in the clink from his earlier prison break. "Dear Agent in Charge," the letter read. "You want Weather Underground fugitives. I want a parole, and some money to start a new life. Interested?! As you're aware, I *can* deliver. There will be, however, certain stipulations that are non-negotiable. The prime requisite—above even the parole and money—is that you agree to take no action that might bring suspicion to bear on me as an informant." Toward the end of the letter Eder reflected, "This is no snap decision on my part. It's taken a great deal of cold, hard thinking to bring me to a point 180 degrees from my previous position on informing."

It is said that no good news comes between midnight and six a.m.

True to this maxim, the FBI's first inkling that its calls were being wiretapped came at 2:01 a.m. on June 24, 1975, in the form of an urgent teletype message from its New York office. The five-page message, wordy by FBI standards, was marked confidential and was encrypted for added security. It described Draper's use of a blue box to wiretap the San Francisco office, gave a quick sketch of Draper's background, and described "'phone freaks,' an underground clandestine group involved in making 'blue boxes.'" It requested FBI headquarters to authorize funds so that Eder could travel to California with Draper and purchase a blue box from him "in order to determine the degree of technology developed by 'phone freaks.'" Finally, it asked the San Francisco office to survey its employees to see if any of them remembered making a telephone call like the one Eder claimed Draper intercepted.

The FBI reacted the same way many large organizations react to surprising and unwelcome news: with disbelief. Informants make crazy claims all the time. This was probably just another one. The sort of thing you're duty bound to check out but nothing to get too excited about.

San Francisco responded that there was little point in asking its employees if any of them remembered making such a call unless the informant could be "pinned down" as to specifics. Perhaps headquarters could check with the FBI Laboratory to see if anyone there knew anything about these outlandish claims.

San Francisco asked friends at Pacific Telephone if they knew anything about this. Was it even possible that some guy in New York could remotely wiretap the San Francisco FBI office? Pacific Telephone told them that this was all nonsense. According to the phone company the only automatic telephone monitoring equipment in northern California was in Stinson Beach, Inverness, and Point Reyes, beautiful rural towns north of San Francisco but far away from the FBI's offices. Though it might conceivably be possible that calls in those small towns could be vulnerable, Pacific Telephone said, firmly, "San Francisco is not serviced by this equipment and calls cannot be monitored" by the procedure Eder claimed Draper had used.

An anonymous source familiar with the investigation summarized it this way: "An informant contacts us and tells us, 'This guy

Draper is bugging your calls.' Our Laboratory Division knows nothing about it and people in AT&T and Pacific Telephone basically say it's not possible, just can't be done." Shrug.

Disbelief notwithstanding, FBI headquarters authorized its New York office to pay for Eder's round-trip airfare to California ("coach," the FBI memo noted) to buy a blue box from Draper. The FBI also felt it needed to inform other governmental organizations of the problem. A July 2, 1975, memo classified SECRET and titled "Alleged Interception of Telephone Call of Federal Bureau of Investigation Field Office" was dispatched to several agencies, including the U.S. Department of Justice and the Secret Service.

> This is to inform that an investigation is currently being conducted concerning an allegation that an interception of communication took place on a telephonic communication in a field office of the Federal Bureau of Investigation (FBI). Information has been received that the device used, described to be a sophisticated "blue box," can not only intercept FBI telephone calls but [*one sentence redacted*] and calls made on the White House "hotline."
>
> Investigation is continuing to obtain this device for examination by our FBI laboratory so that determination may be made as to the capability of the device.
>
> You will be apprised of developments in this matter.

News of such developments would have to wait for the FBI's informant to turn up something more. Fortunately for the FBI, Chic Eder was a varsity player; he was good as a drug dealer, he was good as a hustler, and he was good as an informant. On July 13, he did as his masters bade him: he bought a blue box from Draper. Actually, blue boxes being works of art back in those days, he commissioned the creation of one; it would be ready for pickup in a few weeks. In the meantime, he got Draper again to demonstrate how to eavesdrop on the FBI's San Francisco field office. This time Eder made sure to get details of the conversation they eavesdropped on.

This time, in fact, he got it all on tape.

Now it's one thing to have an informant tell you something fantastic. Oh, you know, some hippie guy from California with an electronic box can somehow magically tap the FBI's phone calls from New York, two thousand miles away. But it is a different thing to have an informant provide detailed information that can be checked against reality. It is all the more unusual when the informant can back it all up with a tape recording.

"All hell broke loose," recalls an anonymous source familiar with the investigation. "AT&T and Pacific Telephone said it wasn't possible. But here's a tape recording of it happening."

"Headquarters wanted this case solved, fast," the source remembers. "In thirty years, it's the most freedom I've ever seen special agents given in a case. All they had to do was sneeze and say, 'I need a Lincoln Continental' and there would be one parked out in front of the building. Headquarters wanted it solved, whatever it would take, and there were no questions asked. Whatever it will take to nail this guy and see to it that it doesn't happen again."

Why the urgency? "The implications from a national security viewpoint, when you consider the consulates that were there in San Francisco, law enforcement, DEA . . . the opportunities were limitless [for wiretapping]. And it could be done from any telephone, anywhere in the country. It became rather evident that if this technology fell into the wrong hands, well, the implications were tremendous."

The freedom of action may have been a pleasant change for the FBI agents but it came at a price. The agents working the case were now under the gun on a case that headquarters wanted results on, today. "You figure this out! Solve this! Figure out what he did, how he did it, who else was involved, who else did he intercept!" is how the source recalls the orders from HQ.

A few days later, on July 18, Los Angeles FBI agents worked with Walter Schmidt—the same General Telephone security officer who had been instrumental in Draper's arrest in 1972—to see if they could duplicate Draper's technique for wiretapping calls with a blue box. They succeeded. According to a teletype from the

Los Angeles FBI office, the group "was able to intercept numerous telephone calls in progress of the San Francisco office [. . .] through utilization of a conventional blue box." As if it wasn't bad enough that the FBI's phone calls could be intercepted at all, the word "conventional" here was particularly chilling. It meant that the box Eder obtained from Draper wasn't "sophisticated" or anything special. In other words, anyone who owned a blue box was able to eavesdrop on San Francisco FBI telephone calls, as well as calls in other parts of the San Francisco Bay Area. All that was needed was the magic code "127" and the telephone number that was to be intercepted.

The Los Angeles office requested additional pieces of silver for Eder: "Los Angeles believes [Eder] has performed a valuable service for the Bureau and accordingly should be compensated," agents wrote, describing Eder's work as "outstanding."

Eder met with his FBI handlers in San Francisco a few days later, on July 21, and turned over the blue box he'd purchased from Draper. He reported that "the phone freak underground has the capability of monitoring calls throughout the country" by using the verification technique.

Eder further reported, "The phone freak underground currently is not selling information obtained from the intercept technique." An FBI memo continued, "[Eder] does not know how widespread the phone freak underground is or who the contacts, if any, are with the telephone companies or the affiliates there. [. . .] As a source of income, the underground is manufacturing and selling 'red boxes' in large quantities. These boxes duplicate the tones generated by coins deposited in pay telephones. Through the use of 'red boxes' an individual is able to make long distance call[s] without depositing money. These boxes cost the underground $6 or $7 to manufacture and are currently retailing on the street at $100. All money obtained from the sale of red boxes is going towards purchase of technical equipment for further research."

Swell. Just swell. A shadowy underground organization made up of technical wizards—wizards who might have spies within the phone company—can monitor your calls from anywhere and who might, if they chose, sell the results of their wiretapping to the highest bidder. And who might that bidder be? The Yippies? The mob? The Russians? Who knows?

San Francisco FBI agents contacted Assistant U.S. Attorney F. Steele Langford to discuss prosecuting Draper for wiretapping. The meeting didn't go well for the G-men. Langford thought there was "insufficient information to consider any action against Draper and that the identity of the 'blue box' manufacturer [was] still unknown." He kicked things upstairs, saying he would defer his opinion on the matter to his bosses in the Department of Justice in Washington.

Part of Langford's reluctance probably stemmed from the fact that the government's star witness in the matter, Chic Eder, was an informant in several different cases. Nobody wanted to put Eder on the stand since it would blow his cover and compromise other investigations.

Meanwhile, Bill Harward, head of the Radio Engineering Section of the FBI lab in Washington, D.C., had been working with Ken Hopper at Bell Laboratories to see if they, too, could duplicate Draper's wiretapping technique. As with Walter Schmidt at General Telephone in California, they found it worked like a charm—at least for intercepting phones in the San Francisco Bay Area—and could be done from the East and West Coasts. It was unclear if this problem existed in places other than San Francisco. Harward reported in a memo that Hopper was "most anxious that this condition be corrected as soon as possible and has stated that Bell resources will be made fully available on the authority of the highest level of management." Harward suggested that the FBI make a formal request to AT&T to assess the vulnerability of the telephone network in other parts of the country and to explain exactly what steps were being taken to fix the problem. In addition, he recommended that every FBI field office be alerted via teletype that phone calls to all offices could be wiretapped and that they should be "extremely cautious in use of the telephone."

As a result of Harward's memo, on July 23, Clarence M. Kelley, the director of the FBI, penned a note to John D. deButts, chairman of the board of AT&T.

Dear Mr. deButts:

I am advised that information just developed and confirmed discloses a condition which permits any knowledgeable person using a blue box to intercept and monitor telephone conversations to and from the San Francisco FBI Office, and other subscribers in that area.

This is a most alarming situation and I request the full cooperation of your organization and its resources to assess the possibility for similar conditions elsewhere and to take immediate corrective action wherever they exist.

It is requested that, for the purpose of this effort, liaison with the FBI Laboratory, Washington, D. C., be established in order that I may be kept advised of pertinent results.

The next day the FBI lab director Jay Cochran received a telephone call from Joe Doherty, AT&T's director of corporate security. Doherty said that AT&T was aware of the problem, that it was now fixed in San Francisco, and that instructions had gone out to remove the capability from any AT&T facilities where it still existed. In a memo to his bosses at the FBI Cochran noted, in his best passive-voice Bureauspeak, "It is pointed out that we have received prior assurances from AT&T that procedures such as discovered [in this case] are not possible. It is also pointed out that the condition developed in this case was developed by FBI investigation and not from any information furnished by the telephone company. [. . .] In view of the past record of AT&T in this area, we feel a stronger, more positive position, must be taken in the absence of any constructive offering from [AT&T]." Cochran later described Doherty's attitude during this call as "rather 'ho-hum' and appeared calculated to downplay the gravity of the situation."

The FBI informally approached the President's Foreign Intelligence Advisory Board to let its members know of the problem. A PFIAB representative said that they "would undoubtedly be sympathetic with any strong initiatives that the FBI might take . . . to insure the security of communications."

Meanwhile another issue came up. Chic Eder needed to get his blue box back from the FBI so he could maintain credibility with Draper. (You can imagine the conversation: "Hey, Chic, where's that box I made for you?" "Oh, uh, sorry, John, I'm sure it's around here somewhere . . . oh, *that's* right, I loaned it to some friends at the FBI! Um, no, I mean, uh. Crap.") A small blizzard of memos bounced back and forth among those in the FBI lab, the Legal Division, HQ, and various field offices to figure out how to handle the situation. Do we really want to give the bad guys back a piece of equipment that they can use to tap our phones? But wait a minute, the bad guys made the equipment in the first place. If we don't give it back they'll just make another one. And besides, Eder is our *informant,* he's not a bad guy. But Eder has friends who might borrow it who *are* bad guys. Plus, wasn't it used in the commission of a crime? Isn't it evidence at this point? How would we maintain evidence chain of custody if we give it back?

This dilemma continued until late August 1975 when FBI agents again met with U.S. Attorney Langford in San Francisco. Per instructions from FBI HQ they explained that Eder was "a most valuable informant to the FBI who will not testify" in any legal proceedings but that they wanted to get the blue box back to him so they could continue their efforts to "penetrate the underground phone phreaks." Langford stated that, as there were no witnesses—or at least none willing to testify—there could be no prosecution. Therefore FBI could dispose of the blue box or any other evidence as it saw fit, so long as the recipient didn't use it.

No prosecution. Really? Draper can wiretap the FBI and just get away with it?

Up the chain of command went the word that the U.S. attorney wasn't going to prosecute. Down came word from the Department of Justice: "Departmental Attorney Kline, after reviewing the matter, desired to know whether any of the telephone companies involved are actively pursuing investigation . . . in order to establish Fraud by Wire investigations." In other words, remember how we got Al Capone for tax evasion when we couldn't get him for murder? If we can't get Draper for wiretapping us, maybe we can take him down for making free phone calls. Let's see if the phone companies don't have something on him in that regard.

The answer was no. Pacific Telephone's security office in Los Angeles said the company was "vitally interested" in determining whether Draper was phreaking, but until Draper moved to Los Angeles and started to phreak there would be no investigating him. General Telephone's security office in Los Angeles said much the same. New York Telephone's security office said its investigators followed Draper's activities by reading the *TAP* newsletter but "did not have him under investigation on specific fraud by wire charges." And Pacific Telephone's San Jose security office—the office in charge of security in the area where Draper actually lived—simply said that it was "not taking any further investigative action" toward him.

AT&T claimed it had fixed the problem, the star witness wouldn't testify, the U.S. attorney had declined prosecution, and not even the phone company was following up on things. A month passed. Somebody at the Justice Department poked someone at FBI HQ. You-know-what rolled downhill, toward San Francisco, Los Angeles, and New York, on November 17, 1975.

> For the information of receiving offices, the [Justice] Department continues to maintain an interest in this matter.
>
> San Francisco should timely submit letterhead memoranda, by cover airtel, reporting results of efforts to penetrate "underground phone freaks" pursuant to instructions set forth in referenced Bureau air telegram, 9/18/1975. These communications should [. . .] relate exclusively to investigation regarding penetration of "phone freaks."

Consideration should be given to potential prosecution for violations of Fraud by Wire Statutes should this become apparent.

The change in strategy was now official. The focus of the investigation was now on penetrating the underground phone phreaks and getting Fraud by Wire prosecutions. The wiretapping business might have started it but that wasn't how it was going to end.

Eighteen

SNITCH

PHONE PHREAKS LIVE to solve puzzles. They spend time observing, gathering data, thinking, and inventing theories about how things fit together. They think up experiments—things they can try—to solve whatever puzzle they're working on. They get a little dopamine hit when they get it figured out. And that dopamine hit is the kick that causes them to rinse and repeat.

What's funny is that you can replace the phrase "phone phreak" with "FBI agent" or "telephone company security officer" in the preceding paragraph and it would be just as true. Figuring out a new phone hack, catching a bad guy: same same, at least as far as the brain's neurotransmitter receptors are concerned.

Phone phreak or cop, most of the observing, data gathering, and experimenting that either one does is a long, tedious process of running down leads—the 99 percent perspiration that made Thomas Edison a wealthy man.

Other times, though, you get lucky and something drops into your lap that cracks things wide open. If you're a phone phreak, this might be a purloined manual that tells you something of how the telephone network works, or perhaps an anonymous voice on a long-distance loop-around circuit who tells you how to do something you had been trying to figure out for months.

For the FBI and Pacific Telephone and their case against John Draper, that lucky break would turn out to be a young phone phreak from Los Angeles.

Wayne Perrin was a Pacific Telephone lifer. That wasn't his plan, it just happened that way. Perrin was a big man, almost six-foot-two and 220 pounds, but he came across as affable and friendly rather than imposing; perhaps his sandy reddish hair, hazel eyes, and easygoing manner helped with this. Perrin had wanted to be a cop, and while waiting for a job with the local police force in 1965 he took a temporary gig with the phone company as a lineman, climbing telephone poles and such. He was good at it and was quickly promoted. He stayed with the phone company and also worked as a reserve police officer for the city of Alhambra, just east of Los Angeles. Then, in 1971 at the age of twenty-nine, opportunity knocked. There was an opening in the telephone company's chief special agent's office in Pasadena. Perrin became a telephone cop.

Along with the other telephone cops in that office, Perrin was responsible for investigating security problems for the phone company in the greater Los Angeles area. Very few of these investigations had anything to do with phone phreaks or electronic toll fraud. More often it was pay phone or office burglaries, petty cash theft, vandalism, or dealing with a traffic accident involving a company vehicle, pretty much the same stuff that security people at all large companies handle.

The latter half of 1975 has been unusually busy. In just six months Pacific Telephone's Los Angeles area had been caught up in a vortex of telephone crime. But it wasn't just that it was unusually busy, it was that the crimes were just plain weird. Someone had figured out a way to hack the 611 repair service phone number to make free phone calls all over the world. Meanwhile, telephone company truck yards were being burglarized, and the things being stolen were items such as telephone company hard hats, tools, and "test sets"—the odd-looking telephones with alligator clips that telephone company repair people always have on their tool belts.

"We didn't have a clue. No clue," Perrin recalls. "We had all these little cases. You knew they were related in a fashion but you couldn't tie them. . . . We had trucks being broken into, we had Dumpster diving, the Valley was just rife with petty thievery. Test sets were taken. Books were taken. Manuals were taken. Wire is taken. Nothing of great value, but they would go in and take this stuff. So you're looking at this trying to figure it out." And not getting anywhere.

Then there were the really strange cases, the ones that made no sense at all. Like the $21,000 worth of telephone calls that had been fraudulently charged to one Dr. Bosley in what appeared to be a giant, multistate, nineteen-hour-long conference call over the course of a weekend. Or the late-night telephone calls to telephone company employees in Pacific Telephone's Simi Valley and Panorama City offices, a creepy mixture of obscene, stalkative calls to operators peppered with threats of physical violence and bomb blasts. Strangest of all, some of the bomb threats were then followed by calls to law enforcement by someone pretending to be a telephone company security officer investigating the matter—or, in some cases, the reverse: calls would be made to the telephone company security office by someone pretending to be a law enforcement officer.

All this left Perrin scratching his head. Who would do this, and why?

Whoever was doing this was calling telephone operators to make these threats simply by dialing 0. You would think that when you call a telephone operator, the operator would have your telephone number. You'd think that the operators would be able to look up Mr. Harassing Caller and hand all of his info directly to security and then Perrin and Company could swoop down on this guy. Problem solved.

Sounds great in theory but in practice it didn't seem to work that way, at least not in 1975 in certain parts of Los Angeles, and at least not with this caller. The one clue they had—that their harassing caller would sometimes identify himself as "Robert P. Norden"—didn't seem to be as helpful as you might think. They didn't seem to be able to find any service records under that name.

On November 19, 1975, at 3:55 a.m., "Norden" called the Panorama City office. This time the phone company held his line. When your line is held it means that you can't hang up. Or, more accurately, you can hang up but it won't disconnect your call. When you pick the phone back up, instead of getting a dial tone you're still connected to the person you called or you get no dial tone at all.

This is a very disconcerting thing, and if you're a telephone prankster it's like a creepy phone call in reverse. Imagine yourself making a late-night harassing phone call, thinking you're powerful and anonymous and king of the world, and then finding that your phone has inexplicably turned on you. You can't hang up. No matter what you do you're stuck. Your intended victim has you by the tail and won't let go.

His line was held for hours and hours. Eventually he got up the nerve to go to another phone and call the telephone company to find out what was going on. He ended up speaking with Perrin's security colleague Bill Cheney and demanded to know why his line was being held. Cheney gave his best telephonic shrug and told him that probably there was trouble on his phone line and perhaps he should call his local repair service. As soon as he hung up Cheney called the test board supervisor and explained the situation. As expected, "Norden" called repair service. He was told that his line was being checked for trouble.

Meanwhile the phone company was feverishly trying to find out whose phone line it was holding. Normally this would be simple. Back in those days every phone line coming into a central office had a "line card," a three by five-inch note card that had on it all the information about the telephone line—information like whose line it was, for example. But his line card was missing. It wasn't in the 611 repair bureau file where it should have been. The next logical place would be the telephone company business office, but that didn't open until later in the morning. And once it opened, employees there said they didn't have it either.

The phone company finally released his line that afternoon, almost twelve hours later. "No one could find any records," Perrin says. As it turned out, a business office representative named Angie had the line card in her desk. "She was having other problems with that guy, so she had locked it up. So we couldn't find anything about it until Angie actually got into the office. Had they had the line card we would have had him right away."

One thing you may have noticed by now about phone phreaks is that they're obsessive. True to form, that night he again called the Panorama City office, this time to complain about his line being held the night before. But this time Perrin was ready and had arranged for a trap on the line that would allow him to trace the call. Finally, he had an address and telephone number for this mystery caller.

"Mr. Norden" must have known the jig was close to being up at that point. "He got scared," says Perrin. Two days later he called the phone company and canceled his telephone service. Three days after that, Perrin says, he seemed to have a full-fledged panic attack. They were on to him, it seemed clear. Better to switch sides now, he must have thought, while the switching was good.

On November 24, 1975, "Robert P. Norden" picked up the phone and called Wayne Perrin. Over the course of a wide-ranging two-hour conversation, Perrin wrote, he "related numerous items concerning toll fraud involving 611 toll trunks, toll fraud concerning the use of call diverters, a scramble-descrambling method used to monitor telephone conversations at any location in the country and his ability to access numerous kinds of telephonically secure systems." That fateful phone call began his new career as an informant, perhaps the single most effective phone phreak informant that the telephone company ever had.

The two met and spoke numerous times over the next several weeks. "Norden" was convinced the phone company was "three days away" from swooping down and arresting him. They weren't, says Perrin, but since "Norden's" worries made him talkative and anxious to cooperate, Perrin wasn't about to correct him in this regard. Perrin described this paranoid phone phreak as being in his "early twenties, five-foot-eleven, approximately 145 to 150 pounds, dark brown hair and eyes, extremely grubby" with hair that "comes to the shoulders, sideburns down to the chin line with a partial muttonchop." Perrin's notes give a bit of insight into his psyche.

> Mr. Norden, often times, loses sight of his perspective, he attempts to keep everything on a "we, he, they" basis but often times gets so involved in his descriptions he changes to "I" and "me" [. . .] If you catch it, he will finally admit to you on a rough basis that he was actually involved or did the act. He is extremely egotistical, very easy to work with if you do not apply any pressure. You can question him subtly, if you question him violently he will react and want to back off. Mr. Norden is extremely nervous about being followed or whisked away by Secret Service or CIA or FBI. He is so paranoid about the situation that he looks over his shoulder at everything and anybody, with the exception of young ladies.

Finally, after many meetings, Perrin learned "Norden's" real name: Paul Sheridan.*

Perrin didn't know what to make of Sheridan, this unkempt and unsettled kid who made outlandish claims about all the crazy things he could do with a telephone. He had mastered all sorts of telephone tricks and was thoroughly plugged in to the Los Angeles phone phreak scene. He seemed to know everyone, from the kids who hung out on LA loop arounds to the John Drapers and Bill Ackers of the world. But Sheridan brought an intensity and an intelligence to his endeavors that not everyone had. He was quick-witted, foulmouthed, verbally gifted, and had a telephonic self-confidence—really more of an arrogance—that made him a talented social engineer. Being able to make free phone calls was apparently the least of his skills. Sheridan admitted to being part of the Santa Barbara nuclear hoax a few years earlier. He said he could wiretap phone calls with a blue box. He bragged of breaking into the military's telephone network and getting the U.S. Air Force Strategic Air Command in Omaha, Nebraska, on

---

*A pseudonym.

the horn. He could scramble nuclear bombers by doing this, he claimed. He said he had a special 800 number that went directly to the White House; he boasted that he could get President Ford on the line any time he wanted. In fact, he claimed, he had spoken to the president several times by phone.

The president? Really?

"We did not believe that," Perrin recalls. So Perrin and his colleague Bill Cheney decided to try it out. They got the 800 number from Sheridan and gave it a try from their office in Pasadena. "Here's two grown adult men, we're sitting in Cheney's office, and we dial that number up and we got right to the second floor of the White House. It scared the crap out of us! We hung up!"

That was the problem, really. It would be easy enough to dismiss these crazy things Sheridan was saying, but they all seemed as if either they actually *were* true or they *might* be true. It was a great combination—claims that were impossible to discount and disturbing as hell.

Among Sheridan's most disturbing claims was that phone phreaks could break into AUTOVON. Though it sounds like a German highway, AUTOVON—short for Automatic Voice Network—was the U.S. military's telephone network. It started in the United States in the early 1960s but later expanded into other countries where the United States had military bases.

For the most part AUTOVON looked and felt like the plain old telephone network that civilians used. This was no great surprise. AUTOVON was built by AT&T, General Telephone, and Automatic Electric, the same companies that built the civilian telephone network, and they reused as much technology as they could. AUTOVON telephone numbers were seven or ten digits long, just like normal ones. Internally, AUTOVON used multifrequency signaling, just as the civilian network did. You could even call into the regular telephone system from AUTOVON, though you weren't supposed to be able to go the other way.

However, AUTOVON had some features that made admirals and generals, network engineers, and phone phreaks salivate.

Put into operation just a year after the Cuban missile crisis, AUTOVON was a child of the cold war, a telephone network designed to withstand a nuclear attack. The civilian telephone system was built on Bell's hierarchical network concept, one in which lower-level switching centers forwarded calls to higher-level ones. The higher-level switches, the brainy ones like 4A crossbars, had lots of trunks to other cities. This approach made economic sense, because it minimized the number of switching centers and long-distance lines you needed. But it made military planners worry. What if the higher-level switching centers got taken out by Russian nukes? Civilian telephone central offices were what the military called "soft targets"; they might be solid buildings but they simply weren't designed to withstand a nearby nuclear blast.

What the military needed, the Pentagon decided, was a "survivable" telephone system, one that could survive a nuclear war. With help from the phone company, the Defense Communications Agency began constructing its own network of telephone switching centers, about seventy of them throughout the United States. Many of these were underground, in hardened bunkers. Unlike the civilian telephone network, AUTOVON was nonhierarchical; there were many more trunk lines between AUTOVON switches than in the civilian network, and they tried to minimize the importance of any one switch. That way the Soviets couldn't take out just a couple of switching centers and bring down the entire military phone system.

The other unique thing about AUTOVON was something called "precedence." In the 1960s, the civilian telephone network wasn't as developed as it is today; there just weren't enough long-distance telephone circuits. So sometimes you'd try to make a long-distance call and you'd be treated to a recording telling you, primly, "We're sorry, all circuits are busy now. Won't you please try your call again later?"

That didn't sit well with the military brass. If you're calling the president to let him know the country was under attack, you don't want to have to listen to any recordings about all circuits being busy. So the Defense Communications Agency and its telephone company contractors came up with a scheme called precedence dialing, the idea being that some calls are more important than others. If you're ordering pizza, that's low precedence. If you're reporting war with the Soviets, that's high precedence. If the network was busy, higher-precedence calls trump lower-precedence calls, automatically booting them and seizing their lines if necessary to get the important traffic through. This led to AUTOVON touch-tone phones having sixteen buttons, not just the twelve we're used to. These extra buttons weren't just any buttons. They were shiny and red, arranged in a neat military column to the right of the keypad. They were labeled, cryptically, "FO," "F," "I," and "P."

That is: Flash Override. Flash. Immediate. Priority. The precedence levels, in other words. Flash Override was the highest precedence, to be used only by the president, secretary of defense, members of the Joint Chiefs of Staff, or commanders reporting an attack on the United States.

Be honest. Who doesn't want a phone on his desk with a Flash Override button? Even if you're just ordering a pizza, wouldn't it make you feel good to press Flash Override first? Nothing says "I'm important" like Flash Override.

AUTOVON was an ego blow job delivered via a sixteen-button keypad. The admirals and generals loved it. So did the network engineers. And so did the phone phreaks. It was, after all, another network—one with cool buttons—to explore.

Perrin struggled with what to do about Sheridan. "He would call in. He would talk so fast, you couldn't write fast enough, so we recorded everything that he gave us and then later on we transcribed it and we just told him that we wrote fast," Perrin recalls. "He was telling you things . . . I mean, he starts telling you stuff about getting into the Russian satellite system and I have no idea about the Russian satellite system. I mean, I didn't even know about AUTOVON. So from the standpoint of its functionality and those kinds of things, he was talking way past what I could understand."

Perrin spent a day or two trying to figure out what to do. Finally he decided to get the FBI involved. The Bureau might have a better idea of how to handle things. And maybe it was hooked up with technical spooks who might be better able to evaluate Sheridan's claims. Perrin met with the FBI on December 5, 1975. He gave their agents an overview of the Sheridan matter and described the various outlandish claims that Sheridan had made. Perrin felt that there was enough information on Sheridan at this point to charge him with threatening to "bomb the telephone company"—remember the creepy late-night phone calls and bomb threats that started this whole thing—but he wasn't sure if that was the right way to go. Perhaps the FBI had some ideas. Maybe they could call Strategic Air Command in Omaha or the Secret Service in Washington and check some of this stuff out?

The FBI agents didn't seem to take things very seriously, Perrin says. They told him that they would get back to him.

Meanwhile, the question of what to do about Sheridan was also making its way up the food chain within the telephone company. Pacific Telephone, where Perrin worked, was the Bell System's West Coast operating company. Like all the local Bell companies, it reported to AT&T, its corporate parent, at 195 Broadway in New York City. Pacific Telephone decided to get AT&T involved, since Sheridan was talking about things that were bigger than just California, things like AUTOVON and defense systems and satellites. In turn, the higher-ups at AT&T corporate headquarters decided they needed to talk to the Justice Department about it, since United States government communications were involved. AT&T higher-ups had throw weight. A meeting was soon scheduled with the attorney general in Washington, D.C., on December 17, 1975. In the meantime, AT&T decided that this matter was to be held in the strictest confidence. And that meant Perrin couldn't talk to anyone about it anymore. Anyone, Perrin asked? Did that include the FBI? Anyone.

Physics teaches us that the fastest thing in the universe is the speed of light. Common sense and organizational politics teach us the fastest thing is actually the rumor mill. So it was no surprise, Perrin says, that the FBI somehow instantly got word that its bosses at the Justice Department would soon be meeting with AT&T officials regarding this Sheridan kid. Suddenly the FBI was very interested. It was suddenly decided the Bureau needed to talk to Perrin immediately. But now Perrin couldn't talk to the Bureau. Perrin put the FBI off until the meeting with the attorney general, where it was decided, predictably, that the FBI was the right agency for the phone company to work with on this matter.

On December 22, 1975, Perrin took Sheridan to meet with Special Agent Bob Jacobs. Jacobs was one of the FBI Los Angeles tech squad or "sound" agents. He and his fellow tech squad agents were responsible for the Bureau's high-tech field ops in the Los Angeles area, things like wiretaps, room bugs, and car tracking devices. Jacobs and Sheridan seemed to hit it off. Among other things they discussed Sheridan visiting Draper in person next week. Could Sheridan bring back information or documents from Draper? Maybe. Could the Bureau help Sheridan out a little bit with his rent? Maybe.

On January 7, 1976, Perrin met with Special Agent Bill Snell, one of Jacob's FBI tech squad colleagues. Sheridan's visit to Draper had born fruit. Snell gave Perrin a four-page typeset technical document that Sheridan had gotten from Draper titled "AUTOVON Access Info." Sheridan even offered to demonstrate the techniques described in the document for the FBI and AT&T if they wanted. Sheridan also told the FBI that Draper had a small assembly line going for red boxes that were to be sold in the near future. He was actively using a blue box from the house across the street from People's Computer Company, or PCC, a small nonprofit in Menlo Park dedicated to teaching people about computers. And

Draper was also red boxing from a pay phone just down the street from PCC, Sheridan reported.

The AUTOVON document caused quite a stir. It described, in detail, how to use a blue box to access the military's phone system from the civilian telephone network via a phreaking technique called guard banding. Guard banding added a higher-pitched tone—usually 3,200 Hz, or seventh octave G—into the 2,600 Hz normally used by a blue box to reset a trunk line. If your call went through several telephone switches, guard banding allowed you to control exactly which switch you were talking to, simply by varying the volume of this higher-pitched tone. This in turn meant that you could stack tandems, building up a call to a particular place one link—in other words, one telephone switch—at a time. This was similar to the tandem stacking technique described in the *Esquire* article, but guard banding was a newer and more powerful method that worked on a wider variety of telephone switches, including the brainy 4A toll tandems.

Sheridan's document explained how guard banding could be used to hack into AUTOVON. First you call directory assistance in Alaska and whistle off with 2,600 Hz. You're now talking to a civilian telephone switch in Alaska that also happened to have connections to the military's AUTOVON telephone network. You'd then use your blue box to tell the Alaska switch to connect you to a military telephone switch at Kalakaket Radio Relay Station in Alaska, originally part of the military's Arctic communication system for the Distant Early Warning line. You'd then use guard banding to send a mix of 2,600 Hz and 3,200 Hz down the line. This skips over the Alaska switch and instead resets your connection to the Kalakaket Creek switch, which then waits for your commands. You now use your blue box to send Kalakaket Creek digits to get you to Pedro Dome Radio Relay Station, also in Alaska. By adding this second link on to your call, you're now fully inside the military's network; as far as Pedro Dome is concerned, you came in from the U.S. Air Force network via Kalakaket Creek station and thus look like a completely legitimate military telephone user. This means you can now tell Pedro Dome to connect you to whatever AUTOVON telephone number you want. You can even set the precedence of your call, from routine up to Flash Override, just by sending the right digits with your blue box.

AT&T representatives met with the FBI in Washington, D.C., on January 9 to discuss the AUTOVON problem. AT&T Long Lines security supervisor Nelson Saxe recalls, "The FBI's biggest concern was: can the phone phreaks scramble fighters by using AUTO-VON?" AT&T hastened to assure them that this wasn't possible; it might be possible to order pilots to their aircraft using AUTOVON, but any orders to actually launch aircraft would have to come over a separate, point-to-point alerting network called JCSAN/COPAN. And the phone phreaks hadn't broken into JCSAN/COPAN. Well, not as far as anyone knew, anyway.

As these things go, it was not the most reassuring of reassurances.

Discussion turned to Sheridan's offer to demonstrate AUTOVON access. The FBI favored a demo in Los Angeles, and soon. Saxe's notes from the meeting show that agents in the FBI's Los Angeles office felt Sheridan was "mentally unstable" and might "go off" at any time. Who knew how long they had to work with him? AT&T attorneys were against a Sheridan demo, arguing that the less contact anyone had with the informant the better. After all, how were they going to successfully prosecute Sheridan if he could later stand up in court and tell the jury, "Not only did the phone company and FBI know I was playing with the AUTOVON network, they asked me to demonstrate it to them!" And since the FBI and AT&T now had a detailed document describing exactly how to break into AUTOVON, why did they need a demonstration from Sheridan? Couldn't the engineers at Bell Labs just duplicate his attack on their own? In fact, it wasn't clear that Sheridan himself had actually ever accessed AUTOVON. He simply may have gotten the information from Draper and might not actually know how to do it himself. It wouldn't help anybody if there really *was* a security vulnerability in AUTOVON, but Sheridan convinced them all otherwise by botching the demo. As Saxe put it, "We're not about to go out to Los Angeles to see Sheridan fail to get a call through on AUTOVON!"

In the end, the FBI was holding all the cards that mattered; the Bureau had the informant and it wanted a demo. If the AT&T people didn't want to attend, well, that was AT&T's business.

AT&T relented. Plans began forming for a joint FBI–AT&T demo of AUTOVON hackery in Los Angeles in a week or two.

Nineteen

CRUNCHED

THE SAME MONTH that Paul Sheridan was starting his career as an informant for both Pacific Telephone and the FBI and being asked to take trips up to the Bay Area to snuffle around John Draper, the December 1975 issue of the phone phreak newsletter *TAP* carried the following letter to the editor.

Dear TAP,
This is Capn. Crunch, I would like to mention a few things.
   First, I'm glad to see you boys back in operation & am curious why you stopped publication for a while. I also want to state my willingness in contacting as many would-be phreaks as possible. In person only & not by mail. Therefore I am offering to anyone who wants to come see me in Mt. View all I know in electronics, computers, & related technologies including freaking of course. However I dislike talking on the phone, nor communication by mail. If you even receive this letter I would consider it a miracle. My current address is: J. T. Draper, 1905 Montecito Ave., Apt. #6, Mt. View, CA 94040 for those who want to set up a meeting by mail. Of course I am not underground. A while back National Review published my phone number in the hopes that people would bug me by calling me at 3 am etc. They didn't realize that I made hundreds of new friends & taught hundreds the art of freaking. Any people who want to visit me are welcome. They can stay with me up to a week (it usually takes that long to teach them). You might want to publish that fact.

The letter, which continued on in that vein, was a wonderful example of why David Condon's circle of Berkeley phone phreaks viewed association with Draper as the "kiss of death." Multiple sources, including General Telephone's security office in Los Angeles, promptly forwarded the December issue of *TAP* to the FBI, where it served as a reminder, as if they needed one, that Draper was still out there, busy minting new phone phreaks. Who knew what tricks he was teaching them?

By January 1976 a dark vibe had begun to spread throughout certain groups of phone phreaks in both California and New York. Phreaks who used to talk freely were now being cagey or simply not returning calls. Discussions that used to be about the latest telephone hacks were now concerned with something more malodorous: who's the rat? Several people believed something unwholesome was happening down in LA, but nobody could prove anything. Paranoia levels were beginning to run at record highs.

In fact, something unwholesome was happening that month down in LA—from a phone phreak perspective, anyway. It was the FBI–AT&T AUTOVON demo, and it took place from Wednesday, January 21, 1976, through Friday, January 23, at the FBI's Los Angeles field office.

Team fed was made up of thirteen heavy hitters. From the FBI there was Jay Cochran, the assistant director of the FBI Laboratory in Washington, D.C.; R. E. Gebhardt, the assistant director in charge of the FBI's Los Angeles field office; Bill Harward, the section chief of radio engineering from FBI headquarters; and Bob Jacobs and Bill Snell, the FBI tech squad special agents who had been Sheridan's FBI handlers. From the local telephone companies there was Bill Bowren, the security director of Pacific Telephone in Los Angeles; Roger Edfast, the security manager of Pacific Telephone in Pasadena; Walter Schmidt from General Telephone; and, of course, Wayne Perrin. From AT&T, there was Chuck Israel, the AUTOVON network manager; Nelson Saxe, the AT&T Long Lines security supervisor; and Ken Hopper from Bell Laboratories. Finally, there was a gentleman from Washington, D.C., who is notable for how his name and organization are blanked out of every government document describing the meeting: a Mr. B. A. Fonger from the National Security Agency.

The two phone phreaks attending, Paul Sheridan and a clean-cut twenty-something phreak described only as Michael,* were heavily outnumbered. Michael was a talented, technically sharp Los Angeles–area phone hacker who had served as a sort of technical adviser to the FBI on a wiretap case some years earlier. The two phreaks were brought in separately so as not to have contact with each other. Figuring the phreaks might be somewhat more talkative if they weren't surrounded by so many feds, the interrogators split into two groups. Harward, Hopper, Israel, Saxe, and the two FBI agents Jacobs and Snell would conduct the interviews in the same room as the subjects. A reel-to-reel tape recorder would record the room conversation as well as any telephone calls that were made. As the reels ran out of tape, every forty-five minutes or so, the tapes would be brought to a second conference room, where they would be listened to by Bowren, Cochran, Edfast, Fonger, Perrin, and Schmidt.

First up was Sheridan, who would give a guided tour of AUTOVON access techniques.

The big question was: could Sheridan really do what he claimed he could? Could he use a blue box to get into the military AUTOVON network? Did this guard banding technique actually work? Sure, everybody understood that he might be able to get in to AUTOVON by fooling an operator; that was slightly troubling but it wasn't nearly as big a deal as being able to do it with a blue box. Sheridan had made lots of claims—lots of hair-raising claims. And now a whole lot of high-ranking people had gone out of their way to see these techniques demonstrated. Recall AT&T Long Lines security agent Saxe's comment a few weeks earlier: "We're not about to go out to Los Angeles to see Sheridan fail to get a call through on AUTOVON!"

---

*A pseudonym.

Of course, Sheridan failed to get a call through on AUTOVON.

Well, that's not entirely fair. In fact, Sheridan was able to get a call through by BSing an AUTOVON operator. And he was able to demonstrate that guard banding worked. He also demonstrated a bunch of other phone phreak techniques. But despite multiple attempts he was unable to get into AUTOVON by the guard banding method described in the paper he had given the FBI earlier in the month. Later that afternoon Michael, the second informant, tried a slightly different guard banding technique for hacking into AUTOVON. It, too, failed.

Yet both phreaks swore their techniques worked.

This situation will be familiar to anyone who has ever had to give or sit through a demo of any new technology. There are entities known in Silicon Valley's high-tech community as "the demo gods." It is said that demo gods can smell fear. An important demo? An audience of VIPs? That's when then demo gods suddenly appear and things mysteriously stop working.

Fortunately for Sheridan and Michael, the more technical members of team fed were familiar with this phenomenon. That evening Fonger, Hopper, Israel, Saxe, and Schmidt adjourned to the General Telephone security laboratory in Santa Monica. Breaking out their (legal) blue boxes and test equipment, they sat down and tried to break into AUTOVON using the techniques they had seen that day. It was a long process; had they been phone phreaks, they might even have enjoyed it. But finally, at 10:30 p.m., they succeeded in accessing AUTOVON using a blue box. Ken Hopper's notes convey the effort they put into it: "Our success in direct AUTOVON dialing came after many, many fruitless attempts, perhaps as many as 100." Given how difficult guard banding was until you got the hang of it, this was not entirely surprising. In addition, apparently part of the problem they had making it work was that that other people had been tying up the lines between Los Angeles and Seattle that very evening. Hopper suspected it was Sheridan and Michael, probably trying to prove to themselves that the techniques they had tried to demonstrate to the FBI earlier in the day still worked.

Perrin remembers being woken up by a late-night phone call that evening from the engineers at the security lab: "It works, it works! This stuff really works!" Perrin wasn't surprised. Despite Sheridan's failure to hack into AUTOVON earlier in the day, Perrin had developed a certain confidence in Sheridan's claims ever since getting the White House on the phone. "What the hell are you calling me about? I already knew that," Perrin recalls telling them. He hung up and went back to sleep.

Just two miles from Stanford University, the 1900 block of Menalto Avenue in Menlo Park was a collection of small storefronts on a tree-lined street in a mostly residential neighborhood. You wouldn't have thought so from a casual glance but it was a nexus of nerdly activity.

A fixture on the block was the electric vehicle pioneer Roy Kaylor. Kaylor was an inveterate tinkerer, a Stanford electrical engineer, an odd blend of hippie and West Point graduate. He had been building electric vehicles since 1965; his "Kaylor Kits" converted Volkswagen Bugs to run on electric motors and batteries. He had a small store on Menalto where he sold electric motorcycles—in 1975. Kaylor's house, just across the street and down the block from his electric motorcycle store, doubled as his shop and laboratory. His garage was filled with electronic test equipment and machine tools, everything to make a geeky heart beat faster.

A few storefronts from Kaylor's electric motorcycle shop was the People's Computer Company. PCC was a sort of computer commune started in 1972 by personal computing pioneers Bob Albrecht and George Firedrake. "Computers are mostly used against people instead of for people; used to control people instead of to free them," read PCC's first newsletter. "Time to change all that—we need a . . . People's Computer Company."

PCC became a watering hole for Silicon Valley's budding personal computer scene. Of course, they weren't called personal computers back then; that term wouldn't be popular for years. They were "homebrew" computers, kits assembled from empty circuit boards and bags of electronic components, built one part at a time with solder and sweat and concentration. They were often enclosed in bulky aluminum boxes or homemade wooden enclosures, that is, when anyone bothered to enclose them in anything at all. The computers weren't powerful; mostly all they could do is blink lights in response to toggle switch inputs. But for those bitten by the bug they were like crack cocaine.

The People's Computer Company took up two storefronts. It had computers around its periphery, a social space with a couch and rug in the center, and a potluck dinner every Wednesday night. The potlucks were a big draw, not to be missed events for microcomputer hobbyists in the Valley in 1975. Steve Wozniak was a frequent attendee; Bill Gates showed up on one occasion as well. Kaylor recalls a PCC potluck in which he tried to convince Wozniak that Woz should sell preassembled Apple I computers directly to the general public instead of as electronic kits to be assembled by computer geeks. Woz thought this was a hysterically funny idea—so funny, Kaylor says, that Woz actually fell off the couch laughing, rolling around on the rug of the People's Computer Company, his belly laugh filling the room.

John Draper became a frequent sight at the PCC, programming computers, building electronic gadgets, hanging out, smoking dope. He and Kaylor quickly became friends. "I was impressed with Draper's diligence, his follow-through, his stick-to-itiveness," Kaylor recalls. He knew Draper was building various colored phone phreak boxes and even let Draper use the electronics lab in his garage to work on them. But Kaylor made a point of not asking Draper too many questions. Kaylor had a security clearance for some defense work he had done, he says, and, as he later put it, "You learn in that environment that sometimes it's better not to know things."

In all, the 1900 block of Menalto was a perfect setup. There were plenty of interesting people to talk to, computers to hack on, soldering irons and multimeters and oscilloscopes to play with. There was a corner market a few doors down where you could buy snacks and soda. The Menalto Market even had a pay phone booth outside where you could call your friends—or test your red and blue boxes to make sure they were in tune. It was everything Draper needed.

"It was decided that the investigation of Draper should be intensified." Thus spake the passive-voice memo to the special agent in charge of the Los Angeles FBI office, summarizing the AUTOVON demo and the skull session that followed. "As such, Assistant Director in Charge Cochran, Section Chief Harward, and Special Agents [. . .] should travel to San Francisco in order to brief the San Francisco FBI Field Office personally of the developments concerning telephone manipulations. In addition, conscientious efforts should be made to establish and cultivate informants in this area with regard to possible prosecution relating to interception of communications, anti-racketeering-interference of government communications, and interstate transportation of stolen property fraud by wire/computer fraud by wire."

A few days later, on January 27, FBI agents met with Pacific Telephone investigators in San Francisco to discuss the Draper investigation. Present were Assistant U.S. Attorney Floy Dawson, the FBI special agent in charge of the San Francisco office, his deputy, the assistant agent in charge, and seven other FBI agents. Three representatives from Pacific Telephone attended. The Pacific Telephone people said they would need to talk to their attorneys to figure out how they could help. For its part, the FBI started spot surveillances on Draper's known haunts to get a handle on his activities. Agents were assigned to check two locations on a random basis. The first was Draper's apartment in Mountain View. The second was the People's Computer Company in Menlo Park.

Draperism. That was John Draper's term for what he viewed as the persistent bad luck that seemed to follow him around like a rain cloud. Draperism was never his fault, never the result of anything he had done. Like the weather, it was a purely external phenomenon, something that just happened.

Whatever it was, the *Wall Street Journal* did Draper no favors when the newspaper ran a front-page story that same day— January 27, 1976—titled "Blue Boxes Spread from Phone Freaks to the Well-Heeled." It described the spread of the hobby from "electronics tinkerers who got a charge out of things like reaching the recorded weather report for Tokyo without paying for the call" to the mainstream, to "people who consider themselves basically honest." It made Draper's hobby sound like the Next Big Thing, one that was spreading like wildfire.

On January 30 the FBI's San Francisco office sent a high-priority teletype message to headquarters. As part of their "intensification" of the investigation against Draper, San Francisco agents had procured a tracking device that they were preparing to surreptitiously install on Draper's car. That same day Pacific Telephone reported that equipment had been deployed that would enable the company to "detect any unusual or illegal telephone usage" at Kaylor's house across the street from People's Computer Company, as well as the pay phone down the street outside the Menalto Market. The FBI continued its "fisur"—Bureauspeak for physical surveillance—of Draper's haunts over the next week.

On February 10 the San Francisco office decided it was time to move the investigation along. "San Francisco has no sources who are phone phreaks," read the draft of an urgent teletype message. Given this, San Francisco requested that Los Angeles send one of its phone phreak informants up to the Bay Area to visit Draper and "accomplish the following objectives."

What might those objectives be? We may never know. The FBI's Freedom of Information Act office suffered an acute attack of shyness and blanked out the entire next page of the draft teletype message. But we can bet the objectives were mundane, certainly nothing exciting, because a few lines later, after the blanked-out material, the draft teletype message noted that Floy Dawson, the assistant U.S. attorney, "advised there would be no entrapment in the above." What a relief!

Except somebody in the FBI drew a line through that sentence on the draft teletype message—striking it out. A copy of the final teletype message as received at FBI headquarters shows that little exculpatory sentence never made it into the actual teletype message that was sent. Apparently Assistant U.S. Attorney Dawson did not advise that there would be no entrapment in the above or perhaps the FBI thought better of checking with him. Here's a suggestion, by the way. If you're ever in a position to document something that might appear to be sketchy—even if it's perfectly legit—don't leave drafts of emails or teletypes or memos in your files. And if you do, try to make sure they don't have sentences that say things like "I checked with our lawyer and he says this is perfectly legal, whoops, actually, no, he didn't say that, let me just draw a line through that sentence." It just doesn't look good.

Whatever the San Francisco office agents were proposing, FBI agents in Los Angeles were not thrilled with it. Still, after some back and forth, Los Angeles finally agreed to send a phone phreak informant up to San Francisco. On Monday, February 23, an urgent teletype message from Los Angeles to San Francisco advised that the informant would drive up the next day and should arrive in the Bay Area late that afternoon. He was instructed to contact FBI agents in San Francisco upon his arrival.

Perrin and Sheridan were spending a lot of time together. "He wasn't a bad kid," Perrin recalls. But, Perrin says, "you couldn't shut him off. You couldn't say, 'Paul, I only talk to you at work,' because he wanted to talk. He wanted a normal life." Sheridan's family situation was a shambles. "It fucked up way back when and it's been fucked up ever since," Perrin recalls Sheridan telling him. Sheridan's parents were divorced and he had attended a reform school in Los Angeles where he had met other teenagers interested in telephone shenanigans.

Perrin says he became a father figure of sorts. Sheridan often dropped by Perrin's house during the investigation. "He'd come over here and he would be comfortable. He played basketball with my son and daughter and talked to them like he was a long-lost cousin. They were very nice to him, they liked him. But they knew he was somebody I was working a case on, and that he wasn't normal. Kids can pick things up like that."

As much as the normalcy that Perrin was providing him, it was clear that Sheridan also liked the attention he was getting from switching sides. Imagine what it must have been like to have telephone company security officers and FBI special agents hanging on your every word, being dazzled by your feats and knowledge, even sending you on spy missions. Then, too, there was the money the FBI was paying him. Finally, Sheridan firmly believed that the phone company had been mere days away from having him arrested. By turning himself in, he must have figured, he was avoiding a much worse outcome.

When Sheridan wasn't playing basketball with Perrin's kids, he could often be found on the couch in Perrin's living room, or in a chair in a conference room at Pacific Telephone, being gently interrogated. "You didn't have to lean on Paul real hard," says Perrin. "Paul wanted you to be his friend. You had to imply that the world was coming to an end. If you threatened him—'listen, you son of a bitch'—it didn't work. But if you said, 'Paul, look, I can't keep these people off you for long, you've gotta work with me.'"

The tape recordings and transcripts of Sheridan's interrogations piled up over the weeks, first a handful, later more than a dozen. Sheridan wanted to please. He went through his notes and address book, combing them for information and then distilling it all down. It got to the point that the sessions were closer to dictation than interrogation—no questions being asked by Perrin, just Sheridan reading into the microphone from preprepared notes. Names and addresses of phone phreaks. Their specific phreaking activities. Recommendations for who should be investigated—"worked," in security parlance—due to their "fucking around." Recommendations for who the phone company should go easy on too. It was all there, all on tape.

The address book Sheridan gave up contained more than sixty names and telephone numbers of phone phreaks. Over hours of interviews he provided additional details on more than fifty of them. Then there were the specific cases that Wayne Perrin and Pacific Telephone needed tied up. Remember the telephone crime wave that had hit the Valley, the burgled phone company trucks, the $21,000 conference call? All of those needed to be explained. The conference call was "Project 21," Sheridan said, a prank against a certain Doctor Bosley who Sheridan and his buddies were pissed at for some reason. They arranged to use some telephone lines that belonged to Bosley over the course of a weekend to call all of their phone phreak friends around the world. It was nice to talk to their far-flung network for nineteen hours but the real purpose was to screw Doc Bosley. Hence Project 21: a goal of racking up $21,000 in phone bills for the good doctor.

Then there were the telephone company employees. If you're a phone phreak, where do you get your information? Dumpster diving, playing with the phone, talking to other phone phreaks? Sure, all that works. But sometimes it's easier just to talk to people who actually work for the telephone company. Big surprise: some telco employees were phone phreaks too. Others just had a soft spot for a bright kid who wanted to know how the telephone system worked.

Sheridan turned in five Pacific Telephone employees and one General Telephone employee, all in the Los Angeles area. Some of these employees were phone phreaks and had black boxes of their own. Some Sheridan claimed would use Pacific Telephone computer systems to turn on or off various features for him on his telephone line. Others provided technical information to him or other phreaks. An employee even gave him telephone company equipment. In at least one case Sheridan actually called a phone technician from Perrin's conference room and got him to divulge confidential company information over the telephone while Perrin was listening from the sidelines.

In the end, two Pacific Telephone employees were fired and two were suspended; the General Telephone employee's name was passed on to GTE security.

FBI headquarters wanted this case solved. Pacific Telephone had blue box detectors and tape recorders and dialed-number recorders and every other god damn thing on every telephone that Draper came anywhere near. FBI agents had Draper under surveillance morning, noon, and night. Draper doesn't have the best judgment to begin with. And just in case Draper's bad judgment can't be relied upon, an informant was being sent up from Los Angeles to move things along.

To this day, Draper maintains that he was framed. He says Sheridan came up from LA and attended a potluck dinner with him at the PCC. Sometime during the evening, Draper claims, Sheridan went outside to the pay phone next to the little market down the street from the PCC and made a blue box call. "I go out to the store and there he is, inside the pay phone booth," Draper says, "but I didn't see the blue box." Draper remembers Sheridan calling him over to the pay phone—"Jim wants to talk to you, here, say hi to Jim"—and passing him the phone. "He hands the phone to me," Draper says. "I say, 'Hi Jim, what's going on?'"

"Well, it turns out he had arranged with the FBI to tap that phone," Draper says. "He told the FBI that I was going to be making a blue box call at that phone at that date and time." The result was that the FBI now had a blue box call on tape with Draper's voice on it.

Given the pressure the FBI agents were under, given the teletype message in which the San Francisco FBI wanted an informant to come up from Los Angeles and "accomplish the following objectives"—the objectives that the assistant U.S. attorney didn't sign off on, whatever they were—this all seems vaguely plausible. A stretch, perhaps, but plausible. But the dates don't line up.

You see, the informant that the Los Angeles office of the FBI sent up didn't arrive in the Bay Area until Tuesday, February 24. The blue box telephone calls that Draper was eventually busted for occurred four days earlier, on Friday, February 20. And on that Friday the Los Angeles informant was still in Los Angeles, enjoying sunny southern California weather or breathing smog or whatever it is that LA phone phreak informants do when they're off duty.

According to Draper's FBI file, an FBI special agent had Draper under surveillance on the Friday that the blue box phone calls were made.

> On February 20, 1976 at 5:23 PM, John Draper was observed in a public phone booth adjacent to the Menalto Market [. . .]. He was hunched over in the booth with his face close to the door, as if he were peering out. He was alone in the booth and no one appeared to be waiting in the vicinity for the booth.

Of course, simply being in a pay phone booth isn't a crime, even if you're John Draper, even if you're hunched over and peering out. But the phone company's monitoring setup finally paid off. It took security agents a few days to review the tapes (it was over a weekend, after all) but on Monday Pacific Telephone presented the FBI with a letter.

> This will serve to inform you that The Pacific Telephone Company has reason to believe that instances of toll fraud are being committed within your jurisdiction (San Mateo County) in violation of Title 18, Section 1343 of the Federal Criminal Code.
>
> We will be pleased to apprise you of certain evidence in our possession which you may acquire pursuant to a duly issued subpoena or letter of demand in accordance with applicable Federal Law.

The phone company had learned much from the Hanna and Bubis cases of ten years earlier. If you have tape recordings of somebody making illegal calls, you don't just hand them over to the FBI. No, you make the FBI demand them from you via a subpoena. That way nobody can make a stink later about how you violated the wiretap laws.

Upon receiving his letter of demand from the FBI, George Alex, the Pacific Telephone security agent for the San Jose region, met with FBI agents the very next day. He provided them with a tape recording and detailed analysis of blue box calls made from the Menalto pay phone on February 20, starting at 4:45 p.m. and continuing until 5:50 p.m., in other words, during the period when the FBI special agent had eyeballed Draper in the pay phone booth, alone and hunched over and peering out. Dozens of blue box calls were made from that line during that time.

Many of these calls were to various internal telephone company test numbers. Some were to numbers in the Bay Area where no one answered. But two calls were enough to hang Draper: one to some friends of his in Pennsylvania and one to his answering service in Mountain View.

For younger readers who have never heard of such a thing as an answering service, come with me on a quick trip down memory lane. Back in the day, long before voice mail, even before telephone answering machines, busy or self-important people would hire an answering service, a company that employed real, live human beings to answer your telephone calls and take messages, handwritten on little pink slips of paper. You could then call in to the answering service, speak to one of these real, live human beings, and retrieve your messages.

The reason the calls to his answering service and his friends were such nails in Draper's telephonic coffin was that they proved it was Draper who had made the calls. In both cases he identified himself as "John." The FBI even went so far as to subpoena the little pink slips of paper and to confirm that it was indeed John Draper who had the account with the answering service, and the service's receptionist said she recognized Draper's voice on the tapes the FBI played for her. FBI agents got Draper's friend in Pennsylvania to listen to the tapes as well; he, too, confirmed that it was Draper's voice.

With all that, why would Draper still maintain to this very day that Sheridan made a blue box call and then handed him the phone in an effort to set him up when the facts seem so clearly to indicate otherwise? Is Draper simply delusional?

Possibly. But it is also possible that Draper's version of events happened too. It is clear from FBI files that, despite knowing about the blue box calls Draper made on February 20, the FBI went through with its plan to send an informant up from Los Angeles. The FBI learned of Draper's February 20 calls only on Monday, February 23, the day before the informant was scheduled to arrive from LA. Agents may not have known that they had enough to convict Draper at that point; if so, sending the informant up from LA might still have made sense to them. This informant may well have been Sheridan. And Sheridan's instructions may indeed have included getting Draper's voice on a blue-boxed phone call.

So Draper may not be delusional. He may actually have been set up. But, if so, the setup wasn't what got him. He got himself, via his own blue box phone calls from three days earlier.

Draper's arrest occurred about a month later, at 7:33 a.m. on April 2. It remains, to this day, a textbook example of how not to deal with the FBI when being arrested. The FBI's after-action report says it best.

> John Thomas Draper, 1905 Montecito, Apartment 6, was advised of the identities of the arresting Agents, as well as the fact that he was being arrested for a federal violation of Fraud by Wire. Draper was advised of his rights [. . .] which he waived as shown on an executed Warning and Waiver form.

Despite Draper's having been arrested on Fraud by Wire charges four years earlier, the report continues,

> Draper inquired as to what a Fraud by Wire violation was and it was explained to him that it involved the use of a "blue box." Draper stated that he never used a "blue box" and why didn't the Agents execute their search warrant and look for one. Draper was

informed that there was no search warrant but that he could vol-
untarily consent to a search. He then agreed to allow his apartment
and his Volkswagen Van to be searched.

Oh dear.

As Draper selected each article of clothing that he desired to wear,
they were first searched [. . .] In the pocket of the pants [the agents]
found a small, black, plastic box approximately one inch by two
inches by three inches with an on/off switch and three buttons
on top.

Oh dear, oh dear.

After Draper completed dressing, he was transported by Bureau
car to the Santa Clara County Jail.

In addition to the mysterious black plastic box (which turned out
to be a red box) the search turned up piles and piles of stuff that must
have looked pretty damning to the FBI agents: bags of electronic
parts, telephone company documents, computer printouts, teletype
tapes, circuit boards, and reels of audiotapes. Oh, and a copy of a
National Crime Information Center (NCIC) computer manual,
the operating manual to the federal criminal computer database.

It turns out that one of the best ways to get the FBI all riled
up, second only to tapping its phones, is to have manuals to the
Bureau's computer systems casually lying around your apartment when FBI agents arrest you. The fact that the agents
didn't have a search warrant but that Draper invited them to
search his apartment anyway just makes it all the more perfect.
Or tragic. Possibly both.

Draper was booked at the county jail and released on $5,000
bail. A public defender was appointed. Twenty days later a federal
grand jury indicted Draper on three counts of Fraud by Wire.

News of Draper's bust raced through the phone phreak community; it was also picked up by the newswires and widely reported in

the press. "Charges Filed Against Electronics Wizard," read one headline; "Wizard Whistles Way into Trouble," said another. For David Condon and his friends, it was a vindication of their policy of staying as far away from Captain Crunch as they could. Others closer to Draper felt a mix of exasperation and dread. "The first thing I thought was, what dumb or crazy stunt did Draper pull this time to get caught?" recalls Dr. Sidney Schaefer,★ a phone phreak friend of Draper's. "Then I began wondering who else might be next, since the bust meant they probably now had my name and number too."

For his part, Draper was well and truly screwed. He was still on probation from his 1972 bust. One of the conditions of that probation was that "Draper shall refrain from illegal use of the telephone or other such electronic devices for fraudulent means," which meant that even if he somehow managed to fight the charges the feds still might be able to get him on probation violations.

On April 22, 1976, Assistant U.S. Attorney Floy Dawson met with Draper's attorney. Dawson proposed that the government would accept a guilty plea to one count of the charges and recommend six months' jail time in return for Draper's complete cooperation with the FBI. He went on to say that, should the government lose at an evidentiary hearing and if Draper didn't cooperate, Dawson "would personally and vigorously pursue every possibility of having Draper's current probation revoked and seeing to it that Draper will spend the remaining one and a half years of his probation in jail." Out of options, Draper agreed, but with two provisos. First, that he be granted immunity for any related crimes he admitted to during FBI interviews. Second, that he not be made to name or incriminate friends.

Draper met four times with FBI personnel over the course of the summer. The interviews focused on understanding exactly

---

★The pseudonym he went by at the time, a tip of the hat to the movie *The President's Analyst*.

what Draper did and how he did it, what the vulnerabilities were in the telephone system, and how to fix them. Draper was mostly cooperative but he couldn't always keep himself from mocking the agents interviewing him. "It was a big joke for him," recalled an FBI source familiar with the debriefings, a joke that inflated Draper's ego to new dimensions.

On August 23, 1976, Draper was "sentenced to the custody of the Attorney General for three years to be imprisoned in a jail-type institution for four months, with the remainder of the sentence suspended and five years probation." On October 4, 1976, Draper arrived at the Lompoc federal prison to serve his sentence. As he walked through the prison gate he added another first to the legend of Captain Crunch: the first phone phreak to serve time in a federal pen.

What of Paul Sheridan, the informant? And what of the phone phreaks he left behind?

On March 5, 1976, Sheridan signed a payment agreement with Pacific Telephone acknowledging that he owed the phone company some $10,851 ($10,000 for his part in Project 21, $457 for fraudulent credit card calls he'd made while in school, and $394 for his final telephone bill as Robert P. Norden). However, the agreement said, he had to pay only about $2,000 of this amount, and he could do it in easy monthly payments over the next six years. Unless, that is, he started phreaking again. If he made fraudulent calls, or wrote articles telling others how to phreak or encouraging them to do so, the entire amount would immediately be due and payable. The agreement required him to report his whereabouts to Pacific Telephone's Pasadena security office every three months.

Wayne Perrin says, "In ninety percent of these cases, with the phone phreaks and the hackers, we had no criminal case. Everything we had was stuff that you could not prosecute them for. Either there was no legitimate crime on the books that you could go after them for or we had only their word that they did it. In other words, there was no tangible evidence that you could go into court and show you that Paul had access to AUTOVON. He showed you how to do it, and he did it, but he did it at your direction. So you had no independent crime that you could go and prove. Now, he didn't know that. And we never told him. So because he was smart, we kind of talked to some people, and we talked to the air force recruiter, and so we got him kind of directed that way. He talked to the recruiter and they accepted him and he went in. Get him the hell out of here!" With that gentle nudge, about two weeks before FBI agents knocked on John Draper's door, Paul Sheridan became Airman Sheridan, joining the United States Air Force and disappearing from the Los Angeles phone phreak scene.

After Draper's arrest, Sheridan's phone phreak colleagues were left to sort through the rubble and try to understand what, exactly, had happened. The sequence of events didn't leave much to the imagination, at least as far as who was responsible. Everyone had been acting paranoid and hinky. Schaefer had tried to reach Sheridan multiple times in February and March but didn't get any calls back. Then one day, Schaefer says, Sheridan called him to say that he had run into a little trouble with the phone company, but not to worry, as he had settled the problem. Sheridan said that phreaking had become boring to him and that he was going to disappear for a while. This struck Schaefer as odd, verging on unbelievable. Two weeks later Draper was in handcuffs. Captain Crunch was sure he had been framed and wasn't shy about saying who had done it.

"The main reaction I had was a deep sense of betrayal," says Schaefer. "I just kept wondering, how *could* he?" Draper's bust also forced Schaefer to think about his involvement in the hobby. "It made me realize how very serious a business this was," he says, "and how I should probably get out while I could. It was no longer fun, and not a game really worth playing anymore. I quickly became less active, I 'lost' my blue box and hid a bunch of files I had. I also couldn't help but feel sorry for John. He'd been kind of a leader and my personal inspiration to become a phreak in the first place. It had all seemed so exciting for a long time, but slowly it became more dangerous and difficult. It just wasn't worth it anymore."

Twenty

TWILIGHT

O N MAY 15, 1976, five and a half months before John Draper would report to the Lompoc prison, AT&T began upgrading its network with a new technology: CCIS, common channel interoffice signaling. Over the course of the next ten years this would spell the end of blue boxes.

CCIS could trace its roots to 1947, all the way back to Bell Labs' invention of the transistor. Transistors enabled computers, which made telephone switches smarter and faster. But these smart switches still had to talk to each other via an old language—the multifrequency signaling system that dated back to the 1940s. The computerized switches still had to sing to one another, slowly, over the same circuits that humans talked over.

Transistors changed that because transistors also enabled modems. Remember modems? If you were around in the early days of the World Wide Web, you may recall dialing up your Internet service provider using a modem and listening to the odd noises it made while it established your connection to the rest of the world. CCIS didn't connect to the Internet or the Web, of course, since those things wouldn't be invented for years. But it did use modems to let the computers in telephone switches communicate with each other digitally, allowing them to quickly trade all the signaling information that they would have sent slowly via MF. Moreover, they could do all this via a separate channel, a channel that phone phreaks couldn't get at. Analog trunk lines would still be used for conversations between humans, but no longer would these trunks resonate with 2,600 Hz when they were idle; no more would the switches serenade each other with musical MF tones to communicate the numbers that customers were dialing. And that meant no more blue boxes.

Bell started experimenting with a CCIS-like system in 1968 and the first trial of CCIS itself began in 1970. Two decades previously it wouldn't have been economically possible, maybe even technically possible, to build a separate computer network for telephone signaling. But now it was, and that's exactly what AT&T did. The company built a CCIS computer network across the nation in which so-called signal transfer points—kind of like routers in today's Internet—were used to gateway telephone signaling information from telephone switches in one region of the country to those in another. CCIS ran at a turtle's pace of 2,400 bits per second by today's Internet standards, but it was plenty fast at the time. In May of 1976 it officially began service between Chicago, Illinois, and Madison, Wisconsin. By 1977 all ten CCIS regions had been switched on, though CCIS coverage of the nationwide network was far from complete.

CCIS, the Bell System said, was about reducing costs, speeding calls, and offering new services; with the new system calls would go through faster and additional information could be transmitted, such as caller ID. But eliminating blue box fraud was a motivation as well. The phone company had also been deploying another innovation—termed CAMA-C—throughout the network. This was a computerized billing system that could be retrofitted into older central offices and was also able to detect blue box fraud. Thanks to computers and modems, made possible by the transistor, the telephone network was becoming immune to blue boxes.

CCIS was a well-timed bit of good news, because Ma Bell had been having a bad decade. There were the service failures in big cities in the late 1960s and early 1970s. There was the EEOC investigation of AT&T's hiring practices in 1970. There was the big strike by telephone workers in 1971. *Esquire, Ramparts,* the

NPR program, and the phone phreaks themselves of course all took their toll. But all of these problems paled in comparison to those represented by three little words that the Bell System would encounter multiple times during the 1970s: competition, antitrust, and scandal.

Competition raised its head in the late 1960s in the form of a Texas rancher turned businessman named Thomas Carter. Carter made his living selling two-way radio systems to oilmen and his fellow ranchers in the Southwest. In the days before cell phones, his customers needed a way to make telephone calls when they were out in the field, on horseback or in a pickup truck, far away from home or office or pay phone booth. Carter invented something called the Carterfone, an electronic widget that connected a telephone line to a CB or other two-way radio system. It allowed a person out in the boonies to make a radio call back to his home base and place a telephone call over the air.

Carter sold thousands of his Carterfones before he showed up on AT&T's radar and Ma Bell began her inevitable crackdown. "The phone companies were harassing my customers—threatening to cut off their phone service unless they quit using the Carterfone," Carter recalled. AT&T had the law on its side, the crystal clear wording of FCC tariff 132: "No equipment, apparatus, circuit or device not furnished by the telephone company shall be attached to or connected with the facilities furnished by the telephone company, whether physically, by induction, or otherwise." If you wanted to attach something to your Bell System telephone line, that something had to come from Western Electric, which was to say from AT&T.

Carter sued the phone company. "The universal comment was, 'You're whistlin' Dixie—you can't win,'" he said. After all, he was but one man against the might of the Bell System, and Bell's case seemed open and shut. But Texas pride and his instinct for self-preservation kept Carter in the fight. "I didn't think it was fair to let them run me out of business," he said. After the usual tortuous legal process, his case came before the Federal

Communications Commission. And on June 26, 1968, something unexpected happened: he won. The FCC decided that the tariff in question was "unreasonable, unlawful, and unreasonably discriminatory." Henceforth, non–Bell devices could be connected to those telephone wires coming out of your wall, just so long as they did not cause harm to the network.

For consumers—and for phone phreaks—this was great news. It would take several years to catch on, but by the mid-1970s you'd finally be able to own your own telephones instead of having to rent them from the telephone company. It even opened the market to outside innovation; it wouldn't be long before fancy new gadgets such as answering machines would become commonplace.

The Carterfone was the first chink in AT&T's monopolistic armor. The next one came less than a year later from a small, scrappy start-up company called Microwave Communications, Incorporated, or MCI for short. In 1969, to the horror of AT&T, the FCC approved MCI's request to construct a point-to-point microwave private line telephone system between St. Louis and Chicago. MCI's product offering was limited. It would not be providing general long-distance telephone service to either businesses or consumers. Rather, it would serve companies who had offices in both cities. MCI would charge these companies a flat monthly fee, one significantly less expensive than AT&T's rates for similar service, to connect their business telephone systems in each city. AT&T executives were furious. The only reason MCI could offer lower prices than the Bell System, they said, was that MCI didn't have to pay for billions and billions of dollars of physical plant, in other words the wires, central offices, repeaters, amplifiers, and telephones that made up Bell's network. By focusing on one thing—building an intercity microwave link—MCI could avoid all sorts of costs and underprice AT&T. The AT&T executives had a term for what MCI was trying to do: *cream skimming*.

Of course, MCI had no intention of stopping with St. Louis and Chicago; why would it? In 1972 the small start-up hit the big time, raising $100 million through an initial public offering. The funds were to be used to build out a microwave network linking 165 cities in the United States, allowing MCI to replicate its St. Louis/Chicago business model across the country. By 1973 MCI had persuaded the FCC to allow it to expand its product offering to include something called foreign exchange, or FX, service. MCI's FX service allowed a big company—an airline, let's say—to offer local telephone numbers that customers could call for free in almost any big city. These were AT&T-provided telephone numbers, but calls to these numbers got routed back to the airline's corporate headquarters over MCI's microwave network. For the airline this was a great deal, because MCI's rates were less than AT&T's. But as far as AT&T was concerned this was FCC-mandated financial suicide. It was bad enough that MCI got to skim cream, but to AT&T it was completely outrageous that MCI's FX service required AT&T to actually help do it by providing the company phone numbers and a connection to Bell's telephone network.

AT&T was not about to go gently into this MCI-scripted good night. The matter quickly wound up in federal court, where MCI won. AT&T appealed. The appeals court vacated the lower court's ruling and kicked the ball over to the FCC, telling the communications commission to handle it. The very next day AT&T began disconnecting MCI's FX lines, cutting off MCI's customers. Less than a week later, in April 1974, the FCC ruled in MCI's favor. AT&T, at regulatory gunpoint, began reconnecting the lines it had just disconnected.

By 1975 MCI expanded its offerings again, this time with something called Execunet. Execunet was revolutionary. With it, you simply dialed a local access number and got a second dial tone. You'd then touch-tone in a four-digit pass code followed by the phone number you wanted to call in one of eighteen metropolitan areas. Your call would be routed over MCI's microwave network and then out into AT&T's local network to complete the call—all for much less than you'd pay for an AT&T direct-dialed phone call. A competitor to MCI, Southern Pacific

Communications Company, launched a system called Sprint that was similar to Execunet.

AT&T hated Execunet and Sprint but businesses loved them. The phone phreaks loved them, too, both those purely interested in exploring a new telephone network to understand how it worked and those purely interested in making free phone calls; the access codes were only four digits and it didn't take long to find a valid one after a bit of time spent dialing numbers on a touch-tone keypad. Paul Sheridan demonstrated Execunet to the FBI during his AUTOVON demo in 1976. Phone phreaks weren't the only ones hacking Execunet, however. In 1977 MCI sued the Hare Krishnas, accusing the religious organization of stealing some $20,000 worth of long-distance calls.

AT&T and MCI continued their legal tussles. MCI sued AT&T, accusing it of monopolistic practices. With that suit AT&T met the second word it would become intimately familiar with during the course of the 1970s: antitrust. Of course, AT&T was no stranger to the term. Ever since the Kingsbury Commitment in 1913, the telephone company and the government had been more or less at peace with each other. With Kingsbury, AT&T changed its stripes from a predatory nineteenth-century monopoly to a kinder, gentler, government-regulated twentieth-century one. Since that time AT&T had largely played by the rules and stopped the sort of behavior that had gotten it in trouble in the early 1900s; for fifty years, Kingsbury had kept the peace and the specter of antitrust lawsuits had seemed contained.

Now, years later, things were different. The Bell System's immense size and sometimes questionable business practices had attracted calls for its breakup. The U.S. Justice Department had gone as far as filing an antitrust lawsuit against American Telephone and Telegraph in 1949, seeking to sever its manufacturing arm, Western Electric. The lawsuit took seven years to go nowhere. In 1956 AT&T and the Justice Department reached an agreement in which AT&T was allowed to keep Western Electric but would have to license its patents to its competitors—of which at the time there were, more or less, none. AT&T would also have to restrict its business to that of communications. Though the government trumpeted the 1956 agreement in the press as a major victory, inside the Justice Department it was considered a travesty. As one historian put it, "The wounds from that 1956 scandal never healed inside the Antitrust division. Many of the division's lawyers believed that AT&T had abused its political power, circumvented the legal process, and cheated the American public. Throughout the 1960s, the division maintained files about AT&T's activities, waiting for the right moment to go after Western Electric again."

The MCI lawsuit provided the right moment. On November 20, 1974, the Department of Justice filed an antitrust lawsuit against American Telephone and Telegraph, the largest company on earth; fittingly, it would turn out to be the largest antitrust lawsuit in the history of the world. The legal action sought nothing less than the total breakup of the Bell System: the separation of AT&T Long Lines, the regional Bell telephone companies, and Western Electric—"severed limbs" was how one Justice Department official would describe their goal.

AT&T lawyers argued that the antitrust laws did not apply to the company. It was, after all, a government-regulated entity; anything it did was approved by the Federal Communications Commission. Given that its every move required permission from the government, how could it possibly be engaged in improper behavior? Indeed, AT&T asked, did the courts even have jurisdiction over AT&T given that the Communications Act made the FCC the phone company's overseer? These questions stalled the lawsuit until 1977, when the Supreme Court settled the issue. AT&T was subject to the same antitrust laws as any other big company, FCC oversight or no. Finally, after three years, the lawsuit could move forward. Due to the case's size and complexity, the pretrial preparation work alone would take almost four more years. It would be 1981 before the trial itself actually started, and longer still before the case would be settled.

The third word the Bell System would become intimately familiar with in the 1970s was *scandal*. In this regard the phone company was in step with the times. From 1972 to 1974 the United States suffered through the Watergate scandal, in which a botched burglary and an even more botched cover-up led to the unraveling of the Nixon White House and culminated in the resignation of the president, the firing of the White House counsel, the resignation of multiple attorneys general, the conviction of two top presidential aides, and the shattering of a nation's trust in its government.

On October 17, 1974, just two months after President Ford attempted to put Watergate behind the country with the words "Our long national nightmare is over," a Southwestern Bell executive named T. O. Gravitt committed suicide. Gravitt, fifty-one, was a vice president and the chief executive for the company's operations in the state of Texas. The suicide note and nine-page memo he left behind accused Bell and its officials of a laundry list of misdeeds. It concluded, "There is bound to be much more. Watergate is a gnat compared to the Bell System." With that note, AT&T found itself embroiled in a scandal of its own, one that would dog the phone company over the next six years.

Gravitt's friend and colleague James Ashley, an assistant vice president at Southwestern Bell in charge of telephone rate cases in Texas, expanded on the charges that Gravitt left in his note. Ashley claimed that Southwestern Bell engaged in rate fixing by manipulating data provided to municipal regulators, that it maintained a slush fund its executives used to make contributions to sympathetic politicians, and that the telephone company engaged in illegal wiretapping against its enemies. For its part, Southwestern Bell denied any wrongdoing and stated that both Gravitt and Ashley had been under internal investigation for improper conduct; the telephone company suspected Gravitt had misappropriated company funds and Ashley had been suspended earlier that month for sexual misconduct. Indeed, Ashley was fired soon after Gravitt's death. That November Ashley and Gravitt's widow together filed a $29 million lawsuit against Southwestern Bell for libel and slander, actions, they claimed, that drove Gravitt to suicide.

The Ashley-Gravitt affair was much in the newspapers that fall and attracted the attention of Louis Rose, an investigative reporter at the *St. Louis Post-Dispatch,* Missouri's preeminent newspaper. Rose had written a series of articles examining the apparently cozy relationship between Southwestern Bell and the Missouri Public Service Commission, its regulator in that state. "I had been looking at all the expenditures and all of the salaries and donations by Southwestern Bell," Rose recalls. James Ashley, he says, "found a convenient thing in me, because I was already looking up these ties."

In January 1975 the Texas scandal spread to North Carolina when a former Southern Bell vice president—another who had been forced out of the telephone company, as it happened—admitted during an interview that he had run a $12,000-a-year political kickback fund for the Bell System. The telephone company soon found itself being investigated by an assortment of agencies: the Securities and Exchange Commission, the Department of Justice, the Federal Wiretap Commission, the FCC, and the Texas attorney general.

The next shoe to drop in the scandal was, in a way, predictable—so predictable, in fact, that Bill Caming, AT&T's patrician attorney for privacy and fraud matters, had predicted it ten years earlier. Caming couldn't say exactly when it would happen, or exactly how it would happen, but he was sure it would happen. Ever since 1965, when he had first learned about AT&T's Greenstar toll-fraud surveillance system, with its tape recordings of millions of long-distance calls and its racks of monitoring equipment kept behind locked cages in telephone company central offices, Caming had maintained it was a matter of when—and not if—the news of Greenstar would eventually leak.

The "when" turned out to be February 2, 1975. The "how" was a front-page headline in the *St. Louis Post-Dispatch*: "Bell Secretly

Monitored Millions of Toll Calls." The article, by Louis Rose, quoted an anonymous source within the phone company and was chock-full of details: a list of the cities where Greenstar had been installed, the specifics of its operation, the stunning news that the phone company had monitored 30 million calls and tape-recorded some 1.5 million of them. Someone—someone high up, it seemed—had spilled the beans. By the next day the story had been picked up by the newswires and the *New York Times*.

Caming didn't need a crystal ball to predict what happened next: a phone call from the chair of the House Subcommittee on Courts, Civil Liberties, and the Administration of Justice. "He said, 'I think we're going to have to have one of your guys come down and explain all this to us.'" Caming knew, as he had known for ten years now, that he would be the guy.

Less than three weeks later Caming found himself before the U.S. Congress, swearing to tell the truth, the whole truth, and nothing but the truth. Seated with Caming were Earl Conners, chief of security for Chesapeake and Potomac Telephone Company, and John Mack, a Bell Labs engineer who was intimately familiar with the technical details of Greenstar. True to his reputation for loquaciousness (or maybe it was his legal training) Caming made sure his colleagues never got to speak more than two dozen words over the course of the three-hour hearing. Caming explained AT&T's motivations for launching the surveillance system, how it operated, and, most important, why it was legal—indeed, not just legal, but in fact the only option AT&T had to combat blue box and black box fraud at the time. Never once did he refer to it as "Greenstar," the name that ten years earlier he said "just *sounds* illegal." Perhaps it was Caming's legal reasoning, perhaps it was his appearance—competent, prepared, confident, yet self-effacing— or perhaps it was 195 Broadway's deft handling of the press on the matter, but AT&T managed to weather the Greenstar storm without much damage. Despite some alarming headlines there was little fallout and no criminal investigation. The Greenstar matter quickly faded away.

The Ashley-Gravitt lawsuit refused to do the same, though. As soon as it got to trial the case erupted in an explosion of headline-grabbing dirty laundry. Multiple Southwestern Bell managers testified under oath that they had made contributions to politicians and then had been reimbursed by filing false expense vouchers; one manager admitted that he had "arranged for a city council-man to purchase some property from Southwestern in order to curry favorable influence in a rate case." On the witness stand Ashley admitted falsifying expense vouchers but said he did it to "disguise political payoffs." Firing back, Southwestern Bell's attorneys produced thirteen female employees who testified to having sex with Ashley or with Gravitt—or who had sex with other men at their direction—in order to be promoted.

The lawsuit turned into something of a legal roller coaster. James Ashley and Gravitt's widow initially won a $3 million verdict against Southwestern Bell, plus another $1 million in a separate suit in which Ashley claimed Southwestern Bell had illegally wiretapped him. But a year later the appeals court overturned both verdicts. On October 22, 1980, the Supreme Court of Texas let this ruling stand, and Ashley and Gravitt's widow would get nothing.

While AT&T was dealing with its decade of competition, scandal, and antitrust lawsuits, something amazing was happening in Silicon Valley, something that, in its way, would turn the light out on blue boxing and phone phreaking even more effectively than CCIS. Ironically, it was something that AT&T itself had made possible. Bell Labs' invention of the transistor enabled not just the computer but also the microprocessor—a computer on a chip. By the mid-1970s the microprocessor had made it possible for you to own a computer of your very own. As it would turn out, the kind of people who would have been interested in hacking telephones would be just as interested—for many, much more interested—in hacking computers.

Back in 1968, Intel was a small start-up focused on making memory chips for computer systems. Its founders, Gordon Moore and Robert Noyce, had both worked at Shockley Semiconductor, the company started by one of the three Bell Labs scientists who had invented the transistor. In 1970 an even smaller company called Computer Terminal Corporation approached Intel about having it manufacture a new chip that CTC had designed. The interesting thing about the new chip was that CTC wanted it to hold an entire computer on a single piece of silicon; in other words, it would be a computer on a chip, something that had never been done before. Bob Noyce allegedly responded that his company could do it, but it would be a dumb business move for Intel, which was in the business of selling chips. "If you have a computer chip, you can only sell one chip per computer," he said, "while with memory you can sell hundreds of chips per computer." Still, money talked; CTC and Intel signed a $50,000 development contract.

The project did not go smoothly. Intel was unable to deliver on time and CTC decided it would rather build its own computer out of separate chips than wait any longer for Intel. Instead of paying Intel for something it couldn't use, CTC kept its money and Intel kept the rights to the chip. The project eventually resulted in something called the Intel 8008, an early eight-bit microprocessor that Intel began selling for $120 each in 1972.

By 1974 Intel had released a new and greatly improved successor, the Intel 8080, a tiny rectangle of silicon some $3/16$ of an inch on a side that contained about six thousand transistors. It was a computer on a chip that executed a few hundred thousand instructions per second. Engineers called it the "first truly useable microprocessor." Intel didn't know it yet but that chip would be the thing that started the home computer revolution and would lead to Intel's eventual domination of the microprocessor market.

In January 1975 *Popular Electronics,* a geeky electronic hobbyist magazine, offered its readers an unbelievable chance to own their own slice of high-tech heaven. "Project Breakthrough!" the cover fairly shouted. "World's First Minicomputer Kit to Rival Commercial Models . . . 'Altair 8800.'" The cover's photo showed a large metal box—blue, as it happened—about the size of three toasters, its nerd-sexy front panel festooned with dozens of tiny toggle switches and red LEDs. The computer had an Intel 8080 processor and 256 bytes of memory. It had no screen or keyboard, not even a teletype. If you wanted to program it, you would be flipping switches on the front panel for some time. But before you could program it you had to build it. It came as a kit, consisting of empty circuit boards and bags full of electronic components you had to solder together. The price? A mere $397, mail-ordered from a company no one had ever heard of: MITS in Albuquerque, New Mexico.

MITS's phone began ringing off the hook. Within weeks thousands of orders were called in for the Altair 8800, more than four hundred in a single day. The *Popular Electronics* editor Les Solomon said later, "The only word which could come into mind was 'magic.' You buy the Altair, you have to build it, then you have to build other things to plug into it to make it work. You are a weird-type person. Because only weird-type people sit in kitchens and basements and places all hours of the night, soldering things to boards to make machines go flickety-flock."

Weird-type people who sit in kitchens and basements, soldering things to make machines go flickety-flock. Hmm. Where have we heard of such people before?

As a hobby, building computers had a huge advantage over building blue boxes: it was legal. Computer hobbyists began to gather in the Silicon Valley—shockingly, without fear of arrest, without the haunting "who's the informant?" paranoia that accompanied phone phreak gatherings. First there were the Wednesday night potluck dinners at the People's Computer Company on Menalto Avenue in Menlo Park—the same place the FBI would stake out in the Bureau's efforts to catch Captain Crunch—and later there were the meetings of the nomadic Homebrew Computer Club. Homebrew hosted its first meeting in March 1975. Its second meeting had some forty attendees; by its fourth meeting more than one hundred people were on its mailing list. The Homebrew Computer Club rapidly attracted the likes of John

Draper and Steve Wozniak, who often hung out together in the back of the meetings. Wozniak would show off his latest hardware hacks and Draper—before his 1976 bust and still on probation from his 1972 bust—would happily give tips on blue box construction and tuning to those who asked.

Hacking on microcomputers had another advantage over hacking phones because you might actually be able to make money at it. The Altair 8800, for example, quickly caught the attention of a couple of undergraduates from Harvard University. Sensing a business opportunity, the duo proposed to write an interpreter for the BASIC computer language, something that would make the Altair far more useful. Upon seeing demo code from the pair, MITS took them up on the deal. The Harvard students—two kids named Bill Gates and Paul Allen—dropped out and started a company called Micro-Soft to pursue the opportunity.

Intel's 8080 found itself at the center of a competitive whirlpool of other companies' microprocessor chips: the Motorola 6800, the MOS Technology 6502, the Zilog Z80. MITS's Altair 8800 spawned a cottage industry of competitors as well, mostly kits, mostly clumsily named: the IMSAI 8080, the Processor Technology SOL-20, the MOS KIM-1, the Southwest Technical Products Corporation SWTPC 6800. Other companies formed to supply accessory circuit boards to these new computers, such as Cromemco, Morrow's MicroStuff, Godbout Electronics, North Star Computers. Every one needed hardware and software hackers to help them. Riches, or promises of riches, or maybe just a fun job that might pay the bills beckoned.

In 1976 former phone phreaks Steve Jobs and Steve Wozniak were selling Apple I computers to their fellow hobbyists. "Jobs placed ads in hobbyist publications and they began selling Apples for the price of $666.66," journalist Steven Levy wrote. "Anyone in Homebrew could take a look at the schematics for the design, Woz's BASIC was given away free with the purchase of a piece of equipment that connected the computer to a cassette recorder."

The fully assembled and tested Apple II followed later that year. By 1977 microcomputers had begun to enter the mainstream. You could stroll down to your local Radio Shack and buy a TRS-80 microcomputer off the shelf, something absolutely unheard of just a year earlier. The microcomputer revolution was fully under way.

Twenty-one

NIGHTFALL

EVER SINCE 1967, when he called directory assistance operators all over the country to find out where each area code was, Bill Acker had been building a map of the telephone network in his head. By 1976 that map was bursting with information. It had long since expanded beyond the borders of the United States and now included countries overseas. In fact, it was now much more than a map; it was closer to a call routing database. When ordinary long-distance operators got stumped by how to make complicated international phone calls they'd call the expert operators at rate-and-route. Certain phone phreaks knew it was faster, and maybe even more accurate, just to call Bill Acker.

One of Acker's close friends had moved to Florida and had a Haitian roommate. Acker's friend had a blue box and wanted to know how to help his roomie call home, so he boxed himself a call to Acker in New York and asked for routing guidance. Acker was happy to oblige. "Well, let's see," Acker said. "Look, the Dominican Republic is on the same island, so why not call Santa Domingo? 171 121 is how you get there and they'll get you through. It should be pretty straightforward."

It was good routing advice but, like so many things in life, it had unintended consequences. In December 1976, the United States of America indicted William F. Acker on the felony charge of conspiracy to commit Fraud by Wire. As it turned out, the telephone company had been investigating Acker's friend for blue boxing and had placed a recorder on his line. Just like in the Hanna case from the 1960s, the telephone company's recorder grabbed several minutes of conversation from the telephone line every time it was activated by a 2,600 Hz tone. Those several minutes were enough to get Acker on tape giving his buddies advice on how best to route their fraudulent call. As Acker put it later, "Apparently being a rate-and-route operator for phone phreaks is considered conspiracy."

Fortunately for Acker, things had tightened up a little bit since the Hanna case a decade earlier. Back then the phone company turned tapes over to the FBI and the feds prosecuted based on whatever was talked about on those tapes—in Hanna's case, his conversations were used as evidence of bookmaking. That wasn't considered kosher anymore. The new legal standard was that tapes resulting from blue box monitoring could be used as evidence of toll fraud, and to identify the people involved, but attempting to prosecute on other charges based on anything else that was said on the tapes was standing on shaky legal ground. Luckily, Acker hadn't actually committed toll fraud—on that call, anyway—and the result was that the conversation on the tape couldn't be used as evidence of conspiracy. Charges against him were dropped on March 14, 1977. His buddy and the roommate weren't so lucky, for they had actually made blue box calls; they were convicted later that month of Fraud by Wire.

That January, a few months before the charges against Acker were dropped, John Draper walked out of Lompoc prison a free man. He had spent a total of three months on the inside, where he slopped pigs at the prison's piggery and tended the prison grounds in a landscaping job. While there, Draper claims, he taught the art of phone phreaking to dozens of other inmates.

Draper soon went to work for his friend Steve Wozniak at Apple Computer, designing an innovative product called the Charley Board. Charley was an add-in circuit board for the Apple II that connected the computer to the telephone line. With Charley and a few simple programs you could make your Apple II do all sorts of telephonic tricks. Not only could it dial telephone numbers and send touch tones down the line, it could even listen to the calls it placed and recognize basic telephone signals as the call progressed, signals such as a dial tone or busy signal or a ringing signal. With the right programming it could be used as a modem.

An Apple II with a Charley Board, in fact, became the ultimate phone phreaking tool. Just as the phone company thought it was natural to mix computers and phone switches, John Draper thought it was natural to mix computers and phone phreaking. Draper was not the first to have this insight; students at MIT in the mid-1960s had interfaced one of the school's PDP-6 microcomputers to the telephone line and used it as a computerized blue box. According to hacker historian Steven Levy, "At one point, [the telephone company] burst into the ninth floor at Tech Square, and demanded that the hackers show them the blue box. When the hackers pointed to the PDP-6, the frustrated officials threatened to take the whole machine, until the hackers unhooked the phone interface and handed it over." Still, the small size and low cost of the Apple II changed the game, and the fact that Charley could listen to a call in progress meant that it could do tricky things like crack codes for WATS extenders. As Wozniak explained it, "A WATS extender is used when a company has incoming and outgoing free 800 lines. Company executives call in on the incoming 800 line and tap out a four-digit code, which gets them on their company's outgoing 800 line. Then they can dial a free call anywhere they want. The only system protection is the four-digit code." Thanks to Charley and some software Draper had written, some of phone phreaking's drudgery was eliminated; what Charlie Pyne and Jake Locke had to do with their index fingers at Harvard in the 1960s—dialing thousands of numbers and listening for dial tones—an Apple II could now do automatically. According to Wozniak, Draper cracked some twenty WATS extenders by Charley's brute-force dialing of codes while Draper was working at Apple.

All this did not sit well with Steve Jobs and the other managers at Apple, who thought the Charley Board product was a bit too risky and, besides, they disliked Draper to begin with. Charley was shelved. Draper left Apple and moved from California to rural Pennsylvania to work at a friend's company designing a product for the emerging cable television industry. He and his like-minded housemates quickly turned their house in the Poconos into a microcomputer laboratory—a Processor Technology SOL-20 microcomputer sat side by side with an Apple II. Wires spilled out from the guts of Draper's Apple II, where a new and improved Charley Board connected his computer to the telephone line. Charley was immediately set to work scanning for numbers.

Draper loved to show off for his friends. Charley was a telephonic tour de force, an opportunity for adulation not to be missed. Draper penned a handwritten flyer on a piece of graph paper inviting his friends on both coasts to come to his housewarming party on October 22, 1977: "There will be plenty of music, fun, and information exchanges going on all day and most of the evening [. . .] along with substances in solid, liquid, and perhaps gassious [sic] states for the head. 'Charley,' the first phone phreak computer, will be on hand to play with [. . .] So, head for the hills, the beautiful Poconos for the first East Coast Capt Crunch Party."

The event attracted more than a dozen of Draper's friends and acquaintances, some from as far away as California. It was midafternoon before the party crashers arrived: the Pennsylvania state police and security agents from Bell of Pennsylvania. Draper soon found himself in an increasingly familiar situation, in handcuffs, sitting in the back of a police car. His Apple II and his housemate's SOL-20 computer were seized and carted off to Bell Laboratories for analysis.

Pennsylvania Bell security agents had been watching Draper like a hawk, having attached a dialed number recorder, or DNR, to his telephone line within a few days of getting word of his arrival in the 717 area code. Unlike a wiretap, a DNR doesn't generally record voice conversations. Rather, it listens for tones and pulses and then decodes and prints out everything it hears—the numbers dialed with a rotary dial, with touch tones, or with the

MF tones generated by a blue box. Within a couple of days the dialed number recorder printouts showed Draper making illegal calls. Some were made via a blue box, others by WATS extending.

For Draper, it was the start of a lengthy nightmare, one that he would, as always, chalk up to Draperism. He spent the next thirty days in the county prison, finally posting bail and getting out around Thanksgiving. Then, the day after Christmas, Draper's venerable VW van blew a tire while driving through the Lincoln Tunnel. Pulling off in Weehawken, New Jersey, Draper called a tow truck, which dropped him and his van off at a service station. "When I come back to the gas station after getting money for the tire the car's gone," Draper recalled. "So I ask the gas station owner what happened to it and they said, 'Call the Weehawken police.'

"I go down to the Weehawken police station," Draper said, "and this detective down there has a bunch of stuff that was found in the car in his office. [. . .] He says, 'Do you know what this is?' I says, "It looks to me like a black box with buttons on it.' He says, 'Yeah. That's a blue box. It's used to defraud the phone company. We found this in your car.' [. . .] How that thing got there is beyond me." Draper was ultimately charged with possession of a red box, although this charge was later dismissed; simply possessing a red box, it turned out, was not a crime in New Jersey.

At Bell Labs, Ken Hopper and his colleagues in the Telephone Crime Lab reverse engineered the Charley card and dissected the Apple programs that made it work, eventually preparing a 180-page evidence report for the prosecution. Hopper had no love for Draper. He was also aware of Draper's legendary paranoia, his fear that the phone company was watching his every move and listening to his phone calls. At one point during the trial, Hopper remembers, he noticed that Pennsylvania Bell had a particularly spooky-looking van, one decorated with the telephone company's unmistakable logo and color scheme and covered in antennas, complete with a futuristic-looking satellite dish on top. Hopper asked his friends at the Pennsylvania telephone company if they wouldn't mind parking that van in the courthouse parking lot whenever Draper was there, just to freak him out a bit. Hopper's friends were only too happy to oblige.

After a lengthy trial filled with failed motions to suppress evidence, Draper agreed to a plea bargain, pleading guilty on June 19, 1978, to one count of possessing a device (an Apple computer!) to steal telecommunication services. He was sentenced to three to six months in jail in Pennsylvania, with credit for the one month he had already served. Once he got out, he would then have to deal with the feds because the Pennsylvania conviction was a violation of his federal probation.

Meanwhile, Joe Engressia had moved from Memphis to Denver a few years earlier. Asked by a reporter why he was making the move, Engressia responded, "I just have a feeling about different areas of the country." Plus, he said, Denver's telephone switching system was "more fully computerized" than the one in Memphis and he looked forward to exploring it. His feeling paid off. In Denver he found a high-rise apartment building with an indoor swimming pool, a living arrangement he had dreamed about since he was a kid. He quickly adopted a new handle: "Highrise Joe."

In Denver Engressia began attending public utility commission hearings, just to keep up to date on what the telephone company was doing. "I was there every hearing, just perfectly quiet all day, listening," he says. On several occasions Engressia heard a Mountain Bell vice president named Lloyd Leger testifying. Leger made an impression on Engressia with his clarity and no-nonsense style. "He sounded like a ship's captain," Engressia remembers. One day after one of the hearings Engressia approached him.

"I got a problem," said Engressia. "Maybe you could help me out."

"What's that?" asked Leger.

"New York. I called them and told them that every line into this particular exchange just gives me free calls. And they just hung up on me. Bunches of lines, it's like thousands of dollars of revenue being lost every day. I was wondering, who would be the right man to talk to about this?"

"I'm the right man," Leger responded. Engressia gave him the details on the defective circuits and Leger got the problem squared away; technicians in New York confirmed that there were twenty-four lines giving free calls and that the phone company was indeed losing thousands of dollars of long-distance revenue. Leger was impressed.

After that, Engressia would periodically tell Leger about network problems he found while wandering the network. In 1977, Leger offered Engressia a job. "You wouldn't believe the pressure AT&T and Southwestern Bell put on me not to hire him," Leger says. The result was that, just about the time John Draper was being arrested in Pennsylvania, Joe Engressia was starting his new job in Denver with Mountain Bell as a network troubleshooter. He worked in the Network Service Center, where he would receive trouble reports from the field, try to figure out what was causing the problems, and then call the people in the central offices to tell them how to fix it. It was the perfect job for a phone phreak, one that fused arcane knowledge with the problem solving that Engressia had always loved. Engressia would finally get paid to do the things he used to do for free—exploring the network, ferreting out trouble, figuring things out. "I feel the Bell insignia on my jacket and I think I'm the luckiest person on earth," he said.

Buoyed by Engressia's success, Acker moved to Denver in March 1979 and began working for Mountain Bell as a telephone operator. What he really wanted, of course, was a job like Engressia's at the Denver Network Service Center, but Mountain Bell didn't need any more people there. "They tried to sell other Mountain Bell places on hiring him," Engressia recalls. "I'd tell them, 'Yeah, he's good, he's my equal, he'll do real good.'" But it was a tough sell and, despite a few promising opportunities, nothing happened.

Operator services was interesting for a while, Acker says, but the job wore on him. As it happened, Engressia's dream job was beginning to wear on him too. At heart, Engressia was a free spirit who didn't like to be told what to do, and the Bell System with its bureaucratic rules and detailed procedural manuals for how to sweep floors was not notable as a place where free spirits thrived. Some things particularly incensed him, such as having been flagged as "being tardy even though you worked seven days a week," he remembers. "They'd call you tardy if you're not sitting at your desk [at the right time], all these little schoolish sort of things that I just wanted to avoid." By 1980, he says, "I was ready to leave and have a different adventure." It was also not lost on Engressia that with two little words—"I quit"—he might well be able to get Acker hired. "I thought, this may be the one time in my life where I can actually do something to change somebody's life for the better for long term," he recalls. Engressia resigned from Mountain Bell in 1980. A few months later, on August 11, Bill Acker joined the Network Service Center.

Ever since his 1976 court case Acker had become much more careful. Now that he was on the inside, however, he knew he had to be scrupulously clean. But, Acker says, he comes from the school of "once a phone phreak, always a phone phreak"; it was just a question of making sure that what he thought of as phreaking was strictly legal. Acker now went to extra lengths to make sure that any network exploring he did, and any conversations he might have with phone phreaks, were above reproach. Besides, it was a good time to get out of blue boxing. AT&T had started to deploy its electronic switching replacement for the venerable 4A crossbar toll switch, the 4ESS, just a few years earlier, and common channel interoffice signaling had continued to expand throughout the network. It was becoming tough to find a "boxable" trunk within the United States, and it grew more difficult with each passing year.

For John Draper, it was also a good time to put phreaking behind him. Draper had completed his prison sentence in Pennsylvania from his 1978 conviction and returned to California to face the music for violating the terms of his parole. Psychiatric evaluations by two different psychiatrists observed that Draper "tend[s] to pass himself off as the victim claiming that he has almost no control over all of the troubles that now beset him" and that he had "numerous paranoid delusions of being especially picked out for persecution because of his power and knowledge"—although, one of the psychiatrists allowed, his paranoia might in fact have some basis in reality given his recent run-ins with the telephone company. Both psychiatrists agreed that a conventional jail would not be a healthy place for John Draper.

In March 1979 Judge Peckham—the very same judge who had presided over Draper's 1972 and 1976 convictions—once again found himself peering down from the bench at Captain Crunch. "Is this not simple? You have to pay for your telephone calls," he told Draper. Given the psychiatric evaluations, Peckham sentenced Draper to a work furlough program for one year, with credit for time already served in prison in Pennsylvania. Oddly enough, this structure seemed to work well for Draper, focusing his energy and attention. He spent his nights in the Alameda County jail writing computer code on paper and his days keying it in to an Apple II computer in Berkeley. The result was EasyWriter, the first word processor for the Apple II.

That April Draper sent an open letter to *TAP* to be read at the newsletter's 1979 Technological Hobbyist Conference (the new, more inclusive title for what would have been the "Third Annual Phone Phreak Convention"), explaining his absence. "For several reasons, I have permanently retired from phreaking," his letter read. "It's time to move on to new areas of legitimate interest, such as professional computer programming." He added: "I wish to have no further contact with phreaks or other individuals who may have similar interests."

TAP had expanded its focus and regularized its printing sched-ule somewhat since 1977 or so when its founder, Alan Fierstein, turned the reigns over to Tom Edison.★ Edison had learned of *TAP* through a column in the *Village Voice* in 1975 and quickly sent in some money for a complete set of back issues. "I was totally blown away," he says, as he remembers reading through those is-sues. "I had become so fascinated with the whole electronics of the

---

★The pseudonym he went by at the time.

phone system, and at that time there just wasn't too much being published even in the straight world about telephones and how they worked . . . I don't think I even slept, I just went through it issue by issue, page by page. It was just fantastic." Before long Edison was sending *TAP* corrections to black box schematics. Not long after, he was volunteering at the recently opened *TAP* office between 28th and 29th Streets on Broadway in Manhattan. Shortly thereafter he found himself running the place. "Al gave me a key and said, 'Here, this is going to be your new home.'"

TAP still covered telephones, of course, but by 1978 it was running computer hacking articles as well. In fact, Cheshire Catalyst★ perfectly captured the shift from phreaking to hacking when he introduced his readers to what he called the beige box. "While intrepidly trekking around the recent West Coast Computer Faire in San Jose, CA," he wrote, "I learned of a new colored box to do wonderful things. The Beige Box is any computer terminal that looks like a Model 33 Teletype to a remote computer." So named for the sandy brown color of teletypes, Cheshire pointed out that with a teletype (or its equivalent) and a modem you could do all sorts of things, including hack remote computers. It was time for the blue box to move over and make room.

It was true that beige boxes (or, as they were more commonly known, home computers with modems) could be used to hack into distant computers, but they were also destined to allow phone phreaks and hackers to communicate with each other rapidly and efficiently. Just a few months earlier two microcomputer hobbyists in Chicago, Ward Christensen and Randy Suess, had developed a program called CBBS, the computerized bulletin board system. CBBS allowed hobbyists with computers and modems to dial into a computer where they could read and post messages and share files. It was a perfect anonymous exchange medium for phreaks and hackers. The first phone phreak/hacker BBSes began appearing within a few years.

★One of the pseudonyms he went by at the time.

Unbeknownst to Tom Edison or Cheshire Catalyst, *TAP* received some additional scrutiny from the FBI as a result of the THC-79 convention. Someone, it seemed, had been handing out atomic bomb plans at that conference. Via an informant these plans rapidly made their way to the FBI. The New York FBI office forwarded them on to FBI headquarters with a cover note that said, calmly and primly, "Enclosed for Bureau are two packages of Xerox pages which, when assembled, comprise the front and back of a chart entitled 'Fission Fever.' Also enclosed is one eight-page Xerox document entitled 'Thermonuclear Explosives Design.' It is requested that the Bureau forward this material to the Department of Energy for its analysis as to whether the information contained therein constitutes a violation of Federal law." The DOE weighed in on the designs and rendered its verdict: "There is a possibility that such a device could give a nuclear yield." The New York office was asked to investigate the source of the documents, but that source had long since vanished.

Nobody knew it at the time, but Acker's tenure with the telephone company would outlast the Bell System itself—and by no small margin. In 1981, less than a year after he had started work at Mountain Bell, the United States government's antitrust suit against AT&T finally went to trial. Judge Harold Greene drew the case his first day on the bench and went on to preside over the largest antitrust case in history and the restructuring of the telephone industry in the United States. The statistics are mind numbing. Over the seven years leading up to and during the trial, AT&T had more than three thousand people assigned to it and spent some $375 million on it; the Department of Justice had 125 people on the case and spent $18 million. The trial saw more than a billion pages of evidence and called hundreds of witnesses. Then, on January 8, 1982, shortly before the trial was supposed to conclude, the government and AT&T reached a settlement. AT&T would be broken up into eight different companies. AT&T itself would retain several parts of its former empire: long-distance services (formerly AT&T Long Lines), Western Electric, and Bell Labs. It could no longer provide local telephone service but would be permitted to enter the computer market. AT&T's twenty-two regional phone companies would be remolded into seven regional Bell operating companies, or RBOCs: Ameritech, Bell Atlantic, BellSouth, NYNEX, Pacific Telesis, Southwestern Bell, and U.S. West. The RBOCs, each covering a different area of the country, would be allowed to provide only local telephone service, not long-distance calls, and were barred from manufacturing equipment or providing computer and information services.

The new world order went into effect on January 1, 1984. On that date, after 108 years, the Bell System ceased to exist.

The divestiture decision was not universally popular with the public, and especially not with the rank and file of the former Bell System, where Judge Greene and the breakup were widely resented. Life in the post-breakup era took some getting used to for longtime telephone company employees. As part of the settlement, for example, AT&T employees were now supposed to be careful about having contact with their former colleagues at the Bell operating companies. After all, those colleagues now worked for entirely separate companies—not quite competitors, perhaps, but now no longer family. Ken Hopper, the Bell Labs network security engineer, recalls a certain impact this had on his personal life. His wife, Barbara, worked for Bell of Pennsylvania, a Bell operating company. As a joke one evening after Judge Greene's decision, Barbara took a length of green ribbon and ran it down the center of their bed, dividing it in half.

The breakup of the Bell System symbolized just how much the phone phreaks' world had changed. The giant cyber-mechanical-human system that was the telephone network, the largest machine in the world, was now almost entirely computers talking to one another via modems. Old analog trunks were rapidly being replaced by digital carrier systems and fiber optics, great news for consumers, for the clarity of digital audio meant that (as the Sprint ads claimed in the late 1980s) you could now hear a pin drop over the telephone. But for phone phreaks, gone was the comforting hiss of analog long-distance trunk lines, gone were the interesting quirks of electromechanical switches, gone were the *clicks* and *clunks* and *beeps* and *boops* that had so captivated them. The obsolescence of the blue box deprived telephonic explorers of the tool they used most to explore the network, and the network's homogenization meant there was less and less of interest to explore.

Phone phreaking would continue in various forms in the decades to come; there is something about the telephone network that still entices certain people, even today. But it would never be quite the same. Sort of like the echoes of the final *kerchink* of a stacked tandem, the golden age of analog phreaking had passed and its memory was fading into history.

EPILOGUE

THE TOWN OF Wawina, Minnesota, lies some sixty miles west of the westernmost tip of Lake Superior. Green and forested, with a giant swamp nearby, it is home to about seventy people spread out over some thirty-six square miles. Wawina doesn't have much of a downtown. It's mostly just a county road, a town hall, a few buildings, and a church. If you want the bright lights of the big city you need to drive a few miles up the road to Swan River, population 775.

One thing Wawina does have is its own telephone company. With about forty subscribers, the Northern Telephone Company was bought by Bob Riddell in 1972 when he was just twenty-five years old. Riddell, a bit of a phone phreak himself (he prefers "phone nut"), grew up in the area and became interested in telephones when he was three. By the seventh grade he had built his own switchboard and by 1976 had amassed a collection of 108 historical telephones. Riddell injected his quirky sense of humor into the town's telephone exchange. If you dialed a nonworking number in Wawina in the late 1990s you might have found yourself listening to his voice making the following recorded announcement: "We're sorry, your call cannot be completed as dialed. Please check the number and dial again, or ask your mother to help you."

Another thing that Wawina had, for a while at least, was something that no other place in the continental United States could claim: the last operational telephone carrier system that used 2,600

Hz and MF signaling. For many years the carrier circuit, called N2, provided trunk lines for Northern Telephone's subscribers. It was the last place in the lower forty-eight where you could whistle off your call with a Cap'n Crunch whistle or dial a number with your blue box. Not to worry, though, you couldn't actually make free long-distance calls that way; the only numbers you could dial with a blue box on the Northern Telephone system were within town.

Then on June 15, 2006, Wawina's N2 carrier system went the way of all flesh and, indeed, of all telephone equipment—it was, as they say, disconnected and no longer in service. Before it was removed, Shane Young at Northern Telephone set up a voice-mail account and quietly requested telephone enthusiasts across the country to pay their final respects to the system by dialing 218-488-1307 and leaving a message. In the weeks leading up to the cutoff he amassed several hours of good-byes from old phone phreaks and telephone enthusiasts, including Mark and Al Bernay, Captain Crunch, and even the old Whistler himself, Highrise Joe.

The messages were poignant testimony to the power of the spell that the telephone had cast over some people. After all, phone phreaking's heyday came and went some forty years ago. And that means we have a bit of catching up to do.

Most of the original phone phreaks—the ones mentioned in this book, anyway—went on to live happy, productive, and fairly conventional lives. Jake Locke, the slacker student at Harvard in 1967, never did get a summer job with the phone company. Instead, he went on to get his PhD and became a respected scientist and academic administrator, demonstrating, he says, that "even callow youths can go on to become stodgy bureaucrats." The students who preceded him at Harvard and MIT back in 1962—Charlie Pyne, Tony Lauck, Ed Ross, and Paul Heckel—all went on to have successful careers in engineering and related fields and are now mostly retired; Pyne even married his high school sweetheart, Betsy, who used to impersonate operators to reach him at his boarding school. Sadly, Heckel passed away in 2005. David Condon, the man who hoodwinked long-distance operators with his Davy Crockett Cat and Canary Bird Call Flute back in 1955, became an accountant and tax preparer. Now eighty and retired, he lives in the San Francisco Bay Area and enjoys traveling by railroad. Ralph Barclay, the inventor of the blue box, was an electrical engineer and entrepreneur for forty-four years before he died in 2009.

The blue box bookies (and one of their attorneys) came to less happy ends. The government finally succeeded in convicting Gil "the Brain" Beckley, its most-wanted layoff bookmaker, in 1967. After lengthy legal wrangling, it looked like he would be going to prison for ten years. But then Beckley failed to make a court date. Some speculated that he had fled the country. Others suggested he had been rubbed out to prevent his cooperating with the feds; if he was tempted to squeal, *Time* magazine wrote, "Gil Beckley would be distinctly more valuable to his friends dead than alive." Kenneth Hanna, the bookie whose blue box use caused FBI agents to kick in his door in 1966, met a more certain end. He was found shot dead and stuffed into the trunk of a car at the Atlanta airport in 1970. Flamboyant mob attorney Ben Cohen was convicted of income tax evasion in 1966 and sentenced to eighteen months in prison; he died in 1979.

Thankfully, most of the phone phreaks profiled in the *Esquire* article, and those who fell in with them later, avoided prison, to say nothing of car trunks in airport parking lots. Bill Acker spent twenty-seven years at Mountain Bell (which, after the AT&T breakup, became U.S. West and then later Qwest) as a network troubleshooter and switch technician; ironically, he even spent some time in the Network Element Security Group. Now largely retired, he lives in Denver, Colorado, where he maintains a version of the Linux operating system that is accessible to the blind; he also hacks on Asterisk, an open-source software-based telephone switching system. Al Gilbertson, whose annoyance at being busted by the phone company set the unintended consequences in motion that culminated in the *Esquire* article, retired after an entrepreneurial career in electronics. He now lives in a house on a vineyard in an idyllic area of northern California where, he says, he tries to do "as little as possible." For almost twenty years Jim Fettgather has been at Alphapointe Association for the Blind in Kansas City where he teaches computer skills to the blind. Denny Teresi continues to love music and radio; he ran an oldies record store for a number of years and recently celebrated his thirty-fifth anniversary at San Jose State University's radio station, KSJS. Mark Bernay switched from engineering to law; he is now retired and lives in San Francisco. Ray Oklahoma, the author of the *Ramparts* article and the discoverer of the 052 conference, went on to become a software developer and computer consultant. Al Diamond, also known as Al Bernay, whose telephone conference lines gave so many Los Angeles phone phreaks their start, was a schoolteacher for many years in southern California. He passed away in 2008.

Joe Engressia traveled a substantially less conventional path. After leaving Mountain Bell's Network Service Center in 1980 he took some time off, only to return to Bell System in 1981 as an operator for about a year. He moved to Minneapolis on June 12, 1982, a date he says he chose because 612 was the area code for Minneapolis. He found a high-rise apartment building where he lived on Social Security disability payments and the occasional odd job, including working as an olfactory panelist (or, as he put it, "smelling pig poop") for the University of Minnesota. He also ran a pair of recorded telephone announcement lines, one called Zzzzyzzerrific Funline (the last entry in the phone book) and the other Stories and Stuff.

Around 1986 he began calling himself Joybubbles. "We were on a retreat at Carleton College, a spiritual retreat, and it went around the room, what name would you like to use for the week?" he told a reporter later. "Suddenly it got around to me and I said, 'Joybubbles.' It was like a breath. You just felt the rightness of it. . . . I guess because it conjures up in my mind joyful feelings."

Several years later Joybubbles decided to become a child. He explained it this way: "I'm a survivor of child sexual abuse at a blind school in New Jersey from 1955"; this was something he had "sort of forgot for a number of years." He continued,

"I think that, and going to school when I was four, and other things contributed to me feeling like I never had a childhood . . . I felt that I was too smart to need to play like other kids did." So, he said, "in 1988 I decided to have a childhood at last." He declared himself eternally five years old and began surrounding himself with toys. He legally changed his name to Joybubbles in 1991. In 1998 he made a few headlines for his pilgrimage to the University of Pittsburgh's library in order to listen to several hundred episodes of the television program *Mister Rogers' Neighborhood*. Fred Rogers, Joybubbles suggested in an interview, was on par with Martin Luther King and Gandhi: "Nobody knows how much peace and love he sowed," he said. He remained interested in telephones and often reported telephone network misconfigurations to the telephone company. Joybubbles died of congestive heart failure in 2007 at age fifty-eight. He left behind a tiny apartment full of toys, a diverse collection of books and magazines on tape, a few telephones, many real-world friends, and several imaginary ones.

For John Draper, things were looking up in 1980. EasyWriter for the Apple II did well enough to be noticed by IBM, which selected it to be the word processor of choice when it introduced the IBM PC in 1981. For the next few years Draper lived high on the hog as president of his own company, Cap'n Software. A 1983 newspaper article described him as a "wealthy executive," one who drove a new Mercedes sedan and hung out on the beaches of Hawaii and Acapulco. But by 1984 his personal fortunes were crumbling. Cap'n Software's distributor, Information Unlimited Software, had introduced its own, entirely separate version of EasyWriter called EasyWriter II—one for which Draper received no royalties. By 1985 Cap'n Software had collapsed and Draper took a more conventional software job. Two years later he was back in the papers for forging tickets to BART, the San Francisco Bay Area subway system; he eventually plea-bargained this charge to a misdemeanor. This was the beginning of twenty-five years of spotty employment, raves and dance parties, failed start-ups, and the occasional where-are-they-now newspaper article. Today Draper is sixty-nine and lives in Burbank, California.

Chic Eder, the drug dealer and informant who gave the FBI the recording of Draper wiretapping their San Francisco office, ended up back in the slammer in 1980 on drug charges, where he died eight years later. Paul Sheridan, the phone phreak spy for Pacific Telephone and the FBI's Los Angeles field office, went on to have a successful and entrepreneurial career in business after his stint in the air force.

Ron Rosenbaum, the man who made the *Esquire* phreaks famous, continues his distinguished writing career. He is the author of nine books and now writes for *Slate*. A reprint of "Secrets of the Little Blue Box" can be found in his collection *The Secret Parts of Fortune* (2000).

TAP, the phone phreak newsletter formerly known as *YIPL,* thrived in the early 1980s, especially thanks to a 1982 article in *Technology Illustrated* magazine. Still, rents being what they are in Manhattan, editor Tom Edison decided to close *TAP*'s New York City office and move production of the newsletter to his condo in New Jersey. Then, over the July Fourth weekend in 1983, while he and his wife were out of town, Edison's home was burglarized and set ablaze. "It was an arson job, they had set fire to three different rooms. But before they set fire to everything they took the computers, the *TAP* information, the mailing lists, everything," Edison says. "The fire department concluded that it was started by person or persons unknown. They agreed it was arson, there were accelerants used, there was no question." To this day Edison believes that the telephone company was behind it. "The stuff that was taken had no value except to the phone company. If they stole the stereo, that would be one thing, but when they stole the paper mailing list and the floppy disks, that has no value to anybody else." Editorship transferred to Robert Osband, aka Cheshire Catalyst. *TAP* ceased publication soon after, in the spring of 1984, after ninety-one issues. As it happened, in January of that same year a new hacker/phone phreak publication, *2600,* appeared on scene.

Alan Fierstein, the original founder of YIPL, was blissfully un-aware of all this drama, having long since retired from the newsletter. Today he is an acoustical engineering consultant in New York City. Edison is retired and lives in New Jersey. Cheshire Catalyst moved to Florida, where he was instrumental in getting area code "321"—the last words astronauts hear before "Liftoff!"—for the Space Coast of Florida.

The Bell System employees described here all went on to have lengthy careers with the telephone company. Ken Hopper, the former head of the Telephone Crime Lab, retired from Bellcore (the post–AT&T-breakup successor to Bell Labs) in 1991 after forty-four years. He and his wife, Barbara, moved to Arizona where he established Rancho Radio—several acres of desert land dotted with telephone poles and strung with long-wire antennas where he could enjoy ham radio. He passed away in 2007 at age eighty. Wayne Perrin, the Pacific Telephone security agent who handled the Paul Sheridan affair, retired from the telephone company in 2000 after thirty-five years; he passed away in 2009 at sixty-seven. Bill Caming, the former Nuremberg prosecutor and AT&T's attorney for Privacy and Fraud, retired in 1984 after thirty-one years with American Telephone and Telegraph. In retirement, he wrote and lectured on international war crimes and freedom of information issues. Today, in his nineties, he lives in New Jersey. As he noted in a letter to Ken Hopper at the time of his retirement, "We fought a great many battles together."

As to Ma Bell, after being broken up by the U.S. Department of Justice in 1984, AT&T and the Baby Bells (a great name for a rock band) went their own ways for a while, and then, gravitational attraction being what it is in a maturing industry, slowly began to reassemble. One of the planetary masses was SBC, formerly Southwestern Bell, which in 1998 and 1999 gobbled up SNET, Pacific Telesis, and Ameritech. Another heavenly body was Verizon, the new name for Bell Atlantic, which by 2000 had glommed on to NYNEX and GTE (the old General Telephone). These two telephonic gas giants orbited around each other for a few years, with Qwest off on the side. Then, in 2005 and 2006, SBC bought the old AT&T long-distance company, the new AT&T wireless company (Cingular), and BellSouth, and renamed itself "at&t." Verizon bought MCI. And that brings us to where we stand today, telephone company–wise: lowercase at&t, Verizon, and CenturyTel (formerly Qwest); at&t now trades on the New York Stock Exchange, not the Boston one, but in a nod to history its ticker symbol remains "T."

Judge Harold Greene, the man who presided over the restructuring of the telephone industry, passed away in 2000.

The telephone network itself, the phone phreaks' electronic playground, continued its evolution, as it had every year since its birth in 1876. Today its core is digital, with bits flowing over fiber optic cables. Increasingly, it is wireless as well. By 2001 the number of wired telephone lines in the United States had peaked and the number of households with wireless service only was on the rise. There is not an electromechanical switch to be found anywhere on the network today, except in museums and the basements of telephone collectors. The last 4A crossbar switch was too large to fit in either of those places and was removed from service sometime in the mid-1980s. No ceremony or newspaper article mourned its passing.

The blue box slowly became obsolete, a victim of technology: the transistor, the computer, the modem, the electronic telephone switch, common channel interoffice signaling (CCIS), and the digital network. Yet it still could be used in other countries that utilized telephone switching equipment from the United States —reports on the Internet claim that blue box calls could be used to explore the network (and, as always, make free phone calls) as late as the 1990s outside of the United States. CCIS, the computerized telephone signaling network that spelled the end for blue boxes, has shuffled off this mortal network. Its progeny, a system called signaling system number 7, lives on. Ironically, SS7 allows caller ID to be easily faked and was, at some level, what made possible the British telephone hacking scandal involving Rupert Murdoch's *News of the World* newspaper in 2011.

As to phone phreaking itself, an old joke comes to mind: "When was the golden age of science fiction?" The answer: "Whenever you were fourteen years old." Blue boxes may not work anymore, and computer hacking may have stolen the lime-light, but some teenagers and young men still seem quite inter-ested in obsessively exploring the telephone network. In 2006, when I was first starting this book, I received an email from a modern-day phone phreak who goes by the handle Lucky225. His email opened with "PHREAKING ISN'T DEAD." He went on (thankfully in lower case) to list a variety of phone phreaking techniques in use today, ranging from using blue boxes on obscure old trunks in various parts of the world to caller-ID spoofing and voice-over-IP hacking. There was still much to explore in the modern telephone network, he said, and he urged me not to let my readers think that "we live in a world where the phone company has learned from its mistakes."

Phone phreaking itself, however, differs from the legacy be-queathed to us by the original phone phreaks. To borrow a phrase from Apple, the phone phreaks "thought different"—and taught us to do the same. Where others saw a rotary phone that connected them to the three towns next door, Charlie Pyne saw a portal to another world. Where others saw a dense article in a little-read technical journal, Ralph Barclay saw a gaping hole. Where oth-ers saw a utilitarian telephone system, Joe Engressia, Bill Acker, John Draper, and their friends saw an electronic playground. They noticed things that others ignored, and they saw joy and opportunity in the otherwise mundane.

Nothing captures this spirit more than the inspiration Steve Wozniak and Steve Jobs found in Ron Rosenbaum's Alice in Wonderland tale of blind kids hacking the telephone network, the two Steves jumping for joy after discovering the blue box frequencies in an obscure technical document in the library at the Stanford Linear Accelerator Center. Their phone phreak col-laboration selling blue boxes door to door in the dorms at Berkeley foreshadowed their later ventures, and phone phreaking was one of the things that formed the basis of their partnership—a collaboration that would give the world the Apple computer and create a company that would go on to produce the iPod, the iPhone, and the iPad. As Jobs recalled later, "It was the magic of the fact that two teenagers could build this box for $100 worth of parts and control hundreds of billions of dollars of infrastructure in the entire telephone network of the whole world from Los Altos and Cupertino, California. *That was magical!*" He concluded: "If we hadn't made blue boxes, there would have been no Apple."

The phone phreaks forced us to consider things we hadn't thought of, sometimes things we'd rather not think about—to ponder questions about who is ultimately responsible for computer and network security, for example, and what to do with people whose curiosity causes them to cross societal lines. The figurative descendants of the phreaks are still forcing us to think about these questions every single day.

In the 1930s and '40s and '50s, the telephone company spent billions of dollars designing and building and deploying an automated long-distance network. The result was a technical accomplishment that pushed the limits of what was possible. Bell Laboratories had a lot on its plate; short of the Apollo space program and the atomic bomb, its researchers were tackling one of the biggest engineering problems that mankind had ever attempted. Computers and automated networks didn't exist then, and there weren't hackers to hack into them, so the technicians didn't think much about security. You can hardly blame them for this oversight.

Fast forward sixty years or so. In 2005 the Boston subway introduced a new system, CharlieTicket, that used magnetic stripe cards as subway tickets. You could add value to your CharlieTicket by depositing money in a fare machine that would rewrite the mag stripe on your card with the new amount. It turned out that the CharlieTicket had no security to speak of; less than three years later MIT students proudly displayed a $653 subway card they had created using a mag stripe card reader/writer they had bought for $300 on eBay. The Boston subway system's response? Sue the students to prevent them from reporting their results at a security conference.

The exasperated cry of Al Gilbertson, the phone phreak whose 1970 bust resulted in the *Esquire* article, seems applicable here: "What the Christ did they think, that there's not any bad guys in this world?"

Whose fault is it when things like this happen? Do you blame the MIT students for being clever? Or do you blame the Boston subway authorities for fielding a system like that in the first place? Is it the fault of the phone phreaks for playing with the telephone system or the fault of Bell Labs for designing a vulnerable system to begin with?

The phone phreaks compelled us to deal with a new class of criminal: the curious. When Charlie Pyne started dialing thousands of telephone numbers out of curiosity, just to find out what would happen, did he do anything wrong? When Bill Acker called the directory assistance operators in every area code, did he cross a line? What about when the 2111 phreaks dialed in to a broken TWX converter and used it as a giant conference call, making it into their home on the network? How about when Joe Engressia whistled telephone calls for his college buddies for a dollar each? At some point a threshold is crossed. But the precise location of that threshold—as well as where it *should* be—very much remains subject to debate.

Then, too, there's the question of what society should do when one of its virtual lines is crossed. Should Engressia be kicked out of school for whistling calls? Should John Draper be fined $1,000 for making a three-minute phone call to Australia? Should he be sentenced to prison for four months for doing it again? And should he get more jail time for programming a computer to dial numbers to break into a WATS extender? How about for remotely wiretapping the FBI, even if he did it just as a lark?

This is not to say that phone phreaks and hackers should get a free pass. There is a difference between mere curiosity and true crime, even if we cannot always clearly articulate what the difference is or what we should do about it when we recognize it. At some level, we as a society understand that there is a benefit to having curious people, people who continually push the limits, who try new things. But we'd prefer they not go too far; that makes us uncomfortable.

In the end the phone phreaks taught us that there is a societal benefit to tolerating, perhaps even nurturing (in the words of Apple) the crazy ones—the misfits, the rebels, the troublemakers, the round pegs in the square holes. Say Wozniak and Jobs hadn't been so lucky when they wound up in the back of the police car that evening back in 1972, when they convinced the cops that their blue box was actually a music synthesizer. Say they had been arrested, possibly gone to jail. We might never have had Apple computer or any of the other things that Apple went on to make. Would we be the better for it?

SOURCES AND NOTES

ON A SUNNY afternoon in November 2005 I found myself giving a sweaty, half-naked man a piggyback ride around the front room of a dingy little apartment in Burbank, California. The man was heavy and my knees strained to hold us up as he shouted directions in my ear, telling me where to turn or how better to support him as I lurched across the room. The man was John Draper and the piggyback ride, which Draper referred to as "energy work," was my introduction to what one author described twenty years earlier as a "Draper initiation ritual that all interviewers must survive before they get anything out of him."*

I survived, knees only slightly the worse for wear. I got little out of Draper that day; actual substantive interviews would come later, he assured me. It was an uncomfortable and slightly inauspicious start to collecting the stories that would eventually turn into this book, and perhaps it should have served as a warning of sorts as to what lay ahead. Had I more sense, I might have stopped there. But over the next five years I would go on to interview more than one hundred people in person or by telephone, and I would correspond with many, many more via email. Phone phreaks, telephone company employees, FBI agents, and their friends and families all shared stories with me. Sometimes they gave me not just reminiscences but stacks of old documents, often

---

*Douglas G. Carlston, *Software People: An Insider Look at the Personal Computer Software Industry* (New York: Simon & Schuster, 1985), pp. 102–103.

documents I couldn't believe they had kept all these years; in one or two instances, I was handed thirty-five- or forty-year-old tape recordings. It had never before dawned on me just how useful packrats are to historians.

Much of my research time was spent tracking people down, sometimes people who had little interest in being found. My first telephone conversation with Ralph Barclay, the inventor of the blue box, went as follows:

Me: "Hi, is this Ralph Barclay?"

Barclay: "Yes?"

Me: "Ralph, you don't know me, but I'm writing a book on phone phreaking. Back in college, were you involved with something called a blue box?"

After a very long pause, and with a distinct lack of enthusiasm in his voice, Barclay replied, "That was a long time ago." It took me more than a year to earn Barclay's trust to the point that I was able to interview him in person.

One connection often led to another, but I learned that these connections happened at their own pace, often the result of a combination of frustratingly skimpy leads and pure dumb luck. A great example was when a phone phreak told me early on, "You need to talk to John." "John? You mean John Draper?" I asked. "No, this is another John, a phreak at Berkeley in 1972. Or maybe '73 or '74. He built a specialized blue box," was the reply. "Got anything else to go on?" "No." But then a year or so later my phone rang and, out of the blue, the caller introduced himself as John Gilbert, "an old phone phreak from Berkeley, just checking in." Sure enough, same John.

Then there were the Freedom of Information Act requests. I filed more than four hundred FOIA requests with the Federal Bureau of Investigation, the U.S. Department of Justice, the Central Intelligence Agency, the National Security Agency, the Federal Communications Commission, the National Archives and Records Administration . . . some days it felt as if the only agency I wasn't spamming with FOIA requests was the Federal Interagency Committee for the Management of Noxious and Exotic Weeds. After reviewing thousands upon thousands of pages of redacted documents, I built up an unenviable level of expertise in filing FOIA appeals and decoding FBI "Bureauspeak." I eventually got to the point where I was sending holiday cards to the FOIA staff at various federal agencies.

All of that leads to this: the chapter notes that follow provide references for quotations and facts mentioned in the text, and, just as important, they expand on various points that were too technical or otherwise esoteric to include in the main body of the book. I hope you enjoy reading them as much as I enjoyed researching them.

GENERAL SOURCES

All present-tense quotations in this book from the following people are taken from in-person or telephone interviews I conducted at the following times: Bill Acker, 2007 and 2008; Ralph Barclay, 2009; Al Bell, 2006; Mark Bernay, 2005; Bill Caming, 2007 and 2008; David Condon, 2009; Al Diamond, 2008; John Draper, 2008; Tom Edison, 2008; Jim Fettgather, 2008; Al Gilbertson, 2008; Bob Gudgel, 2012; Dennis Heinz, 2010; Ken Hopper, 2006; Joybubbles (Joe Engressia), 2006; Tony Lauck, 2007; Jake Locke, 2006; Ray Oklahoma, 2008; Wayne Perrin, 2008; Charlie Pyne, 2007 and 2011; Ron Rosenbaum, 2008; Ed Ross, 2007 and 2008; and Denny Teresi, 2007.

For newspaper articles, AP indicates Associated Press, and UPI indicates United Press International. FBI files are cited by file number and serial number (essentially a document number within a given file).

Scans of some of the documents mentioned below are available on my website. These documents have a "db number" in angle brackets after the citation, e.g., <db23>. To view a pdf of that document, point your browser at http://explodingthephone.com/docs /db23. Unfortunately, for reasons of copyright and confidentiality, not all documents referenced here are available in this manner.

Chapter 1: Fine Arts 13

Much of the material in this chapter comes from author interviews conducted with Jake Locke.

2 **"WANTED HARVARD MIT":** *Harvard Crimson,* March 7, 1967, p. 6 <db461>.

3 **transcribed the reversed lettering:** Locke does not recall whether the letter was actually in Russian or merely in English transcribed into Cyrillic characters.

5 **"you'd have to dial something like 212-049-121":** Locke's recollection of Suzy's dial code for the New York inward may have been somewhat off; the New York City inward was 212-121, since it was a big city. 212-049-121 would likely have gotten you to an outlying city in the New York area.

7 **"Five Students Psych Bell System":** Charles W. Bevard, "Five Students Psych Bell System, Place Free Long Distance Calls," *Harvard Crimson,* May 31, 1966 <db991>.

8 **Locke dug up the Herald article:** Ron Kessler, "Student Dialers Play Their Way to Global Phone Calls, Non-Pay," *Boston Herald,* May 27, 1966, p. 1 <db471>.

10 **"Signaling Systems for Control of Telephone Switching":** C. Breen and C. A. Dahlbom, "Signaling Systems for Control of Telephone Switching," *Bell System Technical Journal,* vol. 39, no. 6, November 1960, p. 1381 <db445>.

11 **used a telephone dial to select the train to be controlled:** Steven Levy, *Hackers: Heroes of the Computer Revolution, 25th Anniversary Edition* (Sebastopol, CA: O'Reilly Media), p. 8.

Chapter 2: Birth of a Playground

14 **the best known was created by Claude Chappe:** J-M Dilhac, "The Telegraph of Claude Chappe—An Optical Telecommunications

Network for the XVIIth Century," IEEE Global History Network, at http://www.ieeeghn.org/wiki/images/1/17/Dilhac.pdf.

15 **In America the inventor was Samuel Morse:** The Supreme Court of the United States declared Morse to be the sole inventor of the telegraph; see Tom Standage, *The Victorian Internet: The Remarkable Story of the Telegraph and the Nineteenth Century's On-line Pioneers* (New York: Walker Publishing Company, 2007), p. 183. But debate continues as to the extent of Morse's inventorship of the telegraph and the code that bears his name; see Gavin Weightman, *The Industrial Revolutionaries: The Making of the Modern World, 1776–1914* (New York: Grove Press, 2007), p. 197.

16 **Victorian Internet:** Standage, *Victorian Internet.*

16 **"net-work like a spider's web":** David Bogue, *The London Anecdotes: Anecdotes of the Electric Telegraph,* 1849, as quoted in Standage, *Victorian Internet,* p. 58.

16 **conveyed news, facilitated commerce, and whispered gossip:** Standage, *Victorian Internet,* p. 105ff, p. 127ff.

16 **90% of all telegraph traffic:** IEEE Global History Network, "Western Union," at http://www.ieeeghn.org/wiki/index.php /Western_Union.

16 **$6.6 million:** *Annual Report of the President of the Western Union Telegraph Company,* 1869. The U.S. Bureau of Labor Statistics inflation calculator goes back only to 1911, but assuming a 3.2 percent inflation rate gives 2011 equivalent revenues of $676 million.

16 **20 million:** Tomas Nonnenmacher, "History of the U.S. Telegraph Industry," Economic History Association, at http://eh.net /encyclopedia/article/nonnenmacher.industry.telegraphic.us. Astonishingly, the number of telegraph messages didn't stop growing until the end of World War II, peaking in 1945 at 236 million messages.

17 **"Nothing, save the hangman's noose":** Tim Wu, *The Master Switch: The Rise and Fall of Information Empires* (New York: Alfred A. Knopf, 2010), p. 22.

17 **"harmonic telegraph":** "The Alexander Graham Bell Family Papers at the Library of Congress, 1862–1939," at http://lcweb2 .loc.gov/ammem/bellhtml/belltelph.html.

17 **He became obsessed with this new idea:** Thomas Farley, *Thomas Farley's Telephone History Series, 1998 to 2006,* "page 3" at http://www.privateline.com/TelephoneHistoryA/TeleHistoryA.htm.

17 **"could never be more than a scientific toy":** Herbert N. Casson, *The History of the Telephone* (Chicago: A. C. McClurg & Co., 1910), pp. 24–25.

17 **"For him the thrill of the new":** Wu, *Master Switch,* p. 22.

17 **"I now realize I should never":** Floyd Darrow, *Masters of Science and Invention* (New York: Harcourt, Brace and Company, 1923), p. 293.

18 **he finally succeeded:** Bell started work on the harmonic telegraph in 1873. Many have claimed inventorship of the telephone: Elisha Gray, Johann Philipp Reis, and Daniel Drawbaugh, to name but three. Each has his adherents, but the fact remains that, rightly or wrongly, Bell's patents carried the day.

18 **unlikely contraption:** John Brooks, *Telephone: The First Hundred Years* (New York: Harper & Row, 1975), pp. 46–50, and John Murphy, *The Telephone: Wiring America* (New York: Chelsea House Publications, 2009), pp. 33–36. For a drawing of the variable resistance setup from Bell's laboratory notebook, see "Bell's Experimental Notebook, 10 March 1876" at http://memory.loc.gov/ammem/bellhtml/bell1.html.

18 **$100,000:** M. D. Fagen, *A History of Science and Engineering in the Bell System: The Early Years (1875–1925)* (New York: Bell Telephone Laboratories, 1975), p. 31. Bell's offering of the telephone patent to Western Union for $100,000 is reported in AT&T's own official history and other sources. Despite this, the evidence for it is thin. See Michael Wolff, "The Marriage That Almost Was," *IEEE Spectrum,* February 1976, p. 41, for a detailed investigation.

18 **"What use could this company make":** Casson, *History of the Telephone,* pp. 58–59.

19 **"It is indeed difficult":** Providence *Press,* undated, quoted in Brooks, *Telephone,* p. 54.

19 **The Bell Telephone Company itself:** Brooks, *Telephone,* pp. 53–55. In this chapter I use the term "Bell Telephone" to refer to any of

the incarnations of Bell's company, which reorganized and changed its name several times during its early years. It was founded as Bell Telephone Company in 1877. It reorganized in 1878, keeping its name but also creating New England Telephone Company. In 1879 it reorganized again, changing its name to National Bell Company. In 1880 it changed its name to American Bell. In 1882 it acquired Western Electric, which became the company's manufacturing arm. In 1885 American Telephone and Telegraph Company (AT&T) was formed as a subsidiary to handle long-distance lines for American Bell. In an 1899 reorganization, the child became the parent when AT&T acquired American Bell. For more information see AT&T's website, "A Brief History: Origins" at http://www.corp.att.com /history/history1.html, or Brooks, *Telephone,* chapters 1–4.

19 **telegraph contractors:** John E. Kingsbury, *The Telephone and Telephone Exchanges: Their Invention and Development* (London: Longmans, Green, and Co., 1915), p. 67, quoting from an 1877 Bell Telephone advertisement. Note that this Kingsbury is not related to the Nathan Kingsbury of the AT&T Kingsbury Commitment.

19 **$20 per year:** Ibid.

20 **"Instead of erecting a line directly":** Kingsbury, *Telephone and Telephone Exchanges,* pp. 90–91, quoting from a letter from Bell to the investors of the Electrical Telephone Company in March 1878.

20 **The switchboard ... telephone central office or exchange:** Telegraph central exchanges were apparently first patented in 1851 and in use by the late 1860s. Multiple parties, including Bell, thought of applying this hub-and-spoke architecture to the telephone. See ibid., pp. 77ff.

21 **"It was believed that they would have the energy":** Murphy, *Telephone: Wiring America,* p. 81.

21 **"warmer human voice":** Ibid.

21 **American Speaking Telephone:** Farley, *Farley's Telephone History Series,* "page 4," at http://www.privateline.com/TelephoneHistory2A /Telehistory2A.htm.

21 **settled the lawsuit:** Kingsbury, *Telephone and Telephone Exchanges,* p. 189, and Brooks, *Telephone,* pp. 71–72.

22 **ticker symbol "T":** Domenic Vitiello and George E. Thomas, *The Philadelphia Stock Exchange and the City It Made* (Philadelphia: University of Pennsylvania Press, 2010), p. 111; AT&T news release, "New AT&T to Begin Trading Under 'T' Ticker Symbol," November 30, 2005.

22 **"During the past few months":** "Correspondence: Philadelphia," *The Electrical Engineer,* April 16, 1890, p. 249.

22 **"I cannot understand":** Ibid.

22 **AT&T's first long-distance line:** AT&T Long Lines Department, *Our Company and How It Operates,* 1960, p. 3.

23 **the engineers persevered:** Kingsbury, *Telephone and Telephone Exchanges,* p. 444.

23 **more than ten thousand subscribers:** Fagen, *Bell System,* p. 496.

23 **Put fifty of these switchboards:** AT&T, *Principles of Electricity Applied to Telephone and Telegraph Work,* 1953, pp. 79–80. The switchboard went through a lengthy evolution with many design iterations; the switchboard described here is just one example.

24 **an operator on a tandem switchboard:** Fagen, *Bell System,* p. 505.

24 **3 million switchboard connected phones:** Brooks, *Telephone,* p. 111.

24 **warehouses full of people:** I am indebted to Paul Heilman for the phrase.

24 **thirty thousand operators . . . hundred thousand:** Fagen, *Bell System,* p. 550.

24 **"a coast-to-coast call":** F. A. Collins, "Telephone Night Habits," *New York Times,* March 19, 1922 <db993>. A coast-to-coast call in 1922 would have cost "a little more than $5 per minute" during the day, some $67 per minute today. There was a 50 percent discount after 8:30 p.m. and a 65 percent discount after midnight.

24 **legend has it:** There are multiple versions of this perhaps apocryphal story. See Brooks, *Telephone,* p. 100, for one.

25 **Strowger's first mechanical telephone switch:** A. B. Strowger, "Automatic Telephone Exchange," United States Patent No. 447,918, March 10, 1891.

25 **To call telephone number 315:** Kingsbury, *Telephone and Telephone Exchanges,* p. 400. The original Strowger patent required each telephone to have five wires: three for dialing, one for hanging up, and one for audio. Ground was handled by a connection to earth ground.

25 **The first automatic telephone exchange:** Roger B. Hill, "The Early Years of the Strowger System," Bell Laboratories *Record,* vol. 31, no. 3, March 1953, pp. 95ff, at http://www.telecomwriting .com/Switching/EarlyYears.html <db992>.

26 **Bell had licensed:** Fagen, *Bell System,* p. 554.

26 **reached its peak:** The percentage of lines connected to step-by-step switches peaked in 1960 at 49 percent. See ibid., p. 612.

26 **more than six thousand:** AT&T, "Milestones in AT&T History," at http://www.corp.att.com/history/milestones.html.

26 **Prices varied:** Kingsbury, *Telephone and Telephone Exchanges,* pp. 465–80.

26 **different phone lines installed:** Brooks, *Telephone,* p. 109.

27 **Bell had about fifteen hundred:** Ibid., p. 111.

27 **"ruthless, grinding, oppressive monopoly":** Ibid., pp. 112–14.

27 **Interstate Commerce Commission:** Letter from Attorney General to Chairman of the Interstate Commerce Commission, January 7, 1913, quoted in *Annual Report of the Directors of the American Telephone and Telegraph Company,* 1913, p. 29.

27 **just like the postal system:** Brooks, *Telephone,* p. 148.

27 **Kingsbury Commitment:** AT&T, *Annual Report of the Directors of the American Telephone and Telegraph Company,* 1914, pp. 24–27; Brooks, *Telephone,* p. 136.

28 **"The trick of the Kingsbury Commitment":** Wu, *Master Switch,* p. 56.

28 50 million telephone calls: AT&T, *Report of the Directors to the Stockholders for the Year 1925.*

Chapter 3: Cat and Canary

Much of the material in this chapter comes from author interviews conducted with David Condon.

31 "verbally informed the operator of his wishes": Fagen, *Bell System,* p. 502.

32 "it is unbelievable that it took so long to invent": Ibid., p. 578.

32 two-letter, five-digit: I have simplified a bit of the numbering history here. Telephone numbering schemes varied from place to place. Some towns had four-digit telephone numbers, others fewer digits. When mixed letter-number dialing arrived in 1922, it started out as three letters and four digits; it changed to two letters and five digits in 1947. See Amos E. Joel Jr., *A History of Science and Engineering in the Bell System: Switching Technology (1925–1975)* (New York: Bell Telephone Laboratories, 1982), pp. 12, 608. An informative website that provides history on telephone exchange names is the Telephone EXchange Name Project, at http://ourwebhome.com/TENP/TENproject.html.

32 had to dial 211: The long-distance access code varied from place to place, but 211 was common in cities with panel or crossbar telephone systems. In places with step-by-step switching equipment, 112 was used; the telephone company offered a phrase to help customers remember this: "dial one-one-two to go straight through." See Joel, *Switching Technology,* p. 123.

34 costs $5.90: Federal Communications Commission, *The Industry Analysis Division's Reference Book of Rates, Price Indices, and Expenditures for Telephone Service,* July 1998, p. 47 ("AT&T Basic Schedule Residential Rates for 10-Minute Interstate Inter-LATA Calls," Table 2.5), at http://www.fcc.gov/Bureaus/Common_Carrier/Reports/FCC-State_Link/IAD/ref98.pdf.

34 double or nothing scheme: Fagen, *Bell System,* pp. 618–19, 629.

35 Josefina Q. Zoetrope: Variations of this scheme (e.g., with collect calls instead of person-to-person calls) were possible as well.

36 phone phreak nickname: Condon had another nickname, bestowed on him by the younger phone phreak Joe Engressia: Manuel Daze, a pun on "manual days" since, unlike the other phone phreaks in the 1960s, Condon had been playing games with the telephone system since the manual days of operators and switchboards.

39 highest classification: Even "unclassified" AT&T documents were often stamped "Not for use or disclosure outside the Bell System except under written agreement."

39 Oak Ridge: George O. Robinson Jr., *The Oak Ridge Story* (Kingsport, TN: Southern Publishers, Inc., 1950).

Chapter 4: The Largest Machine in the World

41 "could not have supported such a work force": Fagen, *Bell System,* p. 613.

42 some 15 percent of telephones: Robert G. Elliott, "Dial Service Is Extending Its Reach," *Bell Telephone Magazine,* Summer 1955, p. 110.

42 70 percent of long-distance telephone calls: AT&T Long Lines Department, *Our Company and How It Operates,* 1960, p. 6.

42 "stone knives and bearskins": *Star Trek,* original series episode 28, "City on the Edge of Forever," April 6, 1967. (Thanks, Mr. Spock.)

43 national numbing plan: AT&T's first national numbering plan divided the country into eighty-six different geographic areas called numbering plan areas (NPAs). Each numbering plan area was assigned a three-digit "numbering plan area code," which is where the more familiar term "area code" comes from. Within the telephone company and, later, within the phone phreak community, area codes were generally referred to as NPAs. See F. F. Shipley, "Nation-Wide Dialing," *Bell Laboratories Record,* vol. 23, October 1945, p. 368; W. H. Nunn, "Nationwide Numbering Plan," *Bell System Technical Journal,* vol. 31, September 1952, p. 851; and Joel, *Switching Technology,* pp. 123–28.

44 machines need to be able to do the billing: For more on the incredible "automatic message accounting" (AMA) system see http://explodingthephone.com/extra/ama.

44 largest machine in the world: I am indebted to the late Robert Hill for the lovely description of the telephone network as the "largest machine in the world, extending as it does over the whole surface of the earth." See Robert Hill, "Days at the Old Bailey," *Interface* (the house journal of Cambridge Consultants Ltd.), vol. 8, no. 1, April 1974, p. 10 <db341>.

46 memory called a sender: L. T. Anderson, "Senders for #5 Crossbar," *Bell Laboratories Record,* November 1949, p. 385. To be fair, it was possible to augment step-by-step switches with memory and brains as well, and this idea found popularity in the United Kingdom in the 1920s with what were called "directorized" step-by-step switches. See the BT Archives at http://www.btplc.com /Thegroup/BTsHistory/1912to1968/1922.htm.

46 "In a word, the switching systems": Joel, *Switching Technology,* p. 3. The boys at Bell Labs were justifiably proud of their intelligent machines and suggested they might be compared to a form of human intelligence. See John Meszar, "Switching Systems as Mechanical Brains," *Bell Laboratories Record,* February 1953, p. 63 <db994>.

46 4A deserved a grander name: The #4A crossbar switch was an advanced version of the original #4 crossbar. The first #4 crossbar was installed in Philadelphia in 1943 and was followed by sister installations in Boston, New York City, Cleveland, Chicago, and Oakland; all of these systems would eventually be upgraded to be more or less the same as a #4A crossbar. The first #4A crossbar was installed in Albany, New York, in 1950. See Joel, *Switching Technology,* p. 180.

46 fifty-nine of them: *Our Company and How It Operates,* p. 6.

47 thin steel cards: Joel, *Switching Technology,* pp. 180–83.

47 "At the end of this era": Ibid., p. 3.

47 less intelligent brethren: By the 1950s the telephone network consisted of about twenty-six hundred long-distance switching centers divided into five different levels of hierarchy. At the top of the hierarchy were the "regional" or class 1 centers—nine in the United States and two in Canada—followed by the "sectional" (class 2) centers, the "primary" (class 3) centers, the "toll" (class 4) centers, and then "toll points" (class 5). At the very bottom of the hierarchy were "end offices"—telephone switching offices that served only subscribers and weren't used for switching long-distance traffic. Lower-level switching machines were said to "home" on higher-level machines, that is, if they didn't have direct trunk lines to some place, they would forward the call to the machine they homed on in the hopes that it did. So, for example, a primary center such as Casper, Wyoming, might home on a sectional center like Cheyenne, and Cheyenne would in turn home on the regional center in Denver, Colorado. Naturally, the brainy 4As would go at the top of the network and less intelligent switching machines, such as crossbar tandems and step tandems, would make up the lower rungs. The telephone company toyed for a time with the notion of a "national center" in St. Louis, Missouri, but this idea never came to fruition. For the evolution of the hierarchical network concept, see H. S. Osborne, "General Switching Plan for Telephone Toll Service," *Bell System Technical Journal,* vol. 9, no. 3, July 1930, p. 429; AT&T, *Notes on Nationwide Dialing,* 1955 <db995>; and AT&T, *Notes on Distance Dialing,* 1956 <db996>. AT&T made its network hierarchy somewhat visible (well, audible) in 1968 when it began assigning specific area–code–based numerical identification codes to each tandem; these identification codes would be played back to customers when they misdialed or when a circuit condition prevented a call from going through. See http://explodingthephone.com/extra/identcodes.

47 **supervisory information:** Fagen, *Bell System,* p. 505.

47 **multifrequency language, or MF:** The earliest published article on MF signaling seems to be D. L. Moody, "Multifrequency Pulsing," *Bell Laboratories Record,* vol. 23, December 1945, p. 466 <db997>. This article disclosed the MF frequencies (700 Hz, 900 Hz, etc.) but did not explain which digits went with which pairs of frequencies; that information didn't appear in a published article until 1949 in an article by C. A. Dahlbom, A. W. Horton Jr., and

D. L. Moody, "Application of Multifrequency Pulsing," *AIEE Transactions,* vol. 68, 1949, pp. 392–96 <db446>. As it happened, however, several earlier Bell Laboratories patents did include this information, for example, Paul B. Murphy of Bell Laboratories, United States Patent number 2,2882,251, "Automatic Toll Switching Telephone System" (filed December 31, 1940, granted June 30, 1942).

48 **used this 2,600 Hz tone:** Not all long-distance trunk ("carrier") systems used 2,600 Hz for signaling, but the majority did. See Joel, *Switching Technology,* pp. 128–30. For SF signaling history, see A. Weaver and N. A. Newell, "In-Band Single-Frequency Signaling," *Bell System Technical Journal,* November 1954, pp. 1309–30 <db447>.

48 **"playing a tune for a telephone number":** "Playing a tune for a telephone number" (advertisement), *Popular Science Monthly,* February 1950, p. 5 <db998>.

48 **educational AT&T movie:** AT&T, *Speeding Speech,* 1950s, at http://www.archive.org/details/Speeding1950.

48 **"sing" to each other:** "'Long Distance Brain,' Now in Operation Here, Hears, Reads, and Sings," *Times-News* (Hendersonville, NC), November 22, 1954, p. 1.

48 **in-band signaling:** Out-of-band signaling was also used on some long-distance trunks transmitted by the N1, O1, and ON carrier systems. See Joel, *Switching Technology,* pp. 129–30.

49 **operator distance dialing:** Ibid., pp. 52–54. Also known as "operator toll dialing," operator dialing of long-distance calls started on a very limited basis as early as the 1920s but suffered from various technical problems in its early days.

49 **"guinea pigs":** "Direct Long Distance Dialing Told Realtors," *Lodi News-Sentinel* (Lodi, CA), May 25, 1955, p. 1.

49 **Englewood, New Jersey:** "Englewood Begins Long Distance Customer Dialing," *Bell Laboratories Record,* December 1951, p. 571 <db999>.

50 **318-GA2-2134:** Ibid. Yes, in the original numbering plan, San Francisco was 318, not 415.

Chapter 5: Blue Box

Much of the material in this chapter comes from author interviews conducted with Ralph Barclay as well as FBI files.

51 **"Signaling Systems for Control of Telephone Switching":** Breen and Dahlbom, "Signaling Systems for Control of Telephone Switching." There is an oft-repeated legend in the phone phreak community that Bell security agents visited university engineering libraries across the country in the late 1960s or early 1970s and either demanded that issue be withdrawn from circulation or, in some versions of the story, used razor blades to slice this article out of the *Bell System Technical Journal*. Ken Hopper of Bell Laboratories denies that this is true, and the existence of the article intact at the Berkeley, Stanford, and MIT engineering libraries suggests that he is right.

53 **dial directory assistance:** Actually, you wouldn't have called it "directory assistance" in 1960. Back then it was known simply as "information." The change to directory assistance came in 1968: "Frankly, the term 'information' has caused a lot of confusion and delay," said a telephone company manager. "Many people call for bus schedules, solutions to homework problems, baseball scores and other information which our operators do not have . . . we feel the new name is more descriptive and should eliminate a lot of customer misunderstanding." See, e.g., "'Directory Assistance' Replacing 'Information' on Telephone Calls," *Observer-Reporter* (Washington, PA), August 24, 1968, p. 6A. By the way, 555-1212 for information wasn't introduced until 1959. See "For Phone Information, Dial 112 212 555 1212," *New York Times,* August 7, 1959, p. 25 <db1000>.

56 **bobby pin into an electrical outlet:** Anita Harris (Ralph Barclay's sister), author interview, 2012.

57 **Touch-tone phones:** AT&T rolled out touch-tone telephone service to the general public in late 1963, although trials of different versions of pushbutton dialing date as far back as 1948. See Joel Jr., *Switching Technology,* pp. 336–42. Interestingly, one of the early prototypes of touch-tone service used the same tones as those in the

351

multifrequency signaling system—and, thus, that blue boxes used. Imagine how much worse AT&T's fraud problems would have been had it inadvertently installed a blue box in every household!

57 **blue box:** Memorandum from J. F. Doherty, AT&T director of security, to H. W. Caming, AT&T attorney, February 13, 1975 <db415>. This memo states that Barclay's was the first "blue box" that AT&T was aware of. Barclay says the choice of color wasn't a conscious decision, that it was simply a standard blue metal enclosure (likely from Bud Industries, Barclay recalls) commonly used in the electronics industry.

59 **set up in his garage:** Barclay remembers, "When that came out later, there were some people who weren't too happy about it."

61 **pleaded guilty:** FBI file 165-HQ-25, September 1961 <db947>; "Young Scientist Warned to Redirect His Talents," *Grant County Journal,* September 18, 1961, p. 1 <db573>; UPI, "Student Accused of Phone Fraud," *Spokane Chronicle,* September 16, 1961 <db575>.

Chapter 6: "Some People Collect Stamps"

Much of the material in this chapter comes from author interviews conducted with Charlie Pyne, Tony Lauck, and Ed Ross, as well as FBI files.

66 **special telephone operators:** For a list of oxx and 1xx operator codes, see http://explodingthephone.com/extra/oxx1xx.

67 **particularly proud of one call:** Tape recording provided by Charlie Pyne, undated but likely 1959 or 1960 <db521>.

68 **It also functioned:** Sam Smith, "Magna Cum Probation: Falling from Grace at Harvard U," from *Multitudes: The Unauthorized Memoirs of Sam Smith,* 1999, at http://prorev.com/mmintro.htm. "The Network" was shorthand for the station's original call letters, WHCN: the Harvard/Crimson Network.

69 **connect their telephone switches:** A privately run telephone system, such as for a university or a big company, was called a "private branch exchange," or PBX. Like early telephone exchanges, these started out as purely manual affairs, with an operator sticking plugs into jacks at a switchboard. As automated switching

developed, it became more common for institutions to have their own automatic switching systems; such an exchange was properly called a "private automatic branch exchange" or PABX.

70 **tie up all the lines:** "Telephone Hackers Active," *The Tech* (MIT student newspaper), November 20, 1963 <db451>. The article notes that "two or three students are expelled each year [from MIT] for abuses on the phone system" and that "hackers have accomplished such things as tying up all the tie-lines between Harvard and MIT, or making long-distance calls by charging them to a local radar installation. One method involved connecting the PDP-1 computer to the phone system to search the lines until a dialtone, indicating an outside line, was found." This article is often cited as the first published use of the word *hacker* in its modern meaning.

71 **Fine Arts 13 notebook:** Charlie Pyne, "Fine Arts 13," 1963 <db917>.

72 **Notes on Distance Dialing:** *Notes on Distance Dialing* became a staple phone phreak technical reference. AT&T published versions of it in 1956 <db996>, 1968 <db1001>, and 1975 <db1002>. A 1955 predecessor was called *Notes on Nationwide Dialing* <db995>, and its 1980 successor was *Notes on the Network*.

76 **sound of the telephone line:** Telephone lines behaved slightly differently—and sounded slightly different—once billing had started. In particular, momentarily depressing the hook switch had a very different sound once billing had started.

76 **black box:** See chapter 8 for details.

77 **Ernie Reid:** Pyne, Lauck, and Ross met Reid through a blind student at Harvard named Robert Holdt.

77 **Heckel also had a nine a.m. appointment:** Pyne recalls Heckel having an appointment with his dean at MIT, but FBI records do not confirm this.

80 **According to an FBI memo:** FBI file 65-HQ-68169, serial 2, April 24, 1963, p. 3 <db1003>.

80 **As the FBI memo put it:** Ibid.

80 **spy ring:** "FBI Smashes Spy Ring," *Boston Globe,* July 3, 1963, p. 1; Seth S. King, "Britain Convicts All Five in Spy Trial," *New York Times,* March 23, 1961, p. 1.

81 **all attended one of their country's top universities:** "New Reports on Philby Spy Case of '63 Vex Britain," *New York Times,* October 8, 1967.

81 **prosecuted for making free phone calls:** FBI file 65-HQ-68169, serial 3, May 1, 1963 <db1003>. The relevance of the federal Fraud by Wire statute (18 USC 1343) would be debated within the Justice Department several times before it was eventually decided that it could be used to prosecute toll fraud cases; see chapter 7.

81 **urgent FBI teletype message:** FBI file 65-HQ-68169, serial 10, May 8, 1963 <db1003>.

81 **remarkably evenhanded:** FBI file 65-HQ-68169, serial 9, May 5, 1963 <db1003>.

83 **solved one final mystery:** The story of Pyne, Lauck, Ross, and Heckel was told, minus their names, on the front page of the *Boston Herald* in 1966. Indeed, this was the story that Jake Locke discovered, as discussed in chapter 1. Three of the four went on to be featured in a photograph in *Fortune* magazine a bit later that same year: "AT&T thought it had an unbeatable system for billing its long-distance phone customers—until a group of college students turned up who cracked it: Charles Pyne, 22, a Harvard engineering senior, Tony Lauck, 22, a '65 Harvard graduate who now programs computers for the Smithsonian Astrophysical Laboratory, and Paul Heckel, 25, MIT '63 and now a systems analyst for G.E. With two other friends, they painstakingly worked out ways calling free to any phone in the US—and some in Europe—first by tracking down the codes they reached internal phone company operators, and later with a home built 'blue box' that rang numbers electronically. They were interested in displaying their analytical prowess, not in bilking the phone company. 'Anything that man can devise can be undevised,' is the way Heckel explains the principle that guided them. 'The undevising is a challenge.'" See Ron Kessler, "Student Dialers Play Their Way to Global Phone Calls, Non-Pay," *Boston Herald,* May 27, 1966, p. 1 <db471>; and *Fortune,* July 1, 1966, p. 34 <db472>.

Chapter 7: Headache

85 more than $1.4 billion: AT&T Long Lines Department, *Our Company and How It Operates*, 1960, p. 98. The $1.4 billion figure represents the difference between AT&T Long Lines plant investment between 1940 and 1960—a low estimate, since it includes depreciation but does not include any investment by Bell Laboratories, Western Electric, or the Bell operating companies.

86 "brilliant but disturbed teenager": UPI, "Lonely Boy Devises Way of Placing Free Long Distance Calls," *Milwaukee Journal*, July 17, 1963, p. 1.

86 Hoyt Stearns, John Treichler: For more information on these two see http://explodingthephone.com/extras/stearns and http://explodingthephone.com/extras/treichler.

86 Louis MacKenzie: Obituary of Louis G. MacKenzie, *Journal of the Audio Engineering Society,* vol. 23, no. 4, May 1975, p. 352.

86 Los Angeles International Airport: Nagy Khattar (president of MacKenzie Laboratories), author interview, 2007. According to Khattar, the voice used for the Los Angeles International Airport recordings belonged to Addison Taylor, MacKenzie Laboratories' then head of sales. Taylor and his wife were also the voice talent used in the spoof of the recordings in *Airplane!*

87 Sensing a business opportunity: Robert LaFond Sr. (an employee of MacKenzie Labs who was arrested with Louis MacKenzie in 1965), author interview, 2007. See also "Engineers Pay Toll for Phone 'Business,'" *Los Angeles Times,* April 9, 1966, p. SG10 <db469>, and Bob DiSteffano, "Pasadena Man, Employee Indicted in Sale of Phone-Bilking Device," *Independent* (Pasadena, CA), December 8, 1965, p. 1 <db749>. Although MacKenzie was correct in stating that selling blue boxes in California was legal in 1963, by 1965 the law had changed, hence his subsequent arrest. I have been unable to locate a videotape of the CBS news interview with MacKenzie's lawyer, despite it being mentioned in a newspaper article and by two interviewees.

87 the mob: Ken Hopper, author interview, 2006. Sometime in the 1960s a security consultant to AT&T named Alan Tritter showed the attaché case blue box to Charlie Pyne, Tony Lauck, and Ed Ross, the telephone hackers from Harvard back in 1963. One of the Harvard trio remarked that it was much larger than it needed to be, in fact, that the blue box they had built with Paul Heckel at MIT was much smaller. True, allowed Tritter. But wasn't it much more impressive this way? If your goal was to sell expensive stuff to the mob and get them to pay top dollar for it, Tritter asked, wasn't this clever packaging? Sadly, the truth appears to be more mundane. In a 2008 email interview, one of the people who had a hand in making these boxes said that they were designed and built around 1962 by a group of five telephone enthusiasts who worked at a navy research lab in Pasadena, California. They were made simply for their own edification, he said, and there was no mob involvement.

88 **"Slash Communication Costs with TELA-TONE"**: Memorandum to Mr. Lesher and Mr. Ohlbaum of the Federal Communications Commission from Donald F. Clark, attorney, AT&T, April 27, 1965 ("the Clark memo"). The Clark memo is Exhibit B of a Memorandum for the Commission from Henry Geller, general counsel, and Bernard Strassburg, chief, Common Carrier Bureau, Federal Communications Commission, May 14, 1965 ("the Geller memo") <db482>.

88 **"TOLL Free Distance Dialing"**: Classified ad, *Popular Electronics,* January 1964, p. 115 <db1004>.

88 **"The advertiser has admitted"**: Clark memo, p. 6.

89 **covered mail fraud:** Two laws protected the U.S. Post Office against fraud: 18 USC 1720 and 18 USC 1722, both of which were passed by Congress after the mail fraud statute (18 USC 1341) was enacted. If 1341 protected the post office from fraud, why did Congress need to add 1720 and 1722? And if 1341 did not protect the post office from fraud, and since 1343 was almost identical in language to 1341, then 1343 must not protect the phone company. As Nathanial Kossack (the Justice Department lawyer who helped write section 1343) forecast, these arguments would indeed be brought up in blue box cases a few years later. See, e.g., Brief

for Appellants, Kenneth Herbert Hanna and Nathan Modell, appellants, v. United States of America, Appellee, Appeal from the United States District Court for the Southern District of Florida, June 22, 1967, p. 19 <db321>.

90 **organized crime:** Geller memo, p. 2.

90 **two-hundred-word run-on sentence:** "Proposed Statute Proscribing the Fraudulent Obtaining of Telecommunication Service," Exhibit A to the Geller memo.

90 **"A criminal sanction is needed":** Clark memo, p. 5.

90 **"too broad a sweep":** Geller memo, p. 2.

90 **"collection agency":** Ibid.

91 **quarter of a billion to a billion:** Bill Caming, author interview, 2007. Testimony of H. W. William Caming in "Surveillance: Hearings Before the Subcommittee on Courts, Civil Liberties, and the Administration of Justice of the Committee on the Judiciary of the United States House of Representatives," February 2, 1975, p. 220 <db480> (hereinafter Caming, "Surveillance").

91 **"no assurance at all":** Ibid.

91 **"You guys created this mess!":** Hopper, author interview, 2006.

92 **blank check:** Ibid.

92 **stamped with a star, dress uniform hat:** Ibid.

92 **began in 1962:** "ALEX Archive Item Report, Item Number FIL-0115-021922," AT&T Archives, Warren, New Jersey. This is a summary sheet to the AT&T Archives file on Project Greenstar development. Unfortunately, the file itself could not be located, but the summary sheet indicates the creation date of the file as June 26, 1962.

92 **"We devised six experimental units":** Caming, "Surveillance," p. 220.

93 **connected to a hundred outgoing long-distance trunk lines:** More details: each Greenstar unit was made up of five subunits, each capable of monitoring twenty trunk lines. Each subunit had one tape recorder, which is why a total of five lines could be monitored simultaneously. See ibid., p. 225, and Louis J. Rose, "Bell

Secretly Monitored Millions of Toll Calls," *St. Louis Post-Dispatch,*
February 21, 1975 <db44>.

93 **As Caming described it:** Caming, "Surveillance," pp. 220–21.

94 **"If Greenstar judged":** Black box calls were initially recorded
for ninety seconds, but this was reduced to sixty seconds in "late
1966 or early 1967." Recording of blue box calls eventually was
limited to five minutes. See ibid., p. 221.

94 **33 million, between 1.5 and 1.8 million:** Ibid., p. 228.

94 **"We had to have statistics":** Ibid., p. 220.

94 **"25,000 cases of known illegality", "350,000 fraudulent
calls":** Ibid., p. 222.

95 **"It was immediately recognized":** Ibid., p. 210.

95 **"Genghis Khan":** Ibid., p. 218.

95 **"decline to prosecute":** Rose, "Bell Secretly Monitored Millions of Toll Calls."

96 **"Change the name":** During my interviews with Bill Caming I often used the term *Greenstar* in our discussions. Ever the
AT&T attorney, he would periodically correct me: "No, that's
not its name. That was an internal code name that we stopped
using." Sometime later I visited the AT&T Archives in Warren,
New Jersey, which maintains a computerized index of old Bell
System files. I typed in "Greenstar" and watched the display
light up like a Christmas tree as it found relevant documents.
When I mentioned this to Caming a few days later, he gave a
rueful laugh and responded, "Well, I guess you can't keep a
good name down."

96 **two parts to Caming's reasoning:** Before 1968, the federal
wiretapping law was Section 605 of Title 18 of the United States
Code. It was a strangely written law. As discussed in the next
chapter, section 605 did not make wiretapping ("interception")
itself illegal. Rather, to commit a crime under 605 you had to
both intercept a communication and then disclose the contents
of the communication to someone else. Clearly when Greenstar recorded a call and a human listened to it, there was an
interception, but because the trained operator listening to the

tapes never discussed the contents of the communication (just the signaling of the call itself), there was no disclosure, and thus, AT&T asserted, no crime. In 1968 the Omnibus Crime Control and Safe Streets Act became the new law that governed wiretapping—but that law had specific carve outs for random monitoring and interception of communications by telephone company personnel attempting to protect the assets of the telephone company.

96 **"imprimatur":** Caming, "Surveillance," pp. 243–44.

96 **Congressional Research Service:** Ibid., p. 234.

97 **"Lonely Boy":** "Lonely Boy Devises Way of Placing Free Long Distance Calls."

Chapter 8: Blue Box Bookies

Much of the background material on bookies, organized crime, gambling, and the FBI's prosecution efforts of same comes from author interviews conducted in 2007 with former FBI special agents Edwin J. Sharp and Warren Welsh and former U.S. attorney Bill Earle, as well as FBI files.

98 **"Hit the door":** Description of Special Agents Heist and Roussell's entry into Hanna's apartment from *United States v. Hanna,* District Court of the United States for the Southern District of Florida, Transcript of Proceedings on Motion to Suppress, September 12, 1966, pp. 62–85 <db306>.

99 **the line:** The description of "the line" given here is for point-spread betting, common among bookmakers and gamblers for sports betting in the 1960s. Today "the line" may also refer to the money line, which is a different way of expressing odds. See Richard O. Davies and Richard G. Abram, *Betting the Line: Sports Wagering in American Life* (Columbus, OH: Ohio State University Press, 2001), pp. 53–57, and Gregory Curtis, "The Wizard of Odds," *Texas Monthly,* December 1973, pp. 78–83.

100 **$20 billion:** "The Conglomerate of Crime," *Time,* August 22, 1969 <db1005>.

100 **"it ends up feeding something else":** Warren Welsh, author interview, 2007.

100 **"bankrollers and kingpins":** "Robert Kennedy Urges New Laws to Fight Rackets," *New York Times,* April 7, 1961, p. 1; Robert H. Boyle, "The Bookies Close Up Shop," *Sports Illustrated,* September 3, 1962 <db1006>.

101 **$250,000 of bets:** "Crime: No. 11 Off the Boards," *Time,* March 2, 1970 <db793>.

101 **"Beckley lived", twenty thousand cards' worth:** FBI file 165-HQ-1999 <db953>; Edwin J. Sharp, author interview, 2008.

101 **cheese boxes:** "'Cheesebox,' Remote Control Phone Device, Leads to Raid on Bookmaking Headquarters," *New York Times,* November 18, 1950, p. 32 <db6>. The 1974 book *Cheesebox* by Paul S. Meskil with Gerald M. Callahan (Englewood Cliffs, NJ: Prentice Hall, 1974), pp. 171–81, claims, incorrectly, that the cheese box was invented five years later in 1955.

102 **empty apartment with a pair of telephone lines:** Gambling and Organized Crime: Hearings Before the Permanent Subcommittee on Investigations of the Committee on Government Operations of the United States Senate, 75th Congress, first session, part 1, August 22, 23, 24, and 25, 1961, pp. 242–99 <db448> (hereafter, "Gambling and Organized Crime").

102 **bribing telephone company operators and technicians:** Some examples: "U.S. Jury Indicts 13 in Betting Ring," *New York Times,* June 28, 1961, p. 20 <db12>, in which Gil Beckley, Benjamin and Robert Lassoff, Myron Deckelbaum, and more than a dozen others were arrested for bribing telephone company employees to make long-distance calls for them; FBI file 92-HQ-4957 serial, 10 <db812>, describing a conspiracy starting in 1952 in which alleged bookies and telephone company employees "endeavored to conceal from IRS the existence and scope of their widespread horse race betting and other gambling activities by securing free unauthorized long distance telephone service, through the services of telephone company longlines repairmen, as a consequence of which no records would be made concerning the phone calls made by defendants . . ."; and, later, in *United States v. Gilbert L. Beckley, John C. Lowe, and James C. Gunter,* United States District

Court, Northern District of Georgia, Criminal No. 24,167, January 7, 1965.

102 bogus credit card numbers: "Bookmaking Raids Staged in 9 Cities," *New York Times,* January 9, 1966 <db17>.

102 legitimate telephone credit cards: FBI file 92-HQ-3051, serials 53 and 54, September 6, 1960, p. 19 <db814>.

102 Walter Shaw: "Gambling and Organized Crime," pp. 242–99.

103 "some type of instrument", "surprising decrease": FBI file 92-HQ-3051, serial 54, page C, September 15, 1960 <db814>.

103 arrested in Miami: UPI, "Inventor Seized as Telephone Cheater," *New York Times,* March 31, 1961, p. 28; see also, "Gambling and Organized Crime."

104 MacKenzie: *United States v. McCay, Brandon, Gautreaux, and Danford,* No. 66-76 Criminal, United States District Court for the Western District of Oklahoma, Transcript of Proceedings, August 8, 1966, pp. 128–35 <db382>.

104 "using devices": FBI file 165-BS-532, serial 1, August 2, 1965 <db922> and <db950>.

104 targeting bookies and organized crime: 18 USC 1084, introduced in 1961.

104 "indicated their desire": FBI file 165-BS-532.

105 The caller told Doyle: Testimony of Gerard J. Doyle in *United States v. Hanna,* pp. 4–49.

105 connect Hanna with TARCASE: FBI file 165-BS-532, serial 8, September 1, 1965 <db922> and <db950>.

107 dash for the bathroom: *United States v. Hanna and Modell,* 66-69-CR, Opinion on Motion to Suppress Evidence, 260 F. Supp 430, September 26, 1966 <db308>.

107 raids in other cities: "Bookmaking Raids Staged in Nine Cities."

107 "used a chauffeur-driven Cadillac": AP, "FBI Says It Broke Up Bookie Ring in Nine Cities," *Lowell Sunday Sun,* January 9, 1966, p. 38.

107 "most successful": FBI file 92-HQ-3625, serial 293, January 8, 1966.

108 all of Bubis's calls: *United States v. Bubis, Loman, and Beckley,* No. 36270-CD, United States District Court, Southern District of

California, Central Division, Complaint for Violation of U.S.C. Title 18 Section 1084, Affidavit of Charles Bitner, May 24, 1966 <db1007>.

108 **"crippling blow":** FBI file 166-HQ-1765, serial 82, May 25, 1966 <db1008>.

108 **mob attorney Ben Cohen:** See, for example, Paul Jewett, *The Mob and the Flock: Memories of a Twentieth Century Shepherd* (Maitland, FL: Xulon Press, 2010), pp. 132–33; Stuart B. McIver, *Touched by the Sun: The Florida Chronicles, Volume 3* (Sarasota, FL: Pineapple Press, 2001), pp. 80–87; and U.S. Senate Special Committee to Investigate Organized Crime in Interstate Commerce, Interim Report on Investigations in Florida and Preliminary General Conclusions, August 18, 1950 (the Kefauver Committee).

108 **$40 million:** Charles L. Fontenay, *Estes Kefauver: A Biography* (Knoxville, TN: University of Tennessee Press, 1980), p. 173; Steven Gaines, *Fools Paradise: Players, Poseurs, and the Culture of Excess in South Beach* (New York: Three Rivers Press, 2009), p. 45.

108 **balding head, etc.:** Cohen description from Fred Othman, "Good Boys Now," *Pittsburgh Press,* August 30, 1951, quoted in FBI file 63-HQ-7046, serial 23 <db1009>.

109 **"We submit":** *United States v. Hanna,* p. 89.

110 **"Now, there is no omnipotence":** Ibid., pp. 90–92.

110 **"[W]hat is the telephone company to do with it?":** Ibid., p. 96.

111 **willfully:** *United States v. Loman, Bubis, and Beckley,* pp. 9–11.

111 **Hanna and Modell were both convicted:** Amusingly, Hanna's attorneys argued that Hanna did not have a "blue box" because the box he had was "black with red buttons." The court was not persuaded: "It is evident that the term 'blue box' is nominative rather than descriptive, that is, it is the term by which the device is commonly known and, except by accident, has no reference to its actual color. [. . .] Implicit in this is the fact that whether blue, black with red buttons, red with black buttons, umber or indigo, the device is still called a 'blue box.'" *United States v. Hanna and Modell.*

112 **"While we realize":** Alvin Bubis, Appellant, v. United States of America, Appellee, United States Court of Appeals Ninth Circuit, 384 F.2d 643, October 20, 1967 <db1012>.

112 **"Congress may have thought":** Hanna and Modell, Appellants, v. United States, Appellee, United States Court of Appeals for the Fifth Circuit, 393 F.2d 700, March 5, 1968 <db325>.

113 **petitioned for a rehearing:** Hanna and Modell, Appellants, v. United States, Appellee, United States Court of Appeals for the Fifth Circuit, Petition for Rehearing En Banc, March 26, 1968.

113 **Within the past few years:** Hanna and Modell, Appellants, v. United States, Appellee, United States Court of Appeals for the Fifth Circuit, Brief of American Telephone and Telegraph as Amicus Curiae, May 7, 1968 <db328>.

114 **"On original hearing":** Hanna and Modell, Appellants, v. United States, Appellee, United States Court of Appeals for the Fifth Circuit, Order on Rehearing, 404 F.2d 405, November 18, 1968 <db330>.

114 **"Outside of an opening salutation":** The appeals court adopted more like three pages of Caming's brief but, nonetheless, it was still a home run.

Chapter 9: Little Jojo Learns to Whistle

As explained in my epilogue, Joe Engressia legally changed his name to Joybubbles in 1991, hence the references to Joybubbles in the notes below. Much of the material in this chapter comes from interviews with Joybubbles (both mine and other published interviews), as well as newspaper articles.

117 **"Hang up the phone":** Toni Engressia, author interview, 2008.

118 **"I won't lie to you":** Ibid.

118 **"Before I was four":** John Fail and Chris Strunk, "A Conversation with Joybubbles," May 9, 1998, at http://www.icewhistle .com/static/joybubbles.html <db972>.

118 **"I didn't like play":** Ibid.

118 **"It was all I could do":** Toni Engressia speaking on the Joybubbles memorial telephone conference, September 16, 2007.

118 **"I used to ask what time it was"**: Tape recording of a speech Engressia gave to an unknown community group, 1974 <db1014> (hereinafter, Engressia speech, 1974).

118 **"I thought, well, if 3 is 3 away"**: Ibid., and tape recording of a speech Engressia gave to a different group, 1978 <db958>.

119 **"The principle of science"**: Richard P. Feynman, Robert B. Leighton, and Matthew Sands, *The Feynman Lectures on Physics: The Definitive Edition,* volume I (Boston: Addison Wesley, 2005), p. 1–1.

119 **"Through the years"**: Engressia speech, 1974.

119 **"His sister recalls"**: Toni Engressia speaking on the Joybubbles memorial telephone conference, September 16, 2007; "emergency room": Joybubbles, "Stories and Stuff," May 8, 2004, at http://audio .textfiles.com/shows/storiesandstuff/joybubbles_-_stories_and _stuff_-_20040508.mp3.

119 **"Most people"**: Engressia speech, 1974.

120 **"We met a phone man"**: Joybubbles, author interview, 2006.

120 **The Engressias moved a lot:** Ibid.; Toni Engressia, author interview, 2008; and other Joybubbles/Engressia published interviews.

120 **"Daddy hated the snow"**: Toni Engressia, author interview, 2008.

121 **"I learned a whole lot"**: Engressia speech, 1974.

122 **"I was seven or eight"**: "A Conversation with Joybubbles."

123 **"I got $2.50 a week"**: Engressia speech, 1974.

123 **Dade County Junior College:** Bill Acker, author interview, 2008.

123 **"I can whistle like a bird"**: Leslie Taylor, "Blind Student Dials Trouble," *USF Oracle,* November 27, 1968, p. 1 <db1015>. Past-tense quotes and material describing Engressia's USF whistling escapades are from the following newspaper articles: "Whistler Started Young," *USF Oracle,* November 27, 1968, p. 1 <db1016>; Harry Haigley, "If You Want Long Distance, Just Whistle," *St. Petersburg Evening Independent,* November 27, 1968, p. 1 <db932>; "Whistle Has Connections," *St. Petersburg Times,* November 28, 1968, p. B1 <db931>; "Hearing Postponed for 'The Whistler,'" *St. Petersburg Times,* December 6, 1968 <db933>; "The 'Whistler'

Back at USF," *USF Oracle;* December 8, 1968 <db1017>; "USF to Rule Today on Whistler's Fate," *St. Petersburg Times,* December 11, 1968, p. 4B <db934>; "Telephone Whistler Connects, Permitted to Stay in School," *Miami Herald-Tribune,* December 12, 1968, p. 10 <db935>; "USF 'Whistler' Stays in School," *St. Petersburg Times,* December 12, 1968, p. B1 <db936>.

124 roughly $17 today: Federal Communications Commission, "Statistics of Communications Common Carriers, 1995/1996," Table 7.1, p. 280, at http://www.fcc.gov/Bureaus/Common _Carrier/Reports/FCC-State_Link/SOCC/95socc.pdf.

125 "Your brother has been doing something illegal": Toni Engressia, author interview, 2008.

126 received a letter in the mail: FBI file 139-HQ-3481, August 27, 1969 <db878>, and FBI file 100-KC-13546, August 27, 1969 <db866>.

126 Engressia's introduction to B. David: By 1969 B. David was no longer going by that particular pseudonym, but for consistency I use that name throughout this book.

127 tricked a switchman: FBI file 139-HQ-3481, serial 15, September 1, 1969, p. 3 <db878>.

127 "a good deal of discussion": Ibid., p. 4.

127 Though he wouldn't tell Bureau agents: FBI file 139-HQ-3481, serial 1, August 27, 1969, p. 2 <db878>. It is possible that the Southwestern Bell security agent was being coy because his source was Greenstar. One of the Greenstar units had been moved to St. Louis, Missouri, in January 1967, just a few hundred miles away from Kansas City. And later, when the Southwestern Bell agent finally did tell the FBI about where the information had come from, an FBI teletype message noted, "Bureau will protect this source's identity because it would jeopardize not only [our] contact's employment but would probably destroy the amicable relations between the phone company and the Bureau." See FBI file 139-HQ-3481, serial 5, August 28, 1969, p. 3.

127 "highly classified, Top Secret": Ibid.

128 "the activities of Engressia and Way": FBI file 139-HQ-3481, serial 3, August 27, 1969, p. 1 <db878>.

128 **posterior-covering letters:** FBI file 139-HQ-3481, serials 11, 12, and 13, August 29, 1969 <db878>.

128 **"not a sufficient indication":** FBI file 139-HQ-3481, unnumbered serial (memo from director, FBI, to assistant attorney general, Criminal Division, Department of Justice), September 3, 1969 <db878>.

128 **"is believed to be totally unreliable":** FBI file 139-HQ-3481, unnumbered serial (memo from FBI Kansas City to director, FBI), September 8, 1969. See also FBI file 139-HQ-3482 <db878>.

128 **"I didn't really know why I had come":** Andrew T. Huse, interview with Joybubbles, University of South Florida Oral History Program, August 23, 2004.

129 **"be a man":** Engressia speech, 1974.

129 **"as a switchboard operator":** Ibid.

130 **"I got desperate":** Ibid.

130 **"I decided":** Ibid.

130 **"This was in late April":** Ibid.

130 **"going to call Russia":** "A Conversation with Joybubbles."

131 **"NORAD":** Engressia speech, 1974.

131 **"I have only until July":** Ibid.

131 **"I remember one time":** Ibid.

131 **"tapping the tappers":** Ibid.

132 **"freely shown":** "Police Apprehend Phone-Addicted USF Whistler," *St. Petersburg Times,* June 4, 1971 <db937>.

132 **"I was gonna call":** Engressia speech, 1974.

132 **"complex telephone equipment":** "Police Apprehend Phone-Addicted USF Whistler."

132 **"I've done wrong":** AP, "Long-Distance Whistler Draws $10 Fine," *St. Petersburg Times,* June 10, 1971 <db940>.

132 **$1 bail:** AP, "Fascinated with Phones," *Montreal Gazette,* June 5, 1971, p. 2 <db938>.

132 **"Some folks are on dope":** "Police Apprehend Phone-Addicted USF Whistler."

133 **"driving them crazy":** AP, "Blind Lad Quits Fraud, Joins Phone Firm," *Sarasota Herald-Tribune,* June 21, 1971, p. 3A <db941>.

133 **"sixty days in jail":** AP, "Long-Distance Whistler Draws $10 Fine."

133 **friendly knock:** Joybubbles, author interview, 2006.

134 **"four job offers":** Engressia speech, 1974; AP, "Several Job Offers Given to Blind Man," *Hartford Courant,* June 12, 1971, p. 2 <db959>.

134 **"I guess they'll have me do":** AP, "Blind Lad Quits Fraud, Joins Phone Firm."

134 **"I don't recommend":** Engressia speech, 1974. For more on Engressia's life at Millington, see http://explodingthephone.com/extra/millington.

Chapter 10: Bill Acker Learns to Play the Flute

Much of the material in this chapter comes from author interviews with Bill Acker.

142 **the tones were distorted:** According to Acker this is typical of crossbar tandem switching equipment.

144 **computer-generated reports of supervision irregularities:** Ken Hopper, author interview, 2006; testimony of Wallace S. Swenson, *United States v. Thomas McCay, Herman D. Brandon, Sylvester E. Gautreaux, Jr., and Glenn S. Danford,* United States District Court for the Western District of Oklahoma, Transcript of Proceedings, August 8, 1966, pp. 188–90 <db382>.

145 **something called an 800 number:** 800 numbers were more properly referred to as "Inward Wide Area Telecommunications Service," or INWATS, and were introduced in 1967. See "AT&T Files Rate Cut of $5 Million a Year for Fixed-Fee Long-Distance Telephoning," *Wall Street Journal,* December 2, 1966.

Chapter 11: The Phone Freaks of America

Much of the material in this chapter comes from author interviews with Bill Acker, John Draper, Jim Fettgather, Denny Teresi, and other phone phreaks.

147 **busy signals that were shared:** Information on busy signal conferences from my interviews with Rick Plath, 2008; Jim Fettgather,

2008; Denny Teresi, 2007; and Bill Acker, 2007. According to Acker, most busy signal conferences were step-by-step PBX equipment, though some were occasionally found on crossbar exchanges.

147 party line broken recording numbers: As with the busy signal conferences, these tended to be step-by-step PBX equipment. Phone phreak Evan Doorbell (a pseudonym) has documented "party lines" in the New York area from the early 1970s in detail in his charming and wonderfully researched audio series "How Evan Doorbell Became a Phone Phreak," available at http://www.phonetrips.com.

148 213-286-0213 and -0214: 213-737-1118 and -1119 would have been more realistic examples. Phone phreaks spent a great deal of time collecting and trading loop around numbers; for a list, see http://explodingthephone.com/extra/loops.

149 Rick Plath: Plath, author interview, 2008.

149 Al Diamond: For more see http://explodingthephone.com/extra/diamond.

150 Mark Bernay: For more see http://explodingthephone.com/extra/markbernay.

150 "It was like CB radio": Ibid.

151 Airman First Class Draper: Draper physical description from FBI file 87-HQ-121189, serial 1, May 4, 1972 <db883>. Background on Draper's childhood from Steve Long, "Captain Crunch: Super Phone Phreak," *High Times,* June 1977, p. 50 <db923>, and Chris Rhodes, "The Twilight Years of Cap'n Crunch," *Wall Street Journal,* January 13, 2007, p. 1 <db990>.

151 expecting a call from an old friend: Over the years Draper has told several different versions of the story of how he first met Denny Teresi. Teresi says he does not remember the details. I have elected to use in my recounting the elements common to most stories.

153 "a chubby kid": Draper notes, undated but circa the mid-1970s.

153 "drove over to Teresi's friend": Recollections differ slightly on this point. Draper says he met Teresi and they drove over to Fettgather's house. Fettgather says he was at Teresi's house to begin with.

154 you had to press two of the six: John Draper, author interview, 2008.

154 Sid Bernay had discovered: Mark Bernay and Sid Bernay email exchange, 2010. Sid Bernay recalls: "I had heard that 2,600 cycles could interrupt long distance. I called a West Covina number, and when it started to ring, blew the Cap'n Crunch whistle and it 'choinked.' I covered one hole, and it still happened. Thus the discovery. I was a freshman at UCLA at the time, so I'm guessing 1964 or 1965. Also, Oscar Meyer whistles worked, too, but not all. Apparently weren't exactly 2,600."

156 the network expanded from there: Author interviews of Acker, Teresi, and Fettgather.

157 The Machine, VERMONT, Z, ZZ, ZZZ, Superphone: For history and recordings of the Machine and other Los Angeles telephone joke lines see "Phone Recordings, Los Angeles Area & Beyond," at http://www.dialajoke.us/.

158 weren't allowed to connect: See the Carterfone case discussion in chapter 20.

158 "The national switched telephone network": John D. deButts quoted in Steve Coll, *The Deal of the Century: The Break Up of AT&T* (New York: Atheneum, 1986), p. 105.

158–159 Hush-A-Phone: "Phone Company Upheld in Ban on Hush-A-Phone," *New York Times,* February 17, 1951, p. 29 <db1018>; "Hush-A-Phone Hits Back at AT&T," *New York Times,* March 24, 1951, p. 25 <db1019>; "Phone Device Ban by AT&T Upheld," *New York Times,* December 24, 1955 <db1020>, p. 20; "Court Removes Ban Against Phone Device," *New York Times,* November 9, 1956, p. 25 <db1021>; and 238 F.2d 266, HUSH-A-PHONE CORPORATION and Harry C. Tuttle, Petitioners, v. UNITED STATES of America and Federal Communications Commission, Respondents, American Telephone and Telegraph Company et al., and United States Independent Telephone Association, Interveners, No. 13175, United States Court of Appeals, District of Columbia Circuit, 99 U.S. App. D.C. 190; 238 F.2d 266; 1956 U.S. App. LEXIS 4023, October 4, 1956, Argued, November 8, 1956, Decided.

159–160 was born the Machine: Tom Politeo, author interview, 2008.

161 called the Old Man: Bill Acker, author interview, 2008.

161 "number five crossbar": Ibid.

162 teletype machines: For a fascinating history of teletypes and the Teletype Corporation, see Teletype Corporation, *The Teletype Story,* 1958, available at http://www.samhallas.co.uk/repository /telegraph/teletype_story.pdf.

165 International Society of Telephone Enthusiasts: Acker, author interview, 2011. Again, B. David was going by a different handle at this point in time, but for continuity I am continuing to use "B. David" as his pseudonym.

166 Mark Bernay Society: For more on the Mark Bernay Society, see http://explodingthephone.com/extra/mbs.

Chapter 12: The Law of Unintended Consequences

Much of the material in this chapter comes from author interviews with Al Gilbertson and Ron Rosenbaum.

171 "Alice in Wonderland": *Hackers: Electronic Outlaws,* History Channel, 2001.

171 "Mr. Intense" and Draper idiosyncrasies: Author interviews with Bill Acker and Jim Fettgather, 2008, and several sources who prefer to remain anonymous.

172 "When I talked to Ron": John Draper, "Cap'n Crunch Comments on the Esquire Article," at http://davesource.com/Fringe /Fringe/Hacking/Phreaking/Blue_Boxes/Blue_Boxes.Esquire _Article.comments <db485>. A three-thousand word analysis of the Esquire article, this was apparently first posted on the WELL conference system around 1998 at http://well.com/user/crunch.

172 "Secrets of the Little Blue Box": Ron Rosenbaum, "Secrets of the Little Blue Box," *Esquire,* October 1971, p. 116.

174 "I thought he spiced it up too much": Gilbertson says that he wasn't selling blue boxes to the mob, as the article described, nor, he says, did he ever claim to be the creator of the blue box.

174 "technical inaccuracies": Draper didn't like them either; Draper, "Cap'n Crunch Comments on the Esquire Article."

174 **"captured the spirit of it":** Bill Acker, author interview, 2010.

175 **crossbar tandems could be tricked:** Crossbar tandems, also called XBTs, should not be confused with 4A tandems—something that is easy to do since, confusingly, 4As also used crossbar switching technology. Crossbar tandems were smaller switching machines originally intended for metropolitan use that were later upgraded with features that made them suitable for handling the more complex job of long-distance switching. They were used in areas where the bulky and brainy 4A wasn't economical. See A. O. Adam, "Crossbar Tandem as a Long-Distance Switching System," *Bell System Technical Journal,* vol. 35, pp. 91–108, 1956.

175 **"wink" signal:** A wink signal was just a momentary absence of the 2,600 Hz signal sent from the switching machine at the far end of your call. The telephone company had electronic filter circuitry that kept subscribers from hearing the 2,600 Hz signal on long-distance calls. These filters worked great, but when there was a transition in the 2,600 Hz signal—for example, when it went away and then came back, as it did during a wink—the circuits resonated for a fraction of a second. This resonance was what made the bright metallic *kerchink* that was such music to a blue boxer's ears.

175 **KP 099 213 ST:** TTC codes were always in the range of 000 to 199 so they wouldn't interfere with area codes and couldn't be dialed (usually!) by customers. For more on TTC and other 0xx/1xx codes, see http://explodingthephone.com/extra/0xx1xx. The call routing described for the tandem stacking example represents the best recollections of Bill Acker and Evan Doorbell, but they caution that it may not be a hundred percent accurate.

176 **sound like hell:** Long-distance calls were typically sent over two pairs of wires—one pair for one direction, say New York to Chicago, and one pair for the reverse direction. Unfortunately, crossbar tandems were able to switch only a single pair of wires at once. An electronic circuit called a hybrid merged the two pairs of wires used for a long-distance trunk into a single pair so they could be switched by a crossbar tandem. The result was a loss in audio quality every time a call went through a crossbar tandem. This cumulative audio distortion limited the number of crossbar tandems you could stack up. In contrast, 4A switches were true four-wire (two pair) switches and didn't have this problem. But for phone phreaks, alas, 4As lacked the bug that allowed them to be stacked up like crossbar tandems. All was not lost, however. See the discussion of guard banding in chapter 18.

176 series of phantomlike kerchinky noises: Evan Doorbell has lovingly narrated a recording of tandem stacking from 1975. See Evan Doorbell, "Classic Tandem Stacking (January, 1975)," at http://www.phonetrips.com.

177 con telephone employees: The term "social engineering" in the phreak/hacker sense seems to have come into vogue in the mid-1980s, although Bill Acker recalls it being used as early as 1974 or so. Prior to that the term was "pretexting," that is, calling someone on a pretext to get information or convince them to do something for you. The inventors of that term? The FBI, which used pretexting to assist in its investigations. "Like any other accomplishment," an FBI manual advised, "a good pretext is a satisfying experience." The phone phreaks surely would have agreed. See Federal Bureau of Investigation, "Pretexts and Cover Techniques," 1956, at http://www.governmentattic.org/docs/FBI_Pretexts_and_Cover_Techniques_May-1956.pdf.

178 "VFG-EXG-270100": This example is based on actual #1 ESS commands but, because there are still a few #1 ESS telephone switches in the wild, the commands have been intentionally altered.

179 95 percent . . . conducted over the phone: Sonny Kleinfield, *The Biggest Company on Earth: A Profile of AT&T* (New York: Holt, Rinehart, & Winston, 1981), p. 14.

180 "I knew right then and there": *Hackers: Electronic Outlaws.*

180 "boy genius": Roy R. Silver, "'Blue Box' Is Linked to Phone Call Fraud," *New York Times,* May 6, 1971, p. 45 <db25>.

180 Case Western Reserve: AP, "Theft Is Charged to Students Who Let Fingers Walk Free," *Blade* (Toledo, Ohio), May 7, 1971 p. 19.

180 **Billings, Montana:** Georganne Louis, "3 Plead Guilty in Telephone Fraud," *Billings Gazette,* September 3, 1971, p. 1; FBI file 65-HQ-73591, June 5, 1970 <db890>.

180 **arrested in Pennsylvania:** UPI, "Phreaks" (newswire item), September 28, 1971 <db615>.

181 **"For Whom Ma Bell Tolls Not":** Maureen Orth, "For Whom Ma Bell Tolls Not," *Los Angeles Times,* October 31, 1971, p. P28 <db29>.

181 **"mildly mentally unbalanced":** UPl, "'Phone Freak' Probe Hinted," *Spokane Daily Chronicle,* November 18, 1971, p. 6; AP, "'Phone Freak' to Be Subject of Jury Probe," *St. Petersburg Times,* November 19, 1971, p. 20A.

181 **internal AT&T memo:** "Toll Fraud," AT&T memo/press backgrounder, May 18, 1977 <db570>.

182 **Telephone Crime Lab:** Ken Hopper, author interview, 2006, and Kenneth D. Hopper, "Bell Telephone Laboratories at Holmdel, NJ 1929–1991 and Certain Other Job-Related Memories," presented to the Holmdel Historical Society, New Jersey, January 31, 1992.

182 **undersea wiretaps:** See, for example, Sherry Sontag and Christopher Drew, *Blind Man's Bluff: The Untold Story of American Submarine Espionage* (New York: Harper Perennial, 2000), p. 189.

182 **Their report to their bosses:** C. J. Schulz, "Appraisal of 'Secrets of the Little Blue Box' Article in the October 1971 Esquire Magazine," Bell Laboratories memo, September 17, 1971 <db397>.

Chapter 13: Counterculture

Much of the material in this chapter comes from author interviews with Alan Fierstein.

185 **May Day demonstrations:** See, e.g., Richard Halloran, "30,000 Protesters Routed in Capital," *New York Times,* May 3, 1971, p. 1.

185 **Marlon Brando:** *The Wild One,* Columbia Pictures, 1953.

185 **"We are a people":** Youth International Party Manifesto, ca. 1970, quoted in Eric v. d. Luft, *Die at the Right Time: A Subjective Cultural History of the American Sixties* (Baltimore: United Book Press, 2009), p. 437.

187 free buffalo: Abbie Hoffman, *Steal This Book,* 2002 reprint, p. 104: "Every year the National Park Service gives away surplus elks in order to keep the herds under its jurisdiction from outgrowing the amount of available land for grazing . . . Under the same arrangement the government will send you a Free Buffalo. Write to: Office of Information, Department of the Interior, Washington, D.C. 20420."

187 largest company on earth: AT&T was the largest company in the world as measured by assets or by employees; others were larger by revenue. In 1974, for example, General Motors had sales of $35 billion to AT&T's $26 billion. But AT&T had $74 billion in assets to GM's $20 billion; even accounting for liabilities, AT&T far exceeded it in size. And AT&T had more than a million employees, at that time, to GM's roughly 800,000.

187 "In a country indissolubly": Kleinfield, *The Biggest Company on Earth,* p. 9.

187 rate hike requests: For a bibliography of AT&T rate increases, see http://explodingthephone.com/extra/ratehikes.

188 $1 per month: Email conversations with members of the Telephone Collectors International mailing list (Yahoo group "singingwires"), June 2011.

188 DUE: Brooks, *Telephone,* p. 299; "Unauthorized Phones Get Their DUE," *Bell Laboratories Record,* December 1974 <db1022>.

188 "warm gooey feelings": I am indebted to Andrea Nemerson for the phrase.

188 "Cries of frustration": William K. Stevens, "Phone Users Cite Service Decline," *New York Times,* September 22, 1969 <db1023>.

189 "A kind of surrealistic": Brooks, *Telephone,* p. 291.

189 PLaza 8: Ibid., p. 290; Craig R. Whitney, "Phone Company Official Admits Increasing Difficulties in City," *New York Times,* October 15, 1969 <db1024>.

189 "lousy": Brooks, *Telephone,* p. 292, quoting a *New York Times* article.

189 "equal to the job": Stevens, "Phone Users Cite Service Decline." See also, "Dial-a-Snafu: Phone Foul-Ups Vex More Users as Volume of Calls Rises," *Wall Street Journal,* February 3, 1969, and Brooks, *Telephone,* pp. 292–95.

189 **An FCC investigation:** "FCC Telephone Probe in Preliminary Phase," *Hartford Courant,* September 24, 1969.

189 **"personification of male chauvinism":** Kleinfield, *The Biggest Company on Earth,* p. 206.

190 **"blacks, women":** Brooks, *Telephone,* p. 288, and AP, "AT&T Chairman Denies Bias in Employment," *Sarasota Herald-Tribune,* December 12, 1970, p. 12-A.

190 **another sweeping investigation:** Christopher Lydon, "F.C.C. Plans a Wide A.T.&T. Inquiry," *New York Times,* January 22, 1971, p. 23 <db1025>. The Western Electric aspect of the investigation revolved around antitrust issues and the idea that AT&T could be hiding profits in its manufacturing subsidiary.

190 **AFL-CIO:** "Half a Million Workers Go on Telephone Strike," *Miami News,* July 14, 1971, p. 1; Philip Shabecoff, "Telephone Strike Scheduled Today," *New York Times,* July 14, 1971, p. 1 <db1026>.

190 **"we call it 'The System'":** Joseph Goulden, *Monopoly* (New York: G. P. Putnam's Sons, 1968), p. 16.

190 **"as little as possible to the imagination":** Kleinfield, *The Biggest Company on Earth,* p. 208.

190 **Bell System Practices:** A. B. Covey, "The Bell System's Best Sellers," *Bell Telephone Magazine,* Summer 1952, p. 88 <db1027>.

191 **"Sweeping, General":** "Sweeping, General," Bell System Practice 770-130-301, August 1952, available from http://long-lines .net/documents/BSP-770-130-301/BSP-770-130-301-p1.html.

191 **"robotic man in a three piece suit":** Irv Slifkin, *Videohound's Groovy Movies: Far Out Films of the Psychedelic Era* (Canton, MI: Visible Ink Press, 2004), pp. 52–54.

191 **"find it hard to fault":** Maurice Rapf, "Bright Debut by Slapstick Satirists," *Life,* January 26, 1968, p. 8.

191 **"If we do not receive payment":** Lily Tomlin, *This Is a Recording,* Polydor Records, 1971.

192 **"They love the character":** Gene Handsaker (AP), "Gal on Laugh-In Talks Spontaneously," *Kentucky New Era,* February 3, 1970, p. 9.

192 **"We don't care. We don't have to.":** Lily Tomlin on *Saturday Night Live,* season 2, episode 1, September 18, 1976. See http://snltranscripts.jt.org/76/76aphonecompany.phtml.

192 **telephone excise tax:** Louis Allen Talley, "Telephone Excise Tax," Congressional Research Service Report for Congress, RS20119, September 15, 2000. The tax was largely gutted in 2006; see "U.S. to Repeal Long-Distance Telephone Tax," *New York Times,* May 26, 2006.

192 **$1.5 billion, 10 percent:** "Telephone Excise Tax Receipts 1899–2005," Tax Policy Center, at http://www.taxpolicycenter.org/taxfacts/Content/PDF/telephone.PDF. The 10 percent estimate comes from Stephen Daggett, "Cost of Major U.S. Wars," Congressional Research Service, June 29, 2010, at http://www.fas.org/sgp/crs/natsec/RS22926.pdf.

192 **make free phone calls and feel good about it:** Interestingly, several years earlier AT&T cited the telephone company's duty to collect the telephone excise tax as one of the reasons it was legally obligated to investigate and prosecute telephone fraud. See Charles Ryan and H. W. William Caming, Brief of American Telephone and Telegraph Company as Amicus Curiae, in Kenneth Herbert Hanna and Nathan Modell, Appellants, v. United States of America, Appellee, Appeal from the United States District Court for the Southern District of Florida, No. 24343, May 7, 1968 <db328>.

193 **"Fuck the Bell System":** "Fuck the Bell System" was another play on words: in 1967 Abbie Hoffman wrote a precursor to *Steal This Book* titled *Fuck the System*, which focused on free and low-cost survival strategies in New York City.

193 **"The response was":** Alan Fierstein, author interview, 2006.

193 **God created pay phones:** AT&T preferred the term "coin telephone" to "pay phone"; as far as AT&T was concerned, all phones were pay phones.

194 **the percentage of uncollectible credit card:** "Credit Card, Third Number and Total Toll Message Uncollectible Study—March

1970," AT&T internal memo, September 10, 1970 <db406> (referred to below as "Credit Card Study").

195 Students for a Democratic Society: See http://blog.historyof phonephreaking.org/2009/06/101973-students-for-a-democratic -society-prank-fbi.html.

195 Steve McQueen: AP, "College Students Use Credit Card for Phone Binge," *Lewiston* (Maine) *Daily Sun,* May 23, 1968, p. 24. AT&T memos discussing this include William P. Mullane Jr., Teletypewriter Message to All Bell System Newsmen, May 22, 1968 <db190>; J. F. Doherty memo to M. Mullane, October 27, 1969 <db524>; "History of 168 Fraud," AT&T memo, February 1970 <db549>; and "Fraudulent Credit Card Usage, Case #C7-13-19," AT&T memo, undated <db548>.

195 It is evident: "Credit Card Study."

195 It is necessary: "Bell System Credit Card Plan–1971 Cards," AT&T internal memo, August 7, 1970 <db405>.

196 "With all the electronic means": Bill Acker, author interview, 2010.

197 The first underground and college newspapers: See, e.g., "Free Phone Calls," *Dallas Notes,* January 24–February 6, 1971 <db536>; the same article was published in a number of college or underground newspapers within a week.

197 "public disservice announcement": Radio TV Reports, Inc., transcript of Abbie Hoffman appearance on the TV program *Free Time* with Julius Lester, April 7, 1971, 10:30 p.m. in New York City on WNET-TV <db672>.

197 rebuttal from Hoffman: Abbie Hoffman, "Dear Russell (Baker That Is)," *YIPL,* no. 2, July 1971, p. 3.

198 "two thousand and three thousand subscribers": Bell, author interview, 2006.

198–199 assumed names and employee home addresses: Ken Hopper, author interview, 2006; Wayne Perrin, author interview, 2008.

199 obtained a copy of this memo: Memorandum from J. F. Doherty, Director, Corporate Security, AT&T, to AT&T Security

Managers, "Toll Fraud—Y.I.P.L. Publication," October 13, 1972, reprinted in "The AT&T Papers," *YIPL,* no. 14, November 1972, p. 3.

Chapter 14: Busted

201 **discount gas station and subsequent descriptions:** FBI file
87-HQ-121189, serial 3, p. 2, May 10, 1972, and serial 8, July 10,
1972, p. 12 <db883>.

202 **wrecking ball to the phone phreaks' home:** The 2111 conference continued to exist. The old Vancouver step tandem was
still in use on the network and its conference could be reached by
dialing (with a blue box) KP + 604 + 059 + 2111 + ST. It took
the phreaks a while to discover this and, once they did, they realized it was less convenient than it had been. You could dial into
the old 2111 conference merely by using a Cap'n Crunch whistle;
the new one required an actual blue box, which not every phreak
possessed.

202 **open sleeve-lead conference:** Telephone lines have two wires,
"tip" and "ring." But inside a step-by-step or crossbar central office
a third wire is added to each line: "sleeve." The names refer to the
positions of the wires on the plug of an operator's cord. The sleeve
lead was used by both operators and automated switching equipment to determine if a line was busy or idle. If a line's sleeve lead
was disconnected, the telephone switching equipment could no
longer determine if a line was in use. The result was that multiple
people could call such a number and "pile on," that is, be connected
in conference.

202 **"Charleston and . . . Benton Harbor":** Bill Acker, author interview, 2008.

202 **time-honored technique of scanning:** According to Bill
Acker, the 2111 gang referred to such exhaustive dialing as "Jan-
ning," in honor of a phone phreak named Jan from the United
Kingdom who was particularly fond of the approach.

203 **its new name was 052:** For audio recordings of the 052 conference from January 1972, see "Phreaks from Esquire Article on '052'
Conference," parts 1 and 2, at http://www.phonetrips.com.

204 650 Bell System security agents: AP, "Though Weaponless, Telephone Security Force Wields Power," *Geneva Times,* December 26, 1974, p. 19 <db42>.

204 Mostly they focused: Background information on typical telephone company security agent concerns from Wayne Perrin, author interview, 2008.

205 "On several occasions": FBI file 87-HQ-121189, serial 3, April 13, 1972, p. 2 <db883>.

206 more innocent days: More innocent up to a point. Access to California DMV records was restricted in 1989 when the actress Rebecca Schaeffer was murdered "after the prime suspect in the case obtained her home address from DMV records." See "In Killing's Aftermath, State Limits Access to Driver's Data," *Sacramento Bee,* August 27, 1989, p. A4.

207 anonymous telephone company employee: Bill Acker and Ray Oklahoma, author interview, 2008.

207 Due to a bug: The blocking of telephone calls to ten-digit telephone numbers that had a 0 or 1 in the fourth digit was called "D-digit blocking," a feature that made it impossible for ordinary telephone subscribers to call numbers like 914-052-1111. A similar safeguard called "E-digit blocking" blocked calls with 0 or 1 in the fifth digit of a ten-digit telephone number, shooting down calls to numbers like 914-415-1212. But D- and E-digit blocking sometimes failed or wasn't implemented properly, meaning that in some places such calls were possible.

208 "numerous multi-frequency signals" and following description: FBI file 87-HQ-121189, serial 3, May 10, 1972, p. 27 <db883>.

208 "overseas sender points": Overseas phone calls used to have to be routed through special switching facilities called overseas senders, which could be done with a blue box. For more on phone phreak international dialing techniques see http://explodingthephone.com/extra/overseas.

208 "not guilty": FBI file 87-HQ-121189, serial 8, July 23, 1972, p. 2 <db883>.

209 **"contemporary folk hero"**: Rick Carroll, "Captain Crunch's Story," *San Francisco Chronicle,* August 16, 1972 <db88>.

209 **big newswires:** See, for example, AP, "Electronic Rigging Charged to Call Long Distance Free," *Bakersfield Californian,* May 5, 1972, p. 4; UPI, "Costly Whistle," *The Sun* (Lowell, MA), November 30, 1972, p. 1.

209 **"Regulating the Phone Company in Your Home":** R. Oklahoma, "Regulating the Phone Company in Your Home," *Ramparts,* vol. 10, no. 12, June 1972, p. 55 <db431>.

209 **circulation 100,000:** Peter Collier, quoted in Pam Black, "Ramparts," *Folio: The Magazine for Magazine Management,* April 1, 2004.

209 **"It expressed":** Ibid.

209 **"heavy, shiny stock":** Ibid.

210 **"plans or instructions":** California Penal Code Section 502.7(b)(2). The specific wording made a criminal of anyone who "sells, gives, or otherwise transfers to another or offers, or advertises plans or instructions for [making a toll fraud device] with knowledge or reason to believe that they may be used to make [such a device]." For information on the 1965 amendments that added the "plans or instructions" clause to the law, see "Bill Seeks Tough Penalties for Phone Call Chislers," *Fresno Bee,* April 21, 1965, p. 12A.

210 **"Telephone company attorneys":** "How the Phone Company Interrupted Our Service," *Ramparts,* July 1972, pp. 10–11 <db271>.

211 **"In the past ten years":** Ibid.

211 **"we were willing":** Ibid. *Ramparts* drew the line at its subscriber list, refusing to hand that over.

211 **some ninety thousand:** "Magazine to Call 90,000 Copies Back," *Los Angeles Times,* May 19, 1972, p. A23 <db34>.

211 **almost $60,000:** "A Ramparts Issue Halted in Dispute; Magazine Withdrawn After Protest by Phone Concern," *New York Times,* May 22, 1972, p. 8 <db1028>.

211 **"Within a week":** "How the Phone Company Interrupted Our Service."

212 **monitoring the phone phreak conferences:** FBI files 87-HQ-121042, serial 2, page B, May 1, 1972 <db856>; see also FBI file 87-OK-17023 <db856>.

212 **"I know it looks easy":** "A Toll Thief's Tale," *Konowa Leader,* September 14, 1972 <db272>.

213 **"Celebration of Change":** *YIPL,* no. 11, June–July 1972, p. 1.

213 **"As some of you might know":** Ibid., p. 4.

214 **An informant, bench warrant:** FBI file 87-HQ-121189, serial 6, July 10, 1972 <db883>.

214 **phone phreak convention had been postponed:** The phone phreak convention's postponement appears to have been the result of legal concerns. According to *Ramparts* magazine, the convention was "postponed and moved to New York where, Yippies said, the laws against phreaking are 'full of loopholes.'" The *Village Voice* reported, "At Abbie Hoffman's invitation he [Draper] flew to Miami to head a phone freak convention, panicked, and flew right out again." See Robert Sherman, "Phone Phreak-Out in Phun City," *Ramparts,* vol. 11, no. 4, October 1972, p. 12 <db175>, and Maureen Orth, "Sore Losers: Mayor Daley, Meet Captain Crunch," *Village Voice,* July 20, 1972, p. 18.

214 **"a tape-recorder and a brown valise":** FBI file 87-HQ-121189, serial 8, July 28, 1972, p. 8 <db883>.

214–215 **basement ballroom of the Hotel Diplomat (and following description):** Sherman, "Phone Phreak-Out in Phun City."

215 **spy from New York Telephone:** FBI file 87-HQ-121189, serial 9, September 18, 1972, p. 10 <db883>. For more on the Hotel Diplomat, see "The Life and Times of the Hotel Diplomat, 1911–1994," at http://thisaintthesummeroflove.blogspot.com/2009/02/life-and-times-of-hotel-diplomat.html.

215 **Over the course of three days:** AT&T memorandum from Dennis Mollura to Bill Mullane, September 28, 1972 <db651>.

215 **"Cheat Ma Bell!":** Don Schroeder, "Beating the Rip-Off Set," Bell System News Features, January 1973 <db653>. An article based on this news release appeared as "Toll Fraud: Beating the

Rip-Off Set," *Bell Telephone Magazine,* November–December 1972 <db410>.

216 **"more than $20 million"**: The $20 million figure is likely inclusive of credit card fraud and does not reflect just electronic (blue box, black box) toll fraud.

216 **fifty-seven electronic toll fraud arrests:** "Toll Fraud," AT&T internal memorandum, May 18, 1977 <db570>.

216 **failed miserably:** "Capt. Crunch Defense Fund Fails," *San Francisco Chronicle,* September 12, 1972, p. 8 <db89>.

216 **"Don't think that didn't give us pause":** Rick Carroll, "They Got His Number," *San Francisco Chronicle,* November 30, 1972, p. 2 <db90>.

216 **"recollection had been refreshed":** See, for example, FBI file 87-HQ-121189, serial 12, November 17, 1972, p. 5 <db883>.

216 **"Draper didn't look very legendary":** Carroll, "They got his number."

217 **"refrain from illegal use" and description of plea deal:** Judgment, *United States v. John Thomas Draper,* United States District Court, Northern District of California, No. CR-72-973 RFP (SJ), November 29, 1972 <db1029>.

217 **"Your electronic gymnastics":** Carroll, "They Got His Number."

Chapter 15: Pranks

218 **"You know how some articles":** Steve Wozniak with Gina Smith, *iWoz: Computer Geek to Cult Icon* (New York: W. W. Norton & Company, 2006), p. 93.

218 **"most amazing thing":** *The Secret History of Hacking,* Channel 4 Television, July 22, 2001. Although produced for British television, this program was seen in the United States on the Discovery Channel with the title *History of Hacking.*

218 **"described a whole web of people":** Wozniak, *iWoz,* p. 94.

218 **"outsmarting phone companies":** *Secret History of Hacking.*

218 **"I kept reading it":** Wozniak, *iWoz,* p. 94.

218 **"I could tell that":** Ibid., p. 95.

218 **"The idea of the Blue Box"**: Ibid., p. 97.

219 **"I couldn't believe"**: Ibid., p. 96.

219 **"I froze and grabbed Steve"**: Ibid., p. 99.

219 **"It's real. Holy shit, it's real"**: Walter Isaacson, *Steve Jobs* (New York: Simon & Schuster, 2011), p. 28.

219–220 **"I started posting articles"**: Wozniak, *iWoz*, p. 100.

220 **vary with temperature**: The phone phreak Jim Roth, a gifted analog circuit designer, built analog blue boxes that cleverly avoided the temperature variation problem. The values of some of the components in his design increased with temperature while others decreased, and the variations canceled each other out. The result, several phone phreaks told me, was that you could tune one of his blue boxes at room temperature and then put it in a freezer for an hour and it would still work perfectly. Roth later received an accolade of sorts from New York Telephone security agent Thomas J. Duffy, who told the FBI that Roth built "excellent quality blue boxes." See FBI file 139-SF-188, serial 179, February 25, 1976, p. 2.

221 **By early 1972**: Steve Wozniak, author interview, 2008. Isaacson, in *Steve Jobs* (p. 28), states that Wozniak had the digital box "built before Thanksgiving," but Wozniak, in my 2008 interview with him, says it wasn't until early 1972.

221 **clever trick . . . to keep the power consumption down, "I swear to this day"**: Wozniak, *iWoz*, p. 102. For electrical engineers reading this book, Wozniak described his low-power design trick in a 2008 email as follows: "I ran the TTL inputs through the diode matrix to the number buttons. I ran the common of this number button pad into a Darlington, which grounded the circuit. I used a couple more diodes to drop a 9v battery the right amount for the TTL to work. Low power TTL worked as well. Even the CMOS version worked. The TTL inputs can be thought of as supplying a small amount of positive current, acting as tiny outputs. This current triggered the Darlington to ground the chips. I'm still a bit amazed how it worked but it worked extremely well and I don't think I came up with anything as off the wall clever again."

It is worth noting that Wozniak may not have been the first phone phreak to build a digital blue box; Brough Turner recalls building a digital blue box shortly after graduating from MIT in 1971. Turner's design was similar to Wozniak's, minus the clever low-power design trick.

221 **"Berkeley Blue", "Oaf Tobar":** Isaacson, *Steve Jobs,* p. 29. Some reports on the Internet say the pair went by the names "Hans" and "Gribble," but Wozniak does not remember this.

221 **"I would have died":** Wozniak, *iWoz,* p. 103.

221 **"Captain Crunch comes to our door":** Ibid., p. 105.

221 **"He turns out to be":** Ibid., p. 106.

222 **"All of a sudden":** Ibid., p. 108.

222 **"A guy named Moog":** Ibid., pp. 109–11.

222 **"sell it for $170 or so":** Wozniak, author interview, 2008.

223 **sales technique was inspired:** Wozniak, *iWoz,* p. 116.

223 **Many of these wound up in the hands:** Adam Schoolsky, author interview, 2011; see below for related FBI files.

223 **"Sales went on through the summer", "low paid salary":** Wozniak, author interview, 2008.

223 **thirty or forty boxes, more like a hundred:** Ibid.; Isaacson, *Steve Jobs,* p. 29.

224 **"It's kind of strange":** Wozniak, author interview, 2008.

224 **disassembled and analyzed:** By the mid-1970s blue box analysis requests were common enough that the FBI Laboratory created a "Blue Box Work Sheet Guide" that prompted its lab technicians to gather the relevant information when inspecting a blue box. Its categories included physical description (keyboard format, size and type, coupling method, power supply), frequency measurements (for digits 0-9, KP, ST, and 2,600 Hz), interior circuitry arrangement and description, and results of a test call using the blue box.

224 **Woz's little bit of paper:** FBI files 87-HQ-130192, 1973; 87-HQ-133306, 1974; and 87-LA-40513, serial 55, February 12, 1975. In particular, an unnumbered serial of file 87-HQ-130192 from 1975 discusses several blue boxes that contained Wozniak's note, and the 87-LA-40513 serial discusses one of the blue boxes discovered

at Bernard Cornfeld's mansion that also contained Wozniak's note; see <db1030>.

224 "The dozen or so students": Wozniak, *iWoz*, p. 64.

225 "[I]n this heavy accent" and description of Vatican prank: Ibid., p. 115.

225 Los Angeles Times: "Santa Barbara Is Still OK; A-Blast Report Just Hoax," *Los Angeles Times*, November 11, 1974, p. A3 <db41>.

226 "nuclear explosion," "continued throughout the day": Ibid.

227 Another place that simultaneous seizure: This situation was called "glare." To make this hack work, a phone phreak had to send 2,600 Hz down the line and then listen until he heard the remote end stop sending its 2,600 Hz. At that point, he had to momentarily stop sending 2,600 Hz, simulating the wink that told the remote end to send the digits of the number to be dialed. See AT&T, *Notes on Distance Dialing*, 1968, section 5, p. 14 <db1001>.

227–228 "We would sit there": Mark Bernay, author interview, 2011.

228 "We didn't even know," "It's not something": Wayne Perrin, notes and author interview, 2008.

228 "all sorts of shortages these days" and subsequent description: Andrew H. Malcolm, "The 'Shortage' of Bathroom Tissue: A Classic Study in Rumor," *New York Times*, February 3, 1974 <db1031>. The perception of a shortage was due to a confluence of factors, not just Carson's joke. In particular, a congressman had issued a press release a few weeks earlier stating that the United States might soon face a serious shortage of toilet paper and that rationing might be necessary. It concluded: "A toilet paper shortage is no laughing matter. It is a problem that will touch every American."

228 "Crunch's prank began" and subsequent description: John Draper, author interview, 2008, and http://www.webcrunchers.com /stories/toilet.html; a similar version of this story is told in Steve Long, "Captain Crunch: Super Phone Phreak," *High Times*, June 1977, p. 51 <db923>. It is hard to know if Draper and his friend did actually reach President Nixon; some of the details line up but some do not. The 800 number mentioned did indeed go to the White House, though it was not in fact the "CIA crisis line" but rather a toll-free telephone number used by White House staff on travel; see FBI file 139-HQ-0-2098, May 20, 1977 <db585>. Draper claims that he discovered the code name "Olympus" by using a verification circuit to eavesdrop on this line. This was technically possible in a few areas of the country (see chapter 18), but no other phone phreak I have spoken to recalls being able to do such a thing in the Washington, D.C., area. Finally, Nixon's Secret Service code name was "Searchlight," not "Olympus"; see "Top 10 Secret Service Code Names," *Time Specials*, at http://www.time.com/time/specials/packages /article/0,28804,1860482_1860481_1860422,00.html.

Chapter 16: The Story of a War

230 **"This is the story of a war":** Jim Russell, "The Telephone Company You're Dialing Has Been Temporarily Disconnected," a one-hour feature from the National Public Radio program *Options,* January 30, 1973. In a November 16, 2007, email Jim Russell recalled that "AT&T tried to stop its distribution by threatening stations all over the country."

230 **peace talks:** Bernard Gwertzman, "Thuy Rejects Peace Talks While U.S. Raids Continue," *New York Times,* December 24, 1972, p. NJ35.

230 **"MF Boogie":** Kim Lingo, author interview, 2012. Lingo says "MF Boogie" was composed on a Wurlitzer electronic piano that doubled as his blue box. A recording is available at ftp://ftp.wideweb.com /GroupBell/MFBoogie1.zip.

232 **first proposals . . . transistor-based telephone switching:** Joel, *Switching Technology,* pp. 203–4.

233 **the transistor itself would not be used:** Bell Laboratories never used the transistor (more accurately, the pnpn diode) as the actual switching element in any production telephone switching system. One of the main problems with using semiconductors for switching telephone lines was their inability to handle the relatively high-voltage ringing signal used in the telephone network. See ibid., pp. 203–4 and pp. 243–45.

233 **"struck by the similarity":** Ibid., pp. 225–27.

234 **world's first electronic:** Bell Telephone Laboratories, *The Electronic Switching System: Trial Installation, Morris, Illinois; General Description,* 1960, at http://www.archive.org/details/TheElectronicSwitchingSystem.

234 **five thousand times slower:** Ibid., p. 270 ("cycle time is about 3 microseconds").

235 **flying spot store:** Ibid.

236 **"traumatic experience":** Brooks, *Telephone,* p. 279.

236 **retained the basic concepts:** Bell Telephone Laboratories, *Bell Laboratories Record,* vol. 49, no., 65, June 1965.

236 **four thousand man years, $500 million:** Brooks, *Telephone,* pp. 278–79.

236 **"Absent competition":** Sheldon Hochheiser, "Bell Labs: Research, Development, and Innovation in a Monopoly" (presentation given at Reed College), December 2011 <db1044>.

236 **"trample it to death":** Brooks, *Telephone,* p. 279.

237 **more than 132 of the 4As:** Joel, *Switching Technology,* p. 321.

237 **physically smaller (and other features):** Robert J. Chapuis and Amos E. Joel Jr., *One Hundred Years of Telephone Switching, Volume 2: Electronics, Computers, and Telephone Switching* (Amsterdam: Ios Press, 2003), pp. 154–60.

237 **rendered black boxes obsolete, eleven seconds:** Bill Acker, author interview, 2011. A later version of No. 1 ESS software, introduced around 1980, added additional anti–blue box features: after seeing a wink from a remote trunk while a call was in progress, the No. 1 would attach an MF digit detector to the line to catch any subsequent digits sent by a blue box.

238 **red box:** *YIPL,* no. 16, February 1973. In fact the term *red box* had been around for at least six months prior to this introduction; it was mentioned, if not described in detail, at the 1972 phone phreak convention.

239 **modified their red boxes:** Through an odd coincidence having to do with ratios of the various tones involved, a Radio Shack touch-tone dialer could easily be turned into a red box simply by

swapping out a single inexpensive component, the crystal oscillator; see http://www.phonelosers.org/redbox/tonedialer.

240 **the month after that, it would be gone:** Evan Doorbell, author interview, 2012.

240 **"No fancy excuses":** *TAP,* no. 21, August–September 1973, p. 1.

241 **"the legal department of [New York Telephone]":** FBI file 100-NY-179649, serial 13, February 22, 1974 <db374>.

241 **Detroit underground newspaper:** "Fifth Estate Charged with Fraud," *Fifth Estate,* September 26, 1974, p. 2 <db553>. The case eventually went to trial and ended about a year later in a hung jury.

241 **sued by Pacific Telephone:** The Pacific Telephone and Telegraph Company, Plaintiff, vs. Jack Kranyak, doing business as Teletronics Company of America; et al, defendants, Superior Court of California, County of Los Angeles, No. NWC45558, July 14, 1975 <db336>. Pacific Telephone seemed to be particularly litigious that summer. It also sued Wayne Green, the publisher of the ham radio magazine *73,* for printing a technical overview of the telephone system that included blue box plans. See Myrna Oliver, "PTT Sues over Story on How to Duck Call Fees," *Los Angeles Times,* June 10, 1975, p. B3 <db52>, and Spenser Whipple Jr., "Inside Ma Bell," *73 Magazine,* June 1975, p. 67 <db318>.

241 **some eight thousand people:** Southwestern Bell memorandum/ Q&A backgrounder titled "Fraud," undated but circa 1977.

242 **"Dear Telephone User":** "Dear Telephone User" letter from Pacific Telephone and Telegraph, mailed May 28, 1976. In the original, the last three paragraphs of the letter were all in capital letters; see http:// pdf.textfiles.com/zines/TEL/TEL_spec2.jpg.

242 **One recipient of this missive:** *Radio Electronics,* 1976.

242 **"serious national problem," "nationwide telephone fraud":** "Free-Phone Racket Inside Post Office," *Sunday Times* (London), January 21, 1973, p. 1.

243 **"men of intellectual stature":** "Phone Fiddle by Bleep Box," *Daily Mirror,* October 4, 1973.

243 **charges went back to 1968:** "Nineteen Accused of Dial-the-World Phone Fiddle," *Daily Telegraph,* October 4, 1973.

243 **exactly three went to live human beings:** Robert Hill, "Days at the Old Bailey," *Interface* (the house journal of Cambridge Consultants Ltd.), vol. 8, no. 1, April 1974, p. 10 <db341>. Hill was one of the Old Bailey 19; partway through the trial, after Hill gave his testimony, the prosecution moved to drop the charges against him. In his recollection of the trial he wrote: "The telephone system is the largest machine in the world, extending as it does over the whole surface of the earth. It is so easy to gain access to it—just pick up a telephone—and having done that, you can then explore ways of finding your way around the world. Some people are interested in the gadgetry of the system; some in gadgetry they can build to affect the system. Some study the system as geographers, some as computer programmers." Hill passed away in 1974 at age twenty-four.

243 **"Your trial is now over":** "Eight Not Guilty of Phone Fraud," *Daily Telegraph,* November 14, 1973. Interestingly, one of the Old Bailey 19, Duncan Campbell, had previously been arrested and fined 200 pounds (plus 200 pounds for court costs) in April 1972 for using a blue box to call "Moscow, Melbourne, Washington, and Los Angeles." See Kenelm Jenour, "The Man Who Dialed the World," *Daily Mirror,* April 15, 1972.

243 **rock star Ike Turner:** AP, "Ike Turner Arrested," *St. Joseph News Press,* March 27, 1974, p. 5A. Turner and two of the individuals arrested with him were later acquitted; one was convicted. See "Sorry, Wrong Voiceprint," *Detroit Free News,* August 8, 1974 <db464>; "came from Wozniak and Jobs": see Michael Moritz, *The Little Kingdom: The Private Story of Apple Computer* (New York: William Morrow & Co., 1984), p. 78.

243–244 **"just missed the shooting of a *Playboy* center spread":** Ted Thackery Jr. and Ronald L. Soble, "FBI Raids Financier Cornfeld's Mansion, Arrests Aide, Seizes Illegal Phone Boxes," *Los Angeles Times,* January 29, 1975, p. A3 <db43>; "Cornfeld Charged with Phone Fraud," *Los Angeles Times,* June 5, 1975, p. B32 <db51>;

Diana B. Henriques, "Bernard Cornfeld, 67, Dies; Led Flamboyant Mutual Fund," *New York Times,* March 2, 1995. There really was a *Playboy* photo shoot at Cornfeld's mansion the day the FBI swooped down, by the way; see FBI file 87-LA-40513, serial 29, January 30, 1975 <db885>.

244 **"He's got the whole world in his hands":** FBI file 87-LA-40513, serial 55, February 12, 1975 <db885>.

244 **Lainie Kazan:** Sanford L. Jacobs, "Blue Boxes Spread from Phone Phreaks to the Well-Heeled," *Wall Street Journal,* January 29, 1976, p. 1 <db53>.

244 **Woz and Jobs:** Adam Schoolsky, author interview, 2011.

244 **Robert Cummings:** Jacobs, "Blue Boxes Spread."

244 **high-voltage electricity:** David Condon and John Gilbert, author interviews, 2009. Called "juicing" or "nerping," the high-voltage technique involved sending a 110-volt AC signal (preferably 80 Hz, but 60 Hz would do) into the telephone line. Though no one is sure exactly how it worked, it had the effect of causing the local central office to reset a call much in the same way as whistling 2,600 Hz would. The benefit was that it could work even on trunk lines that did not use 2,600 Hz signaling, such as a T carrier. For more details, listen to Evan Doorbell's "A HiFi 914 Routing Tape, Part 1" (December 1975), at http://www.phonetrips.com.

245 **Colby Street house, "kiss of death":** Condon, author interview, 2009. Additional details provided by John Gilbert and other members of the Colby Street gang.

245 **"They explicitly excluded me":** Acker author interviews, 2008 and 2011.

246 **The more people who knew:** In the physical world economists call this the tragedy of the commons. The term describes situations in which a natural resource (e.g., fish in the sea, or trees, or grazing land) is overused because it does not belong to any one individual and, as a result of such overuse, disappears. I think of the electronic security equivalent as a sort of "tragedy of the informational commons." A version of this problem also appears in code

breaking (if you break your enemy's codes and then do something with the information you obtain, your enemy is likely to figure out that you've broken his codes and will change them, denying you further intelligence) and is explored in Neal Stephenson's book *Cryptonomicon* (2002). See Garrett Hardin, "The Tragedy of the Commons," *Science,* December 1968, p. 1243, at http://www .sciencemag.org/content/162/3859/1243.full.pdf.

246 **One such phreak in New York:** Author interview with a New York–area phone phreak who prefers to remain anonymous, 2012. Two of the books in question were the *Distance Dialing Reference Guide* and the *Traffic Routing Guide,* both of which described AT&T's network routing in excruciating detail.

Chapter 17: A Little Bit Stupid

249 **entered a telephone booth:** Ken Hopper notes and author interview, 2006.

250 **had been around since the early 1900s:** Joel, *Switching Technology,* pp. 45–48. See also J. Atkins, K. A. Raschke, and D. L. Woody, "Traffic Service Position System No. 1: Busy Line Verification Feature," *Bell System Technical Journal,* vol. 59, no. 8, October 1980, pp. 1397–416.

250 **verification circuits in some places could be reached:** Bill Acker and Ray Oklahoma, author interviews, 2008. An internal AT&T memo acknowledges that blue box access to verification was possible prior to 1971 in Miami: "[We] caught this in Miami when they cut over their TSPS [a relatively new switchboard system used by operators]. They made a vacant area code available to TSPS operators for verification. [We] pointed out at the time that anything available via unused area code was available to blue box users and would compromise verification." See C. J. Schulz, "Appraisal of 'Secrets of the Little Blue Box' Article in the October 1971 Esquire Magazine," Bell Laboratories memorandum, September 17, 1971 <db397>. AT&T claimed that blue box verification access in San Francisco was due to a misconfiguration of its switching equipment.

251 **Eder was a burly, forty-five-year-old:** Chic Eder's real name was Phillip Norman Ader. Description of Eder from author interview of John Draper, 2008, and from Albert Goldman, "What Will Happen When Middle-Class America Gets the Straight Dope?" *New York Magazine*, August 25, 1975, p. 28.

252 **"Dear Agent in Charge":** FBI file 100-LA-82471, serial 22, August 28, 1973 <db963>. The FBI began evaluating Eder as a potential informant and seems to have accepted his offer sometime in 1974.

252–253 **first inkling (and subsequent description):** FBI file 139-SF-188, serial 1, June 24, 1975 <db899>.

253 **"San Francisco is not serviced":** FBI file 139-SF-188, serial 8, June 27, 1975 <db899>.

254 **"This is to inform":** FBI file 139-HQ-4991, serial 6, July 2, 1976 <db367>. This page of Draper's file was actually stored in the "Special File Room," separated from the rest of his file. Curious about the redacted sentence? So am I. Even thirty-five years later the FBI refuses to reveal it, withholding it on grounds of national security.

254 **got it all on tape:** FBI file 139-HQ-4991, serial 30, July 15, 1975 and bulky enclosure E30. Eder's tape of the phone call was obtained under FOIA and you can listen to it at http://explodingthephone .com/extra/edertape.

255 **Walter Schmidt:** Schmidt later received a personal commendation letter from FBI director Clarence M. Kelley for "exceptional assistance . . . to our Los Angeles Office in the investigation of an Interception of Communications case and most significantly for his efforts which facilitated the handling of a very sensitive situation." FBI file 139-HQ-4991, serial 29, July 31, 1975 <db367>.

256 **"valuable service," "outstanding":** FBI file 139-SF-188, serial 31, July 21, 1975 <db899>. Alas, FBI documents do not reveal how much Eder was paid.

256 **"capability of monitoring calls":** Ibid. and FBI file 139-HQ-4991 (serial number obscured), July 21, 1975 <db367>.

256 **"not selling information," "does not know how widespread":** FBI file 139-SF-188, serial 38, July 25, 1975 <db899>.

258 **"extremely cautious in use of the telephone" and preceding description:** FBI file 139-HQ-4991, serial 26, July 22, 1975 <db367>.

258 **"Dear Mr. deButts":** Ken Hopper notes and author interview, 2006. See also FBI file 139-HQ-4991, serial 26, July 22, 1975, and serial 27, July 24, 1975 <db367>.

258 **"It is pointed out":** FBI file 139-HQ-4991, serial 25, July 24, 1975 <db367>.

258 **"ho-hum":** FBI file 139-HQ-4991, serial 35, August 1, 1975 <db367>.

259 **"undoubtedly be sympathetic":** FBI file 139-HQ-4991, serial 33 (serial number obscured), July 29, 1975 <db367>.

259 **small blizzard of memos:** FBI file 139-SF-188, serial 43, July 30, 1975 <db899>.

259 **"most valuable," "penetrate":** FBI file 139-SF-188, serials 64 and 65, 139-HQ-4991, serial 31 <db899>.

260 **"Departmental Attorney Kline":** FBI file 139-SF-188, serial 75, September 30, 1975 <db899>.

260 **answer was no (and subsequent descriptions):** FBI file 139-SF-188, serials 76–82, October 2–15, 1975 <db899>.

260 **"For information of receiving":** FBI file 139-SF-188, serial 85, November 17, 1975 <db899>.

Chapter 18: Snitch

Much of the information regarding Wayne Perrin's investigation of Paul Sheridan comes from author interviews conducted with Perrin in 2008 and Perrin's case notes from the time.

266 **"related numerous items":** Wayne Perrin, author interview and case notes, 2008.

266 **"early twenties, five-foot-eleven":** Ibid.

267 **"Mr. Norden, often times":** Ibid.

268 **could get President Ford on the line (and preceding description):** Perrin, author interview, 2008; FBI file 139-LA-430, serial 1, December 5, 1975.

268 **"got right to the second floor of the White House":** Perrin's recollection may be slightly off, since the second floor of the

White House is the residential area, but the 800 number in Sheridan's possession (also making the rounds of other phone phreaks at that time) definitely did go to the White House.

268 AUTOVON: Definitive historical and technical information on AUTOVON is difficult to come by. The most authoritative source is Records Group 371 (Records of the Defense Communications Agency), National Archives and Records Administration, College Park, Maryland.

270 to be used only by the President: AUTOVON Telephone Directory, as quoted in Telecom Digest email list, June 19, 1992, at http://massis.lcs.mit.edu/archives/reports/autovon.instructions.

272 Bob Jacobs: FBI file 139-SF-188, serial 108, December 23, 1975 <db899>.

273 guard banding: Guard banding seems to have been discovered sometime between 1971 and 1972. John Draper says he invented it, but Bill Acker says this credit belongs to New York phone phreak Jim Roth. It is interesting to note that the *TAP* newsletter did not print an article about it until 1979, which gives some indication of the informational time lag between the more sophisticated phreaks and the newsletter of the phone phreak masses. For more details on guard banding, see Napoleon Solo, "Guard Banding," *TAP,* no. 56, March–April 1979, p. 4.

273 military's Arctic communication system: United States Air Force, "The White Alice Network," 1958, at http://www.porticus .org/bell/pdf/whitealice.pdf. For a more personal recollection, see Bill Everly, "The White Alice Communications System," at http://www.whitealice.net.

273 Sheridan's document explained: Author unknown, "AUTOVON Access Info," undated <db1032>.

274 The FBI's biggest concern: Nelson Saxe, author interview, 2007.

274 JCSAN/COPAN: JCSAN stood for "Joint Chiefs of Staff Alerting Network"; COPAN stood for "Command Post Alerting Network." See W. H. Seckler, "Global Command Post Alerting Network," *Bell Laboratories Record,* November 1964, pp. 371–74.

274 "mentally unstable," "go off": Saxe, author interview and notes, 2007.

275 "We're not about to go out to Los Angeles": Saxe, author interview, 2007.

Chapter 19: Crunched

276 "Dear TAP": "Letters from Readers," *TAP,* no. 31, December 1975, p. 3. Yes, it was true, William F. Buckley Jr.'s conservative *National Review* had printed Captain Crunch's telephone number, and Joe Engressia's too, as part of an article covering the 1973 phone phreak convention. It was payback for *YIPL's* having printed the telephone number of Nixon's law firm. "Call them up the next time you get in at 4 a.m.," the *National Review* article's author suggested. "Collect. Tell them they're stupid." See D. Keith Mano, "Sorry, Wrong Revolution," *National Review,* October 26, 1973, pp. 1183–85 <db184>.

277 a dark vibe: Author interviews with several phone phreaks who, naturally, wish to remain anonymous, 2008.

277 FBI-AT&T AUTOVON demo: Description of the AUTOVON meetings comes from author interviews with Ken Hopper of Bell Laboratories, Nelson Saxe of AT&T Long Lines, Wayne Perrin of Pacific Telephone, FBI special agents who attended the meeting, and Ken Hopper's notes.

278 National Security Agency: FBI file 139-SF-188, serial 159 <db899>, and Ken Hopper, author interview, 2006. Fonger appears to have worked for the Communications Security side of the National Security Agency and wrote several memos, all classified SECRET, summarizing the Los Angeles AUTOVON demos: "Phone Freaks Invade AUTOVON," January 30, 1976 <db902>; "Phone Freaks Invade Computer Networks," February 6, 1976 <db903>; and "Phone Freaks Can Invade Your Privacy," February 13, 1976 <db904>. The memos noted that an NSA investigation of the phone phreak claims was ongoing and that some of the techniques described were a "potentially lucrative source of intelligence."

278 Michael was a talented: Author interview with "Michael," 2009.

279 Hopper suspected it was Sheridan: Hopper, author interview, 2006.

280 Just two miles from Stanford: Description of the 1900 block of Menalto and the story about Steve Wozniak from Roy Kaylor, author interview, 2008. Additional information from John Draper, author interview, 2008.

280 "Computers are mostly used against people": Levy, *Hackers,* p. 142. See also DigiBarn Computer Museum website, at http://www .digibarn.com/collections/newsletters/peoples-computer/ index.html.

282 "It was decided": FBI file 139-LA-430, serial 30, January 29, 1976 <db372>.

282 "agents met with Pacific Telephone" and subsequent description: FBI file 139-SF-188, serial 127, January 27, 1976 <db899>.

282 "Draperism": Draper, author interview, 2008.

283 Wall Street Journal: Sanford L. Jacobs, "Blue Boxes Spread from Phone Freaks to Well-Heeled," *Wall Street Journal,* January 27, 1976, p. 1 <db53>, included in 139-SF-188, serial 131 <db899>.

283 "has no sources who are phone phreaks": The draft teletype message described here is FBI file 139-SF-188, serial 154, February 10, 1976 <db899>. The crossed-out text is on page 3. The teletype message as received at FBI headquarters is FBI file 139-HQ-4991, serial 70, February 10, 1976 <db367>.

284 agents in Los Angeles were not thrilled: FBI file 139-SF-188, serial 161, February 18, 1976 <db899>.

284 send a phone phreak informant up to San Francisco: FBI file 139-SF-188, serial 160, February 19, 1976 <db899>.

284 would drive up the next day: FBI file 139-SF-188, serial 173, February 23, 1976 <db899>.

287 Draper maintains he was framed: A version of this story with slightly different details appears on Draper's website, at http:// www.webcrunchers.com/stories/snitch.html.

288 "On February 20, 1976 at 5:23 pm": FBI file 139-SF-188, serial 175, February 23, 1976 <db899>.

288 "This will serve to inform you": FBI file 139-SF-188, serial 187, February 23, 1976 <db899>.

289 **tape recording and detailed analysis:** FBI file 139-SF-188, serial 183, February 24, 1976 <db899>.

289 **service's receptionist said:** FBI file 139-SF-188, unnumbered serial (FD-302, numbered page 4*), May 4, 1976 <db899>.

289 **friend in Pennsylvania:** FBI file 139-SF-188, unnumbered serial (FD-302, numbered page 2), May 21, 1976 <db899>.

290 **FBI's after-action report (and following paragraphs):** FBI file 139-SF-188, unnumbered serial (FD-302, numbered page 29), April 2, 1976 <db899>.

291–292 **picked up by the newswires:** AP, "Charges Filed Against Electronics Wizard," *Asbury Park Press,* April 23, 1976, p. A6 <db56>; AP, "Wizard Whistles Way into Trouble," *Sarasota Journal,* April 23, 1976, p. 2D.

292 **"The first thing I thought":** Sidney Schaefer, author interview, 2012.

292 **"Draper shall refrain":** *United States v. John Thomas Draper,* United States District Court for the Northern District of California, No. CR-72-973 RFP, Judgment and Order of Probation, November 29, 1972 <db1029>.

292 **Dawson met with Draper's attorney (and following quotes):** FBI file 139-HQ-4991, serial 90, April 22, 1976 <db367>.

292 **with two provisos:** FBI file 139-HQ-4991, serial 92, June 8, 1976 <db367>.

293 **"It was a big joke for him":** Author interview with anonymous source familiar with the debriefing, 2008.

293 **"sentenced to the custody":** FBI file 139-HQ-4991, unnumbered serial (FD-204), September 7, 1976 <db367>.

293 **On March 5, 1976:** Wayne Perrin, notes and author interview, 2008.

293 **"In ninety percent":** Wayne Perrin, author interview, 2008.

Chapter 20: Twilight

296 **On May 15, 1976:** Victor K. McElheny, "New Phone Setup Started to Save Time and Circuits," *New York Times,* May 15, 1976, p. 34 <db1033>.

297 **Bell started experimenting:** Joel, *Switching Technology,* pp. 430–38.

297 eliminating blue box fraud: Ibid., p. 434.

297 CAMA-C: Ibid., pp. 379 and 432. "As of January 1, 1977, 155 of these [CAMA-C] systems . . . were installed in crossbar tandems and No. 4A crossbar offices. Later the programs for these offices were modified to seek out potential troubles and suspected fraud situations based upon the detected supervisory signals."

298 Thomas Carter: Ellen Wojan, "Thomas F. Carter of Carter Electronics: Calling for Competition," *Inc.*, April 1, 1984.

298 Carterfone: "In the Matter of Use of the Carterfone Device in Message Toll Telephone Service; In the Matter of Thomas F. Carter and Carter Electronics Corp., Dallas, Tex. (Complainants) v. American Telephone and Telegraph Co., Associated Bell System Companies, Southwestern Bell Telephone Company, and General Telephone Company of the Southwest (Defendants)," Docket No. 16942; Docket No. 17073, Federal Communications Commission, 13 F.C.C. 2d 420 (1968), 13 Rad. Reg 2d (P &F) 597, FCC 68-661, June 26, 1968 (hereinafter, "Carterfone").

298 "[T]he phone companies were harassing my customers": Wojan, "Thomas F. Carter."

298 FCC tariff 132: FCC tariff 132, April 16, 1957.

298 "The universal comment," "I didn't think it was fair": Wojan, "Thomas F. Carter."

299 "unreasonable, unlawful, and unreasonably discriminatory": "Carterfone."

299 cream skimming: Coll, *The Deal of the Century,* pp. 11–14.

300 The very next day: "AT&T to Cut Off MCI's Connections," *New York Times,* April 16, 1974 <db1034>.

300 AT&T, at regulatory gunpoint: "AT&T Ordered to Give Service to MCI, Others," *Wall Street Journal,* April 24, 1974. In fact, AT&T appealed the FCC's decision and lost; see "AT&T Loses Motion, Will Reconnect MCI's Private-Line Services," *Wall Street Journal,* May 3, 1974.

300 all for much less (and preceding description of Execunet): Philip Louis Cantelon, *The History of MCI: 1968–1988, The Early Years* (Dallas: Heritage Press, 1993).

301 **sued the Hare Krishnas:** "Krishna Units Accused of 'Pirate' Telephone Calls," *Los Angeles Times,* September 24, 1977, p. B6 <db982>.

301 **seeking to sever its manufacturing arm:** Charles Zerner, "U.S. Sues to Force A.T.&T. to Drop Western Electric Co.," *New York Times,* January 15, 1949, p. 1 <db1035>.

301 **reached an agreement:** Anthony Lewis, "A.T.&T. Settles Antitrust Case; Shares Patents," *New York Times,* January 25, 1956, p. 1 <db1036>.

302 **"The wounds from that 1956 scandal":** Coll, *Deal of the Century,* p. 59.

302 **On November 20, 1974:** Peter T. Kilborn, "The Telephone Suit: Competitive Cold Water for the Mighty Bell System," *New York Times,* November 24, 1974, p. 1 <db1037>.

302 **"severed limbs":** Coll, *Deal of the Century,* p. 120.

302 **AT&T lawyers argued (and subsequent description):** "Antitrust Immunity for AT&T Is Barred by High Court Ruling," *New York Times,* November 29, 1977 <db1038>; *United States v. American Telephone and Telegraph,* 427 F. Supp. 57 (1976), United States District Court, District of Columbia, November 24, 1976.

303 **"Watergate is a gnat":** "A Phone Executive Assails Bell System in His Suicide Note," *New York Times,* November 19, 1974 <db1039>; J. Edward Hyde, *The Phone Book: What the Phone Company Would Rather You Not Know* (Washington, D.C.: Regnery Publishing, 1976), pp. 98–112; "Phone Calls and Philandering," *Time,* September 5, 1977.

304 **Ashley was fired soon after (and surrounding description):** Brooks, *Telephone,* p. 309; Kleinfield, *The Biggest Company on Earth,* pp. 267–69.

304 **"I had been looking at all the expenditures":** Louis J. Rose, author interview, 2006.

304 **The Texas scandal spread:** Kleinfield, *The Biggest Company on Earth,* pp. 271–72.

304 **The telephone company soon found itself:** Brooks, *Telephone,* p. 311; Kleinfield, *The Biggest Company on Earth,* p. 272.

305 **"I think we're going":** Bill Caming, author interview, 2007.

306 **"arranged for a city councilman" and surrounding description:** Kleinfield, *The Biggest Company on Earth,* p. 274.

306 **thirteen female employees:** Ibid., pp. 275–77; "Six Women Testify in Texas Phone Suit," *New York Times,* August 28, 1977 <db1040>; AP, "Suit Against Southwestern Bell in 4th Week of Trial," *Times News* (Hendersonville, NC), August 30, 1977, p. 9.

306 **appeals court overturned:** Kleinfield, *The Biggest Company on Earth,* p. 278; "$3 Million Award Is Overturned in a Suit Against Southwest Bell," *New York Times,* November 30, 1978 <db1041>.

306 **Supreme Court of Texas:** *Dixon v. Southwestern Bell,* 607 S.W.2d 240 (1980), No. B-8208, Supreme Court of Texas, October 22, 1980 (Rehearing Denied November 19, 1980). The Texas Supreme Court did not so much uphold the appeals court ruling as simply decide that it did not have jurisdiction to hear the case; Texas law granted its Supreme Court very limited jurisdiction regarding slander cases.

307 **Intel 8008:** Roy Allan, *A History of the Personal Computer: The People and the Technology* (London, Ontario, Canada: Allan Publishing, 2001); S. P. Morse, B. W. Raveiel, S. Mazor, and W. B. Pohimian, "Intel Microprocessors—8008 to 8086," *IEEE Computer,* vol. 13, no. 10, October 1980.

307 **"first truly usable microprocessor":** Lamont Wood, "Forgotten PC History: The True Origins of the Personal Computer," *Computerworld,* August 8, 2008, at http://www.computerworld. com/s/article/9111341/Forgotten_PC_history_The_true_origins _of_the_personal_computer.

307 **"Project Breakthrough!":** *Popular Electronics,* January 1975, cover and pp. 23ff.

308 **"The only word which could come to mind":** Levy, *Hackers,* p. 192.

309 **Wozniak would show off:** Ibid., p. 250.

309 **"Jobs placed ads":** Ibid., p. 253.

Chapter 21: Nightfall

311 **"Well, let's see":** Bill Acker, author interview, 2007.

312 **The new legal standard:** See, for example, United States of America, Plaintiff-Appellee v. Michael William Clegg, Defendant-Appellant, No. 74-2557, United States Court of Appeals, Fifth Circuit, 509 F.2d 605 (1975), March 5, 1975.

312 **Draper walked out of Lompoc:** Peter Gorner and Michael Smith, "They Still Fear Captain Crunch," *San Francisco Chronicle,* June 29, 1977, p. 4 <db91>.

312 **slopped pigs:** John Draper, "Prisons Are the Universities of Crime," at http://www.webcrunchers.com/stories/prisons.html.

313 **PDP-6:** Levy, *Hackers,* p. 95.

313 **"A WATS extender is used":** Stephen Wozniak, "An Apple for the Captain," *Infoworld,* October 1, 1984, p. 57.

313 **Draper cracked:** Ibid.

313 **disliked Draper:** Moritz, *Return to the Little Kingdom,* p. 205.

314 **microcomputer laboratory:** Bell Laboratories, "Evidence Examination Report: Pennsylvania State Police Incident No. N6-39474, Bell Telephone Company of Pennsylvania Case No. 23-50-E77," December 14, 1977 <db1042>.

314 **"plenty of music, fun, and information":** John Draper, handwritten flyer titled "Capt'n Crunch Party," 1977 <db694>.

314 **party crashers (and surrounding description):** Howard Smith and Leslie Harlib, "The Captain Is Crunched Again," *Village Voice,* January 16, 1978 <db65>.

314 **watching Draper like a hawk (and subsequent description):** Bell of Pennsylvania, "Case Summary of John Thomas Draper," September 8, 1978 <db687>.

315 **start of a lengthy nightmare (and subsequent description):** Smith and Harlib, "The Captain Is Crunched Again." Stories vary as to whether the red box was found on Draper's person or in his car.

315 **At one point during the trial:** Ken Hopper, author interview, 2006.

316 **sentenced to three to six months:** Mike Joseph, "'Phone Phreak' Jailed for 3 to 6 Months," *Pocono Record,* August 19, 1978, p. 17 <db71>.

316 **"I just have a feeling":** K. C. Mason (UPI), "Highrise Joe Is a Whiz in Spite of Blindness," *Sarasota Herald-Tribune,* July 4, 1982, p. 8G.

316 **offered Engressia a job:** Description of Engressia's conversation with Leger from Joybubbles, author interview, 2006.

317 **"You wouldn't believe the pressure":** Lloyd Leger, author interview, 2007.

317 **"I feel the Bell insignia":** "The Whistler and the Captain—Veterans of Phone 'Fixing,'" *New York Times,* March 27, 1978, p. D3 <db69>.

318 **4ESS:** Joel, *Switching Technology,* p. 294.

318 **"tend[s] to pass himself off as the victim":** Dr. Robert B. Blumberg, psychiatric evaluation of John T. Draper, August 17, 1978 (included in Draper's 1976 court records).

318 **"numerous paranoid delusions":** O'Neil S. Dillon, MD, psychiatric evaluation of John T. Draper, December 6, 1978 (included in Draper's 1976 court records).

319 **"Is this not simple?":** Pete Carey, "Cap'n Crunch Programs His Way from Jail to Success," *Chicago Tribune,* May 25, 1983, p. D1 <db966>.

319 **TAP:** In 1979 the phone phreak newsletter changed its name again, this time from Technological American Party to Technological Assistance Program. Was this because they were becoming less political? Not so much, said Cheshire Catalyst in 2010. "It had more to do with the difficulty of opening up a bank account when you have the word 'Party' in your name."

319 **Third Annual Phone Phreak Convention:** YIPL ran phone phreak conventions in 1972 and 1973, but a dry spell followed until THC-79.

319 **"For several reasons, I have permanently retired":** John Draper, "Greetings" (open letter to THC-79 attendees), *TAP,* no. 59, September–October 1979.

320 **"While intrepidly trekking":** Cheshire Catalyst, "The News Is In from the West, and It's Beige," *TAP,* no. 51, July 1978, p. 4.

320 CBBS: Ward Christensen and Randy Suess, "Hobbyist Computerized Bulletin Board," *Byte*, vol. 3, no. 11, pp. 150–57.

320 first phone phreak/hacker BBSes: Katie Hafner and John Markoff, *Cyberpunk: Outlaws and Hackers on the Computer Frontier* (New York: Simon & Schuster, 1991), p. 44; see also a description of the 8BBS in Santa Clara, California, which ran from 1980 to 1982, at http://everything2.com/title/8BBS.

321 "Enclosed for Bureau": FBI file 117-HQ-2905, serial "X," April 30, 1979 <db374>.

321 "nuclear yield": FBI file 117-HQ-2905, serial 3, August 24, 1979 <db374>.

321 Judge Harold Greene: In an odd coincidence, in 1980 as part of a totally separate case, Judge Greene "ordered the FBI to stop destroying its surveillance files and to design a plan in which no files could be destroyed until historians and archivists could review them for historical value." As it turns out, large chunks of this book are based on such FBI files, which might well have been destroyed were it not for Judge Greene's order. See William Yurcik, "Judge Harold H. Greene: A Pivotal Figure in Telecommunications Policy and His Legacy," IEEE Global History Network, at http://www.ieeeghn.org/wiki/images/1/1d/Yurcik.pdf. p. 16, and John Anthony Scott, "The FBI Files: A Challenge for Historians," *Perspectives on History*, March 1980, at http://www.historians.org/perspectives/issues/1980/8003/8003new1.cfm.

321 statistics are mind numbing: Yurcik, "Judge Harold H. Greene."

321 broken up into eight different companies: Coll, *Deal of the Century;* Kimberly Zarkin and Michael J. Zarkin, *The Federal Communications Commission: Front Line in the Culture and Regulation Wars* (Westport, CT: Greenwood Press, 2006).

Epilogue

325 The town of Wawina: Bob Riddell, author interview, 2012.

325 108 historical telephones (and surrounding description): Gail Van Horn (AP), "Small Entrepreneur Owns 148 Telephones," *Spokesman Review*, October 3, 1976, p. B3.

325 **"ask your mother to help you":** Telephone World website, "Sounds and Recordings from Wawina, MN," at http://www. phworld.org/sounds/wawina.

325 **no other place in the continental United States:** Note the qualifier "continental." The town of Livengood, Alaska, also had a 2,600 Hz–based telephone system, but it went away sometime in 2011. See "The Death of Livengood" on the Binary Revolution Forums website, at http://www.binrev.com/forums/index.php /topic/44301-the-death-of-livengood.

326 **several hours of goodbyes:** You can listen to them at the Telephone World website, phworld.org.

326 **"even callow youths":** Jake Locke, email to author, 2011.

327 **looked like he would be going to prison for ten years:** "Bookmaking Sentence Against 3 Reimposed," *Miami News,* December 18, 1969, p. 10A.

327 **"Gil Beckley would be distinctly more valuable":** "Crime: No. 11 Off the Boards," *Time,* March 2, 1970.

327 **shot dead and stuffed into the trunk of a car:** AP, "Fugitive Mike Thevis Back in Custody," *Spartanburg Herald,* November 10, 1978, p. B1.

327 **Flamboyant mob attorney:** Frank Murray, "Ben Cohen Cries 'Mercy,' Is Led Off to Jail," *Miami News,* November 30, 1966; "Ben Cohen, Mr. Big Criminal Lawyer, Dies in Miami Beach of Cancer at 76," *Miami News,* August 28, 1979, p. 4A.

328 **612 was the area code:** George Monaghan, "The Child in a Man," *Minneapolis Star-Tribune,* September 19, 1991, p. 1E.

328 **Found a high-rise:** Gene Collier, "There's Martin Luther King, There's Gandhi . . . and There's Fred Rogers," *Pittsburgh Post-Gazette,* March 9, 2003.

328 **began calling himself Joybubbles:** Andrew T. Huse, interview with Joybubbles, University of South Florida Oral History Program, August 23, 2004. Monaghan, in "The Child in a Man," puts the year Engressia began calling himself Joybubbles as 1988.

328 **"We were on a retreat":** Jim Ragsdale, "One Name Says It All," *St. Paul Pioneer Press,* November 27, 2005, p. A1.

328 **"I'm a survivor":** Huse, interview with Joybubbles.

329 **legally changed his name:** Ibid.

329 **"Nobody knows how much peace":** Collier, "There's Martin Luther King."

329 **selected it to be the word processor:** John Markoff and Paul Freiberger, "Visit with Cap'n Software, Forthright Forth Enthusiast," *Infoworld*, October 11, 1982, p. 31.

329 **"wealthy executive":** Pete Carey, "Cap'n Crunch Programs His Way from Jail to Success," *Chicago Tribune*, May 25, 1983, p. D1.

329 **personal fortunes were crumbling:** Alexander Besher, "The Crunching of America," *Infoworld*, June 18, 1984, p. 66.

329 **forging tickets to BART:** Gary Richards, "'Captain Crunch' Charged in Ticket Forgery," *San Jose Mercury News*, January 9, 1987, p. 1B; "John Draper at AutoDesk," DigiBarn Computer Museum interview with John Draper, May 2006, at http://www.digibarn.com/collections/audio/digibarn-radio/06-05-john-draper-autodesk.

330 **where-are-they-now newspaper article:** Chris Rhodes, "The Twilight Years of Cap'n Crunch," *Wall Street Journal*, January 13, 2007.

330 **TAP ceased publication:** See http://artofhacking.com/tap. In 1989 another group not affiliated with the original *TAP* crew restarted the newsletter and printed issues 92 through 107.

330 **a new hacker/phone phreak publication:** "AHOY!" *2600*, January 1984, p. 1.

330 **area code "321":** "3-2-1, Call Cape Canaveral," *New York Times*, November 23, 1999.

331–332 **wired telephone lines . . . had peaked:** *Trends in Telephone Service*, Federal Communications Commission, September 2010, at http://hraunfoss.fcc.gov/edocs_public/attachmatch/DOC-301823A1.pdf.

333 **"It was the magic of the fact":** Santa Clara Valley Historical Association, interview with Steve Jobs from "Silicon Valley: A 100-Year Renaissance," 1998, at http://www.youtube.com/watch?v=HFURM8O-oYI.

334 **MIT students proudly displayed:** Russell Ryan, Zack Anderson, and Alessandro Chiesa, "Anatomy of a Subway Hack," at http://tech.mit.edu/V128/N30/subway/Defcon_Presentation.pdf; Michael McGraw-Herdeg and Marissa Vogt, "MBTA Sues Three Students to Stop Speech on Subway Vulnerabilities," *The Tech*, August 25, 2008.

ACKNOWLEDGMENTS

WRITING IS OFTEN said to be a lonely endeavor. Yet as I look back over the five years I spent researching and writing this book, I am awed and humbled both by the number of people who have been involved and all the things they have contributed. People have shared their stories with me, given me documents and recordings and historical artifacts, made introductions on my behalf, answered my questions, processed my Freedom of Information Act requests, helped me with writing or editing or research, and encouraged me to keep at it.

I am most grateful to those I interviewed or corresponded with to collect their stories; this book would not exist without them. Sadly, not everyone who shared something with me could be featured as a character or even quoted in this book. Regardless, every person I talked to contributed bits of context that I hope I have been able to mold into a collective and coherent history. I would like to thank the following:

The phone phreaks, telephone enthusiasts, telecommunications experts, and their friends and relations: George A., Ralph Barclay, Jack Bariton, Fred Belton, Mark Bernay, Sid Bernay, Trudy Boardman, Ed Buckley, John-Elmer Canfield, Cheshire Catalyst, Colin Chambers, Bob Clements, David Condon, John Covert, Mark Cuccia, Al Diamond, Richard Dillman, Jed Donnelley, Evan Doorbell, John Draper, Ron "Ducks," Stephen Dunne, Tom Edison, Esther Engressia, Toni Engressia, Jim Fettgather,

Alan Fierstein, Don Froula, Al Gilbertson, Bob Gudgel, Grant Gysbers, Anita Harris, Max Hauser, Dennis Heinz, John Higdon, Doug Humphrey, Joybubbles, Roy Kaylor, Nagy Khattar, Francis Kriokorian, David Kulka, Robert LaFond, Tony Lauck, David Lewis, Kim Lingo, Robert Lipman, Jake Locke, Rudolph Loew, Lucky225, Greg MacPherson, Joe Maximetz, John McNamara, Chuck Meyer, Onnig Minasian, Stuart Nelson, Jay from New York, Stephen Owades, Jon D. Paul of the Crypto-Museum, Jerry Petrizze, Rick Plath, M. J. Poirier, Tom Politeo, Jim Prather, Larry Rachman, Jodd Readick, Bob Reite, Bob Riddell, "Rogtag," Ed Ross, Jim Roth, John Sawyer, Adam Schoolsky, Robert Shaw, Bill Squire, Hoyt Stearns, David Tarnowski, Denny Teresi, John Treichler, Brough Turner, Rick Turner, Richard Weissberg, Steve Wozniak, Herb Yeates, and Norm Zimon.

Former employees of the telephone companies and their associates, friends, and families: H. W. William (Bill) Caming of AT&T, Bob Ginnings of Hekimian Labs, Ken Hopper and Amos E. Joel Jr. of Bell Laboratories, Helmut Kaunzinger of Pacific Telephone, Rob Mang of New York Telephone, Bob McLuckie of BC Telephone, Wayne Perrin of Pacific Telephone, Nelson Saxe of AT&T Long Lines, Walter Schmidt (and his son and daughter-in-law, Bill and Julia) of General Telephone, Swede Sorensen of Pacific Telephone, Ed Turnley of Southern Bell and AT&T, and John Whitman and H. Richard Zapf of New York Telephone.

Members of the law enforcement community: Jay Cochran, Bob Federspiel, Dennis Feine, Harold "Skip" Gladden, Bill Harward, Bud Heister, Dick Lytle, Edwin J. Sharp, Bill Snell, Ray Wannall, Warren Welsh, and Jack Wilgus, all formerly with the Federal Bureau of Investigation, Bill Earle, a former Justice Department attorney, and Floy Dawson, a former assistant U.S. attorney.

Members of the press: Wayne Green, Ron Kessler, Louis J. Rose, and Ron Rosenbaum.

Much of the material in this book is based on documents released under the Freedom of Information Act (FOIA) and the civil servants responsible for handling this often thankless task deserve recognition. Since the Federal Bureau of Investigation was the agency that spent the most time investigating phone phreaks, it had the misfortune to receive the lion's share of my FOIA requests, more than 350 in all. Its representatives bore up under this paper onslaught with professionalism and even the occasional bit of laughter. At the FBI I am indebted to Dottie Bailey, Kathleen Boyle, Craig Clevenger, Theresa Fowler, Kim Garver, Margaret Jackson, Moira Lattimore, Kara Lewis, Debbie Lopes, Candy McCulloh, Travis Mumaw, Patricia Nice, Becky Peterson, Tonia Robertson, Loren Shaver, David Sobonya, Mike Stevens, Lori Synnamon, Erin Uptigraph, and Marla Williamson—to say nothing of the many other members of the FBI Record/Information Dissemination Section whose names I don't know and who toiled behind the scenes processing my requests. My thanks, too, go to the staff at the Department of Justice Office of Information Policy, who handled my several FOIA appeals. At the Department of Justice Criminal Division, Kathleen Segui was most helpful. At the National Security Agency, Pamela Phillips and Marianne Stupar and their nameless staff worked diligently on several of my requests, including one that took almost three years to complete. Other historical documents came from the National Archives and Records Administration, where I am particularly grateful to Steven Tilley and Jay Olin for slogging through box after box of records in search of old memos and files.

At the AT&T Corporate Archives, George Kupczak and Bill Caughlin helped with my research requests and were kind enough to let me spend two days at their facility in New Jersey. Sellam Ismail of VintageTech was good enough to open his archives for me as well.

Several people deserve special thanks. One is Bill Acker, a phone phreak and twenty-seven-year veteran of the Bell System who spent hundreds of hours on the phone with me, reliving stories, answering my questions, and patiently explaining bits of telephone network esoterica. Another is Ken Hopper, a former distinguished member of the technical staff at Bell Laboratories and the head of its Telephone Crime Lab; even though he was quite ill at the time, Ken and his wife, Barbara, let me invade their home and spent days with me reviewing documents, remembering cases, answering questions, and making introductions. Charlie Pyne hosted me at his home, answered numerous questions, and worked diligently to track down relevant FBI files and the Fine Arts 13 notebook. John Gilbert, Wayne Perrin, Alan Rubinstein, Steve Sawyer, and Ed Turnley all helped with thoughtful discussions and treasure troves of old documents and recordings. Former FBI assistant director Edwin J. Sharp educated me on the fight against organized crime in the 1960s and introduced me to numerous former FBI special agents, all while keeping my spirits up with well-timed emails of encouragement. Michael Ravnitzky, my Freedom of Information Act guru and an irrepressible researcher, helped craft FOIA requests and appeals, solved missing-person puzzles, decoded FBI files, and dug up amazing bits of relevant history on his own initiative. Mio Cohen imposed order on chaos by developing a filing system that allowed me to actually locate and use the thousands of documents and records I had amassed. Jordan Hayes, the best system administrator in the world, supported my requests for domain names and Web hosting with patience and humor. Jackie Cheong loaned me her quiet office so I could write; her husband, Curt Hardyck, denied me the office wifi password so that I actually would write. Jason Scott of textfiles.com offered invaluable insights, guidance, introductions, and feedback. Steven Gibb, the executor of Joybubbles's estate, graciously provided access to Joybubbles's (né Joe Engressia's) old tapes and documents. Sam Etler, Steph Kerman, and Mark Cuccia became my go-to resources for technical questions about the telephone network of the 1960s and '70s.

Andy Couturier of the Opening and Jane Brunette of flamingseed.com provided invaluable help and coaching with my writing and the book's organization. I was lucky enough to be part of several outstanding writing groups while working on this book; I would like to particularly thank Katrina Alcorn, Novella

Carpenter, Jodi Halpern, Rachel Lehman-Haupt, Martha Snider, and Robin Bishop for their help. Mio Cohen, George Cook, John and Nancy Gilbert, Jake Locke, Charlie and Betsy Pyne, Mary Rowe, Steve Sawyer, and Jason Scott reviewed early drafts of the manuscript and provided thoughtful feedback. Jennifer Eyre White, Katie Hafner, Bobbie Pires, and Dan Shimizu read some of my earliest writing attempts and book proposals.

Don Kennison's careful copy editing of the manuscript prevented me from committing both atrocities of grammar and errors of fact, for which I am grateful; any errors that remain are, alas, my own. At Grove/Atlantic, Isobel Scott ably assisted in the production of the book. My editor, Jamison Stoltz, brought both enthusiasm and focus to the project. He blends a historian's eye for detail with a writer's love for words and an editor's clarity of thought; his touch can be found on every page.

My ultimate gratitude is to my wife, Rachael Rusting, whose belief in this project and love for me was unwavering.

Thank you all.

INDEX

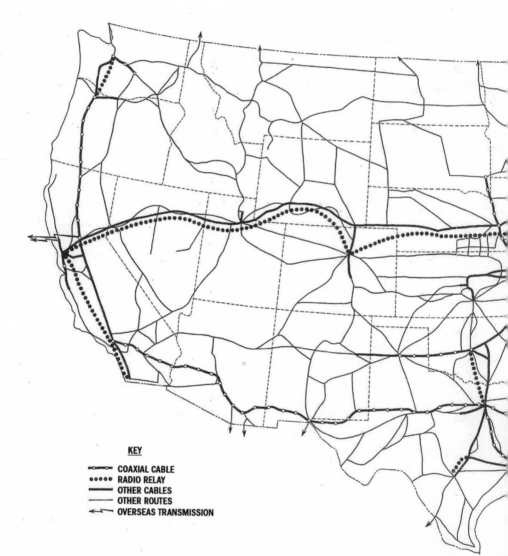

KEY

⊶⊶⊶ COAXIAL CABLE
●●●●● RADIO RELAY
▬▬▬ OTHER CABLES
——— OTHER ROUTES
◄—— OVERSEAS TRANSMISSION